The GaMes BibLE

The GaMes BibLE

OVER 300 GAMES—THE RULES, THE GEAR, THE STRATEGIES

BY LEIGH ANDERSON

WORKMAN PUBLISHING · NEW YORK

For my mother, who's always game.

Library of Congress Cataloging-in-Publication Data is available.

ISBN 978-0-7611-5389-4

Cover design by Janet Vicario / Book design by Rae Ann Spitzenberger

Photo Credits: *Come Out and Play:* Lia Bulaong: 2, 4; Amanda Bernsohn: 3. *Bridgeman Art Library:* 118 top and bottom left. *Fotolia:* Daniel Burch: cover and title page bottom right, 1 (and all subsequent chapter openers), 186, 274, 277; Mannaggia: cover top left, cover center back, viii, 217, 238, 240, 243, 249, 263, 264, 274, 277, 294; Norman Chan: cover top left; Viesturs Kalvans: 11 bottom right; Vladimir Karpenko: cover middle right; Marek Kosmal: 11 bottom left; JLV Image Works: cover bottom center; Sujit Mahapatra: 208. *Getty Images:* photos_alyson: cover and title page middle left. *Superstock:* Superstock: 118 top left, 118 top right; Peter Willi: 118 bottom right.

Workman books are available at special discounts when purchased in bulk for premiums and sales promotions as well as for fund-raising or educational use. Special editions or book excerpts also can be created to specification. For details, contact the Special Sales Director at the address below or send an e-mail to specialmarkets@workman.com.

WORKMAN PUBLISHING COMPANY, INC.
225 Varick Street
New York, NY 10014-4381
www.workman.com

Printed in the United States of America
First printing, August 2010

10 9 8 7 6 5 4 3 2 1

CONTENTS

CHAPTER ONE   1
Putting the Fun
Back Into Parties

CHAPTER TWO   13
Icebreakers
Games to warm people up, calm people down, and mix people together. They'll bring out your most charming selves.

- Your Other Half
- Adult Musical Chairs
- What's Your Line?
- Two Truths and a Lie
- A Knotty Problem
- Divide and Conquer
- Who Am I?
- Name Boggle
- Six-Word Memoir
- Charles Ate a Goat Testicle in Algeria
- Name Game
- Clap and Clapper
- Psychological Scavenger Hunt
- Song Scramble
- Common Interests
- United Nations
- Mr. Hit
- Questions
- Dancing Cheek to Cheek
- Pass the Orange
- Big Booty
- Animal Attraction
- Limbo Dance Contest
- Can I Buy You a Drink? *(New)*

CHAPTER THREE   35
Guessing Games
Guessing games are great equalizers. Winning at these games rarely depends on intellect or smarts, but on how silly and creative you can be.

- Charades
- Race Charades
- Current Events Charades
- One-Word Charades
- TV Charades
- Monster Movie Charades
- Fortune-Cookie Charades
- Noisemaker Charades
- Tabloid Charades
- Tiered Charades
- Tiered Name Guessing
- The Sticky-Note Game
- Botticelli
- Nocturnal Time Completely Lacking Noise
- I Accuse
- Adverbs
- Password (Versions 1 and 2)
- Forbidden Words
- Word Links
- Essences
- Character Guessing
- Celebrity
- Clumps
- Breakfast Combo
- How Why When Where
- She's So Fine . . .
- Match the Match Ad
- Mora
- Telephone Murder
- Psychiatrist
- The Match Game
- Encyclopedia
- Guess the Proverb
- Biography

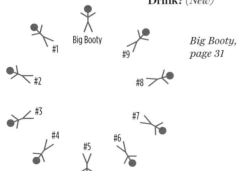

Big Booty

#1 #2 #3 #4 #5 #6 #7 #8 #9

Big Booty, page 31

CHAPTER FOUR 63
Indoor Frolics

This chapter is the antidote to counting cards and calculating odds. It's all about being silly and tumbling about the house in a frenzy of excitement.

- Hallway Bowling
- Four on the Couch
- Sardines
- Up Jenkins
- Pussy Wants a Corner
- Jail
- Balloon Football
- Idiot's Delight
- Brainy Baseball
- Prediction Bingo
- The Lap Game
- Three Words
- Yoga Ball Jousting
- Bubble Wrap Kung Fu
- Physical Word Hunt
- Ministry of Silence *(New)*

Ministry of Silence, page 77

CHAPTER FIVE 81
Conversation Games

In conversation games, the fun is in catching a glimpse of the inner workings of someone's mind—the associations they see, the puns or jokes they make.

- Would You Rather . . .
- I Never
- Walrus
- What Are They Thinking?
- Cage Match *(New)*
- The Dozens
- Shag, Marry, Cliff
- Butterfly or Bumblebee?
- Three Best
- Opposites
- Unfortunately . . .
- One, Two, Three
- Questions, R-and-G Style
- Can You Live with It?
- Band Name, Album Name, or Boat Name
- Group Therapy
- The Ethicist Game *(New)*

CHAPTER SIX 95
Literary & Word Games

If you're a word person, this is the chapter for you—it's all the cleverness and ingenuity you can find in the 26 letters of the alphabet.

- Anagrams
- Syllepsis
- 25 Letters
- Verbatim
- Dictionary
- Fictionary
- "Proverbs" Dictionary
- Medical or Law Dictionary
- Superstitions Dictionary
- Quotations Dictionary
- Slang Dictionary
- Poetry Fictionary
- Cringe Party
- Rhymes About
- Three Lives
- Scrabble Categories
- Associations *(New)*
- Word Logic
- Epitaph
- Definitions
- Contact
- Rewordable *(New)*

CHAPTER SEVEN 111
Right-Brain Games

Enter the drawing, singing, dancing, and performing games for those right-brainers who don't shine at word games.

- Pictionary
- Whisper Pictionary
- Blindfolded Pictionary
- Race Pictionary
- Family Pictionary
- Police Lineup
- Pictionary Down the Lane
- Art Charades
- Literary Rebus
- Old-Fashioned Dance Party
- Profiles
- Karaoke
- Sight Unseen
- Situation Puzzles
- What's the Scoop?
- Who-Where-What
- Exquisite Corpse
- Just a Minute!
- Self-Portrait
- iPod Dance Charades *(New)*

Rewordable,
page 109

CHAPTER EIGHT　　　　　　　**129**
Games of General Cleverness

These games force you to think on your feet. Whether it's word association, visual memory, math and logic skills, or political acumen, you'll find you're clever in more ways than you thought.

- Carnelli
- Read My Mind
- Mafia
- Geography
- Haggle
- Super Babel
- Happy Days
- Guggenheim
- Chain-Link Music
- Save Yourself
- You Don't Say . . .
- Iron Chef Potluck
- Common Ground
- Great Minds Think Alike
- Reversals
- Nomic

CHAPTER NINE　　　　　　　**153**
Victorian Parlor Games

It turns out that repressive Victorian mores are particularly fertile ground for some racy games and goofy flirting.

- Alphabet Minute
- Compliments
- Quotations
- Crambo (Versions 1 and 2)
- Acting Rhymes
- Consequences
- Throwing Light
- French Rhymes
- Squeak, Piggy, Squeak
- The Ant and the Cricket
- Alphabetical Quotations
- Traveling Alphabet
- Given Words
- The Storyteller
- Vowels
- The Cushion Dance
- Hot Cockles

CHAPTER TEN　　　　　　　**169**
Holiday Games

Family events can be fun. They can also make you want to stab your eyes out with grape scissors. As such, you have two choices: You can just show up for Thanksgiving dinner and hope all goes well—or you can plan some games. Please, plan some games.

- Resolutions
- The Yankee Gift Swap, *Survivor*-Style
- Heartbreaker *(New)*
- Valentine's Story Slam
- Mardi Gras Costume Party and King Cake
- Passover Trivia Quiz
- Easter Egg Haggle
- "Reverse" Easter Egg Hunt
- Easter Keg Hunt
- This Is Your Life Trivia
- Human Battleships
- Competitive Picnicking *(New)*
- Taste of America
- Capture the (Waterlogged) Flag
- Priest of the Parish
- Competitive Pumpkin Carving
- Halloween Ball
- Grateful Guessing
- Inheritance Game *(New)*
- Name-Boggle Poetry
- Holiday Trivia
- Family Jeopardy!
- That's the Way It Was
- Baby Shower Games

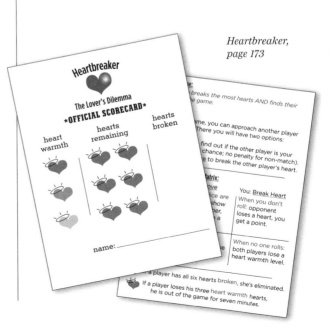

Heartbreaker,
page 173

CHAPTER ELEVEN 201
Games for Gamblers & Bluffers
Love the shot of adrenaline that hits just before the dice rattle against the wall? Then this chapter's for you. If you can calculate odds and keep a cool head, try a dice game.

- Liar's Dice
- Dudo
- Craps
- Liar's Poker
- Rat-Fink
- Blind Man's Bluff Poker
- I Doubt It
- Buzz
- Baseball Bingo
- Brain Teasers
- Arithmetic Croquet
- Secret Signals
- Eleusis Express *(New)*

CHAPTER TWELVE 219
Trivia Games
There's a reason trivia games endure: Nothing beats the feeling of blurting out a piece of information you never thought you knew.

- Multiple-Choice Trivia Game
- Trivia Betting
- Trivia Fictionary
- Trivia Bee
- Hometown Quiz
- Tabloid Trivia
- Current Events Trivia
- Six Degrees of Kevin Bacon
- Quizlinks! *(New)*

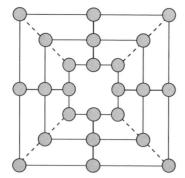

Nine Men's Morris, page 285

Gin Rummy, page 241

CHAPTER THIRTEEN 231
A Card-Game Refresher
Card games are the most elegant of all games, as they perfectly blend strategy, psychology, and sociability. They also boast an infinite variety. If you've got a deck, play it.

- Go Fish
- Old Maid
- Oh, Hell
- Hearts
- Gin Rummy
- 500 Rummy
- Canasta
- Poker: Texas Hold 'Em
- Seven Up
- Pitch
- Blackjack
- Euchre
- Casino
- Pinochle
- Four-Handed Pinochle
- Solitaire
- Spades
- Store *(New)*

CHAPTER FOURTEEN 269
Brainy Games for Two
Get ready for the best pen-and-paper games in the world—games for waiting to see the obstetrician, forty-five minute airplane rides, or the twenty minutes before the casserole is done.

- Expanda-Toe
- Demolition Tic-Tac-Toe
- Sprouts
- Coup d'Etat
- Decipher
- The L Game
- Dots and Boxes
- Depth Charge
- Footsteps
- Battleships
- Poker Squares
- Nine Men's Morris
- Labyrinth
- Reversi
- Mancala

CHAPTER FIFTEEN   **291**

Games for a Weekend Away

Congratulations: You've managed to flee the gritty, stinky confines of town for fresh country air. Of course you'll want to play a few games—especially games that can be enjoyed over a leisurely few days.

- Wink Murder
- 9-5-2
- Tableaux *
- Make Your Own Pantomime
- 1,000 Blank White Cards
- Murder Mystery Games
- Geocaching
- Weekend-Long Forbidden Words *(New)*
- Classic Beach House Games
- Charades *
- Pictionary *
- Nomic *
- Mafia *
- Psychiatrist *
- Assassin *
- Situation Puzzles *

Appears in another chapter

1,000 Blank White Cards, page 299

CHAPTER SIXTEEN   **307**

Impromptu Games

Remember "Not It"? When the last person to put her finger alongside her nose was the person who had to perform some menial task? Impromptu games can start before you even know it.

- Not It
- Not OK
- Punch-Buggy
- El Dorado Omega Johnson
- What?
- Jinx
- Head Splinter
- The Game
- Get Down, Mr. President
- I've Always Thought BBQ Panda Cubs Would Be Delicious

CHAPTER SEVENTEEN   **311**

Outdoor Games

Big games are exhilarating. Plan a few of these for your family reunion, college alumni weekend, or even just for a pickup game in the park.

- Capture the Flag
- Jesse James
- Manhunt
- Assassin
- Yukigassen
- Classic Outdoor Kids' Games
- Variations on Tag
- Frisbee Golf
- Kickball
- Ringoleavio
- Scavenger Hunts
- Urban Bingo *(New)*
- Puzzle Scavenger Hunt
- Museum Scavenger Hunt *(New)*
- Fox and Hounds
- Coast Guard and Smugglers
- Ace-King-Queen
- Kick the Can
- Marco Polo
- No-Equipment Baseball
- Sharks and Minnows
- Slip 'n Slide Curling
- Urban Orienteering
- Triathlons and Relay Races
- Fox and Geese
- Counter Squirt *(New)*
- The Lost Sport of Olympia *(New)*

OUTDOOR GAMES, PART II   **348**

Lawn Games

Is your idea of the great outdoors a manicured garden and cocktails at five? Lawn games let you play without getting your hands—or pants—dirty.

- Croquet
- Horseshoes
- Badminton
- Tetherball
- Bocce

APPENDIX   **357**

ACKNOWLEDGMENTS   **379**

GAMES BY CATEGORY   **380**

INDEX   **386**

Chapter One

PUTTING THE FUN BACK INTO PARTIES

A couple of years ago I noticed that I wasn't having a good time at parties anymore. Every get-together was the same old blur of drinks, finger food, industry gossip, political bickering, and catch-up (How's the job? How's your sister? How's that gluten-free diet working out for you?). It was just a bunch of adults standing around—except for the folks on the couch watching YouTube videos. It had begun to feel like we were all just going through the motions, marking time until we could get home to check Facebook or download a movie.

Then one night at a cocktail party a friend—who obviously shared my boredom—suggested that we play Psychological Scavenger Hunt, in which players compete to discover one another's interesting quirks and tastes. Guests started interviewing each other, hearing one crazy story after another. Suddenly, we were laughing and flirting—*connecting*. From there we moved on to Mafia, a near-perfect parlor game that has you playacting, colluding, and double-crossing your nearest and dearest. Soon I was looking forward to parties again—to teetering on someone's lap in Adult Musical Chairs and digging through the host's underwear drawer in Physical Word Hunt—rather than worrying about endless small talk and how to discreetly slip off my painful shoes. It wasn't just that the games were fun, it was that they immediately dispensed with everything that can weigh a party down—cutting through the inhibitions, formality, and tension that is typically hurdled only by lots of drinking.

Hopscotch Highways from Come Out and Play.

Once my friends' collective memory for games had been exhausted (Celebrity, Dictionary, and Kickball alone kept us going for a few months), I started looking around for a comprehensive guide to games. To my surprise, there wasn't one. Bookstore shelves are crammed with guides to card games, kids' games, and of course volumes of how-to's on sports and video games. But a complete, all-encompassing, exhaustive guide to games for adults, one that included both parlor games and outdoor games? Nada. So I decided to make one myself.

It quickly became apparent why there's no such guide: There are a *lot* of games in the world. The definition of "game" can even get a little slippery: Is it a codified series of steps and rules, with just one winner, like Mean Scrabble? Or can it be an idle, poolside, sun-drenched conversation about who beats whom, Chuck Norris or Jack Bauer (Walrus)? The answer is yes, and yes. Both pit your skills against your fellow players: In the first, your anagramming skills; in the second, your '80s movie recall, your skills at argument, and your sense of humor. Games can showcase your probability skills (Gin) or your ability to improvise (Just a Minute) or your acumen at . . . well, anything (check out Chapter Eight, Games of General Cleverness).

Once the parameters were set, or rather, blown wide open, my research began. It was a *great* conversation starter: The moment I said I was writing a book on games, people's faces lit up. They would lean in and say, "Oh, have you heard of this one? Or that one?" Everyone had a story to tell of games learned from cousins or grandmothers or camp counselors. As my father described Ghost in the Graveyard, an old family favorite, I realized how tightly games are

Human Blackjack from Come Out and Play.

entwined with personal traditions; one family might be a treasure trove of hundreds of unique games unknown to the neighbors right next door. My research had a telescopic effect: Each line of inquiry opened up another, which opened up another . . . until I was thumbing through crumbling Victorian-era parlor-games books in the New York Public Library, finding little old ladies to teach me Canasta, interviewing PhDs who've invented games to make faculty meetings bearable, and insisting that my twelve-year-old cousins spell out in patient detail every game they play at camp and school (their favorite game now is Run Away from Leigh).

I even sought out folks who take play so seriously that they've turned it into a career: game designers. These geniuses have created an entire field, complete with specialties and differing schools of thought and university degrees in game design. (From them I learned fancy terms like "massive multiplayer" and "zero sum" and "collaborative production.") While most of the graduates of those programs are angling to work in the profitable video-game field, they all have an innate love of games in any form, including neo-traditionalists who create new, modern variations of old favorites like Tag and Tic-Tac-Toe. In their spare time, even the most tech-savvy video designers will often develop low-tech parlor games to play with friends during their leisure hours or on road trips. I was lucky enough to convince a number of these talented folks to contribute their newest games for this book. I also discovered people from all walks of life who've invented games, from NYU grads who created a children's picnicking game (Competitive Picnicking) to an IRS attorney who invented The Ethicist Game, to a new generation of game designers and ordinary folk alike who have come up with hip, high-concept, low-cost, DIY board games (see Chapter Fourteen, Brainy Games for Two).

These designers—young and energetic and organized—introduced me to another aspect of the games culture: festivals. Anyone's welcome to participate, so in the name of research, I participated in several Come Out and Play festivals in New York, where I live, and found similar events and festivals in Athens, London, Venice, and Budapest. I also discovered word game weekends at posh hotels (such as one in upstate New York that was moderated by NPR's puzzlemaster, Will Shortz) and murder mystery weekends at bed-and-breakfasts in Vermont.

The latest generation of gamers has also reinvented outdoor play. One of the most exciting trends in recent years has been the growth of enormous organized outdoor games, often with hundreds of participants racing across great wide open spaces or urban grids, transforming cities and towns into large-scale game boards. Adults are taking to the streets, donning sneakers, downloading maps, hiding flags, and sprinting around town looking for hidden treasure. (My favorite of these "public space games" is

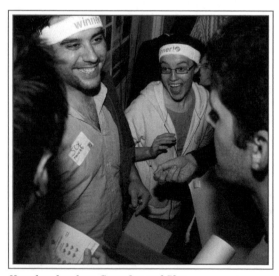

Heartbreaker from Come Out and Play.

Ministry of Silence, in which players have to solve a puzzle in order to find a "spy" hiding in a bookstore, amongst the unsuspecting public.) In 2003 participants moved giant inflatable game pieces around Minneapolis in the Big Urban Game; in 2007 New Yorkers played a game called CounterSquirt, in which they searched through abandoned buildings for a hidden "traitor"—all the while fending off the other teams with high-powered water guns. You'll find 57 seriously fun outdoor games in Chapter Seventeen, an exciting mix of tagging, capturing, hunting, and hiding, often with a backpack, water bottle, and GPS device as required equipment.

Once I started compiling the games for the manuscript, I began testing them on my family and friends—and testing them, and testing them. In fact, all my pals are now roundly sick of games and would rather help me rake leaves than shuffle one more deck of cards. I forced these good people and my long-suffering husband to cut the cards, rip up a million little slips of paper and write down funny things to act out on them, don ridiculous costumes, and repurpose their coffee mugs as dice cups. Gin Rummy in particular was a challenge—at least for me— especially when I tried to launch a game with a group of girlfriends at a pizza parlor in the East Village while competing with pounding hip-hop on the sound system. Games have become part of my family's everyday life; my parents even played Mancala with me while I was in the hospital days after my son was born—we finally found a use for those dozens of Styrofoam water cups that accumulate by your bedside. (Curiously, the baby began playing Tic-Tac-Toe only three days after he was born.)

How to Use This Book

There are enough games here to suit every taste, talent, occasion, and mood—over 349 games in all—for big or small groups, indoors or outdoors, in the car waiting at the drive-thru, walking down a street in your hometown, or dashing around Rome with your kids. We are at the dawn of a new era of play! Instead of storming the newest restaurants and clubs, you can tweet about playing Crambo and Hearts on New Year's Eve. Enliven intergenerational dinner parties with the Sticky-Note Game, or host a Conspiracy Theory party. Whatever your tastes, whoever your friends, you too can be part of this games revolution—just call, e-mail, or tweet your pals, and start planning the best game night ever!

For ease of locating the best games to match your mood and party, this book contains Zagat-like indexes where games are listed by type, occasion, players, mood, etc. (See page 380.) Select games based on your interests: deduction (Coup d'Etat), observation (Police Lineup), probability (Craps), high risk and so on, or the size of your party. Each game description indicates how many players are required—from two to dozens or even hundreds. (Very large games, like CounterSquirt or Can I Buy You a Drink? are best for large-scale events that require planning, and you may need to do a practice run or two before you really hit your stride.) I've also included a bunch of games that can be launched without any plan or party at all—make sure to peruse the Conversation and Impromptu games chapters and commit a couple of these to memory. They are best played when you're doing the dishes with your spouse, or waiting in line for the movies, or really any moment when the current activity is not all you'd hoped it would be. Launching into an impromptu game of Punch-Buggy or Chop-a-Croc has made waiting in line outside my new neighborhood pizza place bearable. After a recent Kentucky Derby, my friend and I, pinned by our sleeping children and unable to reach the remote, unwillingly watched the episode of *Jeopardy!* that aired after the race. Too tired to guess any of the answers, we entertained ourselves with a bout of Shag, Marry, Cliff.

Whatever games you choose, feel free to vary them or even make up entirely new sets of rules. When I was play-testing, I'd realize that what *I* thought was the game was actually a variation, or what I'd thought was a variation was the "real" game. Games have a way of replicating and mutating (in a fun way, not in a killer-virus kind of way), especially as they cross cultures or are passed down through generations. Folks grow up with a set of house rules for certain games, and even to suggest that there might be an alternative can provoke howls of outrage. (It's like suggesting that the way your mother makes meatballs might not be the *only* way to make meatballs.) Hearts with a kitty? Why, I've never heard of such a thing! When playing Charades, you toss unguessed clues back in the hat? Heresy! Capture the Flag with a *jailer*? The indignant splutters are still spluttering in my ears. But to paraphrase Dizzy Gillespie, if it feels good, it is good. If you're having fun, you're playing the right way. And if you *do* feel that your version is tons more fun than the game I've described, please let me know at thegamesbible.com.

Icons

These icons, which appear under the game's title, quickly clue you in to the type of game you can expect. Here's what they mean.

The game is for super game-geeks—the rules will be complicated and/or long, or the game requires special skill or knowledge.

The game is potentially naughty— but it's up to you to figure out how. (I refrained from more explicit instructions, knowing that one man's "naughty" is another's "terribly cheesy.")

The game is even more fun after a cocktail or two.

The game is a great one to play with kids. (Sometimes you'll see a 🍸 and a 👫 side by side. This doesn't mean that kids should be tippling, but that it's an easy, silly game that kids—or adults who have had a cocktail—might enjoy.)

The game can be played online, either via automated programs, like Poker Squares, or with a friend via chat or IM.

The game is noncompetitive.

Tunes are necessary—a stereo or an iPod—to play the game.

The game is silly and guaranteed to generate laughs.

The game is suitable for playing in a car. Refrain from asking the driver to do anything but drive, though—this is for the folks in the backseat.

And finally,

indicates that this is a brand-new game, contributed by a game designer.

HOW TO HOST A GAME NIGHT

Eight for Charades, pizza, and beer? Twenty for cocktails and Haggle? Family reunion picnic with Capture the Flag? Four friends for a sit-down dinner, followed by cards and whiskey? This book isn't just about games—it's about socializing. Games bring people together because, well, most games require more than one player. But behind every fun party game is a great organizer getting everyone excited, giving people the tools, teaching them the rules, generally making the whole thing possible. In other words—a host!

Hosting a game night (or game afternoon) is not rocket science, but disorganized hosting can turn the event into a loud free-for-all, or worse, a boring dud of an evening. That's why I've provided some guidelines to keep the festivities focused and fun. The good news is that you don't have to go too crazy. Game nights, by their very nature, are casual events—even if you want to don a tux, dust off the martini glasses, and make your mother's pot roast. No matter how elaborate your shindig, your guests are not going to judge you for a burnt apple tart or mediocre wine selection when the whole reason they showed up is for the annual Battleship playoffs.

My friend Tamar, an inveterate party-thrower, instructs hosts to approach parties as if they were dogs: "Dogs greet you at the door happily. And make a really big to-do about your arrival. They're happy and inquisitive. They make a mess of the birthday cake. They don't worry about cleaning up. They make out, guilt-free, with other partygoers with no worry about their appearance or their weight or the state of their hair." In short, when hosting, think to yourself, "What would my dog do?"

The bottom line is: Guests will usually have as much fun as you're having. Below are some tips that will not only ensure that your guests will have a good time, but that you will, too!

Make a Match

The real secret to a great game night, like pairing wine with food, is matching the right games with the right people and ambience. Consider the interests of the people you're inviting: If you're an English professor (or even just an English major) your circle of friends will probably enjoy word games like Verbatim, Just a Minute!, or The Storyteller. If your crowd is more analytical, try Arithmetic Croquet, Super Babel, or Nomic. For animated extroverts, propose a round of Police Lineup or a weekend of Make Your Own Pantomime. For the sporty crowd, launch a game of Capture the Flag or Bocce. Select wisely: Don't invite a card novice to Bridge Night and don't expect a pregnant woman to Chicken Fight.

Do a Head Count

Once you choose your games, determine *how many* people to invite and then add a few more—someone will invariably cancel. Most games don't need a precise number of participants, but be sure to check before pulling together your guest list. (If you're worried about too many guests, remember that almost any game can be played in teams.) And in my opinion, the best parties have a 1:1 ratio of people you know and people you don't—so ask your pals to bring a friend or two.

Plan Your Games Like Courses in a Meal

You may want to give everyone a chance to settle in and mill around before the games begin, or you may want to warm up with a cocktail and an Icebreaker that people join as soon as they arrive. In Adam Gopnik's essay on playing Mafia in the book *Through the Children's Gate*, he describes playing a round, breaking for Chinese food while discussing the game, and then launching another round before parting for the evening. Very civilized. A "dessert" game should be short and sweet and played during coffee and after-dinner drinks, like Essences or Consequences. In many parlor games, like Password or a murder-mystery game, "breaks" are built in, as not everyone is continually playing the game at exactly the same time. These games are perfect for after dinner or meals that are served buffet-style. If you're opting for a cocktail party, check out the Icebreakers chapter. If you're doing a large al fresco picnic or potluck, like a family reunion at the state park, check out the Outdoor Games.

Feed Them and They Will Come

The food and drink element of a party can conjure a couple of different kinds of crazy in a host. There's the Alpha Host, who wants to show off and decides to make individual chocolate soufflés for fifteen people. There's the Optimistic Host, who decides it would be fun to roast a turkey for the first time. There's the Ascetic Host, who thinks that a single bag of pretzel rods will satisfy an entire crowd. And then there's the Absent Host, who spends the entire party in the kitchen and mixing drinks. To avoid falling into any of these traps, might I please make a suggestion? Select a menu that's manageable for *you*. If you're used to throwing together finger food for fifty, go for it. If you're more on the take-out side of the culinary aisle, don't pick game night as your moment to experiment in the kitchen. And if you're unsure about how much food you'll need, stock up on some frozen hors d'oeuvres and keep the local pizza place on speed dial. Or, ask everyone to bring a dish, snack, or drink, and your table will be groaning with treats. (The potluck system works with games, as well—ask a few guests to lead with a game or two of their choice. It'll bring variety to the night, and you'll be off the hook for at least part of the evening.)

▶▶ **HOST TIP**
Games that don't require your hands—conversation games, for example, rather than card games—work well at a dinner party. If a paper and pencil is necessary, serve finger foods. Card games and eating don't mix, unless you like your cards crumby and greasy. Either play cards after a meal or just serve drinks on the porch.

Playing by the Rules

As host, you'll likely be playing Master of Ceremonies, which makes you the explainer of rules, the provider of supplies, the organizer of games. (NOTE: You can always pawn that role off on a particularly bossy

The Invitation

For a casual game night, post an invitation about a week before the party. For more involved games that require your guests to do a little prep-work, say Current Events Trivia, send the invite and guidelines roughly two weeks in advance. Don't forget to ask that they RSVP so you can get a head-count and plan accordingly.

When you send out your invitations (whether it's via Facebook, e-mail, snail mail, or courier), make sure your guests know that your party will involve games. Why? Because some people don't like to play games. (Yes, these party poopers walk among us!) Some people are painfully shy. Others think it's a contrived way to spend an evening. Some people just aren't up for it. Game nights are only as fun as the guests are enthusiastic—a little natural selection up front will weed out the less-than-pumped. If one of them slips through the cracks, assign that guest the role of timer or scorekeeper, or exempt him or her entirely by asking for help with serving drinks and food. (Or send them in the other room with a stack of old *New Yorker* magazines and a glass of wine—that's probably what they want to be doing anyway.)

Sample invitations

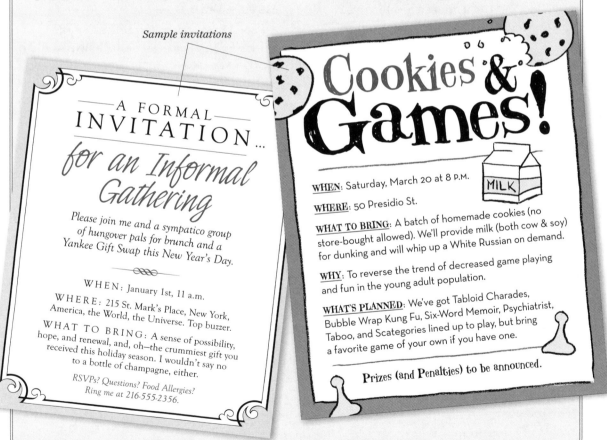

— A FORMAL —
INVITATION...
for an Informal Gathering

Please join me and a sympatico group of hungover pals for brunch and a Yankee Gift Swap this New Year's Day.

WHEN: January 1st, 11 a.m.

WHERE: 215 St. Mark's Place, New York, America, the World, the Universe. Top buzzer.

WHAT TO BRING: A sense of possibility, hope, and renewal, and, oh—the crummiest gift you received this holiday season. I wouldn't say no to a bottle of champagne, either.

RSVPs? Questions? Food Allergies? Ring me at 216-555-2356.

Cookies & Games!

WHEN: Saturday, March 20 at 8 P.M.

WHERE: 50 Presidio St.

WHAT TO BRING: A batch of homemade cookies (no store-bought allowed). We'll provide milk (both cow & soy) for dunking and will whip up a White Russian on demand.

WHY: To reverse the trend of decreased game playing and fun in the young adult population.

WHAT'S PLANNED: We've got Tabloid Charades, Bubble Wrap Kung Fu, Six-Word Memoir, Psychiatrist, Taboo, and Scategories lined up to play, but bring a favorite game of your own if you have one.

Prizes (and Penalties) to be announced.

friend.) Nothing can kill a game buzz like spending forty-five minutes discussing the finer points of Carnelli, so make sure you can simply and clearly explain the game rules— even practicing beforehand if necessary. Depending on the complexity of the game, it may be a good idea to type up or photocopy the rules from this book so players can refer to them throughout the evening. If you're playing with pros, set a time limit on how long you can argue over the rules. These "conversations" are unfortunately inevitable, and though a spirited debate can be part of the fun, it can often drag on way too long. If a player wants to amend the rules (also inevitable), put the matter to a vote. And don't be afraid to lay down the law—one of the many perks of hosting the game night is Host Rule #1: Your party, your rules. When the discussion goes past your time limit, make a ruling and move on.

▸▸ **HOST TIP**
Games that take a great deal of concentration and have a lot of rules, like Nomic, or Canasta, are best started *before* people have had a few drinks—it's hard enough to get through very complicated games with everyone sober.

Play Nice

In games where you're finding things out about people, or sharing things about yourself and others, remind guests that etiquette trumps getting a laugh every time. For example, in Essences, saying that *Frank is the essence of Jabba the Hutt* might be a funny joke to everyone except, well, Frank. Remind people of the "Be Kind Rule" at the start of the game, and keep an eye on the

troublemakers. Another thing to watch out for is the John McEnroe in sheep's clothing. Some otherwise mild-mannered people may turn out to be viciously competitive and yell at their teammates for making mistakes. Do whatever you can to shut down that behavior before it gets ugly: Have one or two noncompetitive games (marked with this icon: ☮) on hand— you can always halt a game and switch to another if things are heading off the rails. And don't be afraid to invoke Host Rule #2: Your party, play nice. Don't be afraid to pull someone into the kitchen and quietly tell him to take it down a notch.

Have a Plan B

All good hosts have alternatives up their sleeve. I like to have a board game like Taboo or Apples to Apples around in case something goes awry with the games I've planned. It's also great to have an extra game in mind, in case the gang is still raring to go even after you've run through everything you've planned.

Relax

Don't be afraid to surrender control. You may be playing games, but your guests aren't six-year-olds. Make it easy for guests to fend for themselves—let them open bottles of wine or dish up more food or run out for more beer if necessary. Throw a terrific game night and everyone will be talking about it for weeks. But the best part is not the glory—it's that your guests will be inspired to host their *own* game nights, thereby ensuring that you'll be invited to many more parties over the next few months. Kind of makes it all worth it, right?

Game Night + Theme Party = Best Night Ever

Game nights can be simple and require no prep. However, the best game nights—the full game experience, if you will—combine a theme with a specific game or games. Below, a few ideas to get you started:

- **English Majors Party:** Plan a few literary games and ask your guests to come in costumes as great figures from literature. Serve tea, comfort food, and cookies.

- **Battleship Party:** Specify that outfits should be sailor-esque; pop a naval war film in the DVD player and launch a Battleship tournament.

- **Cold War Party:** Play Ministry of Silence, Canasta, or *Casino Royale*-type poker, with James Bond movies showing (silently) on the TV and Sinatra on the stereo. Serve classic midcentury cocktails and hors d'oeuvres like martinis, cheese balls, and shrimp puffs. Tell guests to come costumed as pinkos, spies, Bond girls, or any number of famous USSR defectors.

- **Middle-School Dance Party:** Guests come in ill-fitting clothing, one of Dad's ties, and bad hair. Serve pizza and Fresca and host an I Doubt It tournament between dancing (music will correspond to whatever was popular when you were in middle school; for me, every slow song would be "Stairway to Heaven.")

- **Childhood Games for Grown-ups Party:** Go to the park in the afternoon and play Capture the Flag, Marco Polo, and Tag. Head back to the house afterward for a little Slip 'n Slide Curling. Be sure to include balloons in your decor and serve "traditional" American children's food: bologna sandwiches with the crusts cut off, grilled cheese sandwiches and tomato soup, tater tots, and Oreos.

- **Conspiracy Theory Party:** Have a heavily redacted menu or just black out the words on soda or beer bottles. Dress as characters from your favorite conspiracies (JFK, the Roswell alien . . .). Make tinfoil hats for party favors; construct an "all-seeing eye" piñata; and launch a game of Mafia or the board game Illuminati. Place "hidden cameras" (blinking red lights) all around the house, and have a contest to see who can find them all.

- **Bad Sweater Party:** Host a New Year's Day Brunch, complete with a game of Resolutions. Guests have to wear the ugliest sweater they've ever received as a holiday gift or the ugliest sweater they can borrow or buy at a secondhand shop.

- **Titanic Party:** Serve doughnuts and Life Savers and play Victorian parlor games.

- **"Alice in Wonderland" Party:** Play Croquet, of course, and serve tea, crumpets, and cakes.

Chapter Two

ICEBREAKERS

In a perfect world, there'd be no need for icebreakers at a party. No one would exhibit any apprehension or anxiety; no one would compulsively rearrange hors d'oeuvres to avoid small talk; no one would launch into a long nervous story about his latest computer-programming debacle. Our most charming selves would be front and center from the get-go. We would all immediately bond, swap hilarious anecdotes, and discover mutual friends from junior high.

Since it's not a perfect world, icebreakers allow this natural social phenomena to happen a bit faster. When you play an icebreaker game, it's like fast-forwarding through bad first impressions (That guy is really strange! That tie is vile!) to the early stages of discovering a new best pal (That guy is hilarious! That tie is so idiosyncratic!). Games take the attention away from our own nerves and put it squarely on the challenge at hand—unscrambling a puzzle, composing a story, or finding yourself on someone's lap when the music stops.

The games in this chapter are designed to break down the barriers that naturally exist between strangers (and barriers *should* exist between strangers, of course—otherwise everyone, not just your brother-in-law, would be asking you for loans). But at a party, where you want to make friends, or find out why your friends have made (and invited) these other friends, well, you need those barriers torn down, and *pronto*.

You'll find games that require playacting (Your Other Half), a certain amount of silly physicality (Big Booty), and games that can be played over dinner (Two Truths and a Lie). You'll get to know more about your fellow guests—what they do for living (What's Your Line?), how quickly they can undo a half-hitch (A Knotty Problem), and what their cologne smells like (Pass the Orange). And you'll even hear their life stories (Six-Word Memoir or Charles Ate a Goat Testicle in Algeria).

Icebreakers provide an activity so you're not reduced to standing around clutching your fourth drink, wishing that you had the knack for effortless, sparkling conversation. Activities loosen people up: You'll get to know the other guests in silly ways that you experience only with your dearest friends.

Your Other Half

What **better way** to get to know your fellow guests than to pretend to be someone else. Your guests assume the identity of half of a famous duo and must locate the person playing their mate through role-play and quizzes.

PLAYERS: 6–30

THE GEAR: Paper, pencil, a hat.

Preparation

Before your guests arrive, compile a bunch of famous duos: Antony and Cleopatra, Ron and Nancy, Bert and Ernie. You'll need at least one famous couple for each pair of guests. Write the names of the famous couple on slips of paper (one name per slip) and put them in a hat; have each guest grab a name upon arrival. If you'd like to keep a male-female division, put women's names in one hat and men's in another; otherwise, just mix them all together.

The Game Plan

✖ Each guest will assume their new identity and cast about for their "other half"—the person playing their mate. You may do this in two ways: either by asking questions or by acting out your role. Ideally, people will do both.

✖ Players can only ask *indirect* questions—so, if you're Al Gore and you think you're looking for Joe Lieberman, you might ask a fellow partygoer, "Are the Democrats still angry at you for defecting and becoming an Independent?" You may *not* say, "Are you Joe Lieberman?" which would, of course, bring the game to a too-rapid end.

✖ Folks with a dramatic bent may choose to "act out" their roles—whipping out their best Ronald Reagan voice, for example—but this sort of theatrics isn't necessary for the game to be successful. Sometimes a muttered, "Deep Throat left a message for you," can help Woodward find Bernstein.

✖ If you're lucky, these theatrics will be so hilarious that no one will rush to find their counterpart. If someone's intoning "Woman. Friend. Wife," and staggering around like Frankenstein, well, maybe the Bride of Frankenstein will hang back and let her groom amuse the rest of the guests for a bit longer, in ways that only an unholy cadaver can.

NOTE: When you're compiling the duos, you can mix it up by making the "famous" couples slightly more obscure—for example, Neil Armstrong and Buzz Aldrin. ("Are you bitter that your copilot shoved his way out of the spaceship ahead of you, thereby securing his place in history while the world struggles to remember your name?")

A Few Couples to Get You Started . . .

Gene Kelly and Fred Astaire, Britney and Jamie Lynn Spears, Dora the Explorer and her best monkey-friend Boots, Boris and Natasha, Charlie Brown and Lucy, Regis and Kelly, Bonnie and Clyde, Thelma and Louise, Henry VIII and Anne Boleyn, Nicholas Sarkozy and Carla Bruni, Elvis and the Colonel, Tom Brady and Bill Belichick.

Adult Musical Chairs

When playing games, nobody wants to be the first "out"—cast off, eliminated, voted off the island—doomed to wander the host's halls studying generations of family photos while the rest of the crowd shrieks with laughter and meets their future spouses. Not fun. But! There *are* such things as cooperative games—games in which everyone gets to play, all the way to the end. And the best kind of cooperative games are ones in which you sprawl over your fellow players and possibly *your* future spouse. In Adult Musical Chairs, a twist on the traditional childhood game, no one is eliminated when the chair is removed. You *must* find a seat, even if it's on someone's lap. Or several someones' laps.

PLAYERS: 3–15

THE GEAR: Stereo, chairs.

The Game Plan

The game begins like traditional musical chairs, in a circle, with one fewer chair than there are players. Start the music (see page 30 for a list of eminently danceable tunes). Guests must boogie their way around the circle. When you, as the music controller, see fit, stop the music. Dancing ceases; mayhem ensues as everyone scrambles for a seat. Obviously, one person will find herself without a chair—but she *must* still sit down. On the first round, this is probably going to be on someone's lap, and it'll stay this way until the people who don't have chairs outnumber the people who do. The music resumes, and one more chair is removed. That's when the human Jenga begins—people will have to teeter on laps upon laps of people, sprawl lengthwise like the fourth kid in the backseat, or cantilever off someone's knees while holding their wrists. The game continues until there is just one chair left. The final human sculpture might resemble a cheerleaders' human pyramid, or it might resemble a Hieronymus Bosch painting. (It depends on your friends.) Take a photo of the final friend sculpture!

Variation

If you want to make this competitive, award the most points to the person lowest on the chair, or just award points for particularly innovative dance moves.

What's Your Line?

Let's face it—what people do for a living is a critical piece of information about them, but it can be awkward or impolite to ask (there have been times I've been at a particularly stiff cocktail party, asked someone what they did, and been met with silence). Maybe Joe is a wildlife photographer and plays bass in a jazz trio on the weekends for extra money—now there's fodder for at least twenty minutes of chit-chat!—but, since he looks like a mortician, you might never approach him (who wants to talk casket sizes, really?). Do you remember the old TV game show *What's My Line?* in which a panel tried to guess the profession of the guest on the show? And the profession might be snake-charmer or bus driver, cardiologist or game designer? What's Your Line? is a variation in which players have to act out their professions for the rest of the guests!

PLAYERS: 4–10

The Game Plan

* At random, select a guest. (Everyone will have a chance to go, so it doesn't matter who's first.) The chosen guest begins to mime his profession, and players shout out guesses as to what it is. The first person to shout out the correct answer gets a point. Now you may think that some people have it easier than others—ballet dancers or magicians—but c'mon—how many of your friends are magicians? Let's say that one of your guests is a doctor. Sure, she can mime listening to a heartbeat with a stethoscope—but players need to guess her *specific* job. What if she's an orthopedist, or a gastroenterologist, or a dermatologist, or a gynecologist? All of these specialties provide an opportunity for Ms. Serious Doctor to show us what she actually does all day, and perhaps in a pretty hilarious way.

* What's Your Line? gets the awkward what-do-you-do chit-chat out of the way—so you can figure out whose career yin fits with your career yang. And in trying economic times, you'll learn which guests to hit up for job interviews.

Winning

When everyone has had a turn, the player with the most points wins.

Variation

You can also play the way contestants did on the 1950s and '60s TV show *What's My Line?*—by asking yes-or-no questions. The questionee gets a point every time he answers no. If he gets 10 points before the questioners guess his profession, he wins. If a questioner guesses correctly, she wins. To watch an episode of the show, go to www.archive.org.

PARTY RECIPE

Old-Fashioned Lemonade

For a summer cocktail party, make sure to have a special nonalcoholic drink on hand as well.   SERVES 4

INGREDIENTS

Shaved ice	2 liters seltzer
Juice of 8–12 lemons	Orange and lemon slices
8–12 tablespoons powdered sugar	Maraschino cherries

1. Fill a large pitcher with shaved ice.

2. Add lemon juice and sugar and stir well. Pour in seltzer and adjust for taste.

3. Decorate glasses with fruit slices and a cherry. Serve with straws.

Two Truths and a Lie

This game was made famous by *The Howard Stern Show,* but people have been playing it in their devious little hearts forever. Two Truths and a Lie goes in different directions depending on whether you play with friends or strangers. As an icebreaker, it's an excellent way to get to know people.

PLAYERS: 2–15

THE GEAR: Paper, pens.

The Game Plan

✖ Each player writes down three things they have ever done of a daring or unusual nature. Two of the things are true and one is false. The truths, of course, should be counterintuitive—the better to fool your guests with. It's fun to find out which straight-laced MBA is really into Dungeons & Dragons and which long-haired hippie used to be a Young Republican. For some parties, the vibe may head toward the risqué—all the better for quickly getting to know your guests.

✖ The others have to guess which is the lie. Consider these three: 1) I accidentally electrocuted a squirrel. 2) I went Rollerblading in Red Square. 3) I fell asleep during my SATs. Not so easy, right?

Winning

The person who guessed correctly the most times wins (this will be the person whose nonsense antenna is the most finely tuned). An appropriate prize might be a copy of the book *Lies! Lies! Lies! The Psychology of*

Deceit, or Al Franken's *Lies (and the Lying Liars Who Tell Them)*.

▶▶ IF YOU LIKE THIS GAME . . . Try Fib or Not?, a board game.

▶▶ IF YOU LIKE THIS GAME . . . Try Fib or Not?, a board game.

> **AMP IT UP**
> Repurpose an old board game (like Monopoly or Chutes and Ladders). Every time someone gets away with his fib, he gets to move forward a certain number of spaces, say three. Every time someone calls his bluff, that person gets to move forward a lesser, say two, number of spaces. First person around the board wins.

A Knotty Problem

A game for folks who like unraveling knotty problems—and whose patience is rewarded with a charming new acquaintance at the end. Each pair of guests will be given the end of a piece of string and must crawl, twist, and untie to find their partners.

PLAYERS: 4–10

THE GEAR: Lengths of string, like nylon cord. (Thin string, like yarn, tends to tangle.) You should need half as many pieces of string as you have guests. So for a ten-person party, you'll need five lengths of string. Experiment in your space with a 40-foot string and see if you want to go longer or shorter.

Preparation

Thread each piece of string through your living room (or your entire home, or your yard, if you want to go big), looping through things, under things, and over things. Create a sort of obstacle course for each couple. But both ends of the string must be at the front door.

The Game Plan

✄ Once all your guests arrive, distribute one string-end per guest. Each guest must then crawl, climb, and burrow through the space, untangling, untwisting, and unknotting as he goes, until he meets up with the person untangling from the other end.

✄ The first couple to find each other wins, though the game continues until all couples have completed the task. (Players who are finished should help the other players find their partners—by this point many other strings may also be knotted together anyway and it may require a group effort to find each other.) Couples who are strung together are paired off for the rest of the evening's games.

Winning

The first couple to come together wins a small, silly prize, like a how-to book on macramé.

>> **HOST TIP**
If you're trying to make a match, keep track of which string ends go together, so you can make sure that Jane will end up with John as her partner.

Divide and Conquer

Despite its name, Divide and Conquer actually brings your guests together by revealing the interests they have in common. You'll "divide" your guests into groups, using some secret criterion, and they have to interview each other to figure out what that criterion is.

PLAYERS: 4–30

THE GEAR: Paper, pencils.

Preparation

A few days before the party, jot down as many facts about each guest that you can remember—from the banal (Joan likes Labradors) to the absurd (Sally *will not* eat soup). Now try to find connections that will tie (roughly) one half of the party together—everyone once lived in Massachusetts, for example. Do the same for the other half (perhaps everyone in the other group speaks the same second language). If you can't find a connection among more than a few people, divide folks into smaller groups. The facts should be something that *you* know that everyone else probably *doesn't*; for example, that Jim, Jane, John, and Joan have all climbed Everest. (Their first initials are also the same, but that's just too obvious.) Prepare a slip of paper for each guest with the names of the people in his group.

The Game Plan

As your guests arrive, give them their lists of names. They must then circulate and interview each other to figure out what it is they have in common. Do they all like dogs? Did they all vote for Carter? Do they all wear women's underwear? (Less shocking if the group is all women.)

Winning

The first team to correctly deduce their common fact or interest wins. Offer little prizes to the winning players—small bags of jelly beans or boxes of cookies, for example.

Variation

Divide and Conquer may also be played in small groups. Tell your guests that they have something in common with just a few other guests—or even just one guest. You may also decline to tell them who that guest is—thereby encouraging them to talk to as many people as possible! As an incentive, announce at the beginning of the evening that the first guest to find that he has *something* in common with each and every other guest will win the grand prize—which can be a game of Apples to Apples, theater tickets, the latest box set of CDs from a blues musician—whatever your crowd might dig.

▶▶ **HOST TIP**

Don't worry too much if your "connections" aren't airtight. The goal is to get people talking—and when they do, they'll discover that they have things in common that *you* didn't know about—that everyone loves kung fu movies, for example. After all, getting to know each other is the whole point!

Who Am I?

Like 20 questions without the vegetables or minerals, this game elevates the simple yes-or-no question to an art form.

PLAYERS: 4–25

THE GEAR: Paper, pencils, safety pins.

The Game Plan

As your friends arrive, have each one write the name of a famous person—either real or fictional—on a piece of paper. At random, pin one of these papers to the back of each guest. The guests will have to figure out who they are by asking the others yes-or-no questions about their identities. Once a guest has guessed correctly—Am I in politics? Am I a libidinous governor? I'm Eliot Spitzer!—his paper is removed and he is rewarded with, say, a fresh gin and tonic. If he wants to keep playing, quickly make up another name and pin the new identity to his back.

Name Boggle

Sometimes, really, you just want to sit down and work a puzzle. Name Boggle is a great game for when you want to meet people, you want to be social, but you don't have the energy to get off your butt and chat. Name Boggle is a nice quiet get-to-know-you game that can be played from the comfort of your futon.

PLAYERS: 2–6

THE GEAR: Paper, pencils, timer.

The Game Plan

First, one guest introduces herself and spells her full name (first and last). Everyone writes it down. The guests then have one minute to make as many words out of the letters of the name as possible. Players can either make anagrams or smaller words out of the letters. When one minute is up, the next guest introduces himself and the game begins again.

Winning

When everyone's name has been anagrammed, players should read out the words they have made from each name. The person who has generated the most words, total, wins.

Variation

For family events, after you've played the game, make up a poem using those words that expresses something about the family. This may sound sentimental, but poetry can be lighthearted—check out this haiku:

Italians and Jews
So Many Carbs, Little Time
Atkins? Feh. Mangia!

▶▶ **IF YOU LIKE THIS GAME . . . Play Name Boggle at baby showers with the full name of the baby-to-come. For more baby shower games, check out page 198.**

Six-Word Memoir

Memoirs are interesting—you know how gripping *Mommie Dearest* was—but aren't they terribly *long*? So many pages! One gets exhausted just thinking about it. And for a party, of course, no one has time to knock out 600 pages of angst and my-mother-was-a-drunk anecdotes. The solution: The Six-Word Memoir. In short (no pun intended), you have to write your life story in six words, no more, no less. The stories necessarily will be a bit cryptic, and so of course the listeners will want the writers to elaborate. The book that inspired this game, *Not Quite What I Was Planning: Six-Word Memoirs by Writers Famous and Obscure,* is full of six-word cliffhangers—you read the memoir and you're desperate to hear more. If you heard "Stole Wife. Lost friends. Now happy," wouldn't you be begging the author for the whole story?

The brevity of the medium, of course, forces writers to choose their words carefully—when you only have six, every word is critical.

PLAYERS: 2–15

THE GEAR: Paper, pencils.

The Game Plan

As your guests arrive, give them a pencil and paper and ask them to compose their life story in six words (you don't have to write them down, so this game is also good for car trips). Give guests as much time as possible—if you're hosting a sit-down dinner, perhaps let them mull over the assignment during dinner and then ask everyone to read their compositions out loud before dessert. If it's a cocktail party, give people twenty minutes to compose and then read the memoirs to the company. The results will range from the intimate to the flippant and hilarious, and the conversations sparked by the memoirs are 90 percent of the fun. For example, if someone wrote: "Harlan. Silicosis. Benefit. United Nations. Bono!" wouldn't you want to find out a little more about that?

Winning

Though this is not a competitive game, you can make it one. Put all the memoirs in a hat and have the guests try to guess who wrote each memoir. The player with the most correct guesses wins a copy of *Not Quite What I Was Planning.*

A few more samples from recent games:

- *"Struggle Struggle Finally a Winning Streak."*
- *"Left Home. Still Seeking Second One."*
- *"Farm-Raised Free-Range Henny-Penny Nesting Quietly Always."* (In this case, we'll say hyphenated words count as one word, as this was contributed by my mother.)

Variation

The Haiku Memoir: Write your life story in a haiku—a three-line poem in seventeen syllables (the first line has five syllables, the second has seven syllables, and then five again).

|||||||||||||||||||||||||||||||||||||||||||||||||||||||||||||||||||||||||||

Charles Ate a Goat Testicle in Algeria

We've all played **Pin the Tail** on the Donkey, in which you pin a paper tail on a paper donkey. This game is more like Pin the Weird Fact on the Donkey. Players must match obscure little anecdotes with the appropriate guest, and everyone gets to know each other faster than they would if discussing baseball scores.

PLAYERS: 4–30

THE GEAR: Paper, pencils, hat.

The Game Plan

✖ Guests write down three one-sentence tidbits about themselves that even their nearest and dearest don't know—for example, "Until 1st grade, I thought that my pants had to be down around my ankles to use the urinal." The stories (or quirks, like, "I compulsively throw all pennies in the trash") should be one sentence long and as specific as possible. Anecdotes like "I once crashed a car" or "I'm afraid of spiders" are too general because they apply to more than one person. The player pens one sentence per slip of paper. When they're done writing, players toss their three slips in the hat.

✖ Each guest then draws three slips of paper, tossing back any that he wrote. When the host says "Go," everyone begins to interview their fellow guests to match the three stories with three guests.

✖ The only restriction: interviewers *may not* say the pertinent words on the slip of paper. So, if the paper your pal Charles contributed says "I once ate a goat testicle in Algeria" the words *ate, goat, testicle,* and *Algeria* are forbidden by his interviewer. Instead a player might ask of another guest, "Have you ever traveled to Africa?" The hostess should moderate any disputes, but in general guests are on their honor to not ask too-direct questions.

✖ When the hostess feels that everyone has more or less matched their stories with people, she asks each guest in turn to say which person they matched with which anecdote and why. So, Heather might say, "I think it was Charles who once ate a goat testicle in Algeria, because he has traveled to Africa and he is willing to try unusual foods." It's these "whys" that are the crux of the game—even if you're wrong with your guess, you've still learned a few new facts about your fellow partygoers—maybe something even more interesting than what's written on the slips of paper.

✖ Charles will then declare if she's correct—and of course, elaborate on this story for the amusement of the other guests. If she's not

> **▸▸STEALTH STRATEGY ◂**
>
> If the story you draw is potentially embarrassing, be sure to closely watch your interviewee's face. The blush is a dead giveaway.

correct, then she takes another guess. By the end of the game, you'll know a minihistory of your fellow guests—all the better for determining who you want to sit next to at dinner.

Winning

Though the game doesn't require winners and losers, you can make the game a race and instruct your guests to call out "Bingo" when they think they've matched their three stories. The first person to get them all correct wins; if he's wrong, he's lost, but he has to keep trying. Even if he *is* right, the game keeps going to establish second place, third place, etc.

NOTE: For guests who know one another's handwriting quite well, have the players e-mail the hostess ahead of time with the three anecdotes. She can print them out and distribute the slips of paper, thereby keeping all handwriting clues out of the game. Or guests can quickly type them out as they arrive.

Name Game

People don't want to remind you of their names more than once or twice. For those of us who struggle to remember our own children's names, this can make socializing tough. Making friends starts with, well, remembering who they are. The Name Game will help you do just that—and it turns what is normally a chore into a fun activity by making you memorize and list as many people's names as you can without revealing your own.

PLAYERS: 4–30

THE GEAR: Paper, pencil, safety pins.

The Game Plan

✖ As the guests arrive, pin each person's name to his back. Tell the players that the first person to memorize everyone's name will win a prize. Players may not stand with their backs against the wall.

✖ If your guests are straggling in at wildly different times, the earlier arrivals will have an edge—an excellent motivation for getting people to your party on time.

Winning

Be the first person to call out "Done!" and list everyone else's name out loud. Offer the winner a small prize, like a set of ice trays in funky shapes, or Popsicle molds. Offer her a *bigger* prize—like a cookbook or two tickets to the latest movie—if she can repeat the names at the end of the night!

Clap and Clapper

Here's an icebreaker that takes the children's game "hot and cold" to a new and absurd level. Instead of saying "Warmer, warmer," or "Colder, colder," guests decide on a task for an unsuspecting volunteer to perform, and clap hands to indicate his success. The clapping increases in volume as the guest gets closer and closer to performing the task correctly and decreases in volume when he's on the wrong track.

PLAYERS: 3–30

The Game Plan

✖ One person "It" leaves the room while the rest of the group decides on a silly task that he must perform. The tasks can be as low-key (do a jumping jack, pour a fresh drink) or as zany (gather an item of clothing from each guest and put it on, give each guest a kiss) as you want.

✖ Once a task has been decided—let's say it's to gather an item of clothing from each guest and put it on—It returns. He will probably start by wandering aimlessly, a scared little smile on his face (because *God knows* what nutty task his friends have come up with). The rest of the guests begin to clap rhythmically. As It wanders near another guest, the clapping increases in speed and volume. Emboldened by this aural reinforcement, It careens nearer to this guest. The clapping increases. He tentatively stretches out a hand and touches her cap. Clapping becomes louder and louder. He plucks the hat off her head and places it on his own. But! The clapping doesn't stop—so he knows his task is not yet complete. He inches near to another guest and finds the clapping increases when he gets near her shoe. So on and so forth, until It is wearing a whole new outfit.

If the group wants It to do a jumping jack, they might clap slightly louder if he even so much as raises his arms a smidge. This would probably lead to It flapping his arms and eventually hopping up and down. If the group wants It to pour a drink, they might clap louder if he even just leans toward the bar and louder still if he stretches a hand toward the bar.

NOTE: Relatively short, simple, silly tasks are best for this game. Anything too complicated will derail the fun, and eventually the guests will lose their ability to clap with enthusiasm (figuring out how to fix the host's problematic wireless modem connection, for instance, would be too much).

Psychological Scavenger Hunt

On a regular ol' Scavenger Hunt, you run around town looking for certain objects—a manhole cover, a cop on a horse, a cop on a horse on a manhole cover. Well, for a Psychological Scavenger Hunt, instead of *physical* things, partygoers are looking for those *psychological* bugbears that creep in the dark recesses of their fellow guests' minds.

PLAYERS: 4–25

Preparation

Before the party, the host should jot down a bunch of oddball psychological traits—from "afraid of spiders" to "never speeds" or "doesn't ever use an alarm clock." Include a few general quirks—like "eats cereal for dinner" and some commonplace interests such as "likes sailing." Prepare about five facts per guest, making sure they are broad enough so that there's a reasonable chance at least a couple of guests will share that trait. So: "likes dogs, hates cats" is okay, but "blennophobic"[1] is not. Guests shouldn't know what the traits are, so keep mum about the quirks you've thought up. Write each trait on a slip of paper and put the papers in a hat.

[1] *afraid of slime*

The Game Plan

✖ As each guest arrives, have him draw five slips of paper. When you say "go," each guest must interview the others to find a person who matches that trait, with these restrictions:

✖ Guests must ask *indirect* questions in their interviews. So if Jane is talking to Simon, she may not say, "Do you like dogs and hate cats?" She must pose questions like "How do you feel about cockapoos? And if you were getting dressed and saw, say, cat hair on your favorite suit, would you be really enraged or just slightly annoyed?" So once Jane determines that Simon is, in fact, a person who strongly dislikes cats but loves dogs, she can mark Simon's name on the slip of paper and try to find someone else for the next slip. Simon probably will be interviewing Jane at the same time, trying to figure out if she's ever eaten Wheaties for supper.

✖ It's not okay to double up—maybe Simon loves dogs and is also an only child, but he can only satisfy one trait. Remember, the goal is to get to know your fellow guests.

Winning

The first person to match all their traits with five guests should alert the hostess, and she will mark down that person's name as the winner. However, the game continues until everyone has matched their slips of paper with a person; at this point, the hostess will announce that the game's over. One by one, each guest will share his "matches" with the

group. Reading aloud this info with everyone at the end is the most fun part of the game. (Guest A to Guest B: "You think the late afternoon is the best time to fool around? I do too!")

Variation

Psychological Bingo. It's basically the same game, but instead of slips of paper, you make up Bingo cards with traits written in a five-by-five grid ahead of time (see page 372 for a template). This will take a bit of time, as no two guests will have the same Bingo card. You can always ask a willing pal to make up a card or two, as well. Guests play the game as above, but rather than simply matching the traits with a person, they mark the square off on their grid. The first person to get five in a row, either horizontally or vertically, shouts "Bingo" and wins.

Psychological Bingo Sample Card				
Hates corn syrup	Loves Marvin Gaye	Does not recycle	Plays guitar	Went to Montreal
Windsurfs	Tended bar	Reads *Glamour*	Watches *30 Rock*	Does not drive
Has a garden	Cooks	Aunt or uncle	Paints	Loves beets
Has a Wii	Not on Facebook	Handwrites letters	Drinks cocktails	Speaks Spanish
Goes to lectures	Mets fan	Walks to work	Wants folding bike	Has a PhD

Song Scramble

Adapted from *Party Games for Adults,* this is a great icebreaker for people who like to sing. Like the call of sirens, people find their groups by calling or singing out a lyric to the same song. Romantic, no?

PLAYERS: 8–30

THE GEAR: Paper, pens, a hat.

Preparation

✕ When you have a rough idea of how many guests are coming to the party, select a bunch of well-known songs. If you have more than twenty-five guests, choose one song for approximately every four guests. If you have twenty-five or fewer guests, choose one song for every two or three guests.

✕ Before the guests arrive, select two to four lines of lyrics from the songs, and write each line on its own slip of paper. Every guest is then "assigned" one line from a song by choosing a piece of paper from a hat. So Jane might get a slip of paper that reads "This land is your land" and Joe gets one that says "This land is my land" and Fred's reads "from California" and Sally's says "to the New York island."

The Game Plan

Sally, Joe, Fred, and Jane, released into the fray, must find each other. They can do this either by singing their lyric, if they know the song, or reciting the lyrics if they don't. As soon as all four of them have found one another, they begin to sing their song all together.

Winning

The first group to find each other and sing their song wins, but don't stop the game once the first group has found one another—play for second, third, and fourth place! Prizes can be sheet music, mix CDs, or packets of brand-new guitar picks.

▸▸ **HOST TIP**

Check out www.rocktations.com for song lyrics.

Variation

If you're shy about singing and your pals are more literary than musical, try proverbs, poems, or famous quotations.

Common Interests

Ever wish you could know right off the bat which new acquaintances might turn out to be great backgammon players or opera-going pals? Wouldn't it be nice to avoid the guy who's really, really into Second Life *before* you start sharing your first life with him? Common Interests lets you quickly identify the other fly-fishers or find who else really, really appreciates *Gossip Girl* despite being well into her thirties. While the game seems like a getting-to-know-you camp game, the fun lies in what the common interests actually *are.* Maybe someone else's favorite color is green. Great. But did you know that at least four other guests at this party voted for Gore *and* like having their collarbones kissed? (You may find your soul mate!) Common Interests allows guests to find other people who share their (weird, esoteric, idiosyncratic) passions.

PLAYERS: 4–20

THE GEAR: Paper, pens, a hat.

The Game Plan

✖ As your guests arrive, have them jot down, on slips of paper, characteristics or idiosyncrasies that they might have in common with the group. (See "A Few Ideas to Get You Started," right.) Each guest should generate three to five slips of paper and put them in a hat. Choose a moderator or a pair of moderators. (The moderators can become players in the next round.) The group stands in a circle; the moderator(s) stand(s) a little apart from the group with the hat. The moderator then draws a slip of paper from the hat and reads it out loud, followed by "Go!" For example, he might say: "Everyone who likes chocolate, go!" The people who like chocolate must run into the circle, tag hands, and run back out. The moderator then pulls another from the hat and calls out another little factoid, such as: "Everyone who absolutely *must* wear SPF 80 or above, go!"

✖ Because the slips of paper will likely range from the banal to the loony—from who likes pasta and who hails from New Jersey to who washes their feet first in the shower and who thinks that Banana Republic is actually a secret country where all white people dress identically. Guests' oddball traits and preferences and habits become bonding opportunities with other guests, and everyone gets to know everyone's foibles. It's humanizing to know little factoids about someone—that they're

A Few Ideas to Get You Started

Stuck for some common interests—especially the weird, esoteric, idiosyncratic ones? Try these:

- read *Nancy Drew* books as a child
- read *All-of-a-Kind Family* books as a child
- only read comic books as a child
- drives a car that gets more than 30 mpg
- doesn't drive a car
- is a Lakers fan
- is worried that no-iron shirts might be poisoning us
- sometimes eats mac and cheese with ketchup
- remembers when Reagan said that ketchup was a vegetable
- has plastered a wall
- has snaked a drain
- doesn't know what it means to snake a drain
- has experienced a breakup that made him or her lose or gain ten or more pounds
- eats fast food
- eats only fast food while on long road trips
- has a relative who is really, really stupid
- has considered slapping said relative
- has an item of purple clothing
- thinks that as long as one is wearing all blue, regardless of shade, one matches

attracted to Alan Alda or that they like to pour the milk in the bowl before the cereal.

United Nations

A **silly game** that involves gibberish, blindfolds, and collisions. No, it's not a congressional press conference! It's a fun game! Like the Song Scramble on page 26, each group has to find its members—but instead of singing a song, they'll be speaking a common language. Whether anyone actually knows this language is irrelevant: Pretending to be a Russian spy or a French femme fatale brings out the ridiculous in all of us.

PLAYERS: 8–30

THE GEAR: Blindfolds.

The Game Plan

✘ Assign each guest a country and a language: If there are fewer than fifteen guests, assign two people to the same language; for larger parties assign three or more people to a language. Instruct the guests not to reveal their "nationality" before the game starts. When you're ready to begin, have each guest blindfold himself.

✘ At the word "Go," all players must wander about, muttering or yelling, as they see fit, in their best interpretation of what Russian (or Yiddish, or Esperanto) sounds like. People bumping into each other, clutching each other and hollering, "Achtung! Achtung!" while someone else inquires "Et tu, Brute?" can only result in lifelong friendships.

Winning

The first group to find each other wins.

▶▶ **IF YOU LIKE THIS GAME . . . consider a subscription to** *Games* **magazine—this game was created by former editor Phil Wiswell.**

Mr. Hit

M **r. Hit is a game frequently** played as a warm-up before theater rehearsals to keep everyone on their toes. It gets the blood flowing, the legs pumping, and it's great for learning people's names. Similar to a game of tag, when you see "It" (aka "Mr. Hit") running toward you, you have to call someone *else's* name before you're tagged. You'd be surprised how often people call out their own name or the name of the tagger before they're able to remember a name of another player. Even if you're *not* the swiftest at remembering names, you'll still have a blast trying to dodge Mr. Hit before he gets you.

PLAYERS: 6–25

The Game Plan

✘ Introduce the guests to one another.
✘ Select one person to be Mr. Hit. The game always begins with Mr. Hit calling out, "Who am I?" and everyone else answering in unison, "Mr. Hit!" Mr. Hit then tries to tag someone, who can save herself only by calling out the name of another player before Mr. Hit touches her. The player whose name was called then becomes Mr. Hit and immediately tries to tag someone,

who can save herself only by calling out the name of another player before she's tagged . . . and so on.

✖ If a player is tagged before he can call out someone's name, the game starts again with that player as Mr. Hit. He must begin by calling out, "Who am I?"

▶▶ **IF YOU LIKE THIS GAME . . . try Pussy Wants a Corner, on page 68.**

||||||||||||||||||||||||||||||||||||||||||||||||||||||||||||

Questions

An excellent game to play over dinner, this quiet game will spark conversation.

PLAYERS: 2–10

THE GEAR: Paper, pencils, a hat.

The Game Plan

✖ Guests each make up one or more questions that are designed to get people talking, write them down, and put the slips of paper in a hat. The questions can range from the *Sophie's Choice* type—which kid would you choose?—to the comic or banal: how do you get ready for a date?; to Labs or Dachshunds? Why? In turn, guests pull questions from the hat, read them aloud, and answer.

▶▶ **IF YOU LIKE THIS GAME . . . try The Ungame, a noncompetitive board game in which you get to know your family and friends maybe better than you ever wanted to.**

▶▶ **IF YOU LIKE THIS GAME . . . Check out other Conversation Games starting on page 81.**

A Few Ideas to Get You Started

- Would you be willing to move to a distant country for a person you loved deeply, knowing there would be little chance of seeing your friends or family again?

- Do you believe in ghosts or evil spirits? Would you be willing to spend a night alone in a remote house that is supposedly haunted?

- If you were to die this evening with no opportunity to communicate with anyone, what would you most regret not having told someone? Why haven't you told them yet?

- If you could spend one year in perfect happiness but afterward would remember nothing of the experience, would you do so? If not, why not?

- If a new medicine were developed that would cure arthritis but could cause a fatal reaction in one percent of those who took it, would you want it to be released to the public?

- You discover that your wonderful one-year-old child is, because of a mix-up at the hospital, not yours. Would you want to exchange the child to try to correct the mistake?

- Do you think the world will be a better or worse place a hundred years from now?

NOTE: These are from *The Book of Questions,* a great resource if you're looking for inspiration. The answers should spark a discussion, or at least a round of sage nods.

Dancing Cheek to Cheek

Great for literally warming up a party, Dancing Cheek to Cheek gets people moving. Each guest is tied to his partner—which gives your guests a common goal to pursue while they're grooving to the music.

PLAYERS: 4–30

The Game Plan

Pair up your guests. Tie each pair together, back to back, around the waist. Gin up the iPod and pick a song with a funky beat. Each couple must get to the end of the song without collapsing into giggles, still attached to and moving rhythmically with their partners. Of course, there can be more than one winner.

A Few Ideas to Get You Started

- "I Wish I Could Shimmy Like My Sister Kate," Muggsy Spanier
- "My Blue Heaven," Fats Domino
- "I Gotcha," Joe Tex
- "Night Fever," The Bee Gees
- "Kiss," Prince
- "Jailhouse Rock," Elvis Presley
- "Electric Avenue," Eddy Grant
- "Pump Up the Jam," Salt-N-Pepa

PARTY RECIPE

The Icebreaker

A drink always helps the hips shake a little faster. If you're playing in the living room on a cold winter's night, serve this drink with dessert and set the needle on the turntable for the after-dinner dancing portion of the evening.   SERVES 4

INGREDIENTS

4 tablespoons cocoa powder	2 ounces each of peppermint schnapps,
8 tablespoons sugar	Kahlua, and dark
8 tablespoons water	crème de cacao
4 cups milk	Whipped cream, for garnish

Combine cocoa, sugar, and water in a small saucepan. Heat over a low flame, stirring constantly. When a paste has formed (after about 1 or 2 minutes), add the milk. Continue stirring until just at the boiling point, tasting and adding more cocoa or sugar if desired. Remove from heat. Add a ½ ounce each of peppermint schnapps, Kahlua, and crème de cacao to four large warmed mugs. Fill the mugs with hot chocolate, stir, and top with whipped cream.

Pass the Orange

Standard greetings are so cut and dried: a handshake, a peck on the cheek, maybe a fist bump if you're feeling daring. How often do you get close enough to a new acquaintance to really smell his aftershave? Pass the Orange, a favorite at Club Med and other singles-type places, has gotten a bad rap as a cheesy way to cop a feel. But the game is really just another way to break down barriers—to free yourself from standard modes of greeting and speed up the slow process of getting to know new people. At its essence, it's tremendously silly—letting you engage in a task with other guests that has the potential to reduce everyone to giggles.

PLAYERS: 3–20

The Game Plan

✕ The rules are as simple as can be: Stand or sit in a circle (alternating men and women, if you'd like). Have a guest tuck an orange under his neck and pass it to the player on his left, without hands. That player then passes it to the person on *her* left. If you're successful, everyone is rewarded with a little prize—a trinket, or a fresh drink, or a no-bid contract to drill for oil in Alaska (depending on who your friends are).

✕ There's something about a silly little cooperative project that will bring out the utmost in concentration—and that in itself is funny. (My dad, ultracompetitive even in cooperative games, *will not let* the orange drop—as if to do so would be chalked up as a loss on that great scoreboard in the sky.) It's this certain amount of teamwork, combined with some PG-rated touching, that gets a party going: It's hard to be stiff with someone you've smushed chests with.

Variation

Life Saver on a Toothpick. Everyone holds a toothpick between his teeth. One guest threads a Life Saver onto his toothpick and then must pass it to the next guest's toothpick. Careful of your eyes!

Big Booty

Big Booty is a game in which players strive to keep a rhythm as a group. Almost like a dance, Big Booty is a great warm-up for other, more movement-oriented games. The players stand in a circle doing a variation on a rhythmic call and response, and when *your* number is called, you must answer without losing the beat. If you'd like to watch a round of Big Booty, check out thegamesbible.com.

PLAYERS: 3–15

The Game Plan

✕ Everyone stands in a circle. Choose a "Big Booty," or a leader; this person is in the "head" position (where this is is arbitrary as it's a circle). The rest of the group counts off, starting with the person on Big Booty's right. For this example, let's say there are ten players. So you'd have Big Booty and Positions Number One through Nine.

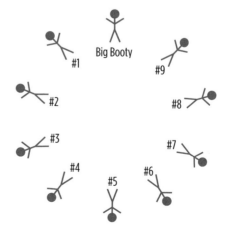

- The leader establishes a rhythm with clapping—starting at a slow tempo. Everyone claps along with this beat.

- Once the rhythm is established, everyone chants together: "Uh huh, Big Booty, Big Booty, Big Booty."

- Big Booty calls out, *in time with the beat,* her position and the position of another person. For example, the leader will call out "Big Booty, Number Three."

- That person whose position was called must respond, *in time with the beat,* with his position and the position of someone else. So in our example, the person in position number three will call out—without hesitating or missing a beat—"Number Three, Number Six."

- The person in position six responds "Number Six, Number [whatever]."

- And so on. The leader, at her discretion, will gradually speed up the tempo.

- If someone hesitates or misses a beat—as determined by the group, though goof-ups are pretty obvious—the game pauses and that person moves to the last position. In our example, let's say the person in position Number Six wasn't paying attention and didn't respond with the beat. She then moves to the last position (Number Nine); everyone who had a number higher than hers shifts down a position. So the person who was in position Number Nine is now in Number Eight, and so on. If Big Booty misses a beat or hesitates, she must move to the end position, and Number One becomes Big Booty, Number Two becomes Number One, and so on.

- To resume play after someone gets demoted, everyone chants together: "Uh Huh. Big Booty, Big Booty, Big Booty," and Big Booty then calls out "Big Booty" and a number.

Winning

Big Booty is technically noncompetitive, though the people who remain stuck in the higher-numbered positions clearly are not going to put "Big Booty expert" on their résumés.

Animal Attraction

If you liked United Nations, you'll love Animal Attraction. It takes the silliness to a whole new level—a crouching, crawling, sniffing level. You're assigned to be an animal, and you have to find your mate or the rest of your pack, or flock, or pride—without words. So get ready to lope and caw and find the other members of the party that are loping and cawing toward you.

PLAYERS: 10–30

THE GEAR: Pencil, paper, hat.

The Game Plan

- Jot down names of animals on slips of paper.

- Make sure there are at least two of each critter; for thirty or more people you can experiment with three or four of a kind. Put the slips of paper in a hat and have guests draw one out. (They shouldn't tell anyone else what animal they've drawn.) When you say go, each "animal" must find his mate (or his pack, for large parties), by pretending to be that animal. Slithering, barking, and gobbling should ensue. As with other "find your partner" games, guests might not want to rush to find their pack, as the sight of staid Aunt Martha slithering across the divan may be too hilarious to cut short. (Keep in mind that your guests might get carried away, so move the china out of the way of the charging bull, and ask the woodpecker to keep moving around the room so he doesn't peck his way through your stereo cabinet.)

Limbo Dance Contest

You may remember the limbo from eighth-grade gym class, or, more recently, from vacations at Caribbean resorts. The dance, in which players bend backwards and shimmy under a pole that is progressively lowered, rewards flexibilty, agility, and a certain amount of daring—you really have to throw caution to the wind and hope your chiropractor is free the next day. (There's a reason why rum is usually served before, during, and after the limbo.) It's perfect for nights when the more cerebral, talky icebreakers are a little too stiff for the wacky gang you've invited over. And while the white sands of the beach are the ideal terrain, you can limbo in the living room, on the front porch, or down Fifth Avenue.

PLAYERS: 6–50

THE GEAR: Chubby Checker's "Limbo Rock," or any Calypso music that catches your fancy. A stick (like a long curtain rod), or a length of rope, suspended horizontally in such a way that it can be lowered as the game progresses.

The Game Plan

✖ Appoint two members of your party—perhaps a couple of your more bashful pals, who would no more limbo than they would streak through the crew races at Henley—to hold the ends of the stick and stand about five feet apart. To begin, they should hold it at a height that will let most people pass under fairly comfortably, and then lower the rope by intervals of about six inches with each round. Cue up your chosen music.

✖ Dancers line up, and traveling in a single file, shimmy their way toward the limbo pole. Dancers must lean backward and dance under the limbo stick without touching it and without falling. After everyone has danced under the limbo stick once, the two stick-holders lower the bar. If a player touches the stick or loses his balance, he's eliminated. With each round, the stick-holders lower the bar a little more. If someone can't quite make it under the stick, but makes an especially valiant and/or ridiculous effort to do so, allow him to stay in for one more round—just to amuse the other guests.

Winning

The last limbo dancer is the winner and is awarded a Gumby doll—or a gift certificate for a massage.

Variation

For double the fun, ask guests to go under the limbo stick in pairs. As the host, you should match up the dancers so that everyone has an opportunity to meet other guests they might otherwise not have connected with yet.

Can I Buy You a Drink?

C an I Buy You a Drink? is played either at a bar or at a private party equipped with a full bar. It's ideal for large parties where no one knows very many of the other guests. Can I Buy You a Drink? gets you circulating faster as you approach guests with their favorite cocktails—and even if you approach the "wrong" person, you'll still be meeting someone new. Everyone wins.

PLAYERS: 20–150

THE GEAR: A large bowl, index cards, pencils. You'll need a full bar at which guests (or a bartender) can mix drinks.

Preparation

Before the guests arrive, set a stack of index cards and a few pencils beside a large bowl.

The Game Plan

✖ As your guests arrive, instruct them to write their favorite drink and their name on two cards and drop them in the bowl. Each guest should then take two cards with two different people's names out of the bowl. These people will be his two "targets."

✖ The player brings a target—or who he thinks is his target—he's guessing here—her favorite drink (or closest approximation) and says, "Hello, can I buy you a drink?"

✖ If he's gotten it right (he has approached the correct person), his target must then give him one of *her* target cards and he will repeat the process with the new target (as well as try with the other one of his original target cards).

▶▶ **HOST TIP**

As guests arrive, have them drop their cards in the bowl, but tell the early arrivals to wait until at least twenty other people have arrived before drawing their two target cards.

Winning

Collect the most cards by the end of the party to win. If you lose both of the target cards you started with—meaning the two people who drew your name found you and bought your drinks—you're out of the game. Even if you've lost, though, people will still be bringing *you* drinks and chatting you up—guessing you are the person named on their target cards—so you'll still be meeting people.

NOTE: If a player can't find a target, he may return it to the bowl and exchange that card for another. Players may only do this three times.

—contributed by Greg Trefry, cofounder of the game-development studio Gigantic Mechanic. For more about Greg, check out www.giganticmechanic.com and www.comeoutandplay.org.

Chapter Three

GUESSING GAMES

Guessing games are great equalizers. It doesn't matter if *you* know Adlai Stevenson's claim to fame—if your teammates don't, you're sunk. And if they're trying to get you to scream *"The Sopranos"* but you haven't watched TV since *CHiPs,* well, you're in trouble. But take heart: Winning at guessing games rarely depends on intellect or smarts or an MBA from Harvard. It has to do with how silly and creative you can get. Are you willing to contort your shoulders into a Richard Nixon stance? How about flopping around on the carpet while demonstrating the Worm? Can you mime the phrase "credit default swaps?" It's these daring risk-takers who mop the floor with their opponents.

If you really want to find out what's going on in your pals' psyches, try a guessing game. For example, in a game like Celebrity—in which everyone quickly generates a hatful of famous names—you'll get a glimpse of what's lurking in the collective subconscious. Call it the "micro-zeitgeist"—in a recent game I played with three friends, all of us put Olympia Snowe's name into the hat. None of us is particularly political; we all shrugged and said sheepishly, "I love her name." It's these little meetings of the mind that make guessing games (and games in general) such a social, connective experience.

How serendipitous to discover that a new acquaintance is also a Chick Corea or *Kids in the Hall* fan!

Fortunately, there are dozens—if not hundreds—of guessing games available, so you can choose one that plays to your guests' strengths—or your own strengths, for that matter. You've got a knack for composing silly stories? Try Match the Match Ad. You're a real ham or master thespian? Charades or one of its nine variations is your game. Word freak? Well, try Nocturnal Time Completely Lacking Noise.

Here we present enough games to keep you guessing until the end of time.

Charades (and its many offspring)

Charades has endured for at least 200 years as a party game because it is *the* perfect social activity—it can be as silly or as serious as the players want, as smart or as dumb, as long or as short—it's infinitely adaptable and malleable and always, always fun. Charades is perfect for parties at which not all the attendees are native English-speakers—as long as the clues are things or people well known to all cultures, anyone can play.

A long time ago, I hosted a Charades New Year's Day brunch in Paris with a bunch of my fellow international students. Hungover oddballs from around the world competed to act out "Marilyn Monroe," an "ironing board," the film *Throw Momma from the Train,* etc. A tall, skinny Swiss girl had us in convulsions with her pantomime of Nelson Mandela: First she got us to guess the country by lurching around and pretending to be an elephant and then tiptoeing and nibbling leaves like a giraffe. Once we hit on "South Africa," she declaimed passionately (in mime) through the bars of her "jail cell." You don't have to be a Swiss ham to enjoy this game, though—you just have to be willing to be silly.

Most everyone knows the basics: Generate a list of things to act out, hop around and contort yourself into weird stances to get your teammates to make guesses, and touch your nose when they've shouted out the correct answer. Did you know just *how many* kinds of Charades exist, though? Plenty, I'll tell you. Below you'll find nine variations.

PLAYERS: 4–30

THE GEAR: A watch, paper, pencils, two hats.

The Game Plan

✄ Divide your group into two teams of at least two people each. Provide both teams with slips of paper (start with about twice as many slips of paper as people playing, but you can experiment with how long or short you want your game to be) and send one team into another room.

✄ Give the teams ten minutes to jot down titles of books, movies, plays, television shows, and songs and drop the slips of paper into a hat. (The group can decide ahead of time if they want the categories

Play Fair

Now, there is a temptation in Charades to make the clues *really, really* hard. And while you may stump the other team, you won't have as much fun—and you might not have any friends when the game is over. (A guest of mine once put "Bhagavad Gita" in the hat—and I've never really forgiven her for it.) Adhere to these guidelines to ensure fair play:

- Only phrases that at least three people on the team have heard of (or both people, if you're playing in groups of two).

- Phrases can't be longer than seven words.

- Phrases can't consist solely of a proper name.

- Foreign phrases are forbidden.

But That's Not How *We* Play!

Charades has a couple of other options for scoring:

1. A team has three minutes to guess a single phrase. When they get it, the timekeeper records how many seconds the players needed to get to a correct answer, and the turn switches to the other team (so your team is acting out only one clue on a single turn, even if you get it in three seconds). If the team *doesn't* guess the phrase in three minutes, the timekeeper announces that the time is up, and records a time of three minutes. The unguessed phrase is discarded. Play continues until each player has had a chance to act out one phrase. The team with the lowest total time at the end wins.

2. If the team guesses correctly within a two-minute time limit, it scores a point. If it doesn't, the other team gets a point for thinking up such a difficult (though still adhering to the "Play Fair" rules on page 37) clue. The teams alternate acting out clues until every player has had a chance to go. The team with the most points wins.

3. Unguessed clues can't be tossed back in the hat, and players may not pass. So if *you* draw "Bhagavad Gita," just do the best you can.

to be more rigid or loose—whether the clues are *just* titles, or if they can be phrases, quotations, famous people, or concepts . . . the sky's the limit.) These words or phrases are target answers to be acted out.

✖ For example, if the answer was *Little House on the Prairie,* you might: Unfold your hands to tell your teammates that it's a book. Hold up five fingers to indicate that the title has five words. Hold up one finger to say that you are about to act out the first word of the title. Lay two fingers on your forearm to indicate that it's a two-syllable word. Mime something little—either by pinching your fingers together, or pretending to be very small, or by miming holding something very tiny in your hands. Once one of your teammates has shouted out "little," you touch your nose to indicate a correct guess. (At this point someone on your team might holler *"Little House on the Prairie,"* in which case you grab another clue from the hat and act that one out, too.) If not, hold up two fingers to indicate you're going to act out the second word. Draw a rectangle in the air with your hands, then draw a triangular roof, and then pretend to be opening the door and walking in. At this point your teammates should be yelling "house!" and then *"Little House on the Prairie!"* and you can grab another slip from the hat and start again.

If you don't know how to act out a word in its entirety—say you've tried to mime *prairie* by spreading your hands wide to indicate a vast expanse, and your team's just not getting it—you can break the words into syllables. For *prairie,* lay two fingers on your arm to indicate "two syllables" and then one finger on your arm to indicate you're working on the first syllable. Then get down on your knees in a prayer position and hope a teammate says *prayer.* The second syllable—*ie*—is tougher, but with any luck your teammates will guess the answer before you have to come up with some way to mime a long *e* sound.

✖ Once all the slips of paper are in the hat, the teams rejoin each other. A player has two minutes to act out as many words or phrases as she can. The first player draws a slip of paper from the other team's hat; the timekeeper (either a neutral party or a member of the other team) says "Go," and the player begins acting out the word or phrase on the paper to his own teammates, probably relying heavily on the shorthand, below. If the player's team guesses the phrase, she grabs another slip of paper from the hat and acts out that word or words, and

so on until two minutes have elapsed and the timekeeper announces that time's up. If the team can't guess an answer before time's up, the slip of paper goes back in the hat. (Now, if unguessed clues are put back in the hat, the person who was giving clues on one round will obviously have the advantage on the next round. This is acceptable. As long as the two batches of clues are reasonably equal in difficulty, each team will probably have a player or two who has seen one or more of the answers. This also means the pace of the game will accelerate toward the end. You'll

Charades Shorthand

To indicate categories:

- **Book title:** Unfold your hands as if they were a book.

- **Movie title:** Pretend to crank an old-fashioned movie camera.

- **Play title:** Mime the curtains of a theater opening.

- **Song title:** Pretend to sing.

- **TV show:** Draw a rectangle with your fingers, as if outlining a TV screen.

- **Quote or phrase:** Make quotation marks in the air with your fingers.

To indicate other things:

- **Number of words in the title:** Hold up the number of fingers.

- **Which word you're working on:** Hold up the number of fingers again.

- **Number of syllables in the word:** Lay the number of fingers on your forearm.

- **Which syllable you're working on:** Hold up that number of fingers.

- **Length of word:** Make a "little" or "big" sign as if you were measuring a fish.

- **"The entire concept":** Sweep your arms through the air.

- **"On the nose"** (i.e., someone has made a correct guess): Point at your nose with one hand, while pointing at the person with your other hand.

- **"Sounds like":** Tug an earlobe.

- **"Longer version of":** Pretend to stretch a piece of elastic.

- **"Shorter version of":** Do a karate chop with your hand.

- **"Past tense":** Wave your hand over your shoulder toward your back.

- **A letter of the alphabet:** Move your hand in a chopping motion toward your arm (near your elbow if the letter is near the beginning of the alphabet, and near your wrist if the letter is near the end of the alphabet).

know that your teammate is trying to act out "Newt Gingrich" by being a tiny frog because you tried to do the same thing five minutes ago. The faster pace will only make the game more exciting. Some rules say that any acted-out but unguessed phrases must be credited to the *other* team—see "But That's Not How *We* Play!" on page 38.)

✖ The other team then has a turn. The first team to empty its hat wins.

NOTE: If you pull a slip from the hat and you don't know who or what it is—let's say it's *Johnny Tremain*—you can throw it back in (passing) and draw another. The only forfeit is lost time. If you get down to the last few slips of paper, you may have to act out the words syllable by syllable or even, if necessary, letter by letter (see "Charades Shorthand," page 39).

Charades Variations

Race Charades

Two teams play in two different rooms, with a moderator stationed halfway between them. The rooms should be far enough apart, and/or have doors, to reduce the chances of the other team overhearing the shouted guesses. The moderator makes up ten phrases and writes each phrase on two slips of paper, for a total of twenty slips of paper. (If the

---

AMP IT UP

When one team has won a round of a guessing game, it may select a member of the losing team and absorb him into their group. When one team has completely absorbed another, the game's over.

---

moderator is unable or disinclined to make up ten phrases, she may ask each participant to make up one or two each and write them in duplicate.) The first player from each team runs to the moderator to receive the first charade (which will be the same for each team) and races back to his team to act it out. When the team has guessed the charade, the second player races to the moderator to get the next clue. The first team to complete all the charades wins, and a new game begins with a new moderator.

Current Events Charades

Have each team jot down a number of current events—from "Scandal-Plagued Senator Steps Down" to "Unemployment Hits a New High" to "Ohio Woman Stabs Husband over Furniture-Rearranging Tiff." Don't get too sticky about whether an event is strictly "current," provided that it's an item that has been in the news over the last six months or so. Players must guess the general gist of the current event—it is not necessary to guess the exact words on the paper.

One-Word Charades

Restrict yourselves to one word. It's pretty hard—but amusing—to mime the word *bacteria*.

TV Charades

Teams act out the titles and/or general themes of various TV shows.

Monster Movie Charades

In this rather specific genre-version of charades, the answers must be monster movies. Of course, you can also play this with any movie titles—romantic-comedy charades, anyone?

Fortune-Cookie Charades

Serve fortune cookies for dessert and have the guests toss the fortunes into a hat; guests then draw fortunes from the hat and act them out.

Noisemaker Charades

Instead of things to act out, have your guests jot down specific noises—car alarm, percolating coffee pot, lemur, etc. Players have to read the slip of paper and imitate the noise described for their team to guess. Have you ever heard the sound-effects guy on *A Prairie Home Companion* imitate a loon? It's darn funny. Check out *Mouth Sounds* by Fred Newman for more ideas.

Tabloid Charades

Collect ridiculous or interesting tabloid headlines over the course of the week before the party and have your guests act them out. Don't get hung up on exact wording— if the headline is "Angelina Jolie Delivers Quintuplets," then "Angelina Jolie Has Five More Kids" is close enough.

Tiered Charades

You'll need paper, pencils, timer, and six hats or other small containers to hold the various clues. Each team should come up with twenty-five easy 1-point answers, like "kiss," "skirt," or "doughnut"; fifteen somewhat challenging 2-point ones, like "daily," "job," or "train tracks"; and ten difficult 3-point answers, like "mercenary," "abstract," or "desperate," for a total of fifty. It is up to the team to decide how difficult each answer is and assign a point value. The two teams put all their 1-point words in one hat, all their 2-point words in another hat, and all their 3-point words in a third. The play proceeds as in Charades, but the clue-giver can choose whether she wants to draw a slip from the easy, medium, or hard hat. Play proceeds in one-minute rounds: Each team has one minute to get as many of the words as they can and then the other team takes a turn.

Winning

For all but Tiered Charades, scoring is as in the regular Charades. Keep some small prizes on hand for the winning team, like mix CDs, fresh, unsharpened pencils, boxes of turtle candies, or gift certificates to your local artisanal doughnut shop.

▶▶ IF YOU LIKE THIS GAME . . . check out Pictionary on page 113.

|||||||||||||||||||||||||||||||||||||||||||||||||||||||||||||||||||||||||||||||||

Tiered Name Guessing

Tiered Name Guessing is a combination of Celebrity and Password. Players try to guess the name of the person someone else is thinking of, with clues that start out hard and get easier.

PLAYERS: 4–10

THE GEAR: Paper, pencils.

The Game Plan

Instruct each player to write down the name of a famous person and six facts about that person, ranging from (in the opinion of the writer) very obscure to very obvious. So if you were to write "Barack Obama," your clues might range from "he likes to play poker" (obscure) to "the 44th president of the United

States" (obvious). Each guest reads out his most obscure clue, and other players write down who they think it is. He then reads out his next-most obscure clue, and guests can write down the same name, if they think they had it right the first time, or change it.

Winning

After everyone has had a turn, players get 6 points for the names they guessed correctly on the first round, five for the ones they guessed on the next, and so on. If a player guesses correctly on an early round and then changes his answer for the second round, and then changes it *back* to the original guess on a later round, he nets *only* the points for the later round. So you can't get 6 points for answering correctly on the first round if you changed your answer on the second and then back again on the third—you would score only 4 points. Each member of the winning team gets a $1 e-gift certificate from iTunes to buy a song by The Guess Who.

The Sticky-Note Game

The Sticky-Note Game is a perfect little appetizer or dessert of a game— it takes only about twenty minutes, requires minimal gear, and can be played by several generations at once around the dinner table.

PLAYERS: 2–10

THE GEAR: Sticky notes, pens.

To start, each guest writes a name (a celebrity, a fictional character, someone you all know— decide on the parameters beforehand) on a sticky note and passes it to another guest. Each player, without looking at the sticky-note, sticks it to her forehead. In order, going in a circle, players ask yes-or-no questions of the other players to determine the name on her own forehead. The questions are posed to the group, and anyone may answer. The first player to guess his own identity wins. Continue playing until everyone has guessed to establish second place, third place, and runners-up.

Botticelli

All of the players are trying to guess what person "It" is thinking of, and It is trying to guess who the rest of the group is thinking, as well. Essentially a two-way guessing game, Botticelli is a game in which one player is pitted against the rest.

PLAYERS: 2–6

The Game Plan

➤ To begin, choose an "It." It thinks of a famous person (or a fictional character, if all players have agreed on this beforehand). A non-famous person with whom all the players are familiar is OK if, again, all players agree ahead of time. The person should be someone It is comfortable answering biographical questions about, and someone he is confident that the other players (the guessers) will all have heard of. This only works well for a group of players who know all the same people, as you have to be sure that everyone is familiar enough with Vince the Super or Dr. Seitz the Sociology/ Anthropology professor to be able to guess.

✕ It then announces the initial letter of the name by which the person is usually known; this is usually the last name. For example, if he chose "Sandro Botticelli," It would announce, "My last name begins with *B*."

✕ Play then proceeds in rounds of *specific* questions and *general yes-or-no* questions.

✕ The guessers, taking turns, think of someone whose last name begins with that letter. Let's say the first guesser thinks of Bill Bryson. He poses a *specific* question to It: "Are you a famous and funny travel writer?" It, guessing who he means, says, "No, I am not Bill Bryson."

✕ The next guesser takes her turn to ask a *specific* question, such as "Are you a famous and reclusive actor?" It might reply, "No, I am not Marlon Brando," or, "No, I am not Alec Baldwin." If It *can't* figure out to whom the guesser is alluding, he must say he is stumped.

✕ The guesser who stumped him then gets to ask a *general yes-or-no* question, such as "Are you a man?" It answers *yes* or *no*; the guessers have gathered a piece of valuable information (that It is thinking of a man).

✕ The questioning then passes to the next guesser, who takes a turn asking a *specific* question now limited to men: e.g., "Were you known as the hardest-working man in show business?" hoping It doesn't know that the answer to this is James Brown. Again, if It is stumped, that guesser gets to ask a general yes-or-no question, like "Are you alive?"

✕ In this fashion, the guessers glean information from It. As they hone in on who It is thinking of—for example, perhaps they now know that he is male and dead— their questions must also narrow. So if the guessers know that It is a man, they *can't* ask "Are you a former child star who became a U.S. ambassador?" because the answer is female—Shirley Temple Black.

Winning
Game play continues until a guesser correctly hits on the identity. That guesser is the winner. It wins if all the guessers give up or if an hour passes, whichever comes first. Reward the victor with a box of Jacques Torres Pure Bliss brownie mix.

Variations
✕ Vermicelli follows the same rules, but is limited to the names of foods.

✕ Bratislava is restricted to geographical names.

✕ Protozoa is restricted to the names of living things, like kingdoms, phylums, classes, orders, families, genuses, or species. Protozoa is perhaps best played by biologists.

||||||||||||||||||||||||||||||||||||||||||||||||||||||||||||||||||||||||||

Nocturnal Time Completely Lacking Noise

I **found this game** on the blog of a playwright acquaintance, Karen Walcott. Can you think of synonyms for "Baby Got Back" or "Single Ladies (Put a Ring on It)"

or "All Along the Watchtower"? An excellent game for long car trips, Nocturnal Time will keep you entertained for at least a few exits along the freeway—and the winner of the game gets to pick the music for the next thirty minutes.

PLAYERS: 2–10

The Game Plan

Each player should think of a well-known song. He should then turn the name into a convoluted, wordy synonym. For example: "Silent Night" = "Nocturnal Time Completely Lacking Noise." He announces the synonym to the group. The first person to guess the correct title gets a point. I recently played with a friend over g-chat, and he came up with "a trip on an enchanted tapestry."[1] I riposted with "the man who stakes money on games of chance."[2] We spent a good half-hour on this game—some might even say we were "not making productive use of our work hours."[3] It was worth it.

[1] *"Magic Carpet Ride," Steppenwolf*
[2] *"The Gambler," Kenny Rogers*
[3] *"Wasting My Time," The White Stripes*

Winning

When all the convoluted, wordy synonyms have been announced and guessed, the person with the most points wins a prize, like a paperback thesaurus or the latest Bob Dylan album. (With just two players, the game is noncompetitive—you'll pose a synonym to your pal, and he'll try to guess it.)

I Accuse

In I Accuse, **players** will choose an identity for themselves—and hope that no one can guess it. The player who correctly identifies the other players' alter egos wins.

PLAYERS: 4–20, plus a moderator.

THE GEAR: A sheet of paper and a pen.

The Game Plan

✖ Select one player to be the moderator and send her into another room with a pen and paper. One by one, the other players leave and give the moderator the name of a famous person or fictional character. A typical list might include the Archbishop of Canterbury, Josephine Baker, Mario Batali, etc. The idea is to pick a name that no one would associate with you. When everyone has given a name, the moderator returns to the room and reads out the list of names.

✖ She then chooses who starts the game. This person decides who is most likely to have chosen a particular name, makes an accusation, and gives a reason for her accusation, saying, for example, "Jane is a dancer, so I accuse Jane of being Josephine Baker."

✖ The accused either acknowledges that this is true (if it is) and is eliminated (and the accuser may accuse someone else), or she will deny the charge and make an accusation herself. Jane might say, "No, I'm not Josephine Baker, but since I know that Fred watches cooking shows all day, he *must* be Mario Batali."

NOTE: You do not have to accuse the person who accused you.

I recently played this with a group of pals, and the names people chose for themselves—Lizzie Borden, Andy Roddick, Frank Gehry, Dr. Frank N. Furter, Cyndi Lauper, and Prior Walter—gave us a snapshot of the micro-zeitgeist of the assembled group (pop culture, sports, architecture).

I was the moderator. One by one, the players came out of the room and gave me their characters. (I had to ask who a couple of these characters were—it turns out that Prior Walter is a character from the play *Angels in America* and Dr. Frank N. Furter is from *The Rocky Horror Picture Show*.) When we all reconvened, I read out the list of characters, and as expected, I had to identify some of the characters—the only person *everyone* had heard of was Cyndi Lauper. As the moderator, I could choose anyone to start the accusing, and I chose Fran.

Fran accused Patrick of being Cyndi Lauper, "Because your hair is as long and luxurious as Cyndi's."

"No," said Pat, "Even though Cyndi was one of the geniuses of the '80s. But I accuse you, Fran, of being Frank Gehry, because you are an architect, too."

"No, I am not Frank Gehry," said Fran. "I accuse Melissa of being Lizzie Borden because she has that 'forty whacks' look about her."

"I am not Lizzie Borden," said Melissa—and here's where, having observed the first few accusations, Melissa proceeded to "run the table," like you do in pool:

"I accuse Angela of being Frank Gehry, because she's a friend of Fran's and he's an architect and she's trying to throw suspicion on him." (Correct: Angela is out of the game, and that was indeed her strategy.)

"Robby, I accuse you of being Prior Walter because you're an actor and the only one who might know who that is." (Correct—Robby's out.)

"Fran, I accuse you of being Cyndi Lauper because you showed your 'true colors.' You were playing an offensive game by accusing Pat of being Cyndi Lauper, right off the bat. (Correct—Fran's out.)

"Pat, I am going to accuse you of being Dr. Frank N. Furter because you seem like the type to dig *The Rocky Horror Picture Show*. (Correct—Pat's out.)

"And finally, Martha, I accuse you of being Lizzie Borden, well, because I'm Andy Roddick."

And so, by a few careful observations, Melissa was able to sweep the game—everyone's out in one fell swoop.

Winning

Eventually, every player but one will be correctly accused and eliminated. The last player left in the game is the winner.

▸▸ **IF YOU LIKE THIS GAME . . .** check out Mafia, a more sophisticated and strategy-oriented game, on page 132, or you might like Clue, available at toy and bookstores.

Adverbs

PLAYERS: 3–20

One player (**the Guesser**) leaves the room; the remaining guests agree on an adverb—let's say it's "lazily." The guesser returns and instructs the other guests to perform certain tasks or actions in the manner of that adverb—for example, "Joe, pour a drink in the manner of that adverb." Joe might then schlump slowly over to the drinks cart, heft the tonic water in a lackadaisical way, and freshen his G&T in a very laissez-faire manner.

The guesser may then guess the adverb, if she likes, or she may instruct other guests to act out various chores in that manner as well. Once she has guessed, another person takes a turn as the guesser.

At one party I attended, the verb was "slowly," which was much too easy. The next one was "atomically," which turned out to be too hard (although prompted many jokes about "giving a wedgie, atomically.") The third adverb we chose, "androgynously," also turned out to be too hard, but led to much bizarre and hilarious mimicry of Annie Lennox and Michael Jackson and one awful rendition of "Karma Chameleon." The guesser guessed "asexually," which we decided was close enough.

Winning

This game is noncompetitive, but if you'd like to *make* it competitive, keep a log of how long it takes the guesser to guess. Lowest time wins.

▶▶ IF YOU LIKE THIS GAME . . . for the perfect combo of guessing and trivia games, check out Current Events Trivia on page 226.

Password (Version 1)

Password **was a TV game show** that aired during the 1960s and '70s. This version, based on the game show, is played by two teams of two players.

PLAYERS: 4, in teams of 2, plus a moderator.

THE GEAR: Paper, pencils, a timer.

The Game Plan

- The moderator, who is also the timekeeper, makes up a word (the "password") and writes it on two slips of paper. (If you don't have a moderator, open a dictionary or newspaper and drop your finger onto a word without looking.) That word will be the password for both teams. One member from each team is given the password.

- Player 1 from Team A must give a one-word clue to his teammate, Player 2. No other words or gestures are allowed. Player 2 will make a guess within five seconds. If he guesses correctly, the team nets 10 points. If he doesn't, the other team has a chance: Player 1 from Team B gives a one-word clue to her teammate, who takes a guess within five seconds. (She also has the benefit of having heard the clue Player 1 from Team A gave his partner.) If she guesses correctly, Team B nets 9 points. If she doesn't, it passes back to Team A for a potential 8 points, and so on.

* The word passes back and forth until someone guesses or until ten clues have been given. On the next round, Team B has the chance to go first; the player who was the clue-receiver becomes the clue-giver.

Winning

A game consists of four words (so each player has a chance to be the clue-receiver and the clue-giver twice). The team with the highest score at the end wins a copy of the Password game.

IIIIIIIIIIIIIIIIIIIIIIIIIIIIIIIIIIIIIIIIIIIIIIIIIIIIIIIIIIIIII

Password (Version 2)

This variation for more than four players has a slightly different strategy. The same word is not "passed" from team to team; instead one member of a couple must guess a word from the one-word clues his partner gives him. He has three tries to do so.

PLAYERS: 4–10, in teams of 2, plus a moderator.

THE GEAR: Paper and pencil, hats or other containers.

The Game Plan

* Divide your guests into teams of two.

* The moderator jots down a bunch of improper nouns on slips of paper. If you want to play without a moderator, give each of your guests slips of paper and have them write down improper nouns; each team will use the nouns generated by the other team(s). Before making up your clues, see "Play Fair" on page 37.

▸▸ **HOST TIP**

When you, as the moderator, are making up the nouns, consider this: Sometimes the simplest words can be the hardest—"dot," for example, proved fiendishly difficult to guess. Though now that I think about it, "polka" and "bikini" might have been good clues to give....

* Mix all the slips of paper in a hat—or, if you are playing without a moderator, give one team all the slips of paper written by the other team.

* A player sits opposite her partner and draws a password from the hat. Let's say she draws the word "cat." She gives a one-word clue to her partner, say, "pet." Her partner then takes a one-word guess, perhaps "dog." The clue-giver may then give another one-word clue, say, "feline." Her partner then guesses *cat*. Because the partner guessed using two clues, the team gets 2 points. If they had guessed it in one try, they would get 1 point. If it takes them three tries, they get 3 points. If they never get it, it's 4 points.

▸▸**STEALTH STRATEGY**

Of course, getting your teammate to say the word in one try is ideal, but sometimes a more conservative strategy, like planning to say two words that will certainly get your partner to guess correctly—is better than to risk getting four points. For example, in a recent game I drew the word "plow." Rather than saying "ox" (the first word that popped into my head) I said "speed." My partner's first guess was "velocity." My second clue was "the," and she guessed "plow." (A popular play on Broadway at that time was *Speed the Plow*, and I was reasonably certain she'd seen it.) So my strategy was to definitely get it in two rather than hoping she'd get it in one with "ox" or "field."

� After the partner has guessed successfully or they have exhausted their three tries, it's another team's turn.

✷ Once each team has gone twice (or, in other words, once each teammate has had the chance to be the clue-giver and the clue-receiver) the round is over and the scores are announced.

Winning

Play an agreed-upon number of rounds. The team with the lowest number of points is the winner.

Variation

Play Password as one large group rather than in teams of two. One player gives clues to the group. The first person to yell out the correct word receives a point and takes over as clue-giver. The first person to get 5 points wins.

||||||||||||||||||||||||||||||||||||||||||||||||||||||||

Forbidden Words

Forbidden Words is a homemade version of Taboo, the board game in which the clue-giver has to get her teammates to yell out the password—but she must *avoid* certain words when giving clues.

PLAYERS: 4–10

THE GEAR: Index cards, pencils, a hat.

The Game Plan

✷ Give each player some index cards. On each card, they will write a noun, proper or otherwise. For each word, they must *also* write, below the main word, five words

that the clue-giver is forbidden to say. For example, if the password were "Ohio," you might not be allowed to say "state," "buckeye," "Cleveland," "Dayton," or "Cincinnati."

✷ Each player should create about five cards. Put all cards in the hat.

✷ Divide into two teams. Choose a clue-giver to go first. She will choose a card and try to get her team to say the word without using any of the "forbidden" words. For our "Ohio" example, above, the clue-giver, instead of saying "this is the Buckeye State," might loudly sing the Neil Young lyric, "Four dead in Blank-Blank-Blank."

✷ A member of the opposing team watches over the shoulder of the clue-giver; if she trips up and uses one of the forbidden words, the opposing team member calls out "Foul!" and the clue-giver throws the card back in the hat and the turn passes to the other team. A team has one minute to guess as many as they can. (A member of the opposing team can be the timekeeper.)

Winning

A team gets a point for each word they guess. When the hat is empty, the team with the most points wins.

▶▶ IF YOU LIKE THIS GAME . . . check out the board game, Taboo.

||||||||||||||||||||||||||||||||||||||||||||||||||||||||

Word Links

In Word Links, one player thinks of several two-word phrases or ideas that each contain a common word. For example, "end run," "run-around," "run out," "run up"—the common word, of course, is *run*. Whoever is "It" presents the *other* word from each phrase as a clue. The players will venture guesses as to the common word.

PLAYERS: 2–10

THE GEAR: Paper and pencil, to keep your train of thought.

The Game Plan

Choose a person to be "It." It thinks of a bunch of phrases that have a single word in common. For example, It is thinking of the word *key*.

　　It: "Stone."

　　Guesser(s): "Henge? Wall? Cold?" They will think for a moment or two and then, when all guessers agree they are stumped, may ask for another clue: "Next clue, please."

　　It: "House."

　　Guessers try to find a common word linking "stone" and "house." They venture guesses until someone hits on the common word or they have to request another clue.

　　It: "Note."

　　Guessers continue trying to find the common word until someone hits on key— "keystone," "house key," "keynote." Obviously, It might need at least five or six words stockpiled for use as clues.

　　I recently played via e-mail with a friend. His first clue to me: "Crash." I guessed "Test?" The answer came back: "No." I guessed again: "Cart?" Nope. I asked for the second clue, which was "Thai." Aha: "crash pad," "pad Thai."

　　I started a new one: "new." He said, "What's?" Nope, I said. He guessed again: "Deal?" Got it in two! If he hadn't gotten it, I would have said "-breaker," and next "No."

NOTE: When playing Word Links via chat or e-mail, you may make only two guesses before

asking for the second clue—and you can't use Google or other electronic tools or a dictionary to find connections!

Winning

If you're playing with more than two people, the first person to guess correctly wins the game and becomes the next It. If you're playing with two people, keep track of how many clues it takes for the guesser to guess the common word. If she gets it with one clue, she gets 1 point. If she gets it with two clues, she gets 2 points. Play four rounds; the player with the lowest score at the end or, if you're playing with three or more, the person who's guessed correctly the greatest number of times, wins a game of Scrabble Apple.

Essences aka Analogies

Essences is a mellow, creative guessing game that's best enjoyed when the evening calls for little exertion, both mental and otherwise: Think post-dinner lounging in a lodge in Vermont, nibbling on ginger cookies (see opposite page) as a blizzard rages outside. You don't need a thing—no paper, no pencils, no jumping around, and no one's trying to double-cross anyone else. Launch a game with some hot chocolate and a roaring fire and you've got the perfect, après-ski activity. Though it's probably easier to play with a group of people that you know well, adding the randomness of a few outsiders can make the game more amusing.

PLAYERS: 6–20

The Game Plan

⚒ One player designates herself the "Seer." This person possesses the ability to see the true spirit—the "essence"—of a person, even if it's a person she's just met. (Think of the Seer as a cross between your mother and a fortune-teller.)

⚒ The Seer secretly selects one member of the group to "spiritually examine"—meaning that the Seer thinks of someone in the group, but does not reveal whom she is thinking of until the end of the game.

⚒ The rest of the group must ask questions of the Seer about that person's *essence*. For example, "If this person were the essence of a color, what color would that be?" The questions can range from the ordinary—"If this person were the essence of an animal, what animal would that be?" to the oddball: "If this person were the essence of a piece of technology, what would that technology be?" The answer to the first might be "a very friendly golden retriever" or "a cheerful songbird"; the answers to the second might range from "the latest iPhone" to "a 1978 Betamax videocassette player."

⚒ The best Seers will take a moment before answering a question, to make sure that their answers are both tactful (see "Etiquette," below) and also exactly right: If someone has asked "If this person is the essence of a particular architect's work, which architect would that be?" then the Seer will want to carefully weigh the differences between the crisp lines of a Frank Lloyd Wright house and the winged, space-age curves of a Santiago Calatrava building.

⚒ After everyone has asked a question, each player takes a guess, out loud, as to whom the Seer has chosen. It's perfectly acceptable to guess yourself—after all, you know better than anyone if you are the essence of a 1978 Betamax videocassette player.

Winning

Whoever guesses correctly wins; there may be more than one winner. Have some small prizes on hand, like a bottle of wine, a box of specialty teas, or a keychain pocketknife.

▸▸ **ETIQUETTE**

The fun lies in the hilarity of the questions and answers. But don't let the quest for a laugh overshadow your tact: If one of your guests believes himself to be the essence of a stallion named Flame, it'll be upsetting to hear that he's really the essence of a lop-eared bunny named Lollipop. On the other hand, Essences is a powerful tool for flirting: If you *do* think a certain gentleman is the essence of a stallion, by all means, let Flame know it.

Variation

One player leaves the room and the rest decide which famous person he represents. When the player returns, he asks questions like, "If this person were the essence of a certain kind of food, what would it be?" The player has to guess what famous person he is embodying.

PARTY RECIPE

Martha Burgess's Ginger Butter Cookies

Essences is the perfect après-ski activity—propose a round while your guests are enjoying a roaring fire, a cup of tea, and a plate of ginger cookies.

MAKES ABOUT 30 COOKIES

1 cup butter (two sticks)	2 cups flour
¾ cup sugar (6 ounces)	¾ teaspoon
1 large egg yolk	ground ginger
2 tablespoons chopped	pinch of nutmeg
crystallized ginger	¼ teaspoon salt

1. In a mixer, cream the butter and sugar until light and fluffy. Add the egg yolk and crystallized ginger and blend. Sift together the dry ingredients and add to the butter mixture. Scrape down the mixer bowl to make sure that the wet and dry ingredients are evenly blended. Mix just until the dough comes together.

2. To shape the cookie, scrape the dough onto wax paper, lengthwise, and roll the paper around the dough to form a sausage shape. (The diameter of the sausage will depend upon how large you would like your cookies to be.) Roll the dough in the wax paper until the sausage shape is even and full. Twist the ends of the wax paper. Place on a flat plate or sheet pan and chill for one hour.

3. Preheat the oven to 350°F. Unwrap the cylinder of cookie dough. Slice the dough into ⅜-inch discs. Place the cookie discs two inches apart on parchment-lined cookie sheets. Bake for 12 to 15 minutes or until lightly golden.

4. Transfer the cookies to a wire rack. They're ready to eat when cool.

Character Guessing

PLAYERS: 3–20

The Game Plan

✖ One player "It" leaves the room and the others come up with a person, real or fictitious. (If playing in a car, have one player jot down a name on a slip of paper and pass it to the other players, excluding It.)

✖ It returns, and the company asks him leading questions about the character he is (that they have chosen). So, if the character were, say, Joseph Smith, a player might ask, "Which one of your wives did you love the best?" It might guess "Am I Henry VIII?" . . . to which the other players will tell him, sadly, no. Another player might then say, "Do you think your upbringing in western New York influenced your religious ideals?" It might say, "Am I John Brown?" to which the other players answer no. It might then remember that Joseph Smith was from western New York, had many wives, and certainly had religious ideals. When he guesses correctly, another person takes a turn at being It.

In a recent game, my husband Fran was It and left the room. We chose "Captain Ahab" from *Moby Dick* as the character, and called Fran in.

I got the ball rolling and asked, "Do you ever feel that you're wasting your life, chasing something you're never going to find?"

Fran thought for a moment. "Am I Hillary Clinton?"

Patrick, hoping to inject a little ye olde New England-ese, said "Why is thy purpose?"

Fran guessed, "Am I Rick Warren?"

Robby asked, "How's your harpoon throwing?"

Finally, Cassie said, "What should we call you?"

"Am I Ahab?" (Never mind that it was Ishmael who instructed us what to call him . . . Fran still got it in four tries, which is pretty good.)

Play Fair

As with all guessing games, you should be reasonably sure that It has heard of the character—don't name someone too obscure for anyone to guess.

Winning

Character Guessing is noncompetitive.

Celebrity

Celebrity is beloved as an after-dinner parlor game because the simplicity/fun ratio is very high. It's the easiest of guessing games: Players write down a bunch of celebrity names and then give clues to try to get their teammates to guess what they are.

PLAYERS: 6–20

THE GEAR: Paper, pens, hat, timer.

The Game Plan

* Each player receives a handful of slips of paper. For a party of six people, roughly ten slips of paper per person will do, though you can experiment with more or fewer. Everyone writes down names of famous people, fictional characters, or other people well-known to all members of the group. (For a two-team game, you'll want to end up with about fifty to seventy names total; add about twenty-five names for each additional team.) Put all the slips of paper into a single hat.

* Divide your players into two or more teams of three or more players. One team is selected to go first and a clue-giver is selected from that team. Start the timer for one minute of game play. The clue-giver draws a name from the hat and begins to give clues to her team to get them to guess the name—for example, "This person is a hockey player . . . Canadian . . . played with the Los Angeles Kings and also the New York Rangers . . ." The clue-giver keeps giving information while her teammates shout out possible answers. As soon as someone on the team shouts out the correct answer—"Wayne Gretzky!"—she sets the slip aside, and draws another name from the hat. When giving clues, she can't use the name on the paper,

Play Fair

In order to keep the game fun, don't write down a name unless you are reasonably sure at least half the members of the group will have heard of the person. "Martin Luther" might be acceptable, but "Jan Hus" probably isn't, unless you're playing with a bunch of divinity students.

obviously, nor can she use any part of the name. So, if she were trying to get her team to say "Robert De Niro," she couldn't say, "this guy is married to Mrs. De Niro." Nor, for Michael Jackson, could she say, "Was a member of the Jackson 5."

✘ When and if the team guesses the name, the slip of paper is set aside to be counted after the minute is up.

✘ The team gets a point for every name they guess correctly in one minute. (If your crowd has chosen difficult names and one minute doesn't seem like enough, you may play in two-minute rounds, as long as everyone agrees.) After the minute is up, the name they were working on when the buzzer sounded gets tossed back in the hat. The names they guessed correctly are counted and taken out of play, and the other team gets their turn.

Winning

The team with the most points when the hat is empty wins a copy of the latest celebrity biography.

I recently played with a bunch of girly-girls and several European men. We played men versus women (for the record, the women won). The men were very sports-oriented and the women weren't, so the clues like "Gayle King" (Oprah's best friend) stumped the men—but obscure tennis champions stumped the women. (Remember, to play fair, you should only put a name in the hat if you're reasonably sure that at least half the players will have heard of it . . . so if you're evenly divided between men and women it's okay to strategize by choosing names that your sex is more likely to know.)

Variation

Optional rounds: Should you so desire, this bout of Celebrity may be considered the first of three. Count up the two teams' scores and write them down.

For round two, return all the names to the hat and set the timer for one minute. For this round, the clue-giver may give just one word as a clue. Remember, you've already heard the names (and the clues used to get your teammates to say them) in round one, so you should be able to say "Oprah!" as a clue and your teammates will shout "Gayle King!" The clue-giver may only say the one word, but may also use hand and body gestures. When the minute is up, the clue-giver tosses the unguessed name she was working on back in the hat and the other team takes a turn for one minute, and so on. When the hat is empty, the scores are tallied again and added to the scores of round one.

For round three, return the clues to the hat, set the timer and start again, but this time, the clues must be given entirely in mime. When the hat is empty, add the scores from round three to the scores of the previous two rounds. The highest score wins.

||||||||||||||||||||||||||||||||||||||||||||||||||||||||||||||||||||||

Clumps

PLAYERS: 6–20

Divide your guests into two teams. One person from each team leaves the room. These two representatives decide upon something to be guessed—this can be an object, the name of a famous person, a concept, a movie title, anything—and reenter the room. Each then goes to his *opponent's* team and is asked yes-or-no questions, such as, for the first few questions: "Is it an object?" "Is it a person?" "Is he or she a famous person?" "Is he or she a movie star?"

The two sides should be separated by some distance, and when guessing, must speak quietly. The first team to guess gets to select a player from the other team. When one team has completely absorbed the other, the game is over.

Winning
The original members of the unabsorbed team are the winners.

Breakfast Combo

PLAYERS: 2–20

Sometimes known as French Toast, Breakfast Combo is a surreal guessing game. Why it's called "Breakfast Combo" (or "French Toast," for that matter) is unclear, given that the game does not have to be about food—the object that "It" is thinking of can be any noun.

Like other surreal games, this one can seem rather arbitrary at first. If you have to give up and ask for the answer, it's OK—the fun is in seeing how your partner thinks, rather than racing to get the right answer. Small children seem to like this game as well, probably because of its randomness—they say things like "Is it the Wiggles? Is it a Cheerio? Is it my Dora the Explorer underwear?"

One player thinks of an object and the other players have to guess what it is, but the answer evolves out of comparisons. For example, Player 1 is thinking of a table saw. Player 2 asks a specific question like, "Is it King Kong?" (The first few questions will be arbitrary and somewhat out of the blue—you could start with "Is it the Sahara?" or "Is it a Chihuahua?" or anything at all.) Player 1 replies, "It is more like King Kong than anything else you've said." Player 2 (or 3 or 4) asks, "Is it a frying pan?" And Player 1 replies, "It is more like a frying pan than like King Kong." (Meaning that it is more like a tool than an animal.) And so a guesser asks, "Is it like a toaster?" and Player 1 might reply, "It is more like a frying pan than a toaster." "Is it a knife?" And Player 1 might say "It is more like a knife than a frying pan." (Meaning that it is a tool for cutting.) And so on, until the guessers arrive at "table saw."

If the guessers are having too much trouble, and the game is flagging, It may give hints: "It is more like a knife, because it cuts," or "It is more like a frying pan because it is round." For the best game, choose something that is somewhat meaningful to the two of you or to the group, like an object from a recent vacation ("Is it the raft that sprang a leak?"), or something that you've laughed about recently ("Is it Grandma's Dixie Cup of Scotch?").

I played recently with a friend via Google chat. I was thinking of "Jell-O." Our conversation proceeded like this:

Is it Sansabelt pants?

It is more like Sansabelt pants than anything else you've asked. (The answer to the first question will always be the same.)

Is it Shake 'N Bake?

It is more like Shake 'N Bake than Sansabelt pants. (This clued her in that it was probably something edible.)

Is it a Western omelet with extra cheese?

It is more like a Western omelet with extra cheese than Shake 'N Bake.

Is it a half-eaten bowl of soggy Cinnamon Toast Crunch? (My friend likes to ask pretty specific questions, but your friends' questions might be more general.)

It is more like a half-eaten bowl of soggy Cinnamon Toast Crunch than a Western omelet with extra cheese.

Is it a cup of coffee with French Vanilla International Delight nondairy creamer?

It is more like a half-eaten bowl of soggy Cinnamon Toast Crunch than a cup of coffee with French Vanilla International Delight nondairy creamer, because it can fit in a bowl. (I started giving hints, because the time between questions started to get longer. Your hints can be as general or as specific as you like.)

Is it a bowl of Skittles?!?!?!!

It is more like a half-eaten bowl of soggy Cinnamon Toast Crunch than a bowl of Skittles because it is wet-ish.

Is it a bowl of maple oatmeal?

It is more like a half-eaten bowl of soggy Cinnamon Toast Crunch than a bowl of maple oatmeal because the texture is smooth-ish, and it is very sweet.

Is it a bowl of tapioca?

It is more like tapioca because it is the same genre as tapioca, and perhaps represents the same cultural implications as tapioca, particularly instant tapioca. It is more like tapioca in that it at once represents the global ascent of American culture and the decline of all things tasty and healthful in this country.

It's Jell-O.

How Why When Where

PLAYERS: 2–20

One person decides on a pair of homophones, two words that sound alike but have different meanings, like *rain* and *rein*. Another player asks a question. "How do you like it?" for example. If the words are *rote* and *wrote,* the answer might be "I like it boringly." The next question might be "Where do you like it?" and the answer might be "I like it on paper." And the answer to "When do you like it?" might be "I like it over and over and over again." And so on until he guesses the words. Players are not required to stick to how, where, when, why questions—they may ask any question they like if they think it will shed light on the words. The players keep guessing until

A Few Ideas to Get You Started

plain/plane, waste/waist, tee/tea, bear/bare, beet/beat, spar (as in boxing)/spar (as in a mast), net (a mesh fabric)/net (profit after expenses), gate/gait, break/brake, steak/stake, rhyme/rime, meat/meet, flour/flower, peel/peal, turn/tern, lie/lye, stair/stare, root/route, mail/male, pair/pare, pole/poll, plate/plait, peek/peak, frieze/freeze, tale/tail, vale/veil, metal/mettle, feet/feat, aunt/ant (only if you're from certain parts of the country that pronounces these words the same), creak/creek someone gets the answer. That player is the winner. If playing with only two people, the game is noncompetitive.

I played with my dad, sitting in his car while we were waiting for a mechanic to replace a part on my car. I came up with son/sun—which turned out to be too ridiculously easy. He came up with heir/air, which took me an embarrassingly long time to get.

We also passed the time with a little wager on how much my car repair was going to cost: I guessed $50; he guessed "a hell of a lot more than that." He one. I mean, he *won*.

Variation

In a simpler version, It just thinks of a word, any word, and the players must ask "How do you like it?" "When do you like it?" etc. First person to guess the word becomes the new It.

|||||||||||||||||||||||||||||||||||||||||||||||||||||||||||||||||||||||||

She's So Fine . . .

You know how you feel great when a friend notices something special about you and compliments you on that trait? It's better if it's a quality you never knew you had—a sweet smile, sultry eyes, a graceful neck. (Even if you secretly think that friend is crazy, being complimented still feels good.) An acquaintance once told me I had a very warm laugh—a compliment I never forgot that endeared him to me forever (no matter that my jeans are inexorably shrinking, no matter that my eyebrows really, really want to meet in the middle . . . in 1997 Guillaume said I had a warm laugh). In She's So Fine, you'll endear yourself to your pals and you'll find out which traits of yours have caught their fancies as well.

Get ready to be complimented: She's So Fine is a guessing game in which players think of another member of the group (not revealing the identity) and then positively describe that person's physical traits. Then everyone guesses the identity of the person being described.

PLAYERS: 6–20

THE GEAR: Paper, pencils, hat or other container.

The Game Plan

✖ Write each player's name on a slip of paper and put the papers in a bowl.

✖ Have each player draw a name. This name will be that player's "target."

✖ Each player must write down three positive descriptions of their target. These descriptions may be of something physical (freckles) or non-physical (a razor-sharp wit). The first description should be of a trait that could apply to more than one member of the group: a confident stride, for example, or a cheerful smile. The second should be something a little more obviously connected to a single person, like glossy hair or delicate fingers or a sweet demeanor, but not totally unique to one member of the group. The third description should be of a physical trait that is (at least in the writer's opinion) unique to that person: the delicate scent of a frangipani blossom at sunset, hair the color and texture of flowing lava, the broad, strong shoulders of a 1950s superhero. (It is okay to be hyperbolic or over the top; you're exercising your creativity as well as your flattery skills.)

✖ Once this is done, Player 1 reads out the first description he wrote down. Everyone jots down the name of who they think is Player 1's target.

✖ Player 1 then reads out his second description. The other players have the opportunity to write down the same name—confirming their original choice—or write down someone else's name.

✖ Player 1 then reads his third description and the players write down their final guess—which could be one of their earlier choices or someone entirely new.

✖ Player 1 then reveals the name of the person on his card. Other players get 3 points if they guessed right the first time and kept their answer unchanged for the next two guesses; 2 points for a correct second guess and keeping the answer unchanged for the third guess; and 1 point if they got it only on the third try. In other words, if you were correct but changed your answer and then changed it back, you only get the point for the latest correct guess.

Winning

Play until everyone's had a chance to read. Then tally up the points; the highest score wins.

▸▸ ETIQUETTE

This game obviously has the potential to hurt feelings. If you wouldn't like to hear that your hands are like a lizard's, neither would someone else. On the other hand, if you think someone has the beatific smile of a Renaissance Madonna, by all means, let her know.

Match the Match Ad

Because this game is essentially a creative-writing exercise, save it for your most verbal and witty friends. Before start of play, collect a bunch of profiles from Match.com and distribute them to the group. Have each player read a profile aloud and ask the players to note what makes an interesting, ridiculous, attractive, etc. personal ad. Then distribute pencils and paper and ask each member of the group to compose a profile for himself. Collect the profiles and read them aloud. As you read them, your guests should jot down their best guesses as to who wrote each profile. At the end, each player discloses which profile she wrote. The players tally up how many correct answers they each had, using the honor system, natch.

PLAYERS: 4–20

THE GEAR: Paper, pencils.

Winning

The player with the greatest number of correct guesses wins.

Optional Second Round

Next, everyone votes on first and second place for the best ads; those players win a prize—like dinner for two at a romantic restaurant, a box of chocolates, or one month's subscription to Match.com.

The ads can range from single sentences to novellas: A recent game produced: "SWF looking for humiliating dating experiences," "SWM looking for woman who is very brave about feral, nonhousebroken dogs," and "SWF looking for same, must be *very very* keen on scrapbooking and the DAR." You can set the parameters based on the personalities within your group: For some gangs, you might want to make a rule that the ads have to be based in truth. For other parties, ones in which the guests are creative, storytelling types, you might want to give them free rein to create an ad that's as funny or absurd as they can write in a short amount of time.

Actually, in our game it wasn't that hard to figure out who'd written what—but the hilarity of how people "advertised" themselves and what they wanted in a mate—was worth the tied-score we had at the end.

Mora

Also known as Fingers, Mora (or Morra) is a guessing game that bears a strong resemblance to Rock Paper Scissors. The object of the game is to correctly guess, in advance, the total number of fingers that will be displayed simultaneously by the two players. How the name "mora" came to be is unclear; it's possibly a corruption of the Latin *micare digitis,* or "to flash the fingers." The game seems to have been around since Roman times.

Players must agree ahead of time on how many games make up a match. Let's say, for our purposes, that it's three.

PLAYERS: 2

The Game Plan

- The two players face each other, each player's right fist resting against his chest.

- They raise their fists at the same time (so that their elbows form a 90-degree angle— almost as if they were about to start shaking their fists at someone) and then snap down their fists simultaneously so that the forearm is parallel to the floor. (The motion is similar to Rock Paper Scissors.) *While the fists are on their way down,* each player opens his fist to display a certain number of fingers and at the same time guesses what he thinks will be the total number of fingers displayed between the two players.

- A player may show as few or as many fingers as he wishes—so the choices are zero to five. The *total* number of fingers displayed between the two players is zero to ten.

- To sum up, three things are happening at once: players are snapping their fists down, opening their fists to show a certain number of fingers, and calling out what they think will be the total number of fingers. So, Player 1 might call out "five" and show two fingers, gambling that his opponent will show three. Player 2 calls out "ten" and displays five fingers, gambling that his opponent will also display five fingers.

Winning

The player who has called out the exact number of fingers displayed, (not the closest number) wins the round. In our example, since the total number of fingers displayed was seven, neither player won the game. Another game follows immediately, and so on, until someone has won three times.

I played Mora on a date while waiting for our food in a trendy New York restaurant—and I couldn't help but notice that we seemed to be having a lot more fun than the couple next to us, who were, like, trying to *make conversation* on their first date. (Shudder.)

Telephone Murder

Remember the game of Telephone where you sit in a circle and whisper a sentence into another player's ear, and by the time it goes around the circle the original sentence is hopelessly garbled? (Where I grew up, in Appalachia, this game was used by our church to teach children the evils of gossip. But it *really* taught me how much I liked it when the boy next to me whispered in my ear.) In Telephone Murder, you're doing the same thing, but in mime. It doesn't provide the thrill of whispering into a boy's ear, sure, but it does let you exercise your inner Mr. Bean.

PLAYERS: 8–20

The Game Plan

✖ Divide into teams of four. Choose a team at random to start; that team leaves the room. Everyone remaining decides on an occupation (of the victim), a location, and a method of murder. For example, "an altar boy, in a blimp, by being baked into a pie." (While this does sound a little bit like Clue, Telephone Murder is more of a mime game than a game of logic and deduction.)

✖ The first person of the team is called back into the room and informed of these three facts. Then Person 2 is called back, and Person 1 must mime the occupation, location, and method to them, one at a time, within one minute. Neither Person 1 nor 2 is allowed to say *anything,* except Person 2 can say "Got it" when she thinks she understands what Person 1 is trying to mime.

✖ When 2 says "Got it," 3 is called in and 2 must now charade to 3, just as 1 did to 2, within one minute. Finally, 4 is called in, 3 charades to 4, again in a one-minute time frame, and 4 gets to deliver the results of their investigation: "The victim was a blind cabdriver, in a submarine, who was killed by a paper cut."

Telephone Murder should lead to absurd acted-out scenarios as your Aunt Kate tries to communicate "bluegrass musician in a deep, dark mine, whacked by a banjo."

In a game I recently played at a picnic (the nonactive players stood behind a large tree until they were called), the scenario started out as "schoolteacher, in a swimming pool, by spearing." The team, after miming the scenario three times, came up with: "painter, ocean, committed hara-kiri with a knife in the chest." The great thing about this game is that you can also (jokingly) argue with each other about who's at fault for losing the game—"How did you get 'ocean' when I was clearly swimming laps? You saw me do the kick turn!" It's fun to apportion blame. It's also fun to mime hara-kiri, even if it's wrong.

Winning

If the message is delivered intact, the team gets 3 points. If they get two parts of the question right, they get 2 points. If they only get one part right, they get 1 point. Once each team has had a chance to play, the team with the most points wins. The winning team gets a little prize, like four tickets to the latest blockbuster horror movie at the cineplex.

Psychiatrist

PLAYERS: 3–15

One guest, called the Psychiatrist, is asked to leave the room while the others (the patients) decide on a pattern with which they will answer questions—perhaps all answers will start with a diphthong, or all answers will be quotes from movies, or each player must tuck his hair behind his ear as he answers. (A good one in my crowd is to answer as if you were a particular person—"Cary Grant syndrome," or "Sarah Palin-itis.") This pattern is the "illness" that everyone in the group is suffering from. The Psychiatrist then returns and must diagnose the patients' ailment by asking questions of the group and observing their behavior. The content of the questions can and should vary widely—the queries may range from "What did you have for breakfast?" to "What is your greatest failing as a human being?" The object is to observe how the patients are answering questions and determine the common pattern. (If playing in a car, have one player pick the ailment, jot it on a piece of paper, and pass it to the other players—excluding, of course, the Psychiatrist.)

I recently played a game in which the players had to respond as if they were Barack Obama—the deliberate pauses, the careful phrasing—which was very amusing but also pretty easy to guess. Another, more difficult one was pretending to be a certain woman in our neighborhood—a woman we had all had various nutty run-ins with. This proved more difficult to guess but also more creatively stimulating, as we had to think before every answer, "How would Batty Maddy answer this question?"

(This is a particularly good game for families—my mother and I once decided that we would answer every question as if we were my grandmother. My dad got it right away: He's able to diagnose "passive-aggressive Southern lady syndrome" anywhere.)

A Few Ideas to Get You Started

- Answer questions with a long "oh" sound.

- Use some kind of sports metaphor in your answers.

- Refer to food in your answers.

- Say something political in your answers.

- Avoid a certain "common" word, or avoid using articles, verbs, or nouns.

- Use a certain word in your answers.

- Answer as if you were a particular movie star.

- Starting every answer with a particular letter.

- Change seats at a certain agreed-upon point—whenever someone mentions food, for example. (Not recommended for car players.)

The Match Game

In a game similar to Mora, each player tries to guess the total number of matches that each player will display.

PLAYERS: 2–6; 6 is best.

THE GEAR: A box of small matches, or a bunch of pennies.

The Game Plan

✂ To start, each player is given three matches. He hides them, either under the table or behind his back. He puts one, two, three, or no matches into his right hand, closes his fist, and brings his fist into view. One player (any player; it doesn't matter who goes first) calls out his guess for the total number of matches that will be displayed. If six people are playing, the total number of matches could range from zero to eighteen.

✂ Proceeding clockwise, the second player makes his guess, the third player makes his, and so on, until everyone has guessed. No player may guess a total that has already been called out. The players then open their fists and the matches are counted.

Winning

If someone has guessed the correct total, she is declared the winner.

If no one guesses correctly: The person who is closest will be the last person to guess in the next round, the person who was the second closest becomes the second to last person to guess, and so on. This is the most complicated part of this rather simple game, but just remember that the person who was most wrong goes first on the next round. If someone *has* guessed correctly and been declared the winner, however, this rule is not observed.

Encyclopedia

PLAYERS: 3–20

THE GEAR: An encyclopedia.

Test your ability to pay attention, your ability to unscramble words, *and* your general knowledge with Encyclopedia, a game created by Dan Rubenstein. One person picks a random encyclopedia entry. You can use a real physical encyclopedia or a virtual one. That person starts reading the entry aloud, backward, at a rather slow speed. You may read backward either word by word, or sentence by sentence. The first person to figure out what the subject is (for example, "Albert Einstein" or "Alberta" or "The United Nations") wins.

It's a great after-dinner game, requiring no physical exertion and merely the smallest amount of concentration. Just let the words wash over you until a picture forms in your mind. Take a look at this encyclopedia entry, reprinted here backward, word-for-word:

"winters long with regions in or islands on found are species few but, worldwide found are They. increment growth each at skin outgrown their shedding, lives . . ."

"Snakes!" screamed Jason, and so he won the round.

Guess the Proverb

PLAYERS: 3–10

Like Botticelli, Guess the Proverb makes all the players—not just the Guesser—think on their feet. If you're playing in a car, have one player jot down a proverb on a slip of a paper and pass it to the others, excluding the Guesser, as obviously no one can leave the room when you're speeding down the highway.

The Game Plan

Select one player to be the Guesser. She leaves the room, and the remaining players agree on a proverb. For example, "Absence makes the heart grow fonder." The Guesser returns and other players tell her they have chosen a proverb that has six words. (For this game, articles and conjunctions count as words.)

The Guesser now has to figure out the proverb by asking questions of the other players, in turn. The first player must include the first word of the proverb in his answer; the second player must include the second word and so on. For example, the Guesser might ask the first player, "Does this proverb have anything to do with money?" And the first player might reply, "Well, it's more about romance than finance, but in any circumstances a surfeit of money is useful and an absence is troubling." The Guesser listens to this answer carefully and then asks a question of the second player, who will bury the word "makes" somewhere in her answer. The Guesser may ask two questions for each word in the proverb, so in our case, twelve.

Winning

If she guesses the proverb correctly after asking her allotted number of questions, the Guesser wins. If not, the players win.

Biography

PLAYERS: 3–10

Whoever's "It" thinks of a famous person and gives hints about them to the assembled company. Players may guess a name after each fact is given.

For example, It, who is thinking of John Adams, might say:

- ✖ I was born in Quincy, Massachusetts.

- ✖ I married my third cousin.

- ✖ My second cousin was a Founding Father of the United States.

If a player guesses correctly, she takes a turn as It.

Winning

The twist for Biography is that it's not the guessers who are trying to win—it's the clue-giver. The person who can list the most facts about a famous person before anyone in the group guesses correctly wins a copy of the latest bestselling historical biography.

> **▸▸STEALTH STRATEGY ◂**
>
> Selection of the name is important, as you want to be able to produce a long list of facts about a character without tipping off the other players.

Chapter Four

INDOOR
FROLICS

S ometimes it rains. Sometimes the chess set is missing
a piece, or the cards are too beat up, or your pals don't
want to learn Fictionary. Or maybe you're just tired of
head games—guessing games and bridge and Scattergories or Trivial
Pursuit. Sometimes you're tired of, well, *thinking*. And, you know,
you shouldn't always *have* to think when you play a game. Kids
never *think* when they're playing—they just play.

   This chapter is the flip side to strategizing, to writing and
rhyming, to counting cards and calculating odds. It's all about being
silly, about clowning, about tumbling about the house in a frenzy
of excitement. Let's face it: for us adults, recreation *outdoors* means

going for a jog and recreation *indoors* means watching a movie or playing a video game. Even when you're playing the other indoor games in this very book, you're still (mostly) sitting still and thinking hard.

These games are for when the mood is silly and the intellect is on hiatus. They're good games for events where alcohol is flowing—or events where both adults and kids need to be entertained. The chapter's called "Indoor Frolics" for a reason: You'll move around a bit—sometimes a lot—and for the more active games, you may even find yourself on the floor, scrambling away from someone trying to tag you. Most of these can be played in an average-sized house or apartment, but some of the large-scale games may be better played in very large living rooms, gyms, or barns (or even outdoors).

Some of the indoor frolics combine movement and strategy in unique ways: Check out Four on the Couch, for a territory-capturing game played on the living-room sofa. Ministry of Silence, a new game designed by Charley Miller, is a code-cracking, information-trading bonanza that takes place (quietly) in a large bookstore or library.

Indoor frolics are the antidote to cabin fever. They're a grown-up version of fort-building. (Remember when you were a kid, and it rained, you'd prop up some sofa cushions and drape a sheet across them?) There's something terribly nostalgic and fun about squeezing into a tiny space and trying to be absolutely silent; about sprawling on the floor, back against the wall, trying to toss cards onto a piece of newspaper; about bowling in the long hallway of your apartment building or dorm.

Take advantage of these games on the days when it's too hot or too cold to go out, or it's sleeting or raining, or you just need to move. You'll gambol in the living room, you'll squish into closets, you'll seek out a fedora-wearing guy in the bookstore and unlock his handcuffs.

Hallway Bowling

Sometimes you just want to throw things. In the house. This is why Nerf basketball games have become so popular. If you're barbecuing on your fire escape and the door's open from your apartment to the hallway, this is an excellent game for keeping your guests amused while you flip burgers. And who doesn't love getting a present before dinner?

PLAYERS: 4–12

THE GEAR: Tennis ball, blindfold, and twelve inexpensive prizes wrapped in boxes. Nothing should be in the least bit fragile, as you may have deduced from the name of the game.

Preparation
Find a long hallway. (If you do not have a long hallway, create an alley in a room by marking two parallel lines with masking tape about three feet wide and twenty feet long.) Mark a foul line, also with masking tape, at the beginning of the hallway or alley.

The Game Plan
Depending on the length and width of your hallway, set up the boxes at random along the corridor. Try to arrange them so that hitting a bunch at once would be difficult or impossible. Player 1 steps to the foul line and blindfolds himself. He then rolls the tennis ball, bowling-style, down the hallway. Any boxes he hits, he keeps. The next player takes a turn, and so on, until all the prizes are gone.

AMP IT UP
Yankee Gift Swaps are usually held after the holiday gift-giving season (for how to host a traditional Yankee Gift Swap, check out page 172 in the Holiday Games chapter). Each guest brings one wrapped gift that she received for Christmas or Hanukkah and that she doesn't want or need. Have one player roll the ball toward a gift. The first gift the ball touches is hers and she should open it. The next player bowls and, if he hits a gift, he may either open this gift or take the already-opened gift from the first player. If he takes the gift from the first player, she may bowl, hit, and open another gift. Then the third player has a chance; upon hitting a box, he may open it or take one of the already-opened gifts from the other players. And so on. Once the last gift has been opened, the game is over and everyone keeps the gift they have in their possession—or saves it for another Yankee Gift Swap.

Variation
If you have sufficient space, set up a miniature golf course, using the boxes as the holes, taking care that you have at least one gift per player. You'll need a miniature-golf club and golf ball for each player. Using a bit of masking tape, mark a "tee" for each "hole" (the wrapped gift). Players take turns putting their balls toward the gifts. The first player to hit the "hole" gets to keep the gift and is out of the game. The player who took the greatest number of shots to hit the gift is the first to tee off for the next hole. Players continue around the course, with one golfer eliminated per hole. For maximum fun, allow the golfers to swap gifts after the round—as the best golfer may not really want a Strawberry Shortcake doll and the worst golfer may not care for her nose hair trimmer.

||||||||||||||||||||||||||||||||||||||||||||||||||||||||||||||||||||||||||

Four on the Couch

Four on the Couch is a group game of strategy and memory in which two teams shuffle seats until one team gains control of all four seats on the sofa, thereby winning the game. The trick to the game is that you are not *you*—you are playing the role of someone else in the group, and someone else is playing you. And each time you change seats, your role changes, too. This is kind of a grown-up version of King of the Hill, in which (in my household, at least) kids wrestle for control of the sofa, frequently rolling off the top and collapsing in a heap.

PLAYERS: 8–14

THE GEAR: A couch, which counts as four seats. If you don't have a couch, pretend that four adjacent seats are a couch. Seats, arranged in a circle, one seat per player, plus one empty seat. The couch (or couch-replacement) counts for four of these seats. Slips of paper, pencils.

The Game Plan

* Divide the players into two even teams. One team should distinguish themselves from the other team by wearing hats, rolling up their pants legs or shirt sleeves, etc. Or, just pit men against women.

* Instruct the players to write their names on slips of paper and put the slips in a hat.

* Each player draws a slip and examines it, but does not reveal the name to the other players. Each player assumes the identity of the name on his or her slip (not to act like or imitate that person—although you could play that way if you want—just remember that if

Eileen's paper says "Mary," Eileen will have to move whenever someone calls "Mary").

* To start the game, have the players sit in the chairs, alternating team members so that no two team members are sitting next to each other. Seat two people from each team on the couch. There will be one empty seat, but not on the couch.

* Play begins with the player to the left of the empty seat, who calls out a name at random. It is permissible to call out either the name of someone on your own team or a member of the other team. (In the beginning, players will not know the "identities" of the other players, so it will be random. If Bob calls out "Mary," he will not know, at this stage, that Eileen's slip of paper says "Mary" and that it will be Eileen who moves when Mary's name is called.)

* Whoever has that name *on his or her slip* must move to the empty seat. His now-vacated seat will be the new empty seat.

* The player who was called trades slips of paper with whoever called him.

* The players who have traded slips of paper assume their new roles—again, not to imitate each other, but just to remember that if Charles's slip says "Fred," Charles must move when Fred's name is called.

▸▸STEALTH STRATEGY◂

If you can't memorize who's playing what role, at least try to memorize who's already on the couch and the roles that those people are playing. Avoid calling out names that would remove your teammates from the couch and do try to call out a name that would put your team on the couch.

Trading the slips of paper every time someone moves makes it more difficult to remember the slips people have.

✱ Play always passes to the player to the left of the empty seat.

Winning

When all four people on the couch are from the same team, the game is over and that team wins.

Sardines

A kind of "reverse" Hide-and-Seek, Sardines is a game in which one player, "It," must hide, and others hide with her when they find her. It's a great game for a post-dinner, had-a-few-drinks kind of gang. To wit, I recently played this at a friend's family house in Maine with a slightly inebriated group of pals. The house was one of those old seaside places with capacious closets and creaky stairwells and an attic filled with trunks of ancient wedding gowns. I was It, the first person to hide, and I chose a spot in the attic behind a stack of boxes. The other five people searched high and low—and fortunately it was my husband who first found me. We had a good ten minutes of very silent smooching under the rafters until person number two joined us, at which point we had to make do with holding hands.

There's something childlike and nostalgic about hiding in a small space, hoping the seekers won't find you (or hoping that they will) and listening for approaching and receding footsteps.

PLAYERS: 5–30

The Game Plan

Select an It. It chooses a hiding place sneaky enough to conceal her, but spacious enough to hold most if not all of the players. The seekers cover their eyes, count to fifty, and then go in search of It. When a seeker finds It, he crawls into her hiding place with her. As seekers one by one discover It, they will cram into her space with her. The last one to find the crowd is It for the next game.

Variation

Sardines, like any Hide-and-Seek game, can also be played outdoors. But there's something much more fun about squishing up against your honey—or an unknown hunk—in the closet.

Up Jenkins

In the TV series *The Office* (season 3, episode 17), Up Jenkins functions as a psychologically revealing plot point. Your version will probably be a little less fraught. It's a game that has been around at least since Victorian times, and like many other silly tests of physical coordination, has evolved into a drinking game. Like other drinking games, the person who remains the most alert and sober is most likely to win—but remaining alert and sober is really not the point, of course.

PLAYERS: 8–20, divided into two teams. Each team will elect a captain.

THE GEAR: A quarter and a long table.

The Game Plan

- Two teams of four to ten people sit in two long lines facing each other across a table. Captains sit at the end of their lines on the same sides as their teams. Flip a coin to see which team goes first. Let's say it's Team A.

- Team A passes a quarter under the table along the line and back again—and the direction may shift at any time—until the moment the captain of Team B says "Up Jenkins."

- At that second, all the members of Team A put their elbows on the table, fists straight up. The quarter is concealed in one player's hand.

- The captain of Team B says, "Down Jenkins"; all members of Team A slam their palms on the table. Players will try to mask the sound of the quarter hitting the table.

- The palms of all the players of Team A are now flat on the table, the quarter concealed underneath someone's hand.

- The players of Team B, one by one, beginning with the player farthest from the captain, now point at the hands, one by one, that they believe are *not* concealing the quarter.

- If the quarter *is* underneath a palm, Team B loses and must drink. If it isn't, and the last palm untapped is indeed concealing the quarter, Team A loses and must drink. (How much the loser drinks is up to you—in my crowd of lightweights it would be a sip; other, more reckless parties may insist the losers guzzle a whole shot or a beer.)

- The team that was playing offense now plays defense: Team B conceals the quarter and Team A looks for the quarter.

Pussy Wants a Corner

I played this game when I was a member of a small theater troupe—we had a bunch of warm-up activities that ostensibly were for building nonverbal communication skills among the actors and establishing trust. I'm not sure how well that worked—in Pussy Wants a Corner, trust is fleeting when players so frequently abandon the person they're supposedly cooperating with. And the nonverbal communication is somewhat inhibited by all the screaming. But it didn't matter because it was *fun*.

If you want a game that uses your cooperative skills, and then your double-crossing skills, and then your sprinting and wrestling skills, try Pussy Wants a Corner (where the name comes from, nobody knows). The basic game is simple: Players beckon to each other, silently agree to switch places, and make a run for it before the person in the middle can dash to one of the suddenly vacated chairs. The game invariably leads to sprawling on each other's laps and screaming with laughter.

PLAYERS: 5

THE GEAR: 4 chairs, one in each corner. If outside, make a square with a clothesline and set the chairs in the corners. If using chairs outside isn't practical, designate T-shirts or trees or anything, really, as bases, as long as they're in four corners.

The Terrain

You need space for this game, like a large living room, a barn, a gym, or a yard.

The Game Plan

* Choose a number to play to, say, 20. The first person to get 20 points wins.

* Four of the five players sit in chairs that are set up in the corners of a large square.

* One player is the "Pussy," or "It," and stands in the middle. Pussy wants to be in a corner (a chair), and the other players want to exchange places with someone else.

* So, while Pussy has his back to Player 1, Player 1 may wink at or beckon to Player 2, indicating, "Let's change places." Players 1 and 2 dash toward each other's chairs while Pussy tries to leap into one of the suddenly vacated chairs.

* If Players 1 and 2 succeed in switching places, they each get a point. If Pussy beats one of them to it, Pussy and the player who succeeds each get a point, and the player who fails is now Pussy.

* A player might wink and silently agree to change places with someone—but if it looks like Pussy is going to beat him to the chair, that player might turn around and try to get back to his original seat—thereby abandoning the other player to her fate.

* Each player keeps track of his own score— honor system—and the first player to get to 20 wins. Have a small prize on hand, like a jump rope or an exercise ball, for the winner.

Jail

Similar to Pussy Wants a Corner, Jail is a game in which people scramble to get seats—but this time you're operating as a couple. This means that everywhere you go, your partner has to go, too. So teamwork is the key here—just like in a marriage, you can't barge ahead without your partner's consent—and if your partner *does* barge ahead, sometimes it's better to just follow without argument. She who hesitates is lost.

PLAYERS: At least 6 couples, plus a moderator.

THE GEAR: A chair for each person.

The Game Plan

* Seat guests in pairs around the room, some with their backs to each other, some side by side. Put one couple in the center and call those two chairs "jail."

* Assign each couple a number. The moderator calls out three numbers—say, 1, 2, and 3, and those three couples scramble to change seats, while the couple in jail also tries to get into a pair of vacant seats. Couples must stay together side by side, but not touching. If the moderator sees them separate more than

a couple of feet, they will lose a point. The moderator's judgment on this is final. Couples who successfully change seats gain a point.

✖ Play is to 10 points, or some other agreed upon number.

|||||||||||||||||||||||||||||||||||||||||||||||||||||||||||||||||||||||||||||

Balloon Football

Real football can be so cruel, so *rough*—too many times a hurtling oblong of pigskin has knocked my glasses off my face before I even saw it coming. But *Balloon* Football can be enjoyed by even the most uncoordinated of game-players; because they're balloons, you have plenty of time to gather your thoughts before something bops you on the head. I wish we'd had Balloon Football in high school.

Like Sardines, Balloon Football can be played indoors or out. I think it's best in a long, narrow living room (think of all those factory conversions that made long skinny apartments with windows only on one end) while the host is roasting a pork loin. Football *is* a fall sport, you know.

PLAYERS: 8–20, plus a referee.

THE GEAR: Around 20 inflated balloons of two different colors—about 10 of each color, 2 pins.

The Game Plan

✖ Divide your guests into two equal teams and assign them one of the balloon colors. Each team selects a goalie, who is armed with a pin and stands on a chair at his team's end of the room.

✖ Each team has one balloon of its color in play at a time. The referee tips the two balloons into the center at the same time. Teams try to bat their balloon toward their own goalie to be popped, while trying to prevent the other team from doing the same. When a goalie pops a balloon, he scores a point for his team.

✖ Players may only tap the balloon to another player—they may not hold it, and if the balloon touches the floor, the last person who touched it gets a foul. Three fouls by one team means a point for the other team. If a balloon is popped by accident, the referee tips in another of that team's balloons to the center, but there is no break in the game—the other team is still trying to bat its balloon toward its goalie while the

PARTY RECIPE

Fall Pork Roast

Football means autumn, and autumn means roasting savory things while whistles blow and announcers chatter. Pop this pork roast in the oven for a cozy November meal. SERVES 6

INGREDIENTS

1 teaspoon salt	2 tablespoons garlic,
1 teaspoon pepper	minced
2 tablespoons sage,	1 2-pound boneless
rosemary, or thyme,	pork loin roast
minced	

Preheat oven to 425°F. Mash together the salt, pepper and herbs in a small bowl. With a small sharp knife, make small slits all over the pork roast and insert bits of the herb mash inside. Roast for 30 minutes. Turn the heat down to 325°F and roast for approximately another 45 minutes. A meat thermometer should read 145–150°F. Let stand for 10 minutes before carving. Serve with applesauce.

referee is putting another balloon into play. Teams are obviously concerned with the offensive aspects of the game (trying to get the balloon to their goalies to score a point) and the defensive aspects (trying to keep the other team from scoring a point).

✖ The first team to get 5 points wins.

Variation

Balloon Volleyball: For this one, you'll need a sheet supported by two players—or string the sheet between two tables or chairs. Players play on their knees. Scoring is the same as in real volleyball.

Idiot's Delight

If you've ever spent an hour or two trying to flick playing cards into a hat, this game will be familiar. Idiot's Delight, however, has the bonus of being competitive and social. (Tossing cards into a hat can be rather lonely.) The whole game takes about ten minutes—perfect to play while waiting for the pasta water to boil.

PLAYERS: 2–4

THE GEAR: A standard deck of 52 cards, a sheet of newspaper.

Preparation

Take a sheet of newspaper and label each quarter 1, 2, 3, and 4 (starting from the bottom left moving counterclockwise). If newspapers no longer exist by the time you're reading this, any large square or rectangular sheet of paper will do, divided into four equal sections.

The Game Plan

✖ Lay the newspaper on the floor about five to ten feet from the players, with the sections labeled 3 and 4 farthest from the players.

✖ Give one player or team the red cards and one player or team the black cards. In a two-player game, each player throws three cards per turn; in a four-person game, each player throws two cards per turn.

✖ Players try to throw the cards into a square on the newspaper. The square labeled "4" earns a player 4 points, 3 points are earned for the "3" square, etc. If a card is on the line between two squares, the players should determine if the card is resting more in one square or another. If the players cannot agree, the points will be averaged; e.g., if a card is precisely between squares 3 and 4, the player is awarded 3.5 points.

✖ As in shuffleboard, one card may dislodge another from the board or move it to another square.

Winning

Once each player or team has thrown all his cards, tabulate the score: Each card in the "4" square gets 4 points, each card in the "3" square gets 3 points, etc. Highest score wins a prize, like a glow-in-the-dark Frisbee.

> **▸▸STEALTH STRATEGY ◂**
> You can experiment with the throwing technique—I like to pinch the card between my thumb and forefinger and flick my wrist like I'm tossing a Frisbee, but I can't say this works any better than the overhand hurl favored by my husband. In fact, in our last round we tied.

Brainy Baseball

Brainy Baseball is a way to inject a little movement into your trivia quizzes. In Brainy Baseball, you have a literal playing field for the game. Rather than just keeping score with a pencil and paper, you can move around in the living room and even heckle the player who's up.

PLAYERS: 10–20, plus a "pitcher" (the moderator).

THE GEAR: Magazines or T-shirts, for bases.

Preparation

Generate a list of true-or-false questions—snopes.com or funtrivia.com are great resources. If you want to make the game a little harder, use cards from a Trivial Pursuit game—instead of limiting the answers to true or false, players have to answer the questions. Lay out a baseball diamond on the floor, using magazines or T-shirts for the bases.

The Game Plan

* Divide your guests into two teams and ask them to decide on a lineup. (In one variation, below, the order of the batters can't be changed.) Anyone who is not on base or at bat should sit in the "dugout," or any space off to the side of the baseball diamond. The "pitcher" sits in the center of the diamond.

* The first member of the team who's up takes his place at home base and is asked a question by the pitcher.

* If he answers correctly, it counts as a base hit and he proceeds to first base; if he's incorrect, it counts as an out and another player goes to bat.

* Three outs means the teams switch places. Runners on base don't score.

* A run is scored when a player returns to home base (or, obviously, when four questions have been answered correctly).

Winning

The first team to get three runs wins.

Variations

* One team may make up the questions for the other team (using the "Play Fair" guidelines on page 37).

* Ahead of time, the host may grade questions as easy, medium, or hard, with medium counting for a double and a hard counting as a home run. In this case, each team may *either* elect a pitcher, who decides which questions he will pose to the batters; *or* you can make a rule that the order of questions and/or the order of batters can't be changed. (So, if the twelve-

---

Test Yourself

Can you answer these true or false questions from funtrivia.com?

1. The "game of kings" is horse racing.

2. Saccharine is derived from coal.

3. "Adam's ale" is a kind of beer.

[1]False. The "game of kings" is chess; the "sport of kings" is horse racing.
[2]True.
[3]False. It is water.

year-old is posed a question about *Hannah Montana,* well, so be it—you can't change the questions around so that Disney Channel topics are given to fifty-year-old investment bankers.)

Prediction Bingo

PLAYERS: 5–25

THE GEAR: Printouts of 3 x 3 grids; one per player.

So you think you know how a party is going to go? Well, now you can win points for your foresight. Give each guest a grid. Ask the players to fill in each square with a prediction for what will happen during the evening—these can be predictions for specific guests or just for general events. For example, a player might write "Jill will cover her mouth when she laughs," or "Someone will try to raise the Venetian blind, and it will go crooked."

Tell the players to keep their grids handy but not visible to other players. Guests will circulate, make small talk, fix drinks—in short, the evening goes on like a normal party. But whenever one of their predictions comes true, they should alert the group: "Everyone? I predicted that Jane would comment that cilantro just *makes* the salsa, and she just did!" and mark off the box. The first person to complete three in a row on his grid—either horizontally, vertically, or diagonally—wins the game.

NOTE: Predictions should be rather specific—so "Fred will act like a jerk" is a little too broad (and also too mean).

A dispute may arise that challenges whether a prediction has actually come about. If the prediction is "Sally will cock her head quizzically," someone might dispute what "quizzically" means. Suffice it to say, this is a lighthearted, subjective game, designed to amuse more than to prompt a hardcore competition. So the one hard-and-fast rule is: Don't be a stick in the mud.

One player's predictions that were made at a recent game:

Allison will discuss healing through nutrition.	Frank will mention how hot a certain female politician is.	Joe and Beth will commiserate over the Red Sox.
Audrey and Rob will discuss obscure French mimes.	Nick will offer one person a dish of his homemade tabbouleh at least three times.	Someone will ask Nick if his tattoo really says "food."
Katie will run out for more beer.	Something will fall off the neighbors' crumbling carport and startle us with a loud bang.*	Charles will ask Stan what year the Gibson guitar on the wall is from.

▸▸ **ETIQUETTE**
This game has the potential to hurt feelings. If you predict that Ryan will "laugh his dying-hyena laugh at Allison's unfunny jokes"—well, you're not going to have many friends left. So keep the forecast light.

Came true! The neighbor's carport is rapidly disintegrating.

The Lap Game

The Lap Game is a great way to get to know your friends—and your friends' laps—better. As questions are asked, players move a certain number of "places," meaning they shift from one lap to the lap two chairs down, for example. You'll learn more about their habits, their peccadilloes, their favorite post-sex foods—whatever your heart desires. Questions can be as innocuous or as ribald, as simple or as complicated, as your group wishes. I observed a game recently where the host liked to mix up very simple, straightforward questions: "If you like fresh tomatoes on your pizza, move two places," with rather complicated ones: "If you think a single-payer health-care system is necessarily more efficient than the fractured health-care system we have now, move three places." He also mixed up the general with the personal: "If you drive an automatic car, move one place. If you wear cotton underwear more than fifty percent of the time, move two places. If you took care to wear nice underwear this evening, move three places."

PLAYERS: 20–40

THE GEAR: As many chairs as you have players.

Objective

The object of the game is to move around the circle of chairs clockwise and get back to your own chair.

The Game Plan

- Make a circle of chairs so that everyone has a seat facing into the circle. There is no limit to numbers, but the game is better with larger numbers (20+) than smaller. Ask players to remember the chair they are in.

- One person is the Caller. She will call out various "if" statements that could apply to the guests. She follows that with an instruction to move a certain number of places clockwise. For example: "If you are wearing white socks, move two places," "If your birthday is in January, move one space," etc.

- If the fact applies to a player, she gets up and moves that number of places to her left, sitting on the chair, if empty, or on the lap of the person (or people) already there.

- If you are currently being sat upon and then are compelled to move, you must carefully take everyone sitting on your lap *with* you, remaining attached as you shift a few chairs down. It is likely that the Caller will take great delight in making sure that this happens—if Sal is on the bottom of the pile and is wearing pants with a whale print, the Caller may make a point of calling out, "If you are wearing whale-patterned pants, move two spaces to your left."

- The Caller may make "negative" statements; if true, the players must go *back* a number of places. For example, "If you didn't brush your teeth this morning, move two places counterclockwise."

- If you're playing a "naughty" version, the caller's instructions will be as tame or as risqué as she wants, for example: "If you like having your collarbone kissed, move one place to your right."

Winning

The first person to get back to her original seat wins.

▶ ▶ IF YOU LIKE THIS GAME . . . check out the Icebreakers chapter. The Lap Game *could* make an interesting icebreaker, but some people really don't like sitting on the laps of people they don't know, so we've saved it for here.

Variation

Have the guests make up the "if" statements ahead of time and put them in a hat when they arrive; the hostess will then draw the slips of paper from the hat and read them out loud.

Three Words

I played this, or a variation of it, a lot in high school and college. For some reason, my friends and I frequently seemed to be sitting in hallways waiting for something—for a lecture hall to open, for the snack bar to open, to get tickets to something that was going to be a once-in-a-lifetime experience. Someone always had a sweatshirt that could be balled up and tossed from player to player.

PLAYERS: 6–15

THE GEAR: A ball—a tennis ball, a kickball— even a rolled-up ball of socks will do. You don't want to break the lamps.

The Game Plan

Seat the players around the edges of the room. The youngest player begins the game as "It." It tosses the ball to a guest and says a three-letter word—say, *dig*—and then immediately begins to count to five. Before It has reached five, the guest to whom the ball was thrown must say three words, each one beginning with a different letter in the word called out by It. If he succeeds, he returns the ball to It. If he fails, he tosses the ball to another guest. So the game might go like this.

It (*throwing the ball to Sadie*): "Dig. One . . . two . . . three . . . four . . ." etc.
Sadie (*catching the ball*): "Dog. Indigent. Garden." (*tosses the ball back to It*).
It (*throwing the ball to Jim*): Ado. One . . . two . . . three . . .", etc.
Jim: "Anger, dot—um, uh . . ."
It: "Five! You're It."

Variation

To make the game slightly harder, guests can be restricted from using words that have already been used. So in the example above, Jim couldn't say "dog" for his *d* word.

Winning

Three Words is noncompetitive, but should you so desire, you may eliminate players if they fail to say the three words in time. The last player to be eliminated is the winner.

Yoga Ball Jousting

Please don't allow children to play this game, and insist that adults go easy, playing on carpeted floor or soft ground and not running too fast toward each other.

PLAYERS: 2

THE GEAR: 2 large exercise balls.

A yoga ball, or large, rubbery exercise ball, is held at waist level by each opponent. The two players start at opposite ends of a room or a yard, or about twenty feet apart. They then run at each other as hard as they can, bounce off each other, and then, inevitably, fall down. If one player does manage to keep his feet, he's the winner. That's the whole game.

Bubble Wrap Kung Fu

I found this game and Yoga Ball Jousting on a blog called "Montague Blister's Strange Games," which is worth checking out if you're interested in weird frolics. Mr. Blister's posts are frequently about games in which strategy and skill play a minor role and the potential for injury is high. Bubble Wrap Kung Fu, however, is not painful and is even somewhat meditative.

PLAYERS: 2–4

THE GEAR: Bubble Wrap, a candle.

The Game Plan

✸ Procure, from an office-supply or packaging store, a long roll of Bubble Wrap. Unroll and make a Bubble Wrap path on a hardwood floor. Players take turns walking barefoot along the length of Bubble Wrap "just like Kwai Chang Caine did on rice paper in *Kung Fu*," says Blister. If a player pops a bubble, he's out.

✸ To add another layer to the game, place a candle at the end of the path. Once they've walked the path, players can take turns testing their strength: A kung fu master can place his hand in the flame and feel no pain. (Please don't actually do this—just pretend.)

✸ For ambience, says Blister, "A non-player can commentate on proceedings using

the words of the masterly Masters Po and Kahn:
What must we say of a mirror that receives tranquility, yet reflects a troubled brow. Discipline your body, Grasshopper, that your mind may find a greater power."

▶▶ **IF YOU LIKE THIS GAME . . . check out Montague's blog: strange-games.blogspot.com.**

Physical Word Hunt

Physical Word Hunt is a combination of an indoor Scavenger Hunt and an anagram activity. It's a great game to launch during the cocktail hour while you're getting the food on the table. It keeps guests moving and playing, rather than standing around, sweating the small talk.

PLAYERS: 2–10, plus a nonplaying host.

THE GEAR: Index cards, a supply of six-letter words.

Preparation

For each guest, make six cards with his or her name on them. On each card, write one letter of a six-letter word. (Each guest gets a different word.) Hide the cards around the house—in books, under the food processor, behind the cotton balls, in your sock drawer.

The Game Plan

When your guests arrive, set them loose to find their cards. They're looking for cards labeled with their names; once they've found all six, they can assemble the word. If they find a card that is *not* theirs, they should return it to its spot undisturbed and tell no one.

Winning

The first person to find all six of her cards and assemble the six-letter word therein wins a small prize, like a Bananagrams! game. A player may also win by guessing her word even before she finds all the letters.

Ministry of Silence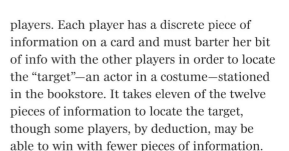

A Big Game About Sharing Information in a Police State

I played this a few years ago at New York's Come Out and Play festival on a blistering summer Saturday. I thought it was my favorite game of the weekend because it took place in a blissfully cool bookstore—but then I realized that the game offered the perfect combination of luck, strategy, tentative trust, and double-crossing that the best games have.

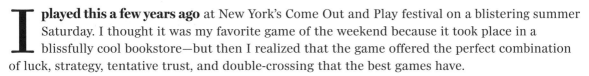

PLAYERS: 14–16, plus you. Twelve people are active players, one person (you) is the moderator, one person is an actor playing the real target, and one to three people are actors playing the role of decoy targets. (You must have at least one decoy target; three is ideal.) The actor roles are best for people who've played the game before, because once you've played, you know how to solve the puzzle and so can't play again.

THE GEAR: ID cards found on pages 357–361; players should bring paper, a pencil, and a cell phone.

The Game Plan

If you are reading this, you will be the moderator, or the MC. You'll be running the game for your group of friends, the competition is among the twelve active players. Each player has a discrete piece of information on a card and must barter her bit of info with the other players in order to locate the "target"—an actor in a costume—stationed in the bookstore. It takes eleven of the twelve pieces of information to locate the target, though some players, by deduction, may be able to win with fewer pieces of information.

You (the MC) will have to prepare by reading these instructions and the cards, collecting props, and briefing your actors on their roles. (But see "Shortcuts," on page 80 if this setup seems too labor-intensive.) Once you all gather at the bookstore, explaining the instructions to the players takes about ten minutes; the game itself takes about an hour.

Objective

To be the first of the twelve active players to find the target, unlock his handcuffs, and then unlock his briefcase to receive the prize inside. In order to do this, each player is given an ID card that has a single clue on it. A player needs to collaborate with other players, learn their clues, and not get caught by a Ministry of Silence Officer to achieve his objective.

NOTE: The players are *not told of the objective*. Only you, the moderator, know. The players are told only that there are clues to solve a puzzle.

The Terrain

The game takes place in a fairly large bookstore, in and around the nonplaying public. Players must be discreet and quiet.

▶▶ **HOST TIP**

If you have more than sixteen people who want to play, you can assign some or all of the twelve active roles to teams of two. Team members may not split up; they are essentially functioning as one person, and must play side by side.

Preparation

Invite fourteen to sixteen people to play Ministry of Silence. Tell them to meet at a specific time in front of a large bookstore. Let them know the game will be played in the bookstore and will take about an hour. Without telling the others, ask two to four of these people to be actors: One will be the real target and the remaining one to three will be the decoy targets. Instruct them to wear long sleeves and/or a coat. Arrange to meet the actors somewhere outside the bookstore, about half an hour before the start of the game.

The moderator must provide:

✖ The set of twelve ID cards (found in the Appendix on page 357).

✖ One locking briefcase for the real target and one locking briefcase for each decoy target, all programmed with the code 345-131.

✖ One red scarf for the real target and one nonred scarf for every decoy target.

✖ One hat for the real target (fedoras are the best hats for spy games) and one hat for each decoy target.

✖ One pair of handcuffs for the real target (and two keys) and one pair for every decoy target.

✖ A note in a sealed Manila envelope inside the real briefcase. It reads: "Congratulations! You win."

✖ One prize inside the real briefcase, such as a spy novel by Alan Furst or John le Carré.

✖ A note in a sealed Manila envelope for each decoy briefcase. It reads: "This is a decoy. You lose."

NOTE: You should not tell any of the twelve active players about this equipment as you are gathering it for the game. If you need help, you should ask one of the people slated to be the target or a decoy target.

The Game Plan, Part II

✖ On game day, meet *your actors* at the appointed time and place. Tell one that he will be the real target and tell the others they will be the decoy targets. (It does not matter if the actors know who is real and who is a decoy.) Give your real target a hat, a red scarf, and a briefcase with the "You win" note and the prize inside. Handcuff him to the briefcase. Give your decoy target(s) scarves, hats, and briefcases with the "You lose" notes inside. Handcuff them to their briefcases. (Your actors' long sleeves and coats should minimize unwanted attention from the other bookstore patrons.)

✖ Instruct your actors as follows: "Circulate slowly in the bookstore and try not to draw attention to yourself for the duration of the game. When a player approaches you with the key to the handcuffs and/or the combo to the briefcase, you must unlock the cuffs and open the briefcase. If you are a decoy and a player approaches you and opens your handcuffs and briefcase, she will find the manila envelope that says 'You lose.' You will then call or text me and tell me where you are. If you are the real target and a player approaches you and opens your handcuffs and briefcase, she has won and the game is over. You will then call or text me and tell me where you are."

✖ Make sure you have the actors' cell phone numbers and they have yours. Send your actors into the bookstore, asking them to remain as far apart from one another as possible for the duration of the game.

✖ When *your twelve players* arrive, distribute the twelve cards and discreetly give handcuff keys to Players 2 and 6. (Hand the keys to the players in the way that you might palm a twenty into a maître d's hand.)

✖ Do not let them show one another their cards. Instruct your players as follows: "Players will have to judiciously barter information with other players to get clues and keys, all of which are necessary to win the game. Do not show one another your cards until the game starts inside the bookstore. A player can *safely* speak

to another player who is one digit away, meaning a player who has the number six ID can 'legally' speak to numbers five and seven (one below and one above, with the numbers nine and one being connected). This rule is printed on all the cards. Players are not *required* to trade information with anyone—so if you offer to trade with someone, you may be rejected. Note-taking is useful for remembering the clues.

✖ "Three of you are Ministry of Silence Officers. These Officers must roam the bookstore trying to catch the other players standing within five feet of each other. If an MoS Officer requests ID, the players must reveal their cards. If an MoS Officer catches a player speaking to another player who is more than one digit away, he takes the numbered card of one of the players and gives his MoS Officer ID to that caught player, who then becomes an MoS Officer. In other words, if an Officer catches two people illegally collaborating, one of the players and the Officer switches cards and roles. Which of the two captured players the Officer switches with is up to the Officer. The other captured player is free to return to the game."

✖ Instruct all your players to speak in whispers and avoid drawing attention to themselves.

✖ Tell each player to start the game in a specific section: Player 1 in Travel, Player 2 by the magazines, Player 3 in the kids' section, etc. This means the players will begin the game spread throughout the store. Tell your players that the game will begin exactly ten minutes from now.

✖ Send them into the bookstore.

✖ The game begins. You should circulate in the bookstore to moderate any disputes and respond to phone calls or texts from your actors. If a player opens a decoy's briefcase, the decoy will alert you. That player is eliminated from the game; you will give the eliminated player's key and ID card to one of the MoS Officers in exchange for his MoS ID card. The "You lose" note and envelope goes back in the briefcase and the decoy target resumes his lurking.

Winning

The first person to find the target, unlock his handcuffs, and unlock his briefcase wins. Anyone who opens a decoy's briefcase or who doesn't have the correct codes loses.

Notes

✖ Make sure to *discreetly* give out the handcuff keys with Players 2 and 6. Don't let the other players see you.

✖ The keys give players 2 and 6 an initial advantage, but they can lose the keys if caught illegally collaborating by an MoS Officer. Or, other players can form an alliance with them to gain access to the keys.

✖ If an MoS Officer confiscates a number 2 or number 6 card, he also will confiscate the handcuff keys.

✖ If all three MoS Officers have been replaced so that no officers remain in the game, end play in twenty minutes as the game possibly could reach a stalemate (this is unlikely).

Shortcuts

✖ The briefcases do not have to *actually* lock. You can inform the actors ahead of time what the code is, and if a player tells them the correct code, they can "unlock" the briefcase. For that matter, you don't even need real briefcases—any bag will do.

✖ You can buy cheap handcuffs at Amazon, but you don't have to use real, locking handcuffs. You can also make handcuffs and keys out of paper or posterboard and the actors can "unlock" them when presented with the key.

—contributed by Charley Miller (a game designer and interactive media producer based in Brooklyn, New York) with Bob Clark. For more about Charley and his projects, check out charleymiller.com.

Key to the ID Cards, on page 357–361, for the MC:

1. One

2. Handcuffs key

3. Thirty-four

4. With ID card #7, player will be able to decipher Target Wears Red Scarf

5. Thirteen

6. Handcuffs key

7. With ID card #4, player will be able to decipher Target Wears Red Scarf

8. 451

9. The order of the digits: 34 451 131. Winner will have to figure out that he must delete duplicate numbers in sequence to get 345-131 for the secret code.

Chapter Five

CONVERSATION GAMES

*T*o the uninitiated, conversation games might seem baffling. There are no winners and losers; there are barely any rules. The games themselves can seem aimless and meandering. But then the questions and answers wander into uncharted territory and reveal surprising new information about your friends and family . . . and you see why the games have endured.

Conversation games have been around since the beginning of time—for as long as the word "hypothetical" has been in our lexicon, for as long as people have posed probing questions to their loved ones from the other side of a pillow. Would You Rather . . . is just a choice between two hypothetical scenarios—but since the follow-up question is always "Why?" the game acts as a portal to seeing into a friend's psyche in unexpected ways. In a recent game, I asked a jock friend if he'd rather be a book of matches or a box of matches. He replied that he'd rather be the box, "because they come in all shapes and sizes, so I'd have a better body." I'd never known that he wrestled with his body image, so this sparked a discussion of a kind we'd never had before—a serious one which marked a turning point in our relationship.

Of course, maybe you don't want serious discussion or turning points, and that's fine—the point of all games is to amuse. While in some games—poker, for example—you are amused by pitting your card skills against your opponents' and Lady Luck, in conversation games, you are amused by the inner workings of someone's mind—the relationships they come up with, the associations they see, the puns or jokes they make. In The Dozens, for example, a facility with verbal humor will always get a laugh: "You're so fat, you eat Wheat *Thicks*." In What Are They Thinking?

a player spontaneously spins a story from a glimpse of a bystander's face—and you may find that your friend is the equal of Garrison Keillor, weaving rich narratives from a single moment in time.

Conversation games require no skills except thoughtfulness and a willingness to think outside the (game) box. They're perfect for long car trips, standing in line at the DMV, or that long, boring stretch of time called "the workday." The object is to have a thoughtful discussion within specific parameters—to explain why you're making a choice, or to narrate to your listeners the inner monologue of the woman in the miniskirt: "She's wishing she'd worn slacks—but she couldn't because she knew she'd be seeing her old flame Doug today, and Doug always loved the freckles on the backs of her knees. . . ."

Fascinating discussions can stem from wildly absurd topics. You'll get to know your friends' goofy, thoughtful sides; you'll get to find out if they consider themselves lovers or fighters; type A's or type B's; meerkats or weasels. It sure beats talking about real estate or swimming pool filters.

Would You Rather . . .

O ne player poses two made-up scenarios—both problematic, and ranging from revolting to horrifying to merely uncomfortable—to the other player or players. Each player must then choose which situation he'd rather find himself in, and then, most importantly, explain *why*.

PLAYERS: 2–10

The Game Plan

At random, choose a player to pose a question to one other player or to the group. He makes up two hypothetical choices that begin with "Would you rather . . . " The other player(s) must choose which of the two they would prefer and why.

The challenge of the game is not only to discuss the thought-provoking, or frightening, or disgusting, but to find the advantages and disadvantages of each scenario and make a judgment call on which seems like the better route. In short, the real treat is the conversation and debate that's sparked. For example, if you were asked, "Would you rather have no sex for the rest of your life, or have cats attached to your hands instead of fingers?" which would you choose? You can ask questions: Are they finger-size kittens, or normal-size cats? Who would have sex with someone who had cats attached to their hands? And can the cats have sex? The mulling over of possibilities can get surprisingly detailed as players break down the potential outcomes of each decision.

A Few Ideas to Get You Started

Would you rather . . .

. . . choose to see your future (without being able to change it)

-OR-

. . . know everyone else's future and not be able to tell them?

■ ■ ■

. . . cheat on your spouse and have nobody know

-OR-

. . . not cheat and have everyone think you did?

■ ■ ■

. . . on a first date, wear a T-shirt that says, "I'm with Stupid"

-OR-

. . . a T-shirt that asks, "Who Cut the Cheese?"

■ ■ ■

. . . be on vacation with your sixty-year-old parents and have your mom insist on wearing a thong bikini

-OR-

. . . have your dad insist on wearing a tiny, Euro-style bikini bathing suit?

■ ■ ■

These are from *Zobmondo!!,* a book of questions that exists specifically for this game. It has plenty of conundrums to start you off.

In a recent game, I started off with, "Would you rather sleep with Bill Maher or Chris Matthews?" (In this game, the questions frequently tended to veer toward the "Would you rather sleep with this person or that person?" but for variety—and of course, if you're playing with kids—try to come up with a wider range of topics.)

My partner refused to choose—he said he'd rather take a bullet—and had to be reminded of the rule of the game: You *must* choose.

So he responded, "They're both awful. But Chris Matthews, I guess, he seems a little more sincere. Bill Maher seems a lot like a squealing weasel."

His own answer evidently influenced him as he made up his next question: "Would you rather marry a wild boar or a squealing weasel?"

And I answered, "The boar, because the weasel reminds me of Bill Maher."

And he said, concurring, that the wild boar would probably be a good provider. Acorns and such.

Then I asked him: "Would you rather be madly in love for twenty years or somewhat in love for fifty?"

And he said—this was my jock friend, now single for longer than he wanted to be—"Madly in love for twenty years. Because I remember being madly in love, and it was awesome. I wouldn't trade that for the world."

▶▶ IF YOU LIKE THIS GAME . . . check out youmustchoose.com, a website that poses user-submitted Would You Rather . . . questions. The site tracks how many people choose each option.

||||||||||||||||||||||||||||||||||||||||||||||||||||||||||||||

I Never

PLAYERS: 2–50

If you came of age in the '80s, you probably remember I Never, a popular drinking game on college campuses.

One by one, players, armed with a beer (or any alcoholic beverage), make a statement of something they've never done: "I've never driven through Nevada," for example, or "I've never had sex in a library." Players who *have* done that—driven through Nevada or had sex in a library—must take a sip of their drinks, thereby both revealing their potentially naughty past actions and rapidly progressing to inebriation. You're on your honor to tell the truth! In college, this game may have seemed puerile—after all, you're coyly nudging people to reveal their sexual escapades as well as encouraging people to drink too much—but the game can be about any adventures at all, not necessarily sexual. And it can be as serious or as silly as you want: "I've never traveled to Algeria," or "I've never peed in the shower," or "I've never had *just* a condiment for dinner." After a few rounds, your most embarrassing and dirty little secrets will be on the table, but so will everyone else's . . . and never have you ever imagined what some of your friends have been doing.

▶▶ IF YOU LIKE THIS GAME . . . try Two Truths and a Lie, on page 17.

||||||||||||||||||||||||||||||||||||||||||||||||||||||||||||||

Walrus

PLAYERS: 3–10

Walrus, also known as Existential Rock Paper Scissors, is a game in which players take turns naming a category and then pitting one item in that category against another. (Why it's called Walrus is anybody's guess.) For example, if the category were "male protagonists of action shows or movies," one player might choose Jack Bauer and the other Walker, Texas Ranger. They must then argue which one "beats" the other. If the category is "kitchen implements," one player might insist that a mandoline "beats" a cast-iron pan because it is slimmer, more vicious, and will certainly slice the fingers of anyone trying to wash it in the sink. A third player acts as the judge and makes the decision once each player has had a chance to make her argument. Once judgment has been rendered, another three players take a turn.

For a whole book devoted to an exercise of this sort, check out *The Enlightened Bracketologist: The Final Four of Everything.* The premise is, in fact, nothing but pitting sixteen members of a category against each other—the best black-and-white TV shows, the best NASCAR phrases ("Rubbin' is racin'" pitted against "one of those racin' deals," etc., with "rubbin' is racin'" winning and then pitted against "boogity boogity boogity.")

The faux-serious discussion of why one member "beats" another is what makes the game amusing. For example, why *does* "rubbin' is racin' " beat "one of those racin' deals"? Well, according to Jeff MacGregor, a senior writer at *Sports Illustrated,* "The phrase *rubbin' is racin'* is laced with the aggression at the heart of the sport. It's what you say after hammering someone out of the way to win. *One of those racin' deals,* on the other hand, is all helpless fatalism, on the order of 'que sera, sera,' what losers say once shunted aside."

PARTY RECIPE

Tea and Shortbread

Conversation games are best played with a hot cup of tea to sip while you ponder your responses. Pair the tea with shortbread, snuggle down into an armchair, and start chatting.

1. Fill a tea kettle with fresh, cold water and place it on a stove burner set on high.

2. When the water is near boiling, warm the teapot by filling it with hot tap water. Empty the pot. For each cup of tea, place 1 rounded teaspoon of leaves into the warmed pot.

3. When the water in the kettle boils, pour it onto the leaves in the teapot. Let steep for 3 to 5 minutes, depending on the type of tea.

4. Place a strainer on the top of a cup, then pour the tea through the strainer to catch the leaves. (A teapot with a removable strainer basket will save you this step.) Add milk, sugar, or lemon if desired. Serve with pecan shortbread, below.

Pecan Shortbread
MAKES 8 WEDGES

INGREDIENTS

2 sticks soft butter	½ teaspoon baking
½ cup confectioners'	powder
sugar	½ teaspoon vanilla extract
2 cups flour	1 cup chopped pecans

1. Preheat oven to 325°F.

2. Combine all the ingredients in a large bowl. Knead until everything is blended into a dough. Press the dough into a round, ungreased pan. Bake for about 20 minutes, or until light brown. Cut into wedges while still warm. Serve with a cup of tea.

What Are They Thinking?

PLAYERS: 2–5

This game is a storytelling exercise in which a narrative is spun from just a glance at a stranger in a public space. One player draws the other's attention to a person in their midst (someone far enough away, of course, that they won't notice they are being discussed) and says, "What is that person [in the yellow hat; with the Labrador; hanging on the porch railing, etc.] thinking?" Another player volunteers to (surreptitiously) examine the "target" and then tell a story about what that person is thinking. The story, of course, can be long or short—from "He's wishing he hadn't had that third doughnut" to "Well, Henry's mulling over the recent dissolution of his marriage, and he's wondering if it had anything to do with that unexpected upset at tennis, a game at which his wife had always bested him. Things had been chilly in the Madsen household since that fateful day . . ."

What Are They Thinking? has no winners or losers. Players have a chance to exercise their imaginative and dramatic skills, relating the inner thoughts of a total stranger based on the smallest of clues: a raised brow, an upturned lip, a wrinkled nose.

Cage Match

Cage Match takes **Walrus** to a new level: It's played in a public place, like a bar, so it's social. Cage Match requires two players and a moderator—but if a player doesn't like the moderator's decision he can appeal to bystanders for a second opinion. This right-to-appeal turns what could be an insular argument into a great way to meet new people.

PLAYERS: From 3 to a whole bar full of people.

To begin, the moderator names a category, say, cereal box mascots. Each player chooses a mascot and makes an argument for which one would beat the other if they were pitted against each other in a cage match. (FYI, a cage match is a bout that takes place inside a mesh steel cage where competitors are trapped and can't come out until one is defeated.)

So, Player 1 might choose the leprechaun from Lucky Charms, and Player 2 might choose the toucan from Froot Loops. Player 2 argues that the toucan has a vicious beak and can fly—but Player 1 counters that the leprechaun, being magical, will always have the edge because leprechauns can appear and disappear at will.

The moderator, after listening to both arguments, makes a decision. If the loser doesn't like the decision, he can appeal to anyone nearby for a second opinion.

—contributed by Charley Miller with David Hoffman, see page 80.

‖‖‖

The Dozens

T he Dozens (or "Yo Momma") originates from American hip-hop culture—but contests of verbal improvisation are centuries old: Flyting, for example, was a battle between poets exchanging abusive poems in sixteenth-century Scotland.

PLAYERS: 2 at a time, plus an audience.

The Game Plan

The Dozens is a battle of wits: One player insults another—either a comment on his age, weight, income status, or looks (or, frequently, the age, weight, income status, or looks of his mother, wife, or girlfriend). The other player then comes up with a counter-insult.

✱ The Dozens showcases originality and wit, the skill to stay one step ahead of an opponent, and a cool temper. While there's no official winner or loser, if a player is getting insulted over and over again and doesn't land any zingers in return—well, the crowd will let him know that his opponent is wiping the floor with him.

✱ The object of the game is to be amusing and clever, not to be truly cruel. It's more like improv than a game. A few examples:

"Your momma's so fat, she fell in love and broke it."

"You're so stupid, you took a knife to a drive-by shooting."

"You're so ugly, your birth certificate was an apology letter from the condom factory."

The game ends when a player is stumped for a comeback.

▶▶ **IF YOU LIKE THIS GAME . . .** go on YouTube and check out *In Living Color* making fun of The Dozens in a game show sketch called "The Dirty Dozens." Just type "living color" and "dozens" into the search bar.

‖‖‖

Shag, Marry, Cliff

PLAYERS: 2–20

A lso known as Do, Date, or Die (actually, it's also known by a few other names that are too raunchy to print), Shag, Marry, Cliff forces players to choose, among three awful options, which person they'd sleep with, which person they'd marry, and which one they'd kill. For example, one player lists three people, say, Dick Cheney, Saddam Hussein, and Paris Hilton. Then the other players must decide who they'd shag, who they'd wed, and who they'd toss off a cliff. Think about the above-mentioned choices. Not so easy, eh? Each player announces his decisions, with the reasons why. As with Would You Rather . . . , the rationales are the point: Maybe you'd choose to marry Dick Cheney because he'd spend so much time hunting that you'd almost never have to see him.

You can add restrictions to the game as you and your pals see fit: The choices can be only celebrities, or only people that you all know, or a combination of the two. You can choose people who have the same first name: Tom Green, Tom Arnold, Tom Cruise. The options can be topical, too: Maybe during primary season you have to choose among the candidates or the talking heads on the news programs. What if your choices were Ann Coulter, Wolf Blitzer, and

Larry King? (Well, if you married Larry King you could borrow all those fun suspenders.)

▶▶ **IF YOU LIKE THIS GAME . . . the writers on the show** *30 Rock* **play a round of Marry, Boff, Kill during a lull in the workday. Check out the clip in nbc.com's video library.**

Butterfly or Bumblebee?

PLAYERS: 2–10

One player poses a question, a choice, like "Are you a butterfly or a bumblebee?" Then another player, chosen by the first, has to answer with what she feels she is, not what she *wants* to be or thinks other people think she is. So she might say she's a bumblebee because she stings but it's not fatal, and because she's cute and useful.

After she answers, the player who posed the choice must answer the question, too. Then it's someone else's turn to offer a choice. That person might say, "Are you a redwood or a sycamore?" You might say a sycamore because you love being by the water and you're pasty white. Someone else proposes a duo to choose between, and so forth. The game, as with many conversation games, is noncompetitive; the point is to understand how players see themselves (unlike Essences on page 49, for example, in which the point is to see how *others* see you). You can choose either similar things: Are you a Prosecco or a Lambrusco?, for example, or dissimilar things: Are you a Lamborghini or a dishwasher?

The acquaintance who told me about this game says, "I love playing the game because you learn things about your significant other that you might otherwise never have known. It's also great because while you're sitting there thinking of what two different items you'll pose that will get a fun answer from your date, you haven't begun to fathom how *you'll* answer the question. So when your turn comes up, sometimes you feel like you got 'hoisted on your own petard,' because the question was, 'Are you eye shadow or lipstick?' and you're a dude—and you didn't really think about what *you'd* say before you asked."

Variation

Experiment with creating more complicated questions like, "If you were a statue, what would it be made of, where would it stand, and what would it represent?" You can pose even wackier questions like, "Why do people throw ice-cream cones at your statue?"

▶▶ **IF YOU LIKE THIS GAME . . . check out Essences on page 49.**

Three Best

PLAYERS: 2–5

It's easy: One player names a category, like sandwiches, holiday destinations, or first dates. The other players must list their three best experiences with the items in that category and, of course, explain *why* their experiences were so wonderful. So if the category was sandwiches, you might answer Wonder Bread and peanut butter by the pool in the late 1970s because your mom made it;

prosciutto crudo on a baguette, because that was what you ate on your first date with your wife; and a muffuletta because it's a sandwich that's the soul of New Orleans.

At heart, this game is similar to Walrus—but in Three Best, you reveal your past and your memories to fellow players. For the "three best cookies"—well, Proust would include the madeleine, of course, and tell the story that accompanies it.

My friend Richard, in answering "three best parks," cites an evening spent in a leafy park in Madrid—an evening in which he was drugged and robbed by a thug. He woke up with no wallet, suitcase, passport, guitar—nothing—to find the Spanish police arresting him for vagrancy. Unable to explain himself in Spanish, still suffering from the aftereffects of the drug, he spent two weeks in a Spanish jail until a bilingual lawyer could be rustled up to state his case before a judge. Now, *why* does Richard include this on his list of three best parks? Well, the experience that began

at that park paradoxically gave him faith in the "system." He was treated fairly in jail, got three square meals a day, and he even made a few friends during his tenure in the clink. In short, what could have been a dreadful experience turned out to be not so bad. It renewed his faith in his fellow man. Except, of course, in the man who robbed him.

Best Portable Food for Car Trips

- A buttered baguette with sliced Serrano ham
- A thermos of gazpacho
- Avocado maki
- Doughnut holes
- Apple slices with small containers of yogurt
- Biscuits with cold sliced chicken
- Bite-sized spanakopitas from Trader Joe's
- Sliced banana bread spread with peanut butter

|||||||||||||||||||||||||||||||||||||||||||||||||||||||||||||||||||||||||||||

Opposites

PLAYERS: 2–4

What's the opposite of black? Well, white. Tall? Of course, short. But what's the opposite of a pufferfish? And this is how the game of Opposites goes: One person, off the top of his head, asks for the opposite of something that does not naturally have an opposite. The game consists of making an argument for why one particular thing is something's opposite. There's no right or wrong: If you convince the other player(s), you win the round. If he has a "better" opposite and you agree, he wins. If you can't agree, it's a draw and you move on to the next question.

While Opposites does technically have a winner and a loser, you shouldn't choose your questions based on whether you think you can win them or not. Let your imagination roam and pose your questions without thinking too much or even at all, about whether you'll be able to "win" the round. If something occurs to you, just blurt it out: What's the opposite of a Brita? A math teacher? A Portuguese Water Dog? A French fry?

Back to the pufferfish: This one originally stumped me in a game, so I broke it down into its parts: OK, well, the opposite of *swimming* is *drowning,* and the opposite of a *fish* is a *cow* (surf and turf, right?). So, a drowning cow is the opposite of a pufferfish.

Then I posed this one to my friend, as we were playing over G-chat: What's the opposite of typing? He pondered a moment (as evidenced by the blinking cursor on my screen) and then answered: "Either hugging or hitting. Typing is articulating feeling through a code (written language). Hugging and hitting are simply transferring feeling via body contact (no code)." I agreed that this did seem like the opposite, and so declined to try to come up with a "better" opposite. One point for him.

Then he asked me, "What is the opposite of a duck-billed platypus?"

"That one's easy," I said. "Its opposite is a loaf of bread, because you know exactly what a loaf of bread is and why God put it on this earth."

▶▶ IF YOU LIKE THIS GAME . . . try Apples to Apples, available at toy and bookstores.

Unfortunately . . .

PLAYERS: 2

A storytelling game, Unfortunately . . . requires players to take the opposite view of whatever was just said. To start, one player makes a statement that is prefaced by "fortunately." For example, "Fortunately, I just won a million dollars." The next player must respond, without pausing, with a sentence that begins with "unfortunately": "Unfortunately, you have to give it all away." The first player then responds again with something prefaced with "fortunately": "Fortunately, it will do a lot of good for the people I give it to." "Unfortunately, you are giving it to Bernie Madoff."

The game continues until one of the players pauses; that player is out and the other player, is, fortunately, declared the winner!

One, Two, Three

A cooperative rather than competitive game, One, Two, Three takes the phrase "great minds think alike" to a new level. It's a free-association game with a twist: You're trying to free-associate to the point where you and your partner say the same word at the same time. You'll learn how your companion mentally makes connections, and you'll try to "psych out" her thought process while she's doing the same to you.

PLAYERS: 2

The Game Plan

Each player thinks of a noun (once you're used to the game you can expand to other parts of speech, but at first, stick with nouns). Out loud, both of you count to three, and then say your words at the same time. Next, you both have to come up with another word that somehow relates the two words you've just said. You count to three again, and say your words at the same time. The game continues until you both blurt out the same word at the same time.

Example:

Player 1	Player 2
1, 2, 3—Ants!	1, 2, 3—Communism!
1, 2, 3—Workers!	1, 2, 3—Red!
1, 2, 3—Firefighters!	1, 2, 3—Firefighters!

Since both said "firefighters" the game is over . . . and you've both won. The prize? A sweet sense of kismet.

Questions R- and-G Style

PLAYERS: 2, plus a judge or audience (optional).

As described in Tom Stoppard's play *Rosencrantz and Guildenstern Are Dead,* the object of this two-player improvisational game is to have a conversation involving only questions. Players have to practice thinking on their feet and showcase their wit, and so it's best played in front of an audience. Statements, repeating questions, and non sequiturs, if caught by the other player (or the judge, if you're playing with one), count as "outs." Three outs and you're out.

An example: "How're you doing?"

"What could be better than today?"

"What about skydiving?"

If you've seen the show *Whose Line Is It Anyway?* (search YouTube for an episode), you know how amusing this game can be.

In the Stoppard play, Guildenstern launches the game, which the two characters

are scoring as in tennis, before Rosencrantz is completely ready:

R: We could play at questions.

G: What good would that do?

R: Practice!

G: Statement! One—love.

R: Cheating!

G: How?

R: I hadn't started yet.

G: Statement. Two—love.

R: Are you counting that?

G: What?

R: Are you counting that?

G: Foul! No repetitions. Three—love.

Can You Live With It?

This variation on the awful-choices games has a new twist of inventing a romantic partner who is entirely and completely perfect for you—except for one awful flaw.

PLAYERS: 2–5

The Game Plan

✖ Describe the perfect romantic partner for another player. Let's say the player's a tennis fanatic, likes blondes, and plays the banjo. So you might say, "Have I got a woman for you. She looks like Anna Kournikova, and she can beat Anna in mixed doubles with one hand tied behind her back—and she's been touring in a bluegrass band with Alison Krauss. But, I'm sorry to say, she has one long curly blue hair sprouting from the center of her chest that she treasures, will not cut or trim, and wants you to call Sweet Blue. So, are you going to go for it or not?"

✻ And the other player will have to say whether he can live with Sweet Blue—and all the other pleasures that the Anna Kournikova/Alison Krauss cross brings—or whether he's going to keep looking for a more ordinary partner whose chest is reasonably hair-free.

✻ Then it's his turn to invent the perfect romantic partner for you—but again, that person has just that one terrible flaw. Can you live with it?

Band Name, Album Name, or Boat Name?

Band Name, Album Name, or Boat Name? is perhaps the quintessential road trip activity. It keeps you alert to your surroundings, your creativity pumping, and the conversation flowing. It sure beats falling asleep with Cheeto dust drooling out of your mouth as you listen to *Blood on the Tracks* for the fiftieth time. Created by Thi Nguyen, Band Name came my way via boardgamegeek.com. Says Thi, "We invented this game when we saw a homey, un-squared-away, sweet little wooden houseboat, with off-center hand-lettering announcing its name: *Well Done*. And I said, 'That's apt—it is, indeed, well done.'"

The Game Plan

As you tool along down the highways and byways, keep your eye out for any unusual words or phrases that could be a band name, album name, or a boat name. These words or phrases could crop up anywhere: on signs in the windows of stores, in the names of little groceries or laundromats, at the lunch counter in a one-horse town in Alabama, or just from your own imagination. As you see or think of a word or phrase that catches your fancy—it can be anything—you point it out to your companions and declare it to be a band name, album name, or a boat name. On Thi's road trip, for example, they decided that "Dave's Laundry" would be an album name, "Your Money or Your Life" would be a band name, and "Loading Zone" would be a boat name. Your companions may disagree—some thought that "Loading Zone" was more of an album name than a boat name, but mild disagreement can only improve the discussion.

Group Therapy

Group Therapy is a game best played with a medium-size group of people who know each other fairly well: You might launch this game in a bar with a group of college friends, on the bus with your Ultimate Frisbee team, or at a family party.

PLAYERS: 4-15

The Game Plan

Randomly choose an "It" and select someone else in the group to pose a question to It. This question may be as silly or serious as the asker wishes, but the answer to the question must be the name of someone in the group.

For example, if Bill is It and Jane is asking the question, Jane might say: "Bill, if you were trapped in the mountains and had to resort to cannibalism, whom in the group would you eat first?"

Bill decides who that would be, but keeps the answer to himself. Then, each player (proceeding clockwise from Bill's left) must state who *he* thinks Bill would choose and why. So Frank might say, "I think Bill would choose to eat Sarah, because she is the thinnest and probably wouldn't last too long anyway." And Sally might say, "I think Bill would choose Henry, because they used to be roommates and Henry knows all of Bill's awful secrets—and would blog about them if he outlived Bill." And so on. Once everyone in the group has stated who Bill would choose, Bill reveals his answer and why he chose that person.

Winning

Anyone who correctly anticipated Bill's answer wins. Another round begins with a new It and a new questioner.

A Few Ideas to Get You Started

The questions can be as mundane, obscene, or bizarre as the questioner likes.

- Who in the group would be most likely to get in trouble with the police?

- Who is the most likely to make a renegade third-party run for president?

- Who is most inclined to try out a wacky new diet?

- Who will marry beneath him/her?

- Who will marry "up"?

- Who will switch political affiliations later in life?

- Who is most likely to accidentally burn down their house?

- Who will die a millionaire?

- If you could pick one person in the room to be stranded on a desert island with, who would it be?

- Who is most likely to be an undercover CIA operative?

- Who would you most want to have as a parent?

The Ethicist Game

The Ethicist Game was invented in a bar in Brooklyn in 2008. An excellent activity for sparking conversation with friends, the Ethicist Game helps you find out how morally upright they really are. A question from *The New York Times Magazine*'s "Ethicist" column is read aloud, and players debate what advice they would offer to the letter writer. It's a pleasant game to play in a bar, as weighty matters of right and wrong are best decided over a nice glass of sherry, but moral issues can also certainly be debated at home, in a car, or on a walk.

PLAYERS: 2–10

THE GEAR: Printouts of some of Randy Cohen's "The Ethicist" columns from nytimes.com.

Preparation

Ahead of time, one player should print out some copies of "The Ethicist" advice column from *The New York Times Magazine,* taking care to fold the paper over the answers without looking at them. Old columns, which you can find online, are best, so your players are less likely to remember how Cohen responded.

The Game Plan

When all the players arrive, take turns reading aloud a question that was posed to the Ethicist. Players take a moment to ponder. Then, in no particular order, they announce what advice they would offer to the letter writer.

Winning

The player whose answer is closest to the Ethicist's wins—or, if the group consensus is that a particular player's answer is *more* ethical that the Ethicist's, that player takes the prize—a small compass on a keychain, for having the strongest moral compass.

—contributed by Heather Southwell, an attorney for the IRS, who knows a thing or two about ethics.

Variation

Try this with other advice columns as well. Etiquette columns are particularly fun, or check out my favorite, "Dear Prudence," on slate.com.

Chapter Six

LITERARY & WORD GAMES

So you're one of the word people. You like crosswords, you make puns, you correct the grammar on bathroom graffiti. Well, is this the chapter for you. It's all about the cleverness and the ingenuity and the creativity you can find in the twenty-six letters of the alphabet.

Word games are an ancient and enduring form of entertainment— you need only skim one of Shakespeare's plays or *Beowulf* to find examples of puns, double entendres, and rhymes galore. These days we picture the punsters and crossword fanatics as bespectacled, bow-tied nerds—but word games used to be aggressive contests of intellect and wit as well as powerful, sexy tools for courtship. In our current sports-obsessed culture, we've forgotten that the ability to be clever with words used to be more respected, and for good reason: Word games reveal an intellect, a creativity, and an agility of mind that other games don't. They test one's understanding of language; they lighten the ordinary process of communicating. They're fun. Word games are infinitely adaptable and suitable for all ages—as long as players are pretty evenly matched, everyone can have fun.

Many parlor games were word games: the parlors of yesteryear were not particularly big, and so even slightly rambunctious games were played outdoors. Well, today's "parlor" is the car—it's the only place where (frequently) the whole family is together, movement is limited, and quiet conversation is possible. Most of these games don't even require a pen and paper, so you can enjoy them on road trips.

If you *are* at home and have a little room to spread out, games that call for a pencil or a heap of Scrabble tiles can also provide an evening's entertainment in the living room. After all, when else can you bust out your knowledge of obscure words like *lagniappe* and *pyx*?

Of course, even word people come with different strengths and weaknesses, and so word games come in many shapes and sizes: Some people might excel at assembling words out of a jumble of letters and then building on them (Anagrams, 25 Letters); others may enjoy the storytelling activities like Syllepsis or Rhymes About. Still others might enjoy another kind of "story" telling: bluffing their way through Fictionary and its many variants. For a great evening, have a few games on deck—try a warm-up of Anagrams and then move to more improv-type games, like Cringe Party. And whatever you do, disport, cavort, gambol, and frolic—in other words, have fun!

▸▸ **ETIQUETTE**

For those of us who are word people, literary and word games are easy and fun. But not everyone, of course, has read *Bleak House* or can make up a limerick at the drop of a hat. Unless you're 100 percent sure that all your guests are as wordy as you are, mix a few other kinds of games into your evening. Card, drawing, strategy, and guessing games will give everyone a chance to shine.

Anagrams
aka Mean Scrabble, or Scramble

Anagrams is fun for two reasons: One, you're making words from a jumble of letters—always a good time. Two, schadenfreude. (For those not fluent in German, *schadenfreude* is that little frisson of pleasure you get at someone else's misfortune.) In Anagrams, you and your opponents make words—*but,* you also get to steal your opponent's words as fast as you can anagram them. Hah, hah! See? Schadenfreude.

PLAYERS: 2–6

THE GEAR: A set of tiles from a Scrabble game, or homemade cardboard Scrabble tiles. (For the amount of each letter to make, see page 105.)

The Game Plan

✖ To start, shuffle the tiles facedown on the playing area. To determine who goes first, each player picks up a tile. The player with the tile closest to the beginning of the alphabet begins.

✖ One by one, proceeding clockwise, players turn over a single tile. As soon as a player spots a word at least four letters long (in English and not a proper noun), she calls out the word, picks up the tiles, and places them in front of herself.

✖ If two players call out a word at the same time, the longer word wins. If the words are the same length, the other players vote on who has made the more clever anagram and thus deserves the letters.

✖ Play continues, with each player turning over one tile at a time. Players may only capture another player's word if they can mix *all* its letters with any number of the upturned tiles to make a new word.

✖ Simply making a word plural is not enough—to capture another player's word you must anagram the word (mix up the letters) and add to it to make a completely new word.

✖ Play continues until a player has made five words. Alternatively, you may choose to end the game when all the tiles have been turned over and no one is able to make another word.

Winning

There are two ways to count up the scores in Anagrams: In the simplest version, the player who ends the game with the greatest number of tiles wins. If you'd like to reward longer words, however, you can square the length of each player's words—i.e., a five-letter word will be worth 25 points. Decide ahead of time how you want to score.

Syllepsis

A *zeugma* **is a phrase** that joins two or more parts of a sentence with a single common verb or noun. A *syllepsis* is a zeugma in which the clauses are not parallel either in meaning or grammar. A syllepsis is usually used for comic or poetic effect. Not an English major? Here are a few examples:

✖ He hastened to put out the cat, the wine, his cigar, and the lamps. —*Flanders and Swann, the British comedy duo*

✖ The levees were broken and so were the promises. —*Anderson Cooper*

✖ [She] went straight home in a flood of tears and a sedan chair. —*Charles Dickens*

✖ You held your breath and the door for me. —*Alanis Morissette*

✖ She was a thief, you got to believe: She stole my heart and my cat. —*Mike Myers,* So I Married an Axe Murderer

---

PLAYERS: 2–20

THE GEAR: Pencils, paper, timer.

The Game Plan

Elect someone to keep the time. This player may, but doesn't have to be, a neutral moderator. If you're playing in a large group, divide into two or more teams and send each one into a different room. Set the timer for five minutes. Each team or individual must come up with as many examples of syllepsis as they can within the time limit; each sentence or phrase will score one point. The goal here is volume rather than making good poetry, but comedy and absurdity *do* count: If someone in the group laughs, flinches, moans, or cringes when the example is read, the person or team who created the syllepsis gets an extra point. In cases of dispute, majority decides what is syllepsis and what isn't.

Winning

When the five minutes are up, appoint a player on each team to read aloud their syllepses; the side that's created the most wins. Award "bonus" points for particularly clever or creative examples of syllepsis, decided by the majority. If you're playing with an intergenerational group, it's best to play the noncompetitive version (pitting a kindergartner against a PhD wouldn't be much fun); just have players call out examples of syllepsis as they think of them.

I played an after-dinner game with some friends recently. The best example of syllepsis, we all decided, was "She teased the child, her hair, and the answer from the reluctant witness." Runner-up was "He cut the cheese, the line, and to the chase."

Variation

To make the game slightly more complicated, create a list of words (five to ten), at least one of which must be incorporated into each syllepsis.

||||||||||||||||||||||||||||||||||||||||||||||||||||||||||||||||||||||||||||||||

25 Letters
aka Crosswords or Word Squares

An excellent "waiting" game— waiting for a plane, waiting for your appetizers, waiting for the anesthesia to kick in. I recently played this at an outdoor film festival in a riverside park under the Brooklyn Bridge—a friend and I had arrived early to secure good spots on the grass—and we lolled on our picnic blanket, playing 25 Letters for an hour in the summer twilight. Then we bought out the concession stand (they had s'mores and a tiny campfire!) and dropped into a heavy food coma on the blanket. I heard the movie was excellent, though I only remember the game and the s'mores.

People with mad Boggle skills like 25 Letters, but it's a great game even for those of us who think Boggle has more to do with visual acumen than word smarts. 25 Letters combines the word-making skills of Scrabble with elements of strategy and luck.

PLAYERS: 2

THE GEAR: Paper and pencils.

The Game Plan

To start, each player draws a five-by-five grid. (For a grid template, see page 372.) These grids should not be visible to the other player, just as one's cards are held close to the chest in a poker game. The object is to make words on the grid, either vertically or horizontally.

The players take turns calling out letters. As a letter is called out, each player plots that letter on his grid *at the time* it's called out. (You can't "save" letters for later—players are on their honor to observe this rule.) The same letter may be called out multiple times. After the twenty-fifth letter has been called out, players share what words they've made. A five-letter word is worth 10 points, a four-letter word 5 points, and a three-letter word 3 points. You can count "words within words," so *abate* would count as 10 points for "abate," 3 points for "ate," *and* 3 points for "bat." You have to identify each word for it to count—if you don't see that "ale" is part of *swale,* you obviously won't get credit for it.

▶▶STEALTH STRATEGY

If you go first, call out a vowel and put it in the center square. You'll have more flexibility to make words as the game progresses.

T	S	C	S	X
O	O	L	A	R
A	B	A	T	E
S	E	M	I	A
T	R	S	N	O

This game produced Abate, Sob, Semi, Bat, Ate, Sober, Toast, Clams, Lam, Satin, Sat, and Tin, for a total of 73 points

AMP IT UP

If this version is too easy, expand the rules to include diagonal or backward words.

Verbatim
aka Word Factory

PLAYERS: 2–20

THE GEAR: Timer, pencils, slips of paper.

One player writes down a moderately long word—at least three syllables with a bunch of vowels—and reads it out loud, spelling it if necessary. Each player has two minutes to write down as many words of three letters or more as he can make from the letters of the original word. So if the word you chose was *attenuate,* some words would be "ten," "ate," "tent," etc. Once the two minutes are up, another player comes up with a root word. You can either tally the score by round or at the end when each player has had a turn to choose the root word. The longest list of words wins.

|||||||||||||||||||||||||||||||||||||||||||||||||||||||||||||||||||||||||

Dictionary

Dictionary has been around for decades and has spawned a bunch of commercial bluffing games like Balderdash, Weird Wordz, and Malarkey. It's a perfect combination of storytelling, b.s.ing, and b.s.-detection. (A friend recently hoped to convince the group that the definition for *surfperch* was "the crest on a wave at the moment it breaks." I believed him, so he won a point. Alas, *surfperch* is a type of fish.)

PLAYERS: 3–8

THE GEAR: Slips of paper, pencils, and a dictionary, natch.

The Game Plan

- ✖ One player (the "reader") chooses an obscure word from the dictionary and reads it aloud. (If anyone *does* know the definition of the word, she must say so and the reader will choose another word.) Each player then quietly writes down a fake (but plausible!) definition, plus the part of speech, in "Webster-ese." The reader doesn't make anything up, but merely copies the real definition. (Many, if not most, dictionary

entries have several definitions; the reader should choose the first (which is usually the most important definition). Players also write their initials in the lower right-hand corner of their slips of paper.

- ✖ All players fold their papers and pass them to the reader; the reader reads them to himself to ensure that he can decipher the handwriting. (In the event that clarification is needed, the player whose handwriting is illegible can whisper in the reader's ear.) The reader then reads out the word and each of the definitions, including the real one, taking care not to stumble or squint or otherwise indicate which definitions are real or fake—unless, of course, he's bluffing.

- ✖ Players then vote for the definition they think is correct, by writing down their guesses, along with their initials, and passing the papers to the reader. The reader keeps track of how many votes each definition receives.

- ✖ When all have voted, the true definition is revealed, and the round is scored. A player gets a point for:

  - ▪ having voted for the true definition.
  - ▪ every vote cast for the definition he wrote.
  - ▪ The reader gets a point only if no one votes for the true definition.

- ✖ After each round, another person takes a turn as the reader. Once everyone has had the chance to be the reader, tally the scores. High score wins. (If you're playing with a very small group, say, three people, you may wish to play to an agreed-upon number of points—10 is good—as otherwise the game will be very short.)

A recent game produced the word *sweven.*

The group created the following definitions:

- ✗ **sweven:** *adj.*, suave; sophisticated
- ✗ **sweven:** *n.*, a flock of birds
- ✗ **sweven:** *n.*, a Scandinavian paradise
- ✗ **sweven:** *n.*, a vision; dream
- ✗ **sweven:** *n.*, a unit of measurement used to note movement in tall buildings
- ✗ **sweven:** *n.*, early New England slang for "goalpost"

Which do you think it is?*

a vision; dream

Dictionary Variations

Fictionary

This game relies on having immediate access to an extensive library of novels, either in hard copy or electronically. One player selects a book and announces the title and the author to the rest of the players. This should be a book that is *not* terribly familiar to the rest of the group—if a player actually knows the real first line of the novel, she should say so and another book will be selected. Each player composes a first line, except for the reader, who writes down the *real* first line. Scoring is the same as for Dictionary.

"Proverbs" Dictionary

Ahead of time, have a nonplaying member print out a number of old sayings or proverbs from a website (I like www.tentmaker.org /Quotes/international_proverbs.htm) and

cut it into slips displaying individual sayings. Put all the slips in a hat. Each person takes a turn as the "Reader." The reader draws one of the slips and reads *only the first half* aloud to the assembled company, for example: "There's an old Japanese saying . . ." If you like, you can give a little more: "There's an old Japanese saying: A good husband is . . ."*

The players must then make up their own second half and jot it down. The reader jots down the real second half. Play and scoring proceeds as in Dictionary.

▶▶ **IF YOU LIKE THIS GAME . . . try Wise and Otherwise, available at toy and book stores.**

". . . healthy and absent."

Medical or Law Dictionary

Use a medical or a law dictionary instead of your trusty Webster's. What does *thalassaemia* mean, anyway? (Of course, this only really works if none—or all—of your company is a doctor or lawyer, otherwise that player would have too much of an advantage.)

Superstitions Dictionary

Use a book or a website of old superstitions; the reader chooses one "real" superstition and gives the theme: "An upside-down horseshoe means . . ." or "A black cat crossing your path means . . ." The rest of the players finish the second half of the sentence, making up plausible superstitions. Play and scoring proceeds as in Dictionary.

Quotations Dictionary

Use a book or website of famous (but not *too* famous) quotations or aphorisms instead of a dictionary. Have the reader read out loud the first half of each quotation: "All's fair in . . . ," for example (though, of course, this particular aphorism is too well known to be playable.) Just as in Dictionary, if a player knows the real quotation, she should say so and another quote will be chosen. Players will compose the second half of the quotation, and everyone votes for the one they think is real.

Slang Dictionary

Ask your kids for the latest slang, or take words from Urban Dictionary (urbandictionary.com) for a game of Dictionary. My latest favorite is *head splinter* (n.): a painfully annoying song that gets stuck in your head, in extreme cases, impeding everyday tasks.

Poetry Fictionary

Use a book of assorted poems instead of a dictionary. A rhyming quatrain is chosen by the reader, who reads the first three lines aloud. A plausible fourth line must be made up by the other players.

▶▶ **IF YOU LIKE THIS GAME . . . try Liebrary, Malarkey, or Balderdash, available at toy or bookstores.**

|||||||||||||||||||||||||||||||||||||||||||||||||||||||||||||||||||||||||

Cringe Party

If you have a bunch of friends who, as teenagers, fancied themselves writers or did a lot of "journaling," you've *got* to throw a Cringe Party. The party started in Brooklyn, New York, a few years ago at a bar near my apartment. It was essentially a regular reading series in which brave souls volunteer "to read aloud from their teenage diaries, journals, notes, letters, poems, abandoned rock operas, and other general representations of the crushing misery of their humiliating adolescence." I attended a few and found it as grimly fascinating as a car wreck—you find yourself watching the readers through your fingers, completely, well, *cringing,* but unable to look away.

PLAYERS: 10–50

THE GEAR: Your friends' adolescent diaries, letters, poems, etc.

The Game Plan

Invite all your friends to your house, offering drinks, snacks, and other goodies. In exchange they must bring some remnant of their teenage writerly selves, like a few pages from a journal or a poem or two, written during the height of adolescent angst. When your pals show up, assign them an order in which to read, ask everyone to quiet down, and sit back. You'll hear discussions of topics you thought you'd left behind—acne, the SATs, MC Hammer. Take it from me: Beer will help you get through it.

▶▶ **HOST TIP**

If you'd like to expand the group to beyond your inner circle, arrange with a local bar to host a "reading series" on an off night, like a Sunday or a Monday, and place an ad in the "free events" section of your local newspaper or website.

Winning

A Cringe Party is noncompetitive, but if you'd like to award a prize to the bravest soul, as determined by a majority vote—have a copy of *Cringe: Teenage Diaries, Journals, Notes, Letters, Poems, and Abandoned Rock Operas* on hand.

Scones

Tea and scones are the perfect accompaniment to any games involving poetry or great literature. The recipe below, adapted from the *Sweet Melissa Baking Book*, produces perfect triangular scones with a crumbly, buttery, not-too-sweet texture. Serve with a pot of English Breakfast tea and you've got a poetry party.   MAKES 8 SCONES

INGREDIENTS

⅔ cup old-fashioned oats	1 tablespoon sugar
1½ cups flour	1 stick cold unsalted
2 teaspoons baking	butter, cut into pieces
powder	⅔ cup heavy cream
½ teaspoon salt	1 large egg

FOR THE GLAZE

2 tablespoons	1 tablespoon sugar
heavy cream	

1. Preheat oven to 350°F.

2. In a food processor, grind the oats into a coarse flour. Add the flour, baking powder, salt, and sugar and combine. Add the cold butter and pulse until it is the size of peas. In a bowl, whisk the cream and the egg together until smooth. Fold the flour mixture into the egg mixture. Turn the dough out to a lightly floured cutting board and pat into a disk about 7 inches in diameter. Cut the disk into eight even triangles.

3. Place the triangles about an inch apart on a cookie sheet lined with foil. To glaze, brush the tops with the cream and sprinkle with sugar. Bake for 30 minutes or until golden. Cool and serve.

Rhymes About

PLAYERS: 2–6

THE GEAR: A book of rhyming poetry.

The leader reads a line of poetry from a book; the players must create a line that matches in rhyme and measure. Whether the line makes sense or not is up to you—the object of the game is to amuse or impress the other players. Not being much of a poet myself, in a recent game I came up with:

"My love is like a red, red rose . . .
And when boozy has a red, red nose."

As an alternative, the leader could assign every *other* line of a poem to an individual player. Each player must create a line that matches the one he's been assigned. Then all lines are read aloud in order, creating a new poem with half of the original lines and half new lines.

Three Lives
aka GHOST or HORSE

PLAYERS: 2–4

Player 1 thinks of a word and says the first letter. The words have to be four or more letters to count. Let's say he's thinking of *catastrophe,* so he gives the letter *c.*

Player 2 thinks of a word beginning with that letter, say, *certain,* and says *e.* Player 3 (or back to Player 1, if playing with only two people) thinks of a word beginning with *c-e* and adds a third letter, like *l,* if he's thinking of *celtic.* And so it goes—but if you finish the word, you lose one of your three lives. And, if you are unable to think of another letter that would make a word, you lose a life as well. If you're bluffing—as in, you say a letter at random—another player can call your bluff and you lose a life. If a player calls your bluff and you're *not* bluffing, that player loses a life. If you lose three lives, you've lost.

Ghost and Horse are simply other names for Three Lives, except in these games you get *five* lives instead of three.

Variation

In Super Ghost, letters can be added to the beginning of the word as well as the end.

Scrabble Categories

Scrabble Categories would optimally be played in a large house or apartment, with a bridge table set up for every four people in the game. In more cramped quarters, seating four in places on the floor, around the coffee table, or at the kitchen table is fine. The game is "progressive," meaning that if you and your partner win against another couple, you physically move to another table (or seat on the floor) to compete against another couple. Players should move clockwise through the tables.

PLAYERS: 8–40

THE GEAR: Scrabble tiles, pencil and paper for each table, and a timer.

The Game Plan

✂ Divide your guests into teams of two. Seat the players in groups of four at a card table (or at a pretend card table, like a space on the floor), with one team of two pitted against the other. Provide a heap of Scrabble tiles, or bits of cardboard with single letters inked upon them (see opposite page), face down on each table.

✂ Give each table their own category, say, "famous mistresses," and start a timer for three minutes. At the word *go,* a player in each group turns over a tile—let's say it's C. The first of the four to name an object of the assigned class that begins with that letter—for instance, Camilla Parker-Bowles—wins a point. Then the next player turns up a letter, and so on for the three minutes allowed at each table. Couples keep track of their own points. (While the game is played in teams, the players don't collaborate—simply add the number of points that Jane won to the number of points Bob won for the total number of points for Team Bob and Jane.)

✂ At the end of three minutes, the couple at each table with the most points progresses to the next table, or, if at the head table, retreats to the foot. (This is assuming the tables are laid out in more or less a straight line, but in more cramped quarters, just make it clear to your guests the order of tables—maybe Table 1 is nearest the front door and Table 6 is nearest the kitchen.) And so the game continues. After twenty minutes, the game ends and the number of moves are tallied. The couple who's moved the most times wins.

▸▸ **HOST TIP**
Make your own Scrabble tiles on bits of cardboard. To the right is the Scrabble tile distribution, so if you're on vacation and don't want to run out and buy *another* Scrabble set, you can draw a grid on a sheet of cardboard, ink the letters on the squares, and cut out the pieces with an X-Acto knife.

Scrabble Tile distribution:

A - 9	B - 2	C - 2	D - 4	E - 12	F - 2
G - 3	H - 2	I - 9	J - 1	K - 1	L - 4
M - 2	N - 6	O - 8	P - 2	Q - 1	R - 6
S - 4	T - 6	U - 4	V - 2	W - 2	X - 1
Y - 2	Z - 1	Blank: 2			

Total: 100

Associations

Associations is an addictive word game that can be enjoyed by a mixed age (12 and up) group, plus a moderator. Perfect for a long car ride, this game requires some low-level mental gymnastics—just enough to distract you if the radio isn't working but not so much that you can't interrupt it with a game of Punch-Buggy (see page 308).

PLAYERS: 4–15, nonplaying moderator

THE GEAR: Paper, pencil.

The Game Plan

The game has two stages. **Stage 1** is a noncompetitive exercise in forming a chain of word associations. The moderator announces a starting word—any word. The first player calls out a word associated with that word; the second player calls out a word associated with the first person's word, and so on. The moderator jots down every word in order. Continue until the group has generated about fifty words. An example: *Love, tennis, court, supreme, Diana Ross,* and so on. The associations must be understood by all players, and punning is allowed.

In **Stage 2,** the players must try to recall all the words in reverse order. (You may choose to tell the players about this stage at the beginning of the game, or not.) So if the fifty-word chain ended with "Diana Ross," as in our mini-chain above, the moderator would say "Stop," give the words "Diana Ross," and ask the next player what preceded it. That player must say "supreme." If he can't, he receives a point, and the next player has a chance to remember the word. If no player in the group can remember the word, the moderator gives the answer and the game continues.

The player with the fewest points at the end of the game wins.

—contributed by Will Shortz, who is the crossword puzzle editor at The New York Times *and the puzzlemaster at NPR.*

PARTY RECIPE

Rosemary–White Bean Dip

Word games mean snacky foods, not full meals. Serve this dip, adapted from Mark Bittman's *Quick and Easy Recipes,* with some savory crackers. Provide napkins so your guests don't get crumbs on their papers, and they will have enough energy for a full evening of literary brainstorming.

MAKES 1 CUP

INGREDIENTS

1 can (15 ounces) white beans like cannellini, drained	3 tablespoons extra virgin olive oil
1 clove garlic, peeled and chopped	1 teaspoon fresh rosemary, minced
Pinch of salt, plus salt and pepper to taste	1 teaspoon lemon zest

1. In a food processor, puree the beans, 1 clove of garlic, a pinch of salt, and 2 tablespoons of olive oil.

2. Transfer the mixture to a bowl, and beat in the rosemary, lemon zest, and the remaining tablespoon of olive oil. Add salt and pepper to taste.

||||||||||||||||||||||||||||||||||||||||||||||||||||||||||||||||||||

Word Logic
aka Jotto

Jotto is unique among word games in that it draws on the players' vocabularies *and* it employs deductive-reasoning skills usually found in more math-oriented strategic games. It's a great game for people who don't think they're word people—people who balk at playing Scrabble but love Battleship, for example. I recently played with a friend who's an SAT math and LSAT tutor, and he *loved* it—because he had to use the same puzzle-solving skills that make him good at his job.

PLAYERS: 2

THE GEAR: Paper and pencils.

The Game Plan

Player 1 writes down (or thinks of) a five-letter word in which no letters are repeated, say, *alive.* This is Player 1's "secret word." Player 2 guesses, by saying aloud, a five-letter word, say, *horse.* (Both players should write down what words have been guessed.) Player 1 must report how many of the letters in the word *horse* are also in the word *alive,* in this case, one (*e*). Player 2 now knows that one of the five letters is either *h, o, r, s,* or *e.* He guesses *navel.* Player 1 answers four, because there are four letters in *navel* that are also in *alive* (*a, l, e,* and *v*). Play continues until Player 2 guesses Player 1's word. Then they switch. Whoever gets the other one's word in the fewest tries wins.

Special Notes

✖ If you guess a word that is an anagram of the opponent's secret word (say his secret word is *grown* and you guess *wrong*) he will answer "five"—but doesn't indicate that you have gotten his secret word—in which case you'd better get busy figuring out the anagram for *wrong.*

✖ In some games, you may choose to play that the secret word *can* have duplicate letters, like *sassy.* If your secret word has duplicates of a letter, like *lulls,* and your opponent guesses a word that has a single *l,* like, *trial,* you would answer "three" for the three *l*s that appear in your secret word.

Variation

Rather than taking turns, both players think of a secret word, and alternate guessing, thus playing the game simultaneously. The first person to guess the other's word wins. I *strongly* prefer this variation to the standard version, as both players are solving a puzzle at the same time.

▶ ▶ **IF YOU LIKE THIS GAME . . . try the board game Jotto.**

Epitaph

A noncompetitive collaborative storytelling game, Epitaph lets you eulogize your friends while they're still alive. (But in a funny way, not in a macabre way!) Because you're writing, well, an *epitaph,* it's best to play this game with people you know pretty well. Consider the activity to be like collectively writing a rhyming biography of your pal.

PLAYERS: 3–10 people who know each other fairly well.

The Game Plan

Have players sit in a circle. One player begins the epitaph of another player: "Here Lies Ken," for example. Proceeding clockwise, each player makes up another line to the epitaph. A recent game created this awful bit of doggerel:

> *Here lies Ken*
> *Ken had a yen*
> *for a high-powered lady named Pelosi.*
> *The Secret Service got nosy*
> *when Ken got so dozy*
> *In the bushes at Nancy's door.*

> *He couldn't explain*
> *So they had to arraign*
> *The judge said "To the pen!*
> *That's five to ten!"*
> *And he rotted away in San Quentin.*

Take turns until everyone's epitaph has been written. Remind your guests that the object is to amuse, not depress.

▶▶ **ETIQUETTE**
Don't hurt feelings—in fact, make it a goal that your epitaphs be as funny and as *kind* as possible. In our crowd, Ken's crush on Nancy Pelosi is well known and fair game for teasing.

Definitions

PLAYERS: 4–10

THE GEAR: A dictionary, index cards, sheet of paper, and a pencil.

Definitions is the opposite of Dictionary: you start with the definition rather than the word. Before your guests arrive, write down definitions of common words on index cards and toss them in a hat, like "an enthusiastic admirer, a fan," for *aficionado.* Number the cards and keep track, on a separate sheet of paper, what word matches each definition. (Try to have definitions for which there are relatively few answers, to reduce squabbling later—so "occurring daily" would work for *quotidian,* but "ordinary" would probably not work as it's a definition for too many words.) Have twenty definitions for groups of nine players or fewer, and forty definitions for groups of ten or more players. To start, have a player draw a card and read the definition. The person who first names the word gets a point and draws the next definition. When the hat's empty, the person with the most points wins.

▶▶ HOST TIP
If your regular word games are getting a little dull, try one of these three Scrabble variations:

Top/Bottom or Left/Right: The first move on the center line divides the board either horizontally or vertically. Each player picks a side and plays on that side for the rest of the game.

Frameless: Players may not make moves along the outside edge, including red squares.

Land Mines: Players may not make moves on any triple score squares (dark blue and red).

Contact

A word-guessing game for three or more players, Contact is a little like Botticelli (see page 42) in that the guessing goes both ways. The objective of the players, who are a team playing against the Wordmaster, is to guess the Wordmaster's word.

PLAYERS: 3–20

The Game Plan

✖ Select one person to be the "Wordmaster." The Wordmaster thinks of a word—an improper noun. Let's say it's *geranium*. The Wordmaster gives the first letter of the word: *g*.

✖ The other players think of words that begin with *g*.

✖ Any player may guess a *g* word. However, she doesn't say the actual word out loud—she provides a clue, hoping that the other players will understand the word she is thinking of and second it by saying, "Contact." So, Player 1 might say, "Is it an elderly person?" thinking of the word *geriatric*. Player 2, understanding that Player 1 is thinking of *geriatric,* will say "Contact."

✖ Once Player 2 has seconded Player 1's clue by saying "Contact," the Wordmaster attempts to identify Player 1's clue. If he thinks he knows it, the Wordmaster will say, "No, it is not _____." In our example, the Wordmaster would say, "No, it's not *geriatric*." The players then go on to propose another clue.

✖ If the Wordmaster *doesn't* understand what the two players are cluing (meaning he doesn't realize the word Player 1 and 2 are thinking of is *geriatric*), or if he just gets it wrong when he says "No, it is not _____," he says, "Challenge."

✖ The purpose of the challenge is to determine that Player 1 and Player 2 *are* in fact thinking of the same word: To prove this, the two of them must say their word simultaneously (they count to three together first—"One, two, three, *geriatric!*"). If they *do* say the same word, even though it's not the correct one, the Wordmaster must give the second letter of his word, *e*. If they *don't* say the same word (i.e., after they count to three, Player 1 says *geriatric* and Player 2 says *geezer*), the Wordmaster does *not* give the second letter. The players continue to propose clues.

Winning

If the Wordmaster's word (*geranium,* in our example) is ever said by any two players during a challenge, the players win and the game is over. Another person, chosen at random, becomes the next wordmaster. If the players propose twenty clues without figuring out the Wordmaster's word, the Wordmaster wins.

Variation

The clues the players give while guessing may be verbal, visual, or aural. In our example above, once the Wordmaster says the first letter is *g,* Player 1 may make a grunting noise— signifying that he is thinking of the word *grunt.* If another player realizes he is signaling the word *grunt,* she says "Contact." If the clue is visual, perhaps Player 1 will exaggeratedly wipe her brow, signifying *gesture.*

Rewordable 😎

NEW GAME!

A **word-building game** with a nasty element of sabotage, Rewordable is the perfect kitchen-table after-dinner activity. (You'll need a bit of space to spread out as the playing area expands.) The cards on pages 362–370—called your *lexicon*—are letters and combinations of letters that you'll use to build words on the table in front of you. Your opponents will also be building words while trying to steal *your* fully-formed words and unused letters. The game is a perfect blend of offensive strategy and Cover Your Ass: Players try to protect their own lexicons by making longer and longer words while simultaneously laying the groundwork to incorporate other players' lexicons into their own. The joy of blowing your opponents' carefully laid plans to smithereens makes Rewordable unique among word games. If you like anagrams—and if you like contests in which you systematically hamper your friends' progress—Rewordable was made for you.

PLAYERS: 3–6

THE GEAR: The deck of cards on pages 362–370. Photocopy and cut these out.

The Game Plan

Shuffle the entire deck. Then count out the number of cards you need for the number of players you have, shown in the table below.

Players	Cards
3	60
4	72
5	80
6	84

Set the other cards aside; you won't need them for this game. From the deck that you just created, deal five cards to each player. Players should hold these five cards in their hands so that other players can't see them. Set the remaining cards from the deck in the center of the playing area as stock.

The player to the left of the dealer begins, and play proceeds clockwise. Each turn has two or three parts:

✴ You must set one card from your hand face up on the table in front of you. These face-up cards, which will gradually grow in number over the course of the game, are your "lexicon."

✕ After you set one card in front of you, you may *also,* if you wish, steal a card or cards from other players' lexicons to form a word (see "Stealing Cards," below).

✕ Draw one card from the stock to replenish your hand. Players should always have five cards in their hands.

Stealing Cards: When you steal a card or cards from rival players' lexicons, you must immediately use them to form a word with one or more cards from your own lexicon.

✕ You may steal an unused fragment or a full word, but the resulting cards in your lexicon must form a full, actual word. You may not steal a portion of a word.

✕ You may insert cards between cards you are stealing, but may not rearrange the order of cards in a stolen word. (For example, you may steal S|OW and insert an N to make it S|N|OW, but you may not make OW|N|S.)

✕ You may, however, rearrange words in your *own* lexicon: for example, if you have CH|IT, you can add a Y and make IT|CH|Y.

✕ You may steal from one or more players in a turn. So if Sally has an unused B and Fred has an unused OW and you have an R in your lexicon, you may take Sally's B and Fred's OW and make B|R|OW. (If Sally has an N, however, she can steal it back on her next turn and make B|R|OW|N. If Fred had an ED he could steal it back on *his* next turn and make B|R|OW|N|ED.)

> **▶▶STEALTH STRATEGY ◀**
>
> Try not to let single cards hang out on the table too long. Multi-card words, and in particular *long* multi-card words—are harder to steal than lone cards.

✕ While you may not steal a portion of a word or rearrange the order of a stolen word, it *is* permissable to split up a word in your or other players' lexicons to make new words. For example, if you have C|AR|E you may steal a TH and make C|AR TH|E.

Winning

When the stock is empty, players play out their remaining five cards in the next five turns without replenishing. When the hands are empty, players should set aside any unused fragments from their lexicons, leaving only cards that make up words (though players may keep single cards which are themselves words, such as BE). Each player counts the number of *letters* they have on word cards, and the player with the most letters wins.

—contributed by Michael Dory and Adam Simon, see page 187.

Chapter Seven

RIGHT-BRAIN GAMES

Let's face it: Game fanatics are frequently word people. They carry around crosswords, they nag you into a quick game of Boggle, they make dreadful, dreadful puns. Of course, there are many games that don't require any verbal facility—a bazillion card games leap to mind—but for some reason it's always the word people that are dragging out the board games or the Scrabble set.

I know these people, because I am one of them. But cue up the karaoke machine and I'm sunk.

Enter the games for the right-brained people: the artists, the actors, the dancers, the improvisers. My husband, an architect, particularly dislikes games in which people ask you questions about history or trivia that you know you *should* know—like who ran against Dewey and Truman in the 1948 election or who wrote *The Master and Margarita*? It's always *just* on the tip of his tongue. . . . But he *loves* drawing games because he can crush an opponent in a matter of seconds. In fact, in a recent game of Pictionary, he had to get his teammates to guess the word "giants." Rather than drawing a little stick figure and then a big stick figure—like any normal person playing Pictionary—he quickly sketched a map of the United States, drew an arrow pointing to San Francisco, and then drew a baseball. "Giants!" screamed his teammate. Show-off.

Another friend really digs the games that are essentially improvisation and performance—he always excels at getting the *bon mot* out with perfect comic timing. Just a Minute! is his favorite way to spend an evening with like-minded friends—and playing with them is like attending a free comedy show right in your living room. He

also recently hosted an Old-Fashioned Dance Party (see page 119) and while some guests who were "real" dancers won, even the amateurs were inspired to try to rhumba to Britney Spears.

For the artists and art historians in your crowd, check out Art Charades on page 117—you'll be able to put your encyclopedic knowledge of art history to good use—or, if you're in school, you and your friends can use the game as a study aid. The key to a successful games party, as always, is to gear the games to your guests' skills and interests. The last thing you want is for anyone to feel dumb or left out.

That said, the good news about these and, in fact, all of the games in this book—is that you don't have to be *good* at anything to have a good time. Games aren't job interviews or raising a baby, or any of the thousand serious things that make up everyday life. You don't really need to be able to draw to have fun playing drawing games, or have perfect pitch to sing karaoke. In fact, as long as you're willing to try, it's more fun if you can't!

Pictionary

Remember *When Harry Met Sally ...?* Remember Baby Fish Mouth? Of course, Pictionary is now a commercially available game and can be purchased just about everywhere. But the game has been around for decades—if not centuries—under various names, and there's certainly no need to shell out $30 for a commercial set when you can easily play with just paper and pencil.

PLAYERS: 4–30

THE GEAR: 2 sketch pads or large pieces of paper, slips of paper, pencils, a timer, and an easel or two (optional).

The Game Plan

There are as many Pictionary variations as there are Charades variations (see page 40), so after you've played the game once or twice you can always branch out. But here are the basics:

* Divide the group into two teams. Give everyone ten minutes to come up with a bunch of movie titles, book titles, aphorisms, places, famous people, etc., write them on slips of paper, and put them in a hat. (See "Play Fair" on page 52 for guidelines.)

* Set up one or both easels, if you have them, or just lay the paper on a table so that all members of the team can see. Flip a coin to decide which team goes first.

* Select a player from that team. That player grabs a clue from the hat and begins

to draw a representation of it while his teammates try to guess. The player may draw pictures but no words. He may draw horizontal blanks at the bottom of the page to indicate how many words are in the clue (So for *Reservoir Dogs,* he might draw one long blank and one short one.) Just as in Charades, the player has one minute to get his team to guess what he's drawing. (He may only draw—he can't nod, or point to things, or use any words.) If they get it before the minute is up, he grabs another clue and draws that one.

* After a minute is up, the team scores a point for every clue they've gotten. Any clue the team hasn't guessed goes back in the hat (one team member will have seen the clue, of course, but as this will happen with both teams, the "advantage" doesn't really go to one team or another).

> **AMP IT UP**
> Teams may play simultaneously, working from the same clue (a player of one team draws a clue, reads it, and then shows it to a player of the other team). The two players then try, at the same time, to get their teams to shout out the clue, and the first team to do so gets the point. (Teams may not peek at the other team's drawing.)

Whisper Pictionary

Rather than having guests generate clues, a nonplaying host can prepare them. Whisper the same clue into two players' ears, thereby eliminating the first ten minutes of the game (the clue-generating phase).

Blindfolded Pictionary

Make the clues relatively simple (belly button, Santa Claus) and blindfold the player after she's had a chance to read the clue. Even the best artists have a hard time drawing when they can't see.

Race Pictionary

Played like Race Charades on page 40.

Family Pictionary

To adjust Pictionary for family events, have all the clues pertain to a certain theme—your last vacation, for example.

Clues might include:

- ✕ crab
- ✕ hotel
- ✕ palm tree
- ✕ sand
- ✕ seaweed
- ✕ seashell
- ✕ wave

Police Lineup

I found this one in Penny Warner's great book *Games People Play*. Police Lineup is a game for those of us who feel guilty *all the time*—who wonder if the store clerk is watching us because we look suspicious, who keep our hands ostentatiously out of our pockets, who flushed when the *other* kids in grammar school got caught in a lie.

A cross between Mafia (see page 132) and improv comedy, Police Lineup lets you play-act and role-play, but with the sole purpose of proclaiming your innocence or concealing your guilt. The game will use all your bluffing and subterfuge skills—as well as call on your improv chops. Basically, you get to find out,

once and for all, whether you still have the sweet, innocent face your grandmother loved to pinch.

PLAYERS: 6–20, plus a moderator.

THE GEAR: Pens and slips of paper or index cards.

Preparation

Ahead of time, you, as the moderator, will write down a bunch of "crimes" ("You stole candy from a baby!" "You said it was homemade but it was really store-bought!" "You voted for Nader!") on index cards. Have one index card (and thus one crime) per player. (See sidebar, right, for more ideas.)

The Game Plan

- ✕ When guests arrive, have each player draw a card, read it to himself, and write his name on the card. (That is *his* crime.) Collect the cards and drop them in a hat.

- ✕ The moderator draws a card, discreetly checks the name on the card, and asks three players (including the "criminal") to come to the front of the room for a "lineup."

- ✕ Read the "crime" out loud. All the other players in the game must now ask the line-up a question. For example, if the defendant stands accused of "Reprogramming my Roomba so that instead of cleaning my apartment, it lectures me about doing something with my life," a question to the lineup might be "How are your computer skills?" or "Do you ever feel compelled to butt into others' business?" Each player must pose at least one question to the line-up but no more than three. Remember, two of the three interrogees are innocent.

A Few Ideas to Get You Started

- You wore white after Labor Day.

- You returned the gift I gave you for cash.

- You removed the "Do Not Remove!" tag from the mattress.

- You double-dipped.

- You put recyclables in with the regular trash.

- You got your peanut butter in my chocolate.

- You reprogrammed my Roomba so that instead of cleaning my apartment, it lectures me about doing something with my life.

- You called amontillado a digestif instead of an apéritif.

- You drank milk straight from the carton.

- You didn't put a new roll of toilet paper on the holder when it was *right there*.

- You wore white socks with black shoes.

- You bogarted the joint.

- You farted in the elevator.

- You are guilty of possession of Crocs (with intent to wear with socks).

- You whistled unnecessarily in your cubicle.

- You claimed *Voyager* was the best *Star Trek* series.

- You served Sauvignon Blanc with filet mignon.

- You used "inferred" when you meant "implied."

- You ordered a Reuben at the kosher deli.

- You shouted "Freebird!" at the symphony.

- You made a Manhattan with bourbon instead of rye.

- You wore a bowtie while under the age of sixty (and not with a tuxedo).

- You made lasagna with cottage cheese in place of ricotta.

- You used Comic Sans in a work e-mail.

- You let the peas touch the carrots.

- You did not put your ducks in a row.

- You started a sentence with "and."

- You ended a sentence with a preposition.

- You made cookies with carob chips.

- You rolled your eyes at your mother.

- You typed "LOL" without actually laughing out loud.

- You did not poke back.

- You re-tweeted without proper credit.

- You're not sure if Bill Paxton and Bill Pullman are different people.

- You tricked Roger Moore into autographing a picture of Sean Connery.

- You are guilty of excessive use of the phrases "going forward" or "skill-set" or "touch base" or "reach out."

✄ Each member of the lineup has to answer the question. As they do, the other players must try to assess who is the guilty party—and remember that the two innocent members of the lineup are *trying* to look guilty: If you aren't guilty of the crime, and someone guesses you *are* guilty, you gain a point.

✄ The players write down their guesses, which are collected by the moderator.

- The guilty party confesses.

- Game play continues until all the "crimes" are solved.

Winning

Everyone who guessed right gets a point. The two nonguilty members of the lineup get a point if someone thought they were guilty. The guilty party gets a point if no one guessed him. The person with the most points, after all the "crimes" are solved, wins. The winner gets a pair of toy handcuffs.

▸▸ **HOST TIP**

When calling the three players up, don't always have the "perp" be first, middle, or last; mix it up a bit so the players can't anticipate what you're going to do.

▸▸ **IF YOU LIKE THIS GAME . . . check out Mafia on page 132.**

‖‖

Pictionary Down the Lane
aka Eat Poop You Cat

Across between Telephone and Pictionary, Pictionary Down the Lane elicits laughs when each player reads the "story" of how her original phrase—"Don't get your knickers in a twist!"—became "Don't pee into a tornado!" In the Victorian era, this parlor game was called "Illustrated Quotations."

PLAYERS: 5–10

THE GEAR: A fair amount of scrap paper, pencils, timer.

The Game Plan

- Players sit in a circle. Give everyone as many sheets of paper as there are players. So if you have ten players, each person gets ten sheets of paper.

- Each player jots down a well-known phrase, aphorism, or idiom on the top sheet of paper. At the same time, each player passes her whole stack of paper to the player on her right. Players read to themselves the phrase written on the sheet, move the top sheet to the bottom of the pile, and attempt to draw a representation of the phrase on the new sheet.

- So for "What goes around comes around," a player might draw a person sending something on a merry-go-round in one direction, with arrows indicating that it's going to return to its starting point.

- After everyone has had a minute or two to draw, they pass the stack to the person on the right. That person examines a probably badly drawn, possibly indecipherable sketch (and does *not* look at the original phrase or aphorism on the page at the bottom of the stack). He then moves the drawing to the bottom of the stack and writes, on the new top sheet of paper, a phrase that represents the drawing he just examined. The players can attempt to make these conform to known idioms, or the new phrases can bear no resemblance to any real aphorisms or sayings. (Hence the alternative name of the game—which I can only surmise came from someone trying to draw "There's more than one way to skin a cat.")

- Continue this pattern until the stack comes full circle. Then each original owner has a little story time in which to recount the various steps that made "Don't get your knickers in a twist" mutate into "Don't pee into a tornado!"

Don't panic if you can't draw—it's funnier if you can't. And even with the best artists, the message will get very garbled.

Art Charades

Art Charades is an excellent game for people who are well-versed in art— but also fun for anyone who likes to act or just be silly. Each player or group of players creates a tableau of a famous statue or painting; the rest of his team must guess the work of art they're depicting. You can adjust its difficulty level depending on who is playing (Munch's *The Scream* would be pretty easy; Renoir's *Girl With a Hoop* might be harder). A large group could tackle da Vinci's *The Last Supper* and an intimate group might arrange themselves like the sculpture *Laocoön*, which would take a while to set up convincingly (but that's half the fun!).

PLAYERS: 4–30 in two teams, plus a nonplaying moderator.

THE GEAR: Art history books or computer with an Internet connection, paper, pencils, 2 hats, timer.

The Game Plan

✖ Divide your players into two teams; give the teams a few minutes to peruse some art books or web sites. Each group will select about five famous statues, sculptures, or paintings and write down the names on slips of paper (see the pictures on page 118 for a few ideas). The group should show their chosen images to the moderator, who should ensure that the teams haven't picked anything too obscure or hard to act out. Put the slips of paper into two hats.

✖ At random, choose a team to go first. One of its members will draw a slip of paper from the other team's hat. If she's unfamiliar with that piece of art, she should alert the moderator, who will help her find the actual image so she knows what she will be acting out.

✖ Once she's seen the image, the moderator starts a two-minute timer. The player will then "strike the pose"; for example, placing her hands beside her face and opening wide to indicate *The Scream*. If it's a pose that requires two or more people, like Michelangelo's *Creation of Adam* on the ceiling of the Sistine Chapel, the player may tap another member of her team to strike the pose with her. The original player cannot tell the new actor what the target answer is. She can only pose him or otherwise indicate what she wishes him to do. The remaining members of the team must shout out their best guesses as to what work is being depicted.

✖ Once the team guesses correctly, the moderator records the time it took for the team to give the answer. If they don't get it in the two minutes, the moderator records the maximum score of two minutes and the clue is discarded. The other team then takes a turn, and so on until the hats are empty.

Winning

When the hats are empty, the team with the lowest recorded time wins.

Variation

Instead of famous paintings and sculpture, act out famous record covers. (*Sgt. Pepper's,* anyone?)

A Few Ideas to Get You Started . . .

Mona Lisa,
Leonardo da Vinci

Self-Portrait with Bandaged Ear,
Vincent van Gogh

Rape of the Sabine Women,
Giambologna

Luncheon on the Grass,
Édouard Manet

Literary Rebus

Literary Rebus combines two great disciplines: drawing and reading. But don't panic: It doesn't have to be great literature—*The Da Vinci Code* is fine. And even if you can't draw, the art show at the end is still a good time, especially for kids. For added authenticity, serve wine, grape juice, and cheese and treat it like a gallery opening. Just like Art Charades, the level of difficulty depends only on your guest list. *To Kill a Mockingbird* would be an easier one (a bird with "X's" for eyes, say) while *Great Expectations* might stump even the yawning Yale literature major in your living room.

PLAYERS: 4–30, plus nonplaying host

THE GEAR: Paper, pencils.

The Game Plan

Give everyone a pencil and a piece of paper and ask them to draw a representation of a well-known book. Guests may choose any book they like, and the drawing can, but doesn't have to be, an interpretation of what the cover might look like—four girls to indicate *Little Women,* a person with a finger pressed to her lips for *The Secret*. Drawings can also be a representation of the theme of the book or a major plot point, like a harpoon for *Moby Dick* or an empty bowl and spoon for *Oliver Twist*. Guests should write the title of the book on the back of the drawings and hand them to the host, who will number the pictures and hang them on the wall. Guests then circulate with a pencil and a piece of paper, noting down the number and their guessed title of each book.

After a period of time, say, a half hour, the hostess reveals the name of the book each drawing is meant to represent.

Winning

The person with the most correct guesses wins a gift card to the local bookstore.

Old-Fashioned Dance Party

For your pals who love to cut a rug (or who just love *Dancing with the Stars*) host a dance party—but not the typical "dance till you drop" kind of contest. Instead, introduce your friends to the social dances of days gone by—the cha-cha, the rhumba, the fox trot—anything that your grandmother might have learned before her debutante ball. Enlist the help of a dancer friend (or hire an instructor for the evening) to give short lessons in each kind of dance. Once everyone's got the hang of the jitterbug and the waltz and whatever else you want to learn, get your playlist going and let the guests cut a rug on their own. Give everyone a half hour or an hour to mingle and dance with everyone else. Then each guest should find a partner and then spend a half-hour

---

AMP IT UP

For the real dance experts, you can put on some very inappropriate music—think 1980s pop—and instruct your guests to try out their ballroom skills. Guests will have to cha-cha to "Thriller" or "Like a Virgin," and the results should keep everyone in stitches.

(or longer if the host feels it's necessary) to dance with their partners and choreograph a short routine. Once the time's up, couples can "perform" for the rest of the crowd and each audience member awards points from 1 to 10 based on rhythm, style, and flair. Guests are "on their honor" to award points fairly, even if it means they themselves are less likely to win. If you can't trust your guests to do this, invite a few nondancers to act as a panel of impartial judges.

PLAYERS: 6–30

THE GEAR: A playlist for social dancing; a dance floor.

Winning

The couple with the highest number of points wins a lesson for two at the local ballroom-dance studio.

Profiles

Tape a large sheet of kraft paper on the wall (found at any craft or art store). As each guest arrives, stand him sideways close to the wall and position a lamp on the other side of him, so that his profile casts a shadow on the paper. Trace the shadow with a pencil, tear off the portrait, write the name of the person on the back, and set it aside until everyone has had their portrait done.

After everyone has arrived and had their profile traced, tack all the portraits to the wall and number them. Each guest must jot down on a slip of paper which guest goes with which portrait. This is surprisingly difficult, and therefore a lot of fun (somehow silhouettes all look the same!) Best of all, once the game is over, your guests can fill in funny cartoon features on each other's portraits.

PLAYERS: 5–50

THE GEAR: Large sheet of kraft paper, a lamp, pencils.

Winning

The guest with the most correct answers wins a set of drawing pencils.

Variation

Tape two seven-foot lengths of kraft paper together width-wise, to create a paper surface big enough for a person to lie on. Make as many of these as you have players. Have guests lie down on the paper and trace the bodies, just like the police do at a crime scene. Try to identify whose outline is whose. (This variation is best for a roomful of no-body-issues–type guests.)

Karaoke

Karaoke, Japanese for "empty orchestra," started in Japan decades ago and has since taken the United States by storm. And while we've come to think of karaoke as a drunken bachelorette-party activity, some people take it quite seriously and consider it an opportunity to perform and show off their vocal chops.

At a karaoke club or with an at-home machine, players sing with musical backing tracks that have had the lead vocals removed. A video screen projects the lyrics to the songs, highlighting which words are to be sung as the song progresses. Your choices for where to sing karaoke are pretty broad: You can find local clubs (Google the name of your city and "karaoke"), sing along with your Wii or PlayStation, or on a stand-alone karaoke machine, available at toy stores or from Amazon. If you have cable TV, check out the On Demand karaoke channel. To play online, check out thisiskaraoke.com or singsnap.com.

PLAYERS: 2–50

THE GEAR: A karaoke machine (see above).

AMP IT UP

If just singing some regular old karaoke is too easy, try a song in a language other than English.

Or, if you'd prefer to let the machine itself be the judge, some karaoke video games, like Karaoke Revolution or SingStar, will award points to the singer for pitch and rhythm. If you like your judgment more personal and you're out at a club, you can appoint a panel of friends (or strangers) to be judges. Award points for things like "gutsiest," "most surprising," or "best-chosen song for performer."

But even without winners and losers, karaoke by itself—listening to your friends sing along with Tom Petty or the Ink Spots—is enough of a good time. A drink or two might help you get up the nerve to belt out a killer rendition of "Eye of the Tiger," but singing is uninhibiting, so once you get going, you don't need alcohol. (And in fact, booze does terrible things to pitch and rhythm!)

If merely singing the songs with your friends isn't enough of a "game" for you, you can stage a karaoke contest: The host selects a list of songs and rates them for difficulty. Players win more points for more complicated songs—or for songs in which the risk of making a fool of yourself is high—and fewer points for "easier" songs.

||||||||||||||||||||||||||||||||||||||||||||||||||||||||||||||||||||

Sight Unseen

Sight Unseen is a drawing game played by couples. And if you can't draw, you're in luck—one-half of the couple doesn't have to. But if you're not the artist, you'll be the person describing the object that your partner is drawing, so your communication skills have to be top-notch. Think of it as a navigator and a driver; they have to communicate and stay friendly or else they end up quarreling on the outskirts of Weehawken.

PLAYERS: 8–12 (must be an even number).

THE GEAR: Two chairs, paper and pencils, a stopwatch, and a bunch of ordinary objects.

The Game Plan

✄ Randomly divide your guests into teams of two and choose one couple to go first. The couple should confer for a moment and decide who will be the artist and who will be describing the object. Seat them back to back in two chairs; they are not allowed to look at each other. Start a stopwatch for two minutes. Give one teammate a regular, everyday object, like a dish brush, a banana, a tire jack, etc. (Don't let his partner see what it is.) The teammate must describe the object to his partner in terms of size, shape, texture, etc. He can't say, "It's a tire jack," or, "This is a thing with which to change tires." The partner draws what is described. It doesn't matter if the artist doesn't ever get what the object actually is; the drawings will be judged on their merit, regardless of whether the artist knew what he was drawing or not, and the results will be even funnier if he doesn't.

✄ When two minutes have passed, the couple writes their names on the drawing. Another couple takes a turn with a new object.

Winning

After everyone's done, each player votes for what he thinks is the "best" drawing—this is totally subjective and doesn't have to be the drawing that most closely represents the original object. The winning team gets a prize of any ordinary object that the host has found extremely useful, like a lemon zester or silicone oven mitts.

Variation

Play in teams of three and keep one person apart from the other two during the describing and drawing phase of the game. Once the drawing is finished, the host invites the third person back into the room. As soon as this third person claps eyes on the drawing, the host starts a stopwatch. The player must guess the object in the drawing; as soon as he correctly guesses, the host notes down the time. The team with the lowest time wins.

Situation Puzzles
aka Murder Mystery Puzzles

Also known as lateral-thinking puzzles or murder mystery puzzles, this game is part riddle and part storytelling. It's great for long train trips—something about the clack of the rails and the passing landscape lends itself to tall tales, puzzles, and lengthy, contemplative silences. The puzzles you'll find online and in books will usually present a murder scene, a couple of details, and a "Why?" at the end.

PLAYERS: 2–50

The Game Plan

✖ One player, whoever wants to go first, decides to be "It." He thinks of a scenario—usually, but not always, one that involves an untimely death—that seems implausible or unlikely or baffling, and informs his audience of this scenario. The player may make up the scenario, if he's creatively inclined, or can use one of the puzzles below. (Googling "lateral thinking puzzles" or "situation puzzles" will also produce a wealth of ideas, and not all of them will be death-oriented.) Beginning with the player to the left of It, the audience then asks yes-or-no questions, one at a time, until they can determine the circumstances that led to the situation.

Here's an example of a well-known situation puzzle:

- A man walks into a bar, and asks the bartender for a drink of water. The bartender pulls out a gun, points it at the man, and cocks it. The man says "Thank you" and leaves. Why?

- The question and answer segment might go something like this:

  Q: Did the bartender hear him accurately?

  A: Yes.

  Q: Was the bartender angry or scared for some reason?

  A: No.

  Q: Did they know each other already?

  A: No, or irrelevant.

  Q: Was the man's "Thank you" sarcastic?

  A: No, or no, he was genuinely grateful for some reason.

  Q: Did the man ask for water in an aggressive way?

  A: No.

  Q: Did the man ask for water in a strange way?

  A: Yes.

Eventually the questions lead to the conclusion: The man had the hiccups and asked for water. The bartender heard the hiccups, guessed the man's need, and chose instead to cure the hiccups by frightening the man with the gun. Once the man got over his fear, he realized his hiccups were gone, was grateful, and didn't need the water anymore.

Below is a sampling of some well-known puzzles to get you started:

Puzzle: A man goes into a restaurant and orders a bowl of albatross soup. He takes one bite, bursts into tears, runs out the door, and throws himself in front of oncoming traffic. Why?

Answer: The man and his wife were two of several castaways after a shipwreck some years earlier. Desperate for food, the ship's cook murdered the man's wife and served her to him and the other castaways, telling them it was albatross soup. When the man ordered the albatross soup in the restaurant, he knew that what he had eaten while shipwrecked *wasn't* albatross soup, and he was able to surmise what had happened to his wife. Overcome with grief, he throws himself in front of oncoming traffic. Tragic! By the way, there's a great little albatross soup place on 43rd Street. . . .

Puzzle: A man is returning from Switzerland by train. If he had been riding in a non-smoking car he would have died. Why?
Answer: The man used to be blind; he's returning from an eye operation in Zurich that restored his sight. The successful surgery has given him a new lease on life, and he imagines all the thrilling possibilities a sighted life will offer. So when the train (which has no internal lighting) goes through a tunnel, he thinks he's gone blind again, and plunges into despair. He nearly decides to kill himself; fortunately, the light of his fellow passengers' cigarettes convinces him that he can still see.

Puzzle: Tim and Greg are having a cup of joe in a café and decide to play a word-association game. Tim says "The land of the free," Greg responds with, "The home of the brave." Tim says, "The terror of flight." Greg says, "The gloom of the grave." Moments later, the coffee shop is raided and Greg is arrested. Why?
Answer: Greg is a spy. His "friend" Tim is suspicious, so he proposes the game. When Tim says, "The terror of flight," and Greg says, "The gloom of the grave," Tim knows Greg is a spy. Any U.S. citizen would recognize lines from the first verse of the national anthem,

but only a spy would have memorized the third verse. (This particular puzzle is from a short story by Isaac Asimov.)

Puzzle: A man lives on the twelfth floor of an apartment building. Every morning he takes the elevator to the lobby and leaves the building. In the evening, he gets into the elevator, and, if there is someone else in the elevator—or if it was raining that day—he goes back to his floor directly. Otherwise, he goes to the tenth floor and walks up two flights of stairs to his apartment. Why?
Answer: The man is a dwarf. He can't reach the upper elevator buttons, so he usually asks people to push them for him, or he can push the buttons with his umbrella.

Puzzle: A man was just doing his job when his suit ripped in several places. Why did he die three minutes later?
Answer: He was an astronaut on a space walk, doing repairs.

Puzzle: Two men are served the same drink at a bar. One lives, but the other dies. Why?
Answer: There are poisoned ice cubes in the drinks. One man drinks his drink slowly, giving the cubes time to melt, but the other man drinks fast and doesn't ingest much of the poison.

Puzzle: A woman proves in court that her husband was murdered by her sister. The judge declares, "This is the strangest case I've ever seen. Though I'm sure who's guilty, this woman cannot be punished."
Answer: The woman and her sister are Siamese twins.

Puzzle: A man is found dead in a field. Next to him lies an unopened package. There is no other creature or thing in the field. How did he die?

Answer: The man had jumped from a plane, but his parachute didn't open. The parachute is the unopened package.

Winning

The player who correctly guesses the situation technically wins. However, situation puzzles are best played noncompetitively, during long train trips.

What's the Scoop?

Pictionary for news junkies, What's the Scoop? is best for guests really up on their current events. Divide the guests into two teams. As in Charades, give the teams ten minutes to come up with current events and to jot them on slips of paper. The current events should be from local, national, or international sources (teams may use newspapers or the Internet to come up with clues, but make sure to follow the guidelines of "Play Fair" on page 37). Alternatively, the host may come up with all the current events ahead of time and write or print them out on slips of paper. Make sure to have a good mix of easy and more difficult news items in the hat. For example, depicting the fire department saving a kitten from a tree might be pretty straightforward. Depicting a banker giving testimony about sub-prime lending to Congress might be more daunting.

PLAYERS: 6–20, plus a timer.

THE GEAR: Paper, pencils, a stopwatch, a hat.

The Game Plan

✖ Put all the slips of paper in a hat. Flip a coin to decide which team goes first. The team will choose a clue-giver, who, when the timer says go, will have one minute to draw the current event he has pulled out of the hat. (He *must* draw that event; there is no passing.) His team will try to guess the event he is drawing. If they do guess correctly, the team wins a point and the clue-giver grabs another slip of paper from the hat and draws that one, and so on until the minute is up.

✖ A clue that is not guessed after a minute is thrown back into the hat, and the other team takes its turn. (Returning a clue to the hat that someone has seen means that his team may have an easier time guessing the next time around, but since this will happen to both teams, neither will have an advantage.) After each person has had a chance to be a clue-giver, the points are tallied and the highest number wins.

NOTE: You don't need to limit the events to current ones—you can use historical events as well—from "Beatles Play Ed Sullivan" to "John Brown Hanged in Charles Town, Virginia."

Variation

Noncompetitive version: The host cuts out or prints out a bunch of headlines or short news stories and starts the game by giving one to each team. The teams then have ten minutes to draw their events. All of the members should participate, so if the headline is "Baby Jessica Rescued from Well," one team member might draw a baby, another team member (on another piece of paper) might draw a firefighter, and the third team member might draw a well.

After ten minutes have passed, the teams present their drawings to each other and must guess the headlines.

▶▶ **IF YOU LIKE THIS GAME . . . check out Current Events Trivia on page 226.**

Who-Where-What

PLAYERS: 5–20

THE GEAR: A stack of index cards (cut in half, if you wish, to save paper), drawing paper, pencils.

Everyone makes up one "Who" card (a person—Susan B. Anthony, Elvis, your mom), one "Where" card (a place—the DMV, Florida, Bill Clinton's bedroom), and a "What" card (action verb—knitting, stealing, running for president). If you're playing with a close-knit group of friends, create cards with relevance to your crowd—like your professors or coworkers. Put the cards in three piles or hats, a "Who" pile, a "Where" pile, and a "What" pile.

Distribute drawing paper and pencils. Each player picks a "Who," a "Where," and a "What" card. Players then get ten minutes to draw a scenario based on their cards. For example, I once drew Ali G negotiating a trade agreement in a Stuckey's restaurant.

After the ten minutes are up, players pass around pictures. Each player must now guess the "Who-Where-What" of their opponents' pictures. If someone guesses correctly, both he and the drawer get a point. This game appeals to the absurdist in us all, and the payoff is an accumulation of surreal sketches

depicting General Custer moonwalking across the Brooklyn Bridge, Plato waiting for the A train, R. Kelly sleeping on Venus (or did he actually do that?).

Exquisite Corpse

Invented by the surrealists in the early part of the twentieth century, Exquisite Corpse was a game that explored the (collective) unconscious. It's similar to the Victorian game Consequences, in which a story is constructed bit by bit, but the players don't know what plot points their fellow storytellers have already contributed. The Victorians, of course, were big gamers, when they weren't gathering around the old harpsichord for a sing-a-long or sniffing the heliotrope and composing poetry on the veranda. Had they had television, a kind of digital Exquisite Corpse on steroids, they would have all been couch potatoes.

PLAYERS: 2–12

THE GEAR: A large pad of drawing paper and pencils.

The Game Plan

Give each player a large sheet of paper and instruct them to each draw the head of something—a mammal, a bird, an alien—at the top of the page. They should then fold down the paper so that just the bottom bit of the drawing is visible and pass the paper to their left. The next player, not being able to see the head of the creature, is told to draw the torso of some other creature, and again fold the paper so that only the bottom bit is showing. Again, the papers are passed to the left. The third player will draw the legs and feet of the creature.

Pictures are then revealed and tacked to the wall; guests should pour themselves a cocktail and discuss the merits of each piece of artwork (the drawings usually look better with each successive cocktail). If your guests are up for another round, play again, mixing up the order of the artists so that the same people aren't drawing the same parts as the previous round. Finally, collect all the drawings and collectively apply for a graduate program in surrealism.

Samples of Exquisite Corpse

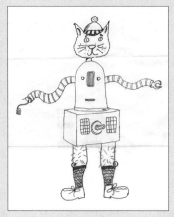

Just a Minute!

This improv game, in which contestants try to speak for one minute on a given topic, is based on the English radio show of the same name. The main object is to display wit, originality, and cogency—and, of course, to amuse your audience. It's great for those of us who missed our callings as stand-up comics—players really have to think on their feet. It's hilarious to see your friends pontificate under pressure and try to disguise that they don't know what's going to come out of their mouths next. Players will inevitably head down verbal rabbit holes and be unable to extricate themselves: Think of Michael Scott on *The Office*. His sentences are always out of his mouth before he even realizes what he's trying to say. To listen to a few clips of the game, search for "Just a Minute" and "BBC" or "Radio 4" on YouTube.

PLAYERS: 4–50 (two improvisers, a moderator, a timer for each round; the rest act as an audience and then take their turns as improvisers).

THE GEAR: Stopwatch, pencil, paper.

The Game Plan

✗ At random, choose two players to go first. Also appoint a moderator and a timer, who will operate the stopwatch, note the time left in the game for each player, and keep track of how long each player speaks.

✗ The moderator decides on a topic, such as "recent NFL draft picks." The timer says

"Go." The first player has to immediately make a one-minute speech about that topic; the goal is to speak for that minute without pausing, hesitating, or repeating anything significant.

✘ The other player may stop him if he hesitates, digresses, or repeats words (other than simple words like *the* and *and*). If the other player spots a mistake in his speech and calls it out, the timer will note down how long the first player spoke—let's say it was twenty seconds—and informs the second player she now has forty seconds in which to make a speech on the same topic.

✘ The timer keeps track of the time and the number of seconds each player has earned.

✘ Let's say the topic is gerrymandering:

- **Player 1:** "Gerrymandering is a real issue. It's a significant problem—congressmen are, um . . ."
- **Player 2:** "OUT! Hesitation!"
- The moderator confirms, with a nod, that that was a hesitation. The timer (quickly) writes down that Player 1 spoke for ten seconds and announces "fifty seconds left."
- Player 2 takes over and attempts to talk for fifty seconds.
- **Player 2:** "I say there's no problem with gerrymandering. People like to be grouped with other like-minded people!"
- **Player 1:** "OUT! Repetition of the word 'people'!"
- **Timer:** "Forty-three seconds left."
- Player 1 now takes over.
- **Player 1:** "Who's to say that gerrymandering isn't actually a good thing? Our country was founded on

principles of equality and fairness, and the founding fathers . . ."
- **Player 2:** "OUT! Digression: He's speaking about the founding fathers instead of gerrymandering!"
- **Timer:** "Thirty-two seconds left." And so on.

Winning

At the end of a minute, the player with the most seconds wins the round.

▶▶ **HOST TIP**

Instruct the timer to note down the seconds earned and restart the clock as fast as he possibly can to prevent contestants from having too much time to plan what they're going to say next.

‖‖‖

Self-Portrait

PLAYERS: 5–20

THE GEAR: Drawing pads, scratch paper, pencils, blindfolds.

Give each player a drawing pad, a pencil, and a blindfold. Players must don the blindfold and, without looking, draw a self-portrait. Once everyone's finished and has written his name on the back of his drawing, the host collects the portraits, numbers them, and hangs them up.

Guests guess whose self-portrait is whose by marking down the number of a portrait along with a name. Players get a point if they guess correctly and/or if their portrait is correctly identified. Fun for the family, especially since everyone comes out looking like the Munsters.

iPod Dance Charades

PLAYERS: 6–30

THE GEAR: A computer, an iPod.

As a group, decide on a playlist of about twenty songs that are familiar to everyone. Put them all on one iPod. Divide the players into two teams. Decide at random which team goes first.

That team dispatches a representative to don the iPod headphones. The rep chooses a song, pushes play and begins to "dance" to that song—acting it out. Her teammates confer about which song she is dancing to, and offer answers. The team has thirty seconds to guess the song. After the thirty seconds, the headphones switch to a player on the other team for thirty seconds of guessing. The headphones pass back and forth between the teams (to the same players) until the end of the song. The team that correctly guesses the song gets 1 point.

Play continues until each team member has had a chance to dance. The team with the most points wins.

—contributed by Greg Trefry
and Mattia Romeo (see page 34).

▶▶ IF YOU LIKE THIS GAME . . . check out Dancing Cheek to Cheek on page 30.

Chapter Eight

GAMES OF GENERAL CLEVERNESS

Sometimes people need games with concrete, readily apparent answers: Thirty-four. Bingo. Gin. But sometimes *getting there* creatively is the most fun part, and this section is full of games that reward the journey and creativity. A bit of play-acting and persuasiveness is required in most of the games, and the winners are usually the folks who throw caution to the wind and fly by the seat of their pants. The games require players to worry less about the ultimate result and to suspend their disbelief and enjoy the ride. If you're looking for a clear-cut result, with a prescribed path for getting there, stick to Bridge. If you want to test the limits of your imagination, go for Nomic or Read My Mind.

You know you're creative. You're the one making the puns at parties and devising new and hilarious activities for bored relatives on rainy beach days. For some of these games you have to come up with various categories yourself, like in Guggenheim, or you have to spin a yarn, fast and under pressure, as in Save Yourself. In Nomic and Mafia, you're essentially creating the game as you go, and you need a grab bag of skills to make it fun: a sense of humor, facility with word association, a sharp visual memory, some skills with math and logic, and political acumen. In fact, both Mafia and Nomic require that you be able to win people over to your side while giving nothing away—and then double-cross the people who helped you in the first place. It's like Poker with a plotline!

My uncle, who is both an unrepentant punster and film buff, was thrilled to discover the existence of Carnelli—finally, a game that combines his two great loves! If you like to shop around, compare prices and then bargain with a shopkeeper, then you might find that Haggle is the game you've been waiting for all your life. If you could teach Julia Child a thing or two about a *roux,* you might like Iron Chef Potluck. If you have a freakishly good memory for pictures, try Geography. Rest assured, whatever you're clever at will be revealed in this chapter.

Carnelli

You've heard of word-association games, right? Well, Carnelli is a *title*-association game—titles of movies, plays, books, and songs. Invented by Jan Carnell, the game is a popular game at Mensa meetings, but you don't have to be a braniac to enjoy it.

PLAYERS: 4–100 (the more the better), plus a nonplaying moderator.

THE GEAR: Timer.

Choose a moderator. This impartial judge (or "Carnelli Master") will decide what titles do in fact have an association with the aforementioned title—for example, *House of the Spirits* following *Bleak House* is a clear association, as they share a word, but what about *Dracula* following *House of the Spirits*. (They both starred Winona Ryder in the movie version.) The Carnelli Master makes these and other tough judgments including hearing challenges (see "Bluffing and Challenging," below) from one player to another; the Master's decisions (according to the official rules at mwm.us.mensa.org/carnelli.html) are "arbitrary, capricious, and final."

NOTE: Players must decide beforehand if they want to limit their titles to a certain genre, say, movies, or also use the titles of books, plays, TV shows, and songs, or some combination of the above.

The Game Plan

- Everyone sits in a circle with the Carnelli Master in the center. The Carnelli Master announces a title (any title that pops into her head—she only has to come up with the first one) and points to a player. That player, within thirty seconds, must name a title that somehow connects to the previously mentioned title. Play continues clockwise and keeps going in a chain. (Players must answer within thirty seconds unless the Carnelli Master feels the game is dragging or going too fast, and may increase or decrease that time.)

- The types of connections permitted are a common word, a common *element* of a word (like following **Post**cards from the Edge with The **Post**man or Romeo and **Jul**iet with The **Jewel** of the Nile), a common author, a common actor in a movie version, a common theme, a common concept (like following *Casablanca* with *Play It Again, Sam*), a common producer, or even a pun— the rules give an example of following *The Trojan Women* with *Condominium* (a novel and TV movie).

- Players do not state the connections, just the title. If a connection is not clear, the player immediately to the left of the speaker may challenge (see "Bluffing and Challenging," below) but runs the risk of being eliminated.

- Players should decide before starting what connections will be allowed, and the Carnelli Master arbitrates disputes that inevitably arise during game play. As mentioned, puns are permitted and encouraged: for example, *Tequila Sunrise* can be linked to *To Kill a Mockingbird* (*tequila* mockingbird, get it?).

Bluffing and Challenging: Bluffing is an important element in Carnelli. If a player can't think of a legitimate connection, he may say any title—or make up a title—and hope that the player immediately after him doesn't challenge him. If he's challenged and is unable to prove the connection, he is out. On the other hand, if he *is* able to prove the connection, the challenger is out.

The Carnelli Master cannot make any challenges (including a repeated or incorrectly stated title); it is up to the players remaining in the game to make the challenge. The Carnelli Master is then the judge, jury, and executioner of the rule, as it were. Like the Supreme Court, the Carnelli Master has no power or authority until a matter is brought to them for consideration.

A player is eliminated from the round if:

* he is unable to think of a connecting title.

* he says a title that another player has already used.

* he misstates the title, like, "The House of the Ghosts" rather than *The House of the Spirits*.

* he challenges and is proved wrong.

* the Carnelli Master rules that his connection is invalid: if he misstates the title or repeats, for example, or if the connection is too tenuous.

Winning

When everyone but one player has been eliminated, that person wins.

Read My Mind

A **game strategically designed** for flirting, Read My Mind allows the leader to creatively and elaborately compliment someone in the room, the better to get to know them, and you know, take them for an egg cream at the local drugstore some Sunday afternoon.

PLAYERS: 4–30

THE GEAR: Paper, pencils.

The leader thinks of someone in the room—perhaps an attractive lady, Jane—among the assembled guests. He then asks the room at large, "Read my mind." The guests—who do not know whom the leader is thinking of—provide nouns or proper nouns, jotted on slips of paper, based on nothing but their own sense of caprice. Let's say one of the answers is "snake." The leader then reveals who is on his mind: "Jane!"—and makes a case for why Jane is like a snake. "Jane is like a snake because she is so charming!" The next player then reveals the word he wrote—let's say it's "Porsche"—and the leader must on the spot say why Jane is like a Porsche (perhaps she's sleek? sporty?) You get the gist. Flirt! Flirt! (If Jane leaves the room, you might want to start thinking of someone else.)

Mafia
aka Werewolf

I **f you like secrecy, collusion,** double-crossing, and a fair amount of blind guesswork that leads to mob hysteria and the sudden death of your friends, then Mafia's the game for you. It was created by Dimitry Davidoff of Moscow State University in the mid-1980s. Like many parlor games,

Mafia's only as amusing as the people who play it, so choose your guests wisely: They should be up for a certain amount of playacting.

In this role-playing game, your group pretends to be a small village in which most people are good but a few are bad—*very, very* bad. These criminals (the Mafia) are assigned by the Mayor and known only to each other. The rest of the players (called Villagers) do not know who the Mafia are. Every night, the Mafia silently collude to kill a Villager, so each dawn the murder of another innocent Villager is announced. As each day passes, the Villagers must vote to eliminate a person they believe to be a mafioso. In order to win (i.e., survive), they must work together to uncover the murderers in their midst and kill them all before they can do any more damage. To that end, accusations are made, alliances are formed, and double-dealings abound. It's every man for himself, and you might just find yourself falsely accusing a loved one in order to save your own skin.

PLAYERS: 6–20. At least five, plus the Mayor, who is a kind of moderator or emcee. The ideal number for Mafia is around twelve; keep the total number of players under twenty, or things start to get too confusing.

THE GEAR: Enough space for the whole group to sit in a circle, with room behind the group for the Mayor to walk. A staff, a stick, a cane—even a wooden spoon, as long as the Mayor can use it to tap people.

Objective

The Mafia's goal is to kill enough Villagers to outnumber them; the Villagers' objective is to find out who among them are Mafia and eliminate them all.

Preparation

Choose one player (ideally someone who's played before and knows the rules) to play the Mayor. The rest of the players begin the game as Villagers—but the Mayor's first task is to secretly designate a minority of these Villagers as Mafia (see "First Night" in the Game Plan). There should be roughly one Mafia member for every two or three Villagers. For example, in a group of ten people, one person is the Mayor, three are Mafia, and six are Villagers.

▶▶ **HOST TIP**

Choose a gregarious, playful person to be the Mayor. A good deal of the fun of Mafia lies in the ability to convincingly pretend that it's nighttime and nefarious doings *really are* afoot . . . and the Mayor sets the tone for how "into it" the other players will be. In a recent game, our Mayor adopted an absurd and terrible Italian accent and invented details of murders that were both gruesome and ridiculous.

The Game Plan

The game is played in rounds, with each round being an imagined day and night in the life of the town.

FIRST NIGHT

- Seat your guests in a circle. The game begins at the phase of the game referred to as "night," meaning that the Mayor tells the Villagers to close their eyes and "go to sleep."

- All players except the Mayor close their eyes. The Mayor walks around the circle and, with his staff, taps the people he's selected to be Mafia members (one-quarter to one-third of the players). The Mayor must do this as stealthily as possible, and ideally he will walk around the circle several times so it won't be easily discernible to the Villagers whom he's tapped.

✖ After the Mayor has made his selections, he instructs *only the Mafia* to open their eyes. The Mafia members make silent eye contact, acknowledging one another as the associates. The Mayor then commands the mafiosi to close their eyes again.

FIRST DAY

✖ The Mayor announces that dawn has broken and instructs *everyone* to open their eyes. The Mayor then reveals that a gruesome murder has been perpetrated during the night. (In this first round, there is no actual victim, but in all subsequent rounds one of the Villagers is "killed" and must leave the game.)

✖ The townspeople must try to suss out who's in the Mafia. The Mafia, of course, will lie to uphold their innocence.

✖ The accusations: Anyone can accuse anyone else of being in the Mafia, and it can be based on nothing more than a gut feeling or a suspicion. But you must give your reasoning to convince the others in the group. For instance, you might say, "I accuse Mary because I felt her twitch when the Mayor was selecting the Mafia members." Or the reasoning can be fanciful and in keeping with the storytelling aspect of the game: "I accuse John because I saw

▶▶STEALTH STRATEGY ◀

Strategy plays a huge part in making these accusations. The person doing the accusing may be a mafioso trying to deflect suspicion from himself and his fellow Mafia. Villagers must stay on their toes and walk a fine line between accusing and staying under the Mafia's radar (or they may find themselves offed during the night). And Mafia players must be careful not to tip their hand.

him exercising his hounds down near the old mill last night at sunset, and didn't the victim live near the old mill?"

✖ Once a charge has been made, the accused mafioso is allowed to speak up in his defense. The Mayor then asks if anyone will second the accusation against that person. If no one does, the charge is dropped. If someone *will* second it, the guilt or innocence of the accused is decided by a vote. At least two people must be accused and the charges seconded before the vote can take place—the vote determines which *one* of the two (or three, or four) of the accused will be executed. Even if you think more than one of the accused is guilty, you may still vote to execute just one.

✖ Once the Mayor senses that all accusations for that round have been made, he takes a vote, via a show of hands, as to who the guilty party is. The accused person who receives the largest share of the vote is "killed" and must leave the game. The Mayor then reveals whether the deceased was Mafia or a Villager.

NOTE: "Dead" players may observe but not participate in the rest of the game. Consider the time to be information-gathering for your next game of Mafia—who giggles when lying, who wildly tosses around accusations, etc.

SUBSEQUENT NIGHTS AND DAYS

✖ Night falls again, and the Mayor tells the players to close their eyes. The Mayor then asks *only the Mafia* to open their eyes and pick a victim. The baddies collude silently—through winks and points and head nods—and settle on someone to

▸▸STEALTH STRATEGY

At this point it's smart to consider what clues the victim's murder can reveal about the status of the surviving Villagers. If the dead person was a mafioso, you can probably deduce that whoever accused them was likely not in the Mafia (although this isn't foolproof) because the Mafia is unlikely to target one of its own. If the victim was an innocent civilian, think back to his behavior on prior rounds. Was it a mafioso who made (or seconded) the accusation? Perhaps they came too close to revealing someone's secret identity and had to be eliminated. Tracking players' alliances and betrayals can pay off—but don't be too obvious about it. If the Mafia thinks you're about to expose one of them, it's you who'll sleep with the fishes.

whack. They silently indicate their choice to the Mayor. The Mayor asks them to close their eyes.

✱ Morning is announced. All players are asked to open their eyes, and the Mayor tells the tale of the vicious murder of the innocent Villager that the Mafia murdered the night before. This time, of course, it's an actual player, and he or she must leave the game. (Again, "dead" players may observe but not participate in the game.)

✱ The accusing and seconding starts all over again. The town takes another vote about which of the accused are guilty, and another suspected Mafia member is lynched before night falls again. Once the accused is killed, the Mayor reveals whether the dead was Mafia or Villager.

✱ Each morning brings news of another murder in the night, and the dwindling number of Villagers becomes increasingly frantic to identify and kill all the Mafia.

Players will gang up—for example, two Villagers might agree that another player is acting suspiciously and so vote to get rid of him, but the next day those same two players might be swayed by a third player's argument and turn on each other. In short, no one can trust *anyone* as the Villagers try to identify and eliminate the Mafia before they themselves are assassinated in a nighttime lynching, and the Mafia tries to eliminate Villagers who are hot on their trail. (But not *too* obviously, as whacking someone who has accused you will only serve to confirm the Villagers' suspicions.) As the game progresses and the group gets smaller and smaller, the arguments get ever more heated, and lies and betrayal are rampant. Everyone becomes a suspect and no one can be trusted.

Winning
The game ends when all of the Mafia are killed (a victory for the Villagers), or when the Mafia outnumber the Villagers (a victory for the Mafia).

Variation
Rather than the Mayor choosing who the mafiosi are, players can draw slips of paper out of a hat. The papers marked with an X designate the Mafia. This has the advantage of randomness, which means the players can't try to psych out the Mayor and guess who he'd pick as Mafia. However, the Mayor will know who the Mafia are and he will still moderate the game.

AMP IT UP
Check out the Wikipedia page on Mafia (Google "Mafia" and "party game.") You'll find dozens of links and optional roles to ratchet up the collusion and double-dealings.

Geography

Test your knowledge of geography (or memory, if you've only *just* looked at an atlas) and maybe you'll finally understand why Pakistan and India are so tetchy with each other. Geography is the kind of game you'd play if you love TV's *Are You Smarter Than a Fifth Grader?* It's a great activity if you want to play something with the family—and give the kids a pretty good chance of winning.

PLAYERS: 3–10

THE GEAR: An atlas or a bunch of maps, timer.

The Game Plan

Allow players (or groups of players, if you're playing in teams) to study a map of the United States for five minutes. When the time's up, the moderator picks a state and calls it out by name. The first player (or team) to call out how many states border that state wins 5 points. If the player wishes to go on, he may name the states that border that state, netting 1 point for every correct state and losing 3 points for every incorrect one. Once you've had enough fun playing with a map of the U.S., expand the game to a map of the world, or contract the game to a county-by-county map of your state.

Winning

After five rounds, the player with the most points wins.

Haggle

Invented by the late Sid Sackson, a renowned game designer, Haggle is an information-trading game. In order to win, you have to build on the information you have, wheedle information away from other players, and hopefully prevent them from gleaning what you know—all while holding a cocktail. For an Easter Egg version of this game, see page 180.

PLAYERS: 15 (if more or fewer, amend the Secret Information, right), plus a nonplaying host.

THE GEAR: Index cards in five different colors: yellow, blue, red, orange, and white. You will need twice as many index cards of each color as there are players in the game. (So for a game for fifteen people, you'll need thirty cards of each color.) Slips of paper, 15 envelopes, and pens.

Preparation

Haggle requires a nonplaying moderator to write or print out the secret information on slips of paper ahead of time and to help score the game at the end. The slips of paper are "secret information sheets" printed with, obviously, bits of secret information.

There are fifteen pieces of secret information, the same as the number of players. If you're playing with fewer than fifteen, don't use the last pieces of secret information. (So if you're playing with thirteen people, use only thirteen pieces of secret information.) Each piece of information will be printed out or copied onto two slips of paper. This will give you, the moderator, a total of thirty slips of paper.

Before your guests arrive, shuffle the index cards and deal them into piles of ten cards each. Place each pile in an envelope along with two of the fifteen pieces of information. (Make sure that duplicates of the secret information are not placed in a single envelope—each player should start the game with two different pieces of secret information.)

The Game Plan

✖ As guests arrive, hand them each an envelope. Tell them that they have the rest of the evening to "haggle," trading information and cards, to try to achieve the most valuable hand.

✖ The players will approach one another and offer to trade information; offers may be declined. Players should also keep an eye on the haggling that *other* players are doing—you may not have wanted the information that Joe had an hour ago, but since Joe traded secret-information sheets with Sue, his newfound knowledge may now be useful. As players obtain information, they will want to gather some different colored index cards and possibly get rid of some cards they're already holding.

✖ Guests will haggle in and around other activities—cocktail hour, dinner, other

Secret Information

- Orange cards have a basic value of 4 and are equal to a red card and a yellow card.

- White cards have the highest basic value and are equal to a red card and a blue card.

- Blue cards have a basic value twice that of yellow and half that of orange.

- If a player has more than three white cards, all of his white cards lose their value.

- A player can only score as many orange cards as he has blue cards.

- If a player has five or more blue cards, 10 points are deducted from every other player's score.

- A set of three red cards protects you from one set of five blue cards.

- The player with the most yellow cards gets a bonus of the number of cards squared (for example, if the most yellow cards are five, the bonus is 25). If two or more players tie for yellow, they are eliminated and the bonus goes to the next highest.

- If a player hands in seven or more cards of the same color, he is eliminated from the game.

- Each set of five different colors gives a bonus of 10 points.

- If a "pyramid" is handed in with no other cards, the value of the hand is doubled. A pyramid consists of four cards of one color, three cards of a second color, two cards of a third color, and one card of a fourth color.

- The player with the most red cards doubles their value. In case of a tie, no player collects the extra value.

- Each set of two yellow cards doubles the value of one white card.

- Each set of three blue cards quadruples the value of one orange card.

- No more than thirteen cards in a hand can be scored. If more are handed in, the excess will be removed at random by the host.

games—though players may occasionally take a quiet moment to sit in the kitchen and assess the data they've gathered.

* At an appointed hour, say, midnight, the game is over. Players arrange their final hands in front of them for scoring. (Since only 13 cards will be counted, players may wish to hold back some of their cards.) The host then reads out the basic point values of each of the cards (which can be deduced from the first three information sheets) yellow = 1, blue = 2, red = 3, orange = 4, and white = 5. Players come up with a preliminary tally. Then the host reads out all fifteen pieces of information, in order, and players adjust their totals accordingly.

Winning
Highest score wins.

|||||||||||||||||||||||||||||||||||||||||||||||||||||||||||||||||||||||

Super Babel

Created by **Robert Abbott,** Super Babel is a little like Haggle, but without the secret information sheets. Super Babel is cool because it's hectic and noisy, like Friday afternoon at the stock exchange. The spirited trading of cards is the main fun here; most card games are so quiet!

PLAYERS: 6–30. Fifteen or more is best, plus a nonplaying moderator/scorekeeper.

THE GEAR: Several decks of cards (the number of decks should be about one-third the number of players), the chart (right) for each player, a score sheet for the scorekeeper, with each player's name at the top of a column.

The Objective
To assemble ten-card hands that will let you "go out," meaning to finish a round and get a new hand. Copy this chart for each player:

FIVE-CARD HANDS (TWO ARE NEEDED TO GO OUT)		
HAND	**POINT VALUE**	**DESCRIPTION**
straight	5	any five cards in sequence
flush	7	any five cards of the same suit
full house	10	three cards of one rank and two cards of another rank
four of a kind	15	four cards of the same rank plus one of any other card
straight flush	20	five cards of the same suit in sequence
royal flush	21	Ace, King, Queen, Jack, and 10 of one suit
TEN-CARD HANDS (ONE IS NEEDED TO GO OUT)		
double straight	20	any ten cards in sequence
double flush	40	ten cards of the same suit
double straight flush	80	ten cards of the same suit in sequence

The Game Plan
Shuffle all the decks together and deal them into piles of ten cards each.

Set a time limit, such as twenty minutes, and say "Go." Players barter cards with each other simultaneously (they don't take turns), attempting to form ten-card hands (or two five-card hands), according to the chart, that will let them go out. (Example: "Who needs an ace of spades? Who needs an ace of spades!? I'll trade you for any club! Any club! I need a club here!")

When a player goes out, he hands in his cards to the scorekeeper for scoring and receives a new packet of ten cards so he may resume playing. As players hand in their packets of ten, the scorekeeper should shuffle them together and make new packets of ten cards to hand out.

Winning

When the time is up, the scorekeeper adds up all the scores, announces the winner, and tells everyone to quiet down—the baby's sleeping!

—I got Super Babel from Wayne Schmittberger's great book New Rules for Classic Games.

Happy Days

So you spent your youth playing the piano, cultivating an interest in art history, writing new software, and starting companies before you were fifteen? Well, most of us spent our youth sprawled on the sofa watching *Happy Days, Laverne and Shirley,* and even *Joanie Loves Chachi.* Those were happy days, indeed!

This game tests the memory of all those TV shows you used to watch. If your guests all came of age during the same decade, like the '70s, your frame of reference will be similar and the game will be easier. If you're playing an intergenerational game—with folks who were watching TV when TV was still a novelty, as well as with kids who don't remember much before Hannah Montana—you may be stumped more frequently.

PLAYERS: 3–30

The Game Plan

Players sprawl on a regulation couch, feet on coffee table, chips and beer near at hand. A player kicks off the game by naming an old TV show, like *M*A*S*H* or *Taxi* or *Frasier* or—God help you—*Melrose Place* (if you're playing with kids, you can expand the time frame to include current TV shows, but don't let them have the beer). That player must then name a character from that show; the player to his left must immediately name another character, and so on. The play continues clockwise around the circle until someone is stumped; that player is eliminated.

If you are or were a soap opera fan, this can be a hilarious way to reminisce with friends about plotlines that started in the Reagan administration.

Winning

The last player to be eliminated wins an iTunes gift card for the latest episode of a favorite sitcom.

Guggenheim

Also known as "Categories," this is an excellent pencil-and-paper game for two or more players. The fun of Guggenheim lies in creating the categories as a group and arguing over what's appropriate. Let's say a category is "disasters." The *Titanic* works, sure, but what about Björk's swan dress at the Oscars a few years ago? Some people might put that under "triumphs." Or the Kevin Costner movie *Waterworld.* I'm going to go with "disaster."

PLAYERS: 2–10

THE GEAR: Paper, pencils, timer.

The Game Plan

Guggenheim may be played in teams, provided that the groups are sufficiently removed from one another that they can't hear the other team's discussion.

To play, each player draws a five-by-five grid, and across the top writes the same five-letter word, like HORSE. (For a grid template, see page 372.) For the vertical axis, come up with five categories, such as names of rivers, dog breeds, hair accessories, past presidents, and folksingers. Players have five minutes to fill in the grid.

The host says "Go"; players begin filling in the squares. (For example, the top left square, which is the intersection of H and "rivers," might be filled in with "Housatonic.") Words like *a, the, an, and, of,* and *in* do not count as first words; in answers of two words it is the first letter of the first word that counts; and in proper names the first letter of the last name counts.

In a recent game, one of our categories was "people who would be terrible to collaborate with." The five-letter word was MAKES. I got 5 points for "Bernie Madoff"; my friend got 5 points for "Sam Kinison"; another pal scored with "Benedict Arnold." Other categories I've used in recent games are: "appliances you don't need"; "words that only people under forty say" ("Twitter"); "words that only people over forty say" ("typewriter"); "workplace gaffes"; "quotes from *Monty Python*"; and the "special skills that VHS repairmen now put on their résumés."

Scoring

If you have a word in one of your squares and no one else has the same answer, you gain 5 points. If two people have it, you each gain 3 points; if three people have it, none of the three gains a point. If you think of a

	H	O	R	S	E
Names of Rivers					
Dog Breeds					
Hair Accessories					
Past Presidents					
Folksingers					

Sample Grid for Guggenheim

two-word answer in which each word begins with the same letter—*Mamma Mia,* at the intersection of "M" and "plays," for example—and no one else has it, you gain 10 points. If another person has it, you gain only 5 points. If more than one other person has it, you gain nothing.

Winning

The player with the most points wins.

A Few Ideas to Get You Started

- Parts of the body
- Romantic places
- Misdemeanors
- Dog breeds
- Movie titles
- Foods you think are healthy but aren't (these subjective ones can be difficult, but just adhere to the rule that a majority of players must agree that the answer fits in the category)
- Psychotropic drugs
- Illegal drugs
- Vacation destinations

Variation

Players decide on a list of categories—about ten or more—and write them down in a column along the left side of the paper. A letter of the alphabet is chosen at random and players have a set time limit to think of an entry that starts with the letter for each of the categories. After the time limit (say, five minutes) is up, the players read out their words. A word that no one else has gets 2 points; a word that other players also have gets 1 point. A majority of players have to agree that a word is an appropriate fit for that category. The player with the most points wins.

AMP IT UP

Guggenheim Outdoors is also fun to play on the move in your city or town, like a Scavenger Hunt. You don't need the five-letter word to play this way, just the five categories, and the first person to come up with five examples wins.

A recent game I played with a friend in Brooklyn had these categories:

- ostentatious displays of wealth
- absurd baby gear
- inappropriate clothing on men who should know better
- marauding teens
- evidence of the end of the world as we know it

My pal quickly captured an "inappropriate clothing" square for his spotting of a not-skinny man in very skinny jeans. But, I managed to fill in the "evidence of the end of the world as we know it" when I spied an $18 cocktail, offered at a newly upscale bar that previously had catered to a rather grimy and wild-eyed clientele.

In order to have something "count," both players (or a majority of players, if you're playing with more than two) have to see the person or thing and have to agree that what you've spotted fits the category. Remember, don't be too much of a jerk about what fits, or your opponent will soon retaliate.

Chain-Link Music

A gentle, very casual game that's great for passing the time when engaged in another ongoing activity (driving, hiking, cooking), with endless variations that will leave you surprised by how many song titles (or book titles, or movies, etc.) you have saved and unconsciously cataloged in your noggin over the years.

PLAYERS: 2–10

The Game Plan

The first person names a song title. The next person has to name another song title with one of the words, or a part of a word, from the first person's title. For example, Person A starts out with "Baby Got Back," so Person B says "I Got You, Babe," and Person C says "Oh, Babe, What Would You Say," etc.

I played Chain-Link Music with my husband, Fran, and our friend Charles (of Goat Testicle fame—see page 22) while I was cooking dinner and they were noodling on their guitars in the kitchen. I kicked off the game with a Simon and Garfunkel favorite and it took off from there:

"Parsley, Sage, Rosemary, and Thyme"
"Time After Time"
"Time Is on My Side"
"Let Me Be Your Sidetrack"
"Tracks of My Tears"
"There'll Be No Teardrops Tonight"
"Tears of a Clown"
"Death of a Clown"
"O Death"
"O Susannah"

"O Canada"
"Canadian Railroad Trilogy"
"Railroading on the Great Divide"
"Across the Great Divide"
"Hot Cross Buns": This song, for some reason, stumped my husband. Charles heckled him unmercifully—I mean, do you know *how many* songs have the word "hot" or "cross" in the title? Charles was incredulous that he couldn't come up with anything. "Think of *any* hymnal from *any* Christian church." Finally, finally, Fran hit on "The Old Crossroads."
"The Old Home Place"
"The Old Folks at Home"
"Homeward Bound"
"Alabama Bound"
"Alberta Bound"
"Alberta"
"You Can Call Me Al"
"Call Me the Breeze"
"Baby Breeze"

. . . and then Charles started picking out "Alberta" on his guitar, and the game ended with music and spaghetti Bolognese.

Winning

If you're stumped, you're out of the game. The last person standing wins.

Variation

Pick a topic, any topic, and take turns singing songs that include that topic. The person who comes up with the most wins. Good topics to start with are colors, food, animals, names, references to real people, references to real places, dreams, etc. These games can last for as long as you want; in fact, they never have to end at all!

PARTY RECIPE

Jelly Doughnut Pudding

This dessert was created at Eli's on New York's Upper East Side. It's a good reason for living.   SERVES 8 TO 10

INGREDIENTS

8 large eggs	1½ cups plus
4 egg yolks	2 tablespoons sugar
1 tablespoon vanilla	14 doughnuts filled with
extract	raspberry jam or other
3½ cups heavy cream,	jam or jelly
at room temperature	Butter, for greasing
1½ cups whole milk,	the pan
at room temperature	Boiling water

1. Preheat oven to 325°F. In a large bowl, combine eggs, egg yolks, vanilla, cream, milk, and 1½ cups sugar. Whisk.

2. Slice the doughnuts from top to bottom in ¼-inch pieces. Butter a 9-by-12-inch baking pan and sprinkle with 1 tablespoon sugar. Pour about ½ inch of the cream mixture into the pan. Arrange a layer of sliced doughnuts in the pan, overlapping slightly. Top with another layer, pressing down slightly to moisten. Spoon a small amount of the cream mixture on top.

3. Arrange 2 more layers of sliced doughnuts. Pour the remaining liquid evenly over top. Press down gently to moisten and sprinkle with the remaining 1 tablespoon sugar. Cover the pan tightly with foil, and place in a larger pan. Fill the larger pan with boiling water until it's three-quarters up the side of the pudding pan.

4. Bake for 1 hour 50 minutes. Remove the foil and continue to bake until the top is golden brown, about 15 minutes. Turn off the oven, open the door slightly, and let the pudding sit for an additional 10 minutes. Serve warm or at room temperature.

Reprinted by permission of Eli Zabar

Save Yourself

Essentially an exercise in storytelling, Save Yourself is a great way to get to better know your friends—and to learn why you shouldn't throw them overboard, even if you could.

PLAYERS: 2–10

The Game Plan

The premise is this: Your lifeboat is overloaded and someone's got to go. Each guest has one minute to make a case for why he should be allowed to live. These reasons can be true or not—the aim is to amuse and convince the other players: Maybe you're the only person who really, truly understands banking regulations in the United States— and if you die, the world economy dies, too. Maybe you know exactly where Osama bin Laden hangs his hat. Maybe you're Eli Zabar, who developed the recipe for Jelly Doughnut Pudding (for crying out loud, this person should live!).

At the end everyone votes to cast someone off. It's kind of like a storytelling version of *Survivor.* Even after you've been eliminated, you continue to vote others off. When all players but one have been voted off, that player is declared the winner. This game should be lighthearted and much, much funnier than the Alfred Hitchcock film *Lifeboat.* But that shouldn't be too hard, assuming that a Nazi won't be crashing your party.

You Don't Say . . .

PLAYERS: 2–50

Some games can be played for the *duration* of a party, or in and around other games. It is extremely helpful to know a few games like this that can provide an ongoing activity, a kind of insurance policy that the party won't bog down and become dullsville. Decide ahead of time on a few words that will be taboo—for example, *yes, no, black, white,* etc. Announce these words to all the guests. (Limit the taboo words to four, as people will quickly forget them if there are too many.) Randomly choose someone to be "It"—preferably someone social and gregarious. It will spend the party trying to get the other guests to say one of these words—through any means necessary. If someone slips and says the word, he's out. (If someone slips and It is not around to hear it, anyone may point it out and eliminate the speaker.) The last person to be eliminated wins, and becomes the next It, if there's enough time for a second round.

Variation

Forbidden Letter. Seat guests in a circle, as at a dinner table, and randomly select someone to be It. It announces that some letter of the alphabet is now off-limits—and that all answers to his questions must be crafted without benefit of that letter. Let's say it's *B.* (Note: It may use the letter in his questions.) So It might ask a player: "So, Joe, which do you like better, the birds or the bees?" and Joe must answer, *without pause,* "Well, I

prefer the little insects, as a matter of fact." If a player makes a mistake, he gains a point. If he hesitates—any pause longer than would occur in natural conversation, as determined by the group—he gains a point. After a predetermined number of rounds (say, five) the points are tallied. Lowest score wins.

Iron Chef Potluck

Maybe when you play games you work up an appetite. So why not make dinner part of the game? I know, I know, you're not supposed to play with your food—but tell that to the Iron Chef people. A game for serious foodies, the goal of Iron Chef Potluck is to make the most delicious dish using a predetermined ingredient or ingredients.

PLAYERS: 2–10

THE GEAR: Paper and pencils to write comments and critique the food.

The Game Plan

✕ Set a date for a dinner party. At least a week ahead of time, tell your guests what the featured ingredient(s) is going to be: pumpkins, tomatoes, chocolate and cheese . . . choose one or more. (For novice cooks, designing a tasty dish around a single ingredient is challenging enough; for parties with more experienced chefs, you can assign a combination of ingredients.) Of course, paying attention to what's in season will result in the most delicious dishes— as well as avoiding anything considered particularly vile. (You might think it's funny to feature "pork rinds," but once you've eaten nine dishes showcasing pork rinds, you'll be sorry.)

✖ Randomly assign guests (and yourself) to bring an entrée, appetizer, or dessert featuring that ingredient. While the featured ingredient need not be the *main* focus of the dish (i.e., if you make pumpkin stuffed with bread cubes, cheese, garlic, and cream, the pumpkin is secondary to the stuffing), it must be clearly present. So if you just put a smidge of pumpkin in a chocolate cake to satisfy the rules, but it's *really* just a regular old chocolate cake, you're out. I mean, I'll still eat your chocolate cake, but you're disqualified.

✖ On the day of the party, have everyone arrive with enough time to heat up their dishes or add last-minute touches. Then dig in! You'll be surprised at how ingredients can be creatively combined—chocolate and cheese, for example, could produce enchiladas with a *mole* sauce, or a chocolate and brie panini. Or Velveeta fudge, but I am Not. Eating. That.

✖ After you've had your fill, everyone votes for the best-tasting and most creative dish. The winner gets to take home the leftovers; the hostess may also offer a small prize, like a copy of the latest celebrity-chef cookbook.

Common Ground

A team game for people who have an interest in history, places, pop culture, politics, science, or industry and like finding obscure connections among topics. Players create lists of words that have *something* in common—and the other team has to guess what that something is. Common Ground is great for parties because it gets smaller groups of people interacting right away. But it will also work on a family camping trip or on a retreat for speech pathologists.

PLAYERS: 4–10

The Game Plan

✖ Divide your players into two teams, taking care to separate husbands and wives, best friends, siblings, etc. Put the two teams in different rooms, or at least out of earshot of each other. Each team comes up with five things, ideas, people, or places (or any combination of these) that have a connection—Washington, plumbers, Ben Bradlee, President Nixon, and Mark Felt, for example, for a connection of "Watergate." (Follow the "Play Fair" guidelines on page 52: Make the examples and connections something that at least half the team has heard of, to give the other team a fair shot.)

✖ Reconvene the teams. Team A reveals its first clue—in our example, it's "Washington."

✖ Team B has a moment to confer and then states what they think the connection is going to be. Let's say they guess "politics."

✖ Team A then reveals its second clue—"plumbers." Team B confers and changes its answer to "Watergate."

✖ Team A then reveals its next three clues; each time Team B decides to keep its answer as "Watergate."

✖ At the end, Team A reveals that the connection was indeed "Watergate." If Team B had changed its answer on, say, the fifth clue, they would get 0 points, despite having guessed correctly on the second, third, and fourth clues. So even if a team gets the answer right early on, the other team should not acknowledge it and continue to give clues until all five have been revealed. There's always a chance that a team will change a correct answer to an incorrect one.

✖ The teams then switch as clue-givers and clue-receivers. Play continues until a predetermined number of rounds have been played—three is a good number.

Winning
Scoring is from 0–5: If the team guesses the connection on the first clue, that team receives 5 points. If they guess it on the second clue (as our example team did) they

>>STEALTH STRATEGY

Try to come up with three or four items that have a connection *other than* the connection between the five total items. Name these three or four items first, thereby throwing off your opponents with a false connection.

receive 4 points, and so on. If they never guess the connection, they get 0 points. Highest score wins.

Great Minds Think Alike

Like to get inside the heads of your friends? Great Minds Think Alike, created by Penny Warner, encourages players to do just that with their teammates. You and your teammates will draw a single category from a hat. Then, individually, you'll generate a list of examples in that category. (For example, if the category is *breakfast foods,* you might list *poached eggs, waffles, oatmeal,* etc.) When the time's up, you'll compare your answers to those of your teammates and count up the number that you have in common. Beware: It's delightful to find out that you and your date think exactly alike, but it can be alarming to discover that you and your batty Aunt Sally were apparently separated at birth.

PLAYERS: 4–16, plus a nonplaying moderator.

THE GEAR: Slips of paper, pencils, hat.

The Game Plan
✖ Divide players into two teams. On slips of paper, the moderator writes down ten categories, for example:

- things you find at the mall
- things you might eat at a carnival
- things that women like
- famous Ponzi schemes

- best honeymoon destinations
- recurring women's-magazine stories
- recurring men's-magazine stories
- standard criticisms of women in politics
- best excuses for not doing your homework
- best excuses for calling in sick

Toss the slips into a hat.

✱ Have one person draw a category from the hat and read it aloud. Everyone on both teams then has one minute to write down all examples of that category he can muster up. When the minute's up, teammates compare answers.

✱ For every answer a player has that *at least half* of his teammates also have, the team gains a point. So if your team is six people, and you wrote "surf's up" for "best excuses for calling in sick," then two of your teammates must also have that example in order to gain the point.

✱ There has to be some flexibility in what constitutes the "same" answer, and disputes will be decided by the moderator. For example, in a recent game, someone wrote "The F train stopped running," another teammate wrote "The subways aren't running," and a third wrote "The train broke down." The moderator ruled that these were essentially the same things, and so the point was allowed.

Winning

The game continues until the hat is empty. At the end, the team with the most points wins.

Reversals

PLAYERS: 2–6

THE GEAR: Pencils, paper.

Give Reversals a try when you've got friends or kids to entertain during a flight delay at Thanksgiving—it'll take them a good ten or twenty minutes to generate the first twenty-six names and up to half an hour to come up with the second twenty-six.

The Game Plan

Each player should write, in alphabetical order by first name, a list of twenty-six celebrities or historical figures. So a player might write down Angelica Huston, Brad Pitt, Christopher Wren, etc. When they've got all twenty-six, they must then reverse the initials of each person and think of another famous person with *those* initials. So next to "Angelica Huston" a player might write "Horatio Alger." If you really want to be diabolical, don't tell the players about the second half of the game until they've finished the first.

Winning

The first person to finish wins.

Nomic

Here's the whole point of Nomic: *The game consists of changing the rules with every player's turn*. Yup. In the words of Peter Suber, Nomic's creator, "The primary activity of Nomic is proposing changes in the rules, debating the wisdom of changing them in that way, voting on the changes, deciding what can and cannot be done afterward, and doing it. Even this core of the game, of course, can be changed."

In short, Nomic was created as a way of understanding, teaching, and maybe even spoofing the legislative process. Lawmaking is treated as a game, and it's a game in which changing the rules is the move. You win points if your rule change passes. Sometimes you get points if you vote *against* a rule change that is going to pass even without your support—just like a Congressman might vote against a slam-dunk amendment just to curry favor with the constituents back home.

When you propose a rule change, you'll have to convince the other players that your amendment is in their best interests, too—or you'll have to agree to support the amendment they are planning to propose. With backroom wheeling and dealing, players jockey for power—you might try to take points away from players wearing eyeglasses or plaid shirts, for example, or gain points for you and your blond-haired cronies.

A QUICK NOTE ON THE RULES: Nomic's initial rule set is long and complex—a substantial part of the game is simply keeping track of the rules and hoping that other people

won't. You'll start with a given set of laws (see page 151)—some that you are allowed to change (mutable) and some that you aren't (immutable). If you want to change a mutable law, you must make a proposal and try to win the other players over. If you want to change an immutable law, you must first propose changing it to a mutable law. Then on your next turn, you'll propose a more specific change to the content of the law.

PLAYERS: 4–100, one of whom will also be a note-taker. The game may be played individually or in teams.

THE GEAR: A die, a copy of the rules (see pages 151–152) for each player, paper, and pens.

The Game Plan

* To play, gather a group of four or more players and get comfortable, either in the living room or at a kitchen table. (FYI, Nomic is a game that doesn't ever *have* to end—some games have been played continuously online literally for years, and there's no reason why a group of friends or family couldn't keep a game going—with pauses for life activities, of course—for a very long time.) If you wish and your group is large enough, you may divide people into teams of two. Give each player or team a copy of the twenty-nine rules.

* Read aloud the list of twenty-nine rules (see pages 151–152) and make sure everyone understands the difference between *mutable* and *immutable*. (Mutable means the rules can be changed; immutable means they can't; however, it *is* possible to change an immutable law into a mutable law—see rule #109.) It's best to have one player read one

rule aloud, have another read the next rule aloud, etc.; this will keep your players from spacing out. Stress to your players that it's not critical that they understand every single rule—if they try something that's against the rules, another player will point it out to them. And if another player *doesn't* point it out, hey, they've gotten away with something.

✖ Each player's turn has two parts: 1) the player will propose a rule change. 2) The player will roll a die, accruing points. (But, as the game progresses and a new rule is proposed, voted upon, and enacted—say, for example, if a proposal passes that everyone wearing blue jeans automatically forfeits any points he or she has accrued so far—points may be rapidly gained or lost.) Ganging up on people pays off, but remember, your alliances can and will shift.

✖ Appoint one player to take notes about which rules have been proposed, changed, and added (assigning numbers to new rules), and to keep track of points. Players will probably want to take their own notes, as well.

A few sample moves: In a recent game of Nomic, the first proposal was that we change rule #203—that rule changes must be approved by a unanimous vote—to read that rule changes must be approved by a simple majority. This was quickly approved. The player rolled the die and got a six. The note-taker noted the rule change and the player's score of six. Another player quickly proposed that we abolish the rule that forbids conspiring (#210), which also passed.

As unanimity was no longer required, the field was open for forming alliances and trying to disenfranchise other players. The conspiring began, and frankly there's nothing more

Why I Like Nomic

For me, Nomic is all about rapid, casual game design. A great thing is the amount of silly jargon that arises during play—it's stuff you've made up very quickly with some friends, but it's just as weighty and valid as the terminology in chess or Magic: The Gathering.

And the politics and rule scamming are a lot of fun, of course: Spotting a route to power or victory, and trying to subtly alter the rules to let you get there, or recruiting other players to help you out, without anyone else realizing what you're up to. And when someone announces a clever coup, the other players immediately start poring over the set of rules to see if they can find a mistake or a loophole that will invalidate the win. As a game designer, it's taught me a lot about how to break a game, and how to stop people from breaking mine.

—KEVAN DAVIS, GAME DESIGNER

annoying than hearing people whisper when they're conspiring. So the next player proposed that "if you must conspire, you must conspire in the open and in a falsetto voice." This was approved, with one or two players implying that they would vote for it and at the last second, voting no—thereby netting themselves a quick 10 points each (see rule #204) and irritating the rest of the players.

And thus began open and craven collaborations (if you support my measure, I'll support yours) among people conspiring in falsetto voices—it was like listening to ten Betty Boops haggle for corn subsidies on the Senate floor.

A particularly silly member of the group proposed that everyone choose a nickname, and that the rest of the group must address and refer to players by their nicknames—no personal pronouns allowed. So instead of saying "I," a player must refer to himself by his nickname, or instead of saying "He proposed . . ." the player must use the nickname of that player (i.e., "Captain Underpants proposed . . ."). Any slips would be penalized by 5 points going to the first player who noted that another player had slipped—prompting all players to listen carefully to everyone else, screaming, "Gotcha!" when someone slipped. This amendment passed. Ridiculous nicknames were chosen.

Nomic will take on the flavor of the personalities involved: silly, legalistic, devious, scatterbrained, rational . . . but it always requires paying attention. After a few turns players are barely hanging on—especially if they've had a few beers. Couple that with the sneaking suspicion that someone is patiently launching some kind of long-range plan to disenfranchise the others, and you end up with the kind of confusion, paranoia, and total lack of rationality that makes for a terrific game (or session of Congress).

Winning

The "official" way to win or lose is outlined in rule #213. However, Nomic can go on for a very long time—as I said, years even—without establishing a winner or loser. In our game, in which using personal pronouns was outlawed, one player "fell on his sword" by screaming "I, I, I, I, I!" until he'd lost enough points to eliminate himself from the game. This was, however, after hours of play, many drinks, and several phone calls from his wife telling him to come home. The rest of us crowned ourselves the winners. It's very possible, even likely, that you will play Nomic for an evening and find that the game doesn't really end. That's fine—just remember (hah!) any rule changes, keep all your notes, and start up the game at the same place another evening. Or continue the game online.

▶▶ **IF YOU LIKE THIS GAME . . . for more information on Nomic, check out nomic.net and www.earlham.edu/~peters/writing /nomic.htm.**

NOMIC :: INITIAL SET OF RULES

Immutable Rules

101. All players must always abide by all the rules then in effect. The Initial Set consists of Rules 101–116 (immutable) and 201–213 (mutable).

102. Initially rules in the 100's are immutable and rules in the 200's are mutable. Rules subsequently enacted or changed from immutable to mutable, or vice versa, may be immutable or mutable regardless of their numbers.

103. A rule change is any of the following: (1) the enactment, repeal, or amendment of a mutable rule; (2) the enactment, repeal, or amendment of an amendment of a mutable rule; or (3) the transmutation of an immutable rule into a mutable rule, or vice versa.

104. All rule changes shall be voted on. They will be adopted if and only if they receive the required number of votes.

105. Every player is an eligible voter. Every eligible voter must participate in every vote on rule changes.

106. All proposed rule changes shall be written down before they are voted on. If they are adopted, they shall guide play in the form in which they were voted on.

107. No rule change may be applied retroactively.

108. Each proposed rule change shall be given a number for reference.

109. Rule changes that change immutable rules into mutable rules may be adopted if and only if the vote is unanimous among the eligible voters.

110. In a conflict between a mutable and an immutable rule, the immutable rule takes precedence and the mutable rule shall be entirely void.

111. If a rule change as proposed is unclear or if it is otherwise of questionable value, then the other players may suggest amendments or argue against the proposal before the vote. A reasonable time must be allowed for this debate. The proponent decides when to end the debate and the final form in which the proposal is to be voted on.

112. The state of affairs that constitutes winning may not be altered from achieving n points to any other state of affairs. The magnitude of n and the means of earning points may be changed, and rules that establish a winner when play cannot continue may be enacted and amended or repealed.

113. A player always has the option to forfeit the game.

114. There must always be at least one mutable rule.

115. Rule changes that affect rules needed to allow or apply rule changes are as permissible as other rule changes. Even rule changes that amend or repeal their own authority are permissible. No rule change or type of move is impermissible solely on account of the self-reference or self-application of a rule.

116. Whatever is not prohibited or regulated by a rule is permitted and unregulated, with the sole exception of changing the rules, which is permitted only when a rule or set of rules explicitly or implicitly permits it.

Mutable Rules

201. Players shall alternate in clockwise order, taking one whole turn apiece. Turns may not be skipped or passed, and parts of turns may not be omitted. All players begin with zero points.

202. One turn consists of two parts in this order: (1) proposing one rule change and having it voted on, and (2) throwing one die once and adding the number of points on its face to one's score.

203. A rule change is adopted if and only if the vote is unanimous among the eligible voters. If this rule is not amended by the time everyone has had two turns, it automatically changes to require only a simple majority.

204. When rule changes can be adopted without unanimity, the players who vote against winning proposals shall receive 10 points each.

205. An adopted rule change takes effect at the moment of the completion of the vote.

206. When a proposed rule change is defeated, the player who proposed it loses 10 points.

207. Each player always has exactly one vote.

208. The winner is the first player to achieve 100 (positive) points.

209. At no time may there be more than twenty-five mutable rules.

210. Players may not conspire or consult on the making of future rule changes unless they are teammates.

211. If two or more mutable rules conflict with one another, or if two or more immutable rules conflict with one another, then the rule with the lowest number takes precedence.

212. If players disagree about the legality of a move or the interpretation or application of a rule, then the player preceding the one moving is to be the Judge and decide the question. Any player may request judgment, called "invoking judgment." (See sidebar, below.)

213. If the rules are changed so that further play is impossible, or if the legality of a move cannot be determined with finality, or if by the Judge's best reasoning, not overruled, a move appears equally legal and illegal, then the first player unable to complete a turn is the winner.

    This rule takes precedence over every other rule determining the winner.

Judge's Judgment

When Judgment has been invoked, the next player may not begin his or her turn without the consent of a majority of the other players.

The Judge's judgment may be overruled only by a unanimous vote of the other players taken before the next turn is begun. If a Judge's judgment is overruled, then the player preceding the Judge in the playing order becomes the new Judge for the question, and so on.

Unless a Judge is overruled, one Judge settles all questions arising from the game until the next turn is begun, including questions as to his or her own legitimacy and jurisdiction as Judge.

New Judges are not bound by the decisions of old Judges. New Judges may, however, settle only those questions on which the players currently disagree and that affect the completion of the turn in which Judgment was invoked. All decisions by Judges shall be in accordance with all the rules then in effect; but when the rules are silent, inconsistent, or unclear on the point at issue, then the Judge shall consider game custom and the spirit of the game before applying other standards.

Chapter Nine

VICTORIAN PARLOR GAMES

When we think of the Victorians, we think of, let's see . . . sexual repression, covered piano legs, imperialism, and maybe some architecture in Newport that we can't afford. But we don't necessarily think of romps through the parlor, stolen kisses . . . or games that instruct you to bury your face in a lady's lap.

Yes, that one made me do a double-take too, but it turns out that very repressive cultural mores are particularly fertile ground for games. Heidi Julavits, writing about Victorian parlor games in *The New York Times,* said, "These games are compelling precisely because they allow people to pop their psychic corsets and indulge their rowdy inner selves." Nowadays, we're certainly less repressed than the Victorians—see *Girls Gone Wild, Celebrity Rehab,* or any number of lascivious governors for evidence—but for us ordinary folks, the demands of jobs and kids can leave us more than a little uptight. Sometimes we need a reminder of just how silly we can be— and that's what this chapter is for.

What's notable about these particular games is how they function as a kind of Rorschach test for the players. Because the instructions in the old books are fairly short, we can imagine that the flavor of each game varied with the guest list. In French Rhymes, for example, players compose poems using a list of words generated by the group— and if the group is collectively looking to rip its psychic bodice, that's obviously going to be revealed.

The Victorians were not so different from us, but they did have fewer options for an evening's amusement. Before the Internet, TV, radio, movies, phonographs, before *everything,* people relied on their own wits to amuse themselves. These days, bombarded with endless digital stimulation, we're looking for amusements that don't involve screens, plugging in, waiting for something to download, or composing a message in 140 characters. At heart, we want what the Victorians wanted: to get to know our friends better; to find new ways of looking at the world; to flirt in a goofy way. (See Compliments for the *ne plus ultra* of goofy flirting.)

A few Victorian games are still going strong, so I've included them in other chapters—Pictionary, for example, which used to be called Drawn Charades, is one of the most popular parlor games on the market today. Some Victorian-era games have even survived the leap from parlor to soundstage: Just a Minute! (in Right-Brain Games) is based on a British radio show, which in turn was based on a Victorian storytelling game called Impromptu. In this chapter you'll find those games that haven't been snapped up and marketed or used as fodder for comedy shows. Although largely forgotten, these games are still a lot of fun. I've weeded out the Victorian games that sound dated or are just plain dangerous—William Tell, for example—and selected those games that are the most fun, the most surprising, and the really quite racy.

Alphabet Minute

PLAYERS: 2–20

THE GEAR: Paper, pencils, hat.

The Game Plan

✖ Have everyone write a general topic of conversation, such as "great moments in NFL history" or "spectacular political blunders," on a slip of paper and place the topics in a hat. Use other slips of paper to create a pile of letter tiles. (Scrabble tiles may also be used for this game.)

✖ One person picks a topic from the hat and a letter from the pile. That player starts a conversation on the topic, beginning the first sentence with the letter on the slip of paper.

✖ If a group is playing, proceed clockwise—so Player A will speak a sentence beginning with that letter; Player B will immediately continue the conversation with a sentence starting with the *next* letter of the alphabet; Player C will respond to Player B with a sentence starting with the next letter, and so on, until the players have cycled completely through the alphabet. (Every player is competing with every other player.)

All the players must continue the conversation through the alphabet, ending back at the letter the group started with. Anyone who hesitates or doesn't follow the flow of the conversation (as judged by the other players), or starts a sentence with the incorrect letter, is out. The challenge for the group is to make a single topic last through twenty-six letters.

In a game played over Sunday brunch with a few friends, the letter picked was *Z* and the topic was "famous pets." We sipped mimosas and conversed like this:

"Zeus did not have any pets."

"Abe Lincoln had a really famous pet, but I can't remember the name of it."

"Benny the chicken."

"Correction: The chicken's name was Mike."

The fifth player couldn't come up with a sentence beginning with *D* within a second or two, so she was out, and the person to her left had to quickly think of a sentence beginning with D. (So if the person before you stumbles and is out, you have to be quick to come up with a sentence beginning with her letter.)

Winning

Once there are two people left, they go back and forth until one of them falters. The remaining person is the winner. If you want to play a noncompetitive version, don't eliminate anyone, just keep playing until the group has cycled through the alphabet. Then switch topics and start again.

Great Literary Moments in Gaming

In Jane Austen's *Emma,* Frank Churchill uses the game Alphabets to communicate with his secret paramour, Jane Fairfax. Emma has written the alphabet on small slips of paper—a kind of early version of Scrabble tiles. In the game, a player makes a word with the slips of paper, then rearranges the letters, and passes the jumble of letters to another player to figure out the original word. Frank creates the word "blunder" as an apology to Jane for a mistake he's made.

PARTY RECIPE

Dark and Stormy

Ginger beer was a popular soft drink in Victorian times, but it's even better with rum.   SERVES 4

INGREDIENTS

8 ounces of rum	Lime juice (optional)
4 12-ounce bottles of ginger beer	Lime slices, for garnish

Pour two ounces of rum over ice in highball glasses and top off with ginger beer. Add a splash of lime juice and garnish with a slice of lime.

Compliments

Victorians were really good at flowery, yet sincere, compliments, *my dearest reader whose eyes are the color of autumn,* but it seems like a lost practice these days. This game marks the comeback of the elaborate compliment. Depending on the crowd, the game can be sincere or irreverent, ironic, and ultimately really funny. (The great turn-of-the-century comic strip *Alphonse and Gaston* centered around two guys who did nothing but compliment each other, competing to give the other the most extravagant praise, to the point that they ignored the house burning down in the background. So there's a precedent for funny, competitive compliments.)

Compliments could also be interpreted as an elaborate courtship ritual because it allows you to openly praise some attractive member of your party. It goes beyond the standard, workaday compliments like "Hey, pretty dress" or "Your hair smells like a strawberry." How

sincere you are, of course, depends on what you want: You can aim to be silly, gun for a laugh, or, you know, just try to get laid. You can make someone feel wonderful: At a games party that my then-new boyfriend attended, he told me I was like a screen door because touching a screen door (he's from the South) means he's home. Reader, I married him.

PLAYERS: 3–20

The Game Plan

In a circle, seat ladies and gentlemen alternately. One lady says, "I should like to be [such and such]"—an animal, a piece of furniture, etc.

The gentleman to her right must find some resemblance between that object and the lady, voiced in some complimentary way. The more ridiculous or grotesque the thing the lady states, the more creative the gentleman must be to compliment her. So if the lady says, "I should like to be a rocking chair," the gentleman might respond, "Well, of course! That's because you're so inviting!"

Then the gentleman states what he'd like to be, and the lady on his right must compliment *him* in some elaborate way. The game continues until everyone has had a chance to compliment and be complimented.

Quotations

This is one of those games that was obviously created for a group of people who were not only well-educated, but educated similarly. In other words, a party of folks who would have all the *bon mots* of

Catullus on the tips of their tongues. In our loosier-goosier times, frames of reference might be more dissimilar or just more lowbrow. So rather than sticking to really famous quotes, like "Once more into the breach, dear friends," your group can mix in contemporary media snippets, from "I did not have sex with that woman!" to "Not that there's anything wrong with that!" The game should spark laughs and discussion—Does anyone else remember that episode of *Seinfeld?* Did you really think that Bill Clinton was feeling your pain or just your breasts?

PLAYERS: 4–10

THE GEAR: Paper, pencils.

The Game Plan

One person thinks of and recites a quotation. Everyone else writes down the name of the person to whom they attribute the quotation.

Let's say Joe stands up and says, "The only thing we have to fear is fear itself." The other players would write down "FDR" (if they knew it was FDR who said it) and "Joe" (just to keep straight which player has recited which quotation). Then Jane rises and says, "I'm not an athlete, I'm a baseball player." And the rest of the players would write down "John Kruk" (if they did know it was John Kruk) and "Jane." If a player doesn't have the faintest idea to whom to attribute the quote, he just takes his best guess. After everyone has recited, the players will reveal the source of their quotation. In some games—and this depends on the mix of quotes—a theme may emerge. If your crowd is literary, you may have a lot of "Call me Ishmael"; if they're a gang of politicos, you might have a bunch of "The ballot is stronger than the bullet."

Winning

Players "grade" their own papers; the person who has the greatest number of correct attributions wins a small prize, like a bunch of striped candy sticks you might find in a late-nineteenth-century sweet shop, or some orange Popsicles in honor of John Kruk (he loved them and even once insisted that a supply of them be included in his new contract).

If you'd like to make the game noncompetitive, scrap the writing down of your guesses and just ask everyone to recite a quotation. The other players guess at random. For people who don't excel at this kind of game, this is a good way to save face and still enjoy themselves.

Crambo (Version 1)

A game for the very verbal people in your circle of friends, Crambo makes players think on their feet and come up with a poem at a moment's notice. It's the "moment's notice" part of Crambo that makes it exciting: You've got to churn out a few lines of doggerel—or more than a few lines, if you can—that make a reasonable amount of sense and answer a particular question. The time pressure and the competition can turn out some doozies.

PLAYERS: 2–20, plus a leader.

THE GEAR: Slips of paper in two colors, pens, and a stopwatch.

The Game Plan

Each player writes a noun on one slip of paper and a question on another. (Use paper of different colors for the noun pile and the question pile.) The papers are returned to the leader and shuffled. Each player then receives one noun and one question. The players have five minutes to compose a rhyming poem that both answers the question and incorporates the word. The poems are then read out loud.

Winning

After all the poems are read, players vote for the best one. The winner gets a copy of Rudyard Kipling's collected poems.

▶▶ HOST TIP

The time limit, paradoxically, reduces the pressure. Anyone trying to compose a poem in five minutes or less is not going to do a great job. Still, this is a game for particularly word-oriented people. Mix in some card, guessing, improv, or storytelling games for the other guests. The goal, of course, is not to make anyone feel horrid for being a terrible poet, even if they know it.

PARTY RECIPE

Cucumber Sandwiches

Nothing is more dainty and Victorian than cucumber sandwiches at tea time. YIELD: 10 PIECES

INGREDIENTS

2 cucumbers	20 pieces thinly sliced
½ cup white wine	white bread with the
vinegar	crust cut off
1 stick butter	

1. Peel and thinly slice the cucumber. In a bowl, drizzle the cucumber slices with vinegar and let marinate for a half-hour or so. Drain the slices and pat dry with a paper towel.

2. Spread the butter lightly on the bread. Place a thin layer of cucumber between two slices of bread. Slice diagonally and serve with afternoon tea. Do *not* serve with Doritos.

Crambo (Version 2)

PLAYERS: 2–10

This game has rhyming in common with Crambo, but it's primarily a guessing game. One player thinks of a word, say, *gird,* and says, "I am thinking of a word that rhymes with *bird.*" Another player says, "Is it ridiculous?" And the first player needs to guess what he means and says, "No, it is not *absurd.*" This continues until either the first player is stumped, in which case the game starts over with the player who stumped him thinking of a word, or the right word is guessed, and the person who guessed correctly then takes a turn thinking of a word.

I recently played this on g-chat with my friend Melissa. She said, "I am thinking of a word that rhymes with *sad.*"

I said, "Is it a renamed and then un-renamed Russian city?"

"Yes, it is *Stalingrad.*"

That was a quick game. I guess we were more in tune with each other than I'd thought.

Then I took a turn as the clue-giver. I was thinking of the word *boat* and said, "I am thinking of a word that rhymes with *float.*"

Melissa: "Is it a weasel-like creature?" [long, long pause]

Leigh: "No, it is not a *goat*?"

Melissa: "A goat is nothing like a weasel. Think *Wind in the Willows.*"

Leigh: "*Trote*?"

Melissa: "*Trote* is not a word."

But I was stumped, because I couldn't come up with the word *stoat,* so she got to think of a new word. (Just FYI, weasels and stoats teamed up and took over Toad Hall in *The Wind in the Willows,* a novel really all about Victorian virtues.)

Winning

If you're stumped, you lose.

▶▶ IF YOU LIKE THIS GAME . . . try Botticelli on page 42, another two-way guessing game.

Acting Rhymes

Acting Rhymes is like Crambo, Version 2, but with pantomime. Instead of giving verbal clues, you act out the word you're thinking of. Your friends will twist about, pretending to be spaghetti, hoping the other team will say, "Yes, it is *noodle.*"

PLAYERS: 4–10

The Game Plan

Divide the players into two teams. One team (Team A) leaves the room and the other (Team B) decides on a word—let's say it's *lair.* Team A returns and Team B reports that they have come up with a word that rhymes with *air.* Team A consults and pantomimes some word that rhymes with *air,* like *square.* Team B, guessing that they are miming *square,* says, "No, it is not *square.*" The guessing continues until the word *lair* is reached or one of the teams is stumped. Then send the other team out of the room.

Consequences

aka How They Met

Mad Libs, those notepads of blank-ridden stories in which you fill in parts of speech to spin a nonsensical tale, clearly descends from this game. Elements of a short story are written separately by the members of a group—a paper with headings to be filled in is passed and a zany story is constructed.

This game was adapted by the surrealists in the early twentieth century and turned into a drawing game called Exquisite Corpse (see page 125). It's curious that the Victorians and the surrealists hit upon the same activity—a game that seems rather bland on the face of it, but reveals the currents of subconscious thought among your friends as you play.

PLAYERS: 4–20

THE GEAR: Paper, pencils.

The Game Plan

Give a piece of paper to each player and instruct everyone to write *a woman's name* (any name, famous or not) on the top. Once they have done so, they fold the paper over so that the woman's name is not visible and pass the paper to their right. The next player writes down *a man's name,* folds the paper over, and passes it to his right. The next player writes down *a place of meeting,* folds the paper, and again passes it to his right. The next player writes down *what he said,* folds, and passes. The next player writes down *what she said;* the player after that writes *what the world said*. The final player writes *the consequences*. Everyone passes their papers to the hostess.

The hostess reads the little seven-line "stories" aloud to the group. Of course, you may want to choose different headings to fill in, and the results will be as ridiculous or naughty as your party wishes.

I played at a dinner party once, right after we had played a rousing game of Dudo (see page 204). Nearly every person filled in "Dudo!" for the *what he said* and *what she said* blanks—except for one person, who, totally randomly, wrote, "You know what's a really hard song to play on Guitar Hero?"

The *woman's name* and the *man's name* were all people we knew and were obviously people we wanted to poke a little fun at. The whole exercise took a total of five minutes after dinner, and my friend Alexis said it was the perfect post-coffee amusement, like a tiny, delicious square of dark chocolate.

Example from Victorian-Era Parlor Games Book:

Lydia Pinkham

and John Sullivan

Met in London

He said: "How wonderful!"

She said: "It must be true!"

The world said: "I told you so!"

The consequences were: They were very happy.

Throwing Light

Throwing Light is one of my favorite old-fashioned games, because the punishment for making a mistake is to sit with a handkerchief over one's head, which, one presumes, must have been the height of silliness to the Victorians. It's a pretty difficult game, so don't be too stingy with your clues and hints, and feel free to reveal the answer if the questions are going on too long.

PLAYERS: 3–20

The Game Plan

Two people decide on a word with more than one meaning and begin a conversation calculated to shed light on it. The other players try to guess. If someone thinks he has it, he may join in the conversation, making remarks that will indicate to the two leaders that he's discovered the secret. If they think he doesn't know it, they'll question him in a whisper. If he's right, he joins in the conversation. If he's wrong, he must sit with a handkerchief over his head until he figures it out.

If you're playing with only three people, two people are in on the secret and the third must try to guess.

My husband, Fran, and I visited friends in the south of France one particularly chilly April. As the fire in the stone hearth of the dining room crackled, Camilla, our hostess, prepared a dinner of duck magret, fingerling potatoes, and asparagus. Norval, our host, played Throwing Light with Fran and me while the cat, Sophie, snored in Camilla's chair. It was Norval and Fran against me, with Camilla occasionally contributing from the kitchen.

Norval and Fran secretly decided on *rifle*. (Rifle, the gun, and rifle, the verb, as in, "to rifle through someone's stuff.")

Norval: "Well, Fran, how do you feel about this word?"

Fran: "I sure like to do it to other people, but I don't like it done to me" (meaning, he likes to rifle through people's stuff but doesn't want his stuff rifled through).

Me: "Tickling. You like to tickle, but not be tickled."

Fran: "No. Norval, what are your thoughts on this word?"

Norval: "I like to shoot it."

Me: "Ducks. And Fran likes to duck under people, but doesn't like people to duck under him."

Fran: "That doesn't make sense."

Me: "Guns. You shoot guns, and you gun for something."

Fran: "Still not making sense."

Camilla: "Rifle. You shoot a rifle, and Fran likes to rifle through things."

Everyone: "Dinner! Yay!"

French Rhymes

Similar to **Crambo,** French Rhymes requires players to compose an impromptu poem incorporating a certain number of words.

PLAYERS: 2–10

THE GEAR: Paper, pencils, and timer.

The Game Plan

Each person writes down two words that rhyme. The slips are collected and the pairs read aloud; players should jot down all the words. Everyone then has five minutes to compose a poem incorporating all the rhyming words.

Below is a poem that resulted from a game I played poolside with a few friends. We lolled under an umbrella, discreetly sipped our G&T's, and composed our poems. The one below came from a friend who had spent a miserable week struggling to potty train his child. Maybe this poem exhibited wishful thinking.

The words: dinner, winner, be, tea, subtract, act, drenching, quenching, skip, trip, dread, bed, set, wet.

A poem:
Little Caleb had problems in bed
And viewed the nighttime with dread.
What could it be?
Too much water or tea?
He decided to act:
From his evening he'd subtract
Any fluids, that is, stuff that's wet.
An alarm for midnight he'd set
And wake for a trip
To the loo—and hopefully skip
The nightly drenching
His bed got due to quenching
His thirst after dinner.
This plan was a winner.

Fine, no one's going to be nominated for poet laureate. But the different results from the same few rhyming words often reveal something from the subconscious of the poet, just like what happened all the time with Coleridge, Wordsworth, and those other dudes.

Squeak, Piggy, Squeak

Squeak, Piggy, Squeak *could* be an icebreaker—but your pals would have to be a pretty friendly sort, as it involves crawling all over the other party guests. So reserve this one for a group where everyone knows one another well.

Squeak, Piggy, Squeak is one of those games you read about in crumbly old books called things like *Wholesome Activities for Young Ladies.* But as you cast your eye over the description, you do a double-take because it seems rather, well, *racy*—especially for the Victorians. Really, when was the last time you got to sit in someone's lap?

PLAYERS: 6–12

The Game Plan

All players sit cross-legged in a circle on the floor. One player is selected to be the "Farmer." He is blindfolded and spun around in the center of the circle until he is sufficiently disoriented. He then crawls, dizzy and blind, toward the edge of the circle until he can establish himself on someone's lap. That person must squeak—or make some kind of barnyard noise—continuously until the Farmer is able to guess the identity of the person on whose lap he is sitting. Of course, if he *likes* where he's sitting, he might take his time guessing the right answer.

The Ant and the Cricket

The Ant and the Cricket is essentially a guessing game—but *you're* trying to guess what the *other* players will guess before they guess it—and so remain in the position of the "Cricket," or the leader.

PLAYERS: 4–10

The Game Plan

- Draw straws to choose a Cricket. The rest of the players are Ants.

- The Cricket thinks of a category and an example of that category. Let's say he's thinking of "salty snack foods," and his example is "pretzel." He jots down "pretzel" on a piece of paper, which he keeps hidden from the Ants. He then says, "Oh, Ants, I am so hungry—can you suggest a salty snack food?"

- Each Ant, in turn, must name a salty snack food: potato chips, cheese puffs, popcorn, etc. If an Ant names what the Cricket has written down—pretzels—that Ant wins and immediately becomes the Cricket for a new round.

- If no Ant succeeds, the Cricket remains the Cricket for the next round.

With each round, the category and the example changes. A conservative strategy for the Cricket is to choose an obscure example of the category—like *edamame* for salty snack foods. But the Cricket might find that the Ants may be pretty good at coming up with obscure examples—and so the Cricket might try to psych out the Ants by choosing a very *obvious* example of that category. Let's say the category is "'80s fashion missteps." "Parachute pants" would be a pretty obvious answer, and the Cricket might jot that down, gambling that the Ants will all be saying, "Members Only jackets, moon boots, asymmetrical haircuts," etc.

For categories that are subjective, like "fashion missteps" or "political gaffes," there might be a certain amount of argument (*Were* parachute pants a misstep? Or were they a serious contribution to the sartorial world?). If a debate threatens to derail the game, appoint an impartial judge to settle disputes.

‖‖

Alphabetical Quotations

PLAYERS: 2–40

You've got to rack your brain for just about anything noteworthy anyone's ever said in this game. Two teams or people compete to come up with quotations or aphorisms—and what's even more difficult, players have to speak them in alphabetical order by the first word of the quote. This is another game, like Quotations on page 156, that presumes that your players weren't sleeping through history and literature classes and have a good memory for this kind of thing: In an actual Victorian games book describing Alphabetical Quotations, Person A

begins by saying, "Absence of occupation is not rest / A mind quite vacant, is a mind distrest." Person B counters with, "But evil is wrought by want of thought / As well as want of heart."

If your knowledge of famous quotations isn't terribly broad, you can substitute lines from movies or books. If playing competitively won't work for your group, you can just try coming up with alphabetical quotes or sayings as a group.

The Game Plan

You might start with "All's fair in love and war." The second person or team then comes up with a quotation that begins with *B:* "Bankers will lend you money only if you can prove you don't need it," and so on. The first team or person to delay more than thirty seconds thinking of an aphorism or quotation is eliminated from the game; play continues until only one person is left. In a noncompetitive game, players can just chime in when they've thought of an appropriate quote.

How pithy can you be under pressure? Can you think of something for, say, the letter *Q?* Try this one: "Quotation, *n:* The act of repeating erroneously the words of another." —Ambrose Bierce

In a recent, noncompetitive game on a long car trip, we started with *P:*

"Pride goeth before a fall."

"Quitters never win, and winners never quit."

> **▸▸STEALTH STRATEGY ◂**
>
> Think ahead. Even when you're only at *C,* dredge up some quotes beginning with *M* or *N:* "Marry in haste, repent at leisure," and "Neither a borrower nor a lender be."

"Recession is when your neighbor loses his job. Depression is when you lose yours."

"Speak softly and carry a big stick."

"There is no 'I' in 'team.'"

"United we stand, divided we fall."

. . . and so on. Going through the alphabet kept us busy for about forty minutes (with some significant, thought-filled pauses) of a three-hour car trip. Not bad.

Traveling Alphabet

PLAYERS: 2–6

Many Victorian games appear in books geared for adults but are actually great for the whole family. Traveling Alphabet can keep both adults and kids occupied for rather long stretches of freeway. (Victorians, sadly, didn't live long enough to experience the joys of the open road, with its endless Ramada Inns and Stuckey's.)

Player 1 mentions the name of some city, beginning with *A,* and asks his neighbor what he should do there. The neighbor must make an answer in which all nouns and verbs begin with *A.* For example, in Amsterdam, you will "admire all apples." That player then names a city beginning with *B,* say, Baltimore, and asks the next player what he will do there. And the answer might be "berate bold bagladies." If a player hesitates (what counts as "hesitation" can be defined by the group, but a good general rule is that more than three seconds is too long), he's out. This game, like French Rhymes, can be revealing:

Players won't necessarily take that critical moment to *think* before a sentence flies out of their mouths because they are under time pressure. And so you might hear your crush say: "In London, loll with Lotte Lenya lookalikes." So, if you're rather small and funny-looking, you're in like Flynn.

Given Words

Like a verbal treasure hunt, you have to find the "given" word—which should be a rather odd or unusual word—but it's buried among so many *other* odd or unusual words that it might not immediately leap out at you. In this game, your understanding of the verbal tics of your teammates will aid your quest.

PLAYERS: 3–20

The Game Plan

✕ Every player whispers a single word to his right-hand neighbor—the more difficult the word for introducing it into an ordinary sentence, the better.

✕ When everybody knows his word, one player begins by asking a question of his neighbor to the left. This question can be as simple—What did you have for dinner last night?—or as complicated—What's your opinion of the new tax-reform proposal?—as the players want them to be. The neighbor then must compose a sentence with the given word, as adroitly as possible, to avoid detection by his interrogator. He is allowed one sentence to answer the question.

✖ The player who asked the question then guesses which word was the given word. If he guesses right, he gets a point. If he doesn't, the other player gets a point.

✖ After everyone has had a chance to ask a question and answer one, all the players who have garnered points are runners-up; if anyone has garnered two points, he is the winner. Ties may be broken in a run-off if winners do not wish to share the glory.

Suppose the word given is *idiosyncrasy,* and that the person questioning asks, "Do you like to play games?" A suitable reply would be: "When hurricanes howl and icicles form, I enjoy games like this; but it is an idiosyncrasy of mine not to rapturously admire out-of-door sports with the thermometer at ninety in the shade."

By using several other equally unnecessary words for an ordinary reply to the question, one may successfully conceal the real word. If you know the person who has whispered the given word to the player, it might help you in guessing which word is the right one.

> **STEALTH STRATEGY**
>
> Sometimes simple words, like *dot* or *frock,* can be the hardest to pick out.

The Storyteller

Remember *Little Women*? Wasn't that just about the best book you ever read? If you're like me, you read it about a thousand times—and maybe wished you had as many sisters and beaus and fun times as

the March girls. Remember when the girls and Laurie and Mr. Brooke and Laurie's guests from England (the Vaughns) go on a picnic? Well, they play The Storyteller! (They also play Croquet, and one of the Vaughn boys cheats and nudges the ball with his foot, but we'll save that story for the Outdoor Games chapter.) The Storyteller is like Consequences (page 159) in that you're creating a story collectively.

PLAYERS: 2–20

The Game Plan

One person begins a story, and just as he has told enough to intrigue his listeners, he points to another member of the group, who must continue the tale without pause for thought. No hesitations allowed, or you're eliminated from the game! Since you can't stop and think, the twists and turns of the story need to fly out of your mouth—with frequently absurd results.

The game continues until everyone in the group has had a chance to contribute to the story. Think of this game the next time you're around a campfire at night—especially if the story you're weaving is a ghostly one.

Let's say you're on a camping trip in the Catskills, and someone begins a story:

"Not many people know that the old millhouse is haunted. Yes, it's true, it's haunted by the ghost of . . .

"Millicent! An old woman who cleaned there and kept the place in order. She went missing in the late 1950s—the last person to see her said she was headed down . . .

"Route 112, dragging an old wagon wheel. Why a wagon wheel, you ask? It *is* a little strange, given that people were certainly not using wagons for transportation in the 1950s in New York. Well, she was dragging a wagon wheel because . . .

"Everyone knows you have to remove the wheel and bring it with you after you chain up the wagon, or people will steal it. And Millicent was certainly still using her wagon to get around in the 1950s—in fact, the dizzying pace of progress had bothered her for some time, bothered her enough to actually try to do something about it. Which is why . . .

"She'd hatched a plan to turn the old millhouse back into a working mill. There was just one opponent to the project."

And so on. A story, some marshmallows—what's better on a fall night under the stars?

Vowels

The game Vowels seems to be based on something rather nit-picky: You try to compose a sentence without using a particular vowel, and if you trip up, you've lost. Though the aim of the game is to avoid a forbidden letter, its point is also in *what you say*. The fun of this game lies in the ingenuity of the players: You're trying to adhere to the rules (avoid a certain vowel) but also tell an interesting story.

One day last summer, I'd planned a games party for what was supposed to be a rather crummy beach day. Well, the weather was unexpectedly gorgeous, and by 11 A.M. the cancellations were rolling in. In order to fill out the guest list, my friend Simon brought his parents, who were visiting from out of town. We also pressed our odd, recalcitrant neighbor—a man who apparently feels

that boxer shorts are perfectly acceptable lawn-mowing attire—into service as well. I confess I felt a tremor of misgiving at this mismatched crew—Would everyone like everyone else? Would there be anything to talk about? I read out the rules, we started a game of Vowels . . . and it was great. People avoided the vowels mostly (there were some slip-ups and a bunch of *gotcha*s), but in the course of composing sentences with no *a*, for example, we learned about Simon's mom's defection from Russia, Simon's dad's work as a professor of economics, and the neighbor's model-train hobby. (Not being able to say "train," he managed to get out "the thing which runs on two lines with ties in between.") So the moral of the story? Include a mix of people at your event, people of all ages and walks of life, and people whose stories you don't already know. The results will be ten times more fun than if all your guests went to Virginia Tech, have 2.3 kids, and are "consultants."

PLAYERS: 2–20

The Game Plan

Each player must answer five questions posed by different members of the party—without using words containing certain vowels designated by the questioners. So the first questioner might say to the questioned, "Why did you come here tonight? Answer without *a*." And the answer might be, "For fun." And the next questioner might say, "What are your plans for Friday night? Answer without *e*." The answer could be "I'm going bowling!" and so forth, until someone slips up or hesitates. If they do, they're eliminated from the game; the other players continue until all but one has been eliminated. (If you don't want to cut people out of the game, assign a point every time someone slips up; the first person to get to five loses, and a new game begins.)

In our game, the questions got progressively more personal—Masha's defection, for example—and therefore much more interesting. Again, in games like these, everything depends on the players. The questioners in particular have to ask probing questions without being disrespectful or too intrusive; if you sense that someone is uncomfortable, back off. But in general, remember that most people *like* to talk about themselves, and almost everyone has a zany story or two up their sleeve. It just takes some coaxing.

So don't be afraid to ask leading questions and pay attention to where the stories are going. And when you're answering the questions, don't worry too much about the rules: If you're only coming up with monosyllabic "correct" answers, the game might get a little boring. Let your mind skip

A Few Ideas to Get You Started

If you are concerned that conversation might flag, try *The Book of Questions* by Gregory Stock, Ph.D., for interesting topics of discussion. Here are some fun ones:

"When was the last time you stole something?"

"If you knew there would be a nuclear war in one week, what would you do?"

"You are given a million dollars to donate anonymously to charity or to a stranger. How would you dispose of it?"

a little ahead of your mouth—try to avoid the vowels, but also try to answer the questions in a way that will let your fellow guests get to know one another.

The Cushion Dance

Let's say you were the kind of child who liked to play tag for the sheer joy of grabbing members of the opposite sex and *wrestling them to the ground*. Well, it turns out there were people who liked to do this in Victorian times, too, and they even made a weird little game out of it. Kind of like those "Oops, I fell on you! And now we're kissing!" moments in crummy romantic comedies.

PLAYERS: 4–8

THE GEAR: A hassock or cushioned footrest.

The Game Plan

Place a hassock in the middle of the floor. Divide the players into two teams. Team members join hands in a line; then the people at the ends of the line join hands with ends of the other team's line. This will form a rough circle around the hassock, but with one team mostly on one side and the other team mostly on the other. The two teams, facing each other and joined on the ends, begin by dancing around the hassock three times—everyone counting together, "One, two, three." After the third round, each side will try to force the other side forward by leaning backward and pulling (still linked at the hands), so as to make one member of that team touch the hassock. The first person to touch the hassock loses the game for her team.

The Cushion Dance is essentially a group wrestling game—a trial of strength and flexibility and team work—but also racy and intimate for people who don't know one another. Think of all the opportunities for accidentally falling on someone!

Hot Cockles

PLAYERS: 6–20

Okay, we've saved the weirdest and raciest game for last. The salient feature of Hot Cockles is that a gentleman *kneels in front of a lady and hides his face in her lap*—now here's a game I can get on board with—while the other players, one by one, slap his hand, which is resting palm-up on his back. With each slap, he must guess who of the other players has administered the slap.

Once he has guessed correctly, he may get up, and the game continues with another gentleman and lady. This is the entire game. Of course, if the gentleman *likes* where he is, he may choose to deliberately guess wrong, netting himself a few extra moments warming the cockles of the lucky lass.

We've included this game primarily as a point of historical interest about the Victorians: They were sexier than we think. When I first read about Hot Cockles, I imagined young Victorian ladies saying innocently, "Anyone want to play a game? I know a really fun game . . ."

A Victorian-era writer says of Hot Cockles, "The origin of the title of this game is lost in the mists of antiquity," but I think we can guess. I mean, why *wouldn't* her cockles be hot?

Chapter Ten

HOLIDAY GAMES

H olidays are supposed to be a time for celebration, reflection, and family. Too often, though, they can feel like a forced march on a tight schedule. Planes must be caught, presents bought, dietary restrictions accommodated . . . and yet somehow, *within* the frenzy of gift-wrapping and cleaning and picking up people at the station, a lot of downtime creeps in. You find yourself plopped on the couch, clutching a drink, locked in a staring contest with your silent aunt. You feign interest in your niece's fourth-grade play, a stage adaptation of *Breaking the Waves*. The strongest of us make small talk, arrange endive leaves, and toss a football with the kids. The weakest lurk in the yard palming cigarettes and nursing a bottle of rye.

It doesn't have to be this way. In this chapter, you'll find games that will fill that downtime with more fun than you thought possible. No more strained small talk while you're waiting for the Haggadah to be read or the lamb to be carved—try Passover Trivia Quiz! No more derisive questions about your "so-called career" while you're fending off an overly affectionate cat and a slobbery dog—try Grateful Guessing! These games offer quick, easy, indoor entertainment so that you can actually *enjoy* the holiday with your family.

Now, certainly not all holidays are family holidays—thank goodness. But those, too, have pitfalls: New Year's Day, for example, can tend toward, well, sodden self-reflection: Did you accomplish your goals this past year? Will you in the coming year? The best New Year's Day I've had was spent playing Resolutions, a two-part game that took us from a late-morning brunch to late-afternoon coffee. The game yanked me from a kind of maudlin (and hungover) feeling of "What am I doing with my life?" to a

focus on friends and *their* stories and goals and accomplishments. It was a shared feeling of beginning the year together, in good company, with people who were also "taking stock."

And, of course, there's Valentine's Day—the anxieties around February fourteenth are well documented: Are you single? Good luck getting through the fourteenth without a twinge about your status. Coupled up? The sheer oppressive focus on romantic love can give you a moment's pause—are you really, really, as *in love* as you can possibly be? Well, did you at least buy her a diamond tennis bracelet? The best way to approach V-Day is with a game to make you laugh—because God knows you're going to need it. Try a haiku contest or a story slam and welcome the day with humor rather than dread.

This chapter is arranged by month, with a specific game assigned to a holiday. Of course, feel free to mix and match—Taste of America would work as well on Easter as it would in July, and a costume party is terribly fun on any day of the year.

Let's start at the beginning: January 1.

JANUARY

Resolutions

We all make resolutions at New Year's. But what if you made resolutions for *other* people? Resolutions was created by Melissa Kirsch, the author of *The Girl's Guide to Absolutely Everything,* for a New Year's Day brunch in 2009. Six of us met at 11 A.M. at Balthazar, a restaurant in the heart of New York's Soho. Despite the air of hangovers and dissipation, the mood was festive and optimistic. As we worked our way through French toast and eggs and mimosas (hair of the dog) everyone wrote down an improving resolution on a slip of paper and dropped the slips in a sugar-packet caddy.

Each person then drew a slip from the caddy, taking care not to take his own. (Paper of different colors can prevent this, otherwise, just toss it back in and take another if you draw your own.) Everyone then read the resolution they'd drawn and promised to adhere to it for a year, no matter how bizarre. I drew one that read "Practice the art of listening." Another friend got "Every morning, as soon as I wake up, I will bend over and touch my toes ten times, then throw out my hands to the side, wiggle them in a 'jazz hands' motion, and shout 'It's Showtime.'"

Then, the person who wrote each resolution identified himself.

After we'd finished our meal, we went off to shop for a gift for the person who'd written our resolutions, based on the resolution *they* had received. So Bernie, who wrote "Practice the art of listening," which I drew, had drawn "I will include more music in my daily life."

So I dashed to the secondhand bookshop and got a beginner's book on music theory for him. (The price limit was $10 and we had an hour to shop before meeting again at three for a cup of coffee.)

All in all, a lovely way to shake off the old year and ring in the new.

PLAYERS: 4–50

THE GEAR: Slips of paper, pens.

Variation

Resolutions 2: Give everyone three slips of paper and have each person write down a resolution for himself or herself on each slip. These resolutions should be things that the player *does* actually want to work on—to practice yoga for twenty minutes a day, to call her mother once a week, to eat more spinach. (Warn players that these resolutions are going to be revealed to the group, so players shouldn't make any resolutions they don't want read aloud.)

Put the slips of paper in a hat and mix them up. Have a player draw a slip of paper, read it aloud, and guess who made the resolution. If he guesses correctly, he gets a point. If he's wrong, the player to his left guesses, and so on, until someone guesses correctly and gets the point. Then have another player draw a slip of paper and take a guess, until the hat is empty. The player with the most points wins. You think you know what your friends want to improve about themselves (and you probably think you could give suggestions about what they should improve), but you'll learn something new every time: that your straight-laced sister wants to start playing the bass and that your carnivorous dad is finally considering learning some vegan recipes.

Variation 2

Advice: This is a variation on Consequences (see page 159), where one thing is written on a piece of paper, which is then folded over and passed around to be added to by each player.

Seat guests in a circle. Give each player a sheet of paper and ask them to jot down a difficult problem they need help solving. These can range from "My kitchen sink keeps clogging" to "I always choose emotionally unavailable men."

Each player then passes his/her paper to the person on the right. That person reads the problem and writes a solution underneath it. Then have the players fold the paper so that the solution is hidden but the original problem is still visible. Pass the paper to the right again, and that person composes a solution to the problem, folds over the paper, and passes it again.

When the papers return to their original owners, have the players read aloud their problem and all the various solutions.

▶▶ **HOST TIP**

If players are familiar with one another's handwriting, have your guests type out their resolutions.

The Yankee Gift Swap, *Survivor*-Style

Ever heard of a Yankee Swap? It's generally played on New Year's Day and lets people unload the white-elephant gifts they got for Christmas or Hanukkah.

PLAYERS: 10–20

THE GEAR: Slips of paper, pencils, hat.

The Game Plan

For this variation, invite a bunch of people and tell them to bring a wrapped present; pile the presents on a table or in the middle of the room. Each player puts his name in a hat. The hostess randomly draws a name and calls it out. That player chooses a gift and unwraps it.

The hostess draws a second name; that player may either open a new gift or try to take the gift the first guest opened. If he wants to take the first guest's gift, he must make an argument (hopefully a funny argument; this is supposed to be a lighthearted game, not an organ-donor swap) about why he is more deserving of the gift. The first guest may then counter-argue. The rest of the group votes on who deserves it more; the winner gets the gift.

The hostess draws a third name; that person either opens a new gift or tries to take one of the already-opened gifts, again making an argument for why she's most deserving. The game continues until all the gifts are opened. One rule: If a player wins an argument three times as to whether she deserves a particular present, she can no longer be challenged for her gift.

▶▶ IF YOU LIKE THIS GAME . . . see Save Yourself, on page 143.

AMP IT UP

Launch a game of Mafia (see page 132 for the rules) with this twist: Every time someone is offed, they can choose and open a gift. The next person who's offed can choose and open a gift; if they like a gift better that was previously opened, they can offer to trade, but the current owner of that gift is under no obligation to do so.

FEBRUARY

NEW GAME!

Heartbreaker

When playing Heartbreaker, players must develop a strategy that involves elements of trust, backstabbing, and/or a mix of the two. Throughout the game, players will come together in pairs in front of a judge. This means that a player must simply approach someone else playing the game and ask him or her to "roll the dice." (BTW, Heartbreaker also makes an excellent icebreaker game.) By rolling the dice, they do one of two things: Find out if the other is the true love match, or break the other's heart.

PLAYERS: 10–150. You will also need non-playing "judges"—about one for every ten players.

THE GEAR: A scorecard for each player (photocopy the scorecard on page 174, and fold along center line to give it a front and back), a pair of dice for each judge, pencils.

Objective

To break the most hearts *and* find your true love.

Scorecards

Players are given a scorecard with three levels of heart temperatures, six hearts, and a place to note how many hearts they have broken.

- Any player that has all six of his hearts broken is eliminated from the game.

- Any player whose "core heart temperature" drops—meaning that he has crossed off all three of his "heart warmth" hearts—is frozen for seven minutes. After seven minutes, the player may then return to the game at full core temperature—he regains his three "heart warmth" hearts.

The Game Plan

- One player will ask another to roll the dice; these two players present themselves in front of a judge. (Since players have to roll the dice with as many other players as possible in order to play the game, it's unlikely—even impossible—that a player would be rejected.)

NOTE: In games of more than ten people, there will be more than one judge, so many couples will be playing at once.

- The judge gives them each a die. The judge counts to three. Exactly on three, each player either rolls his or her die or not.

- Possible outcomes:

  1. When both dice are rolled and the numbers are the same, the players are a "true love match." The two players should note on their cards that they have found a true love match.

  2. If one player rolls and the other does not, the player who rolled gets his heart broken. He must cross off one of his six hearts on his scorecard. The other player gains a point and should note it in the "hearts broken" section of his scorecard.

  3. When both dice are rolled and the numbers are different, there is no penalty and no point gain.

4. If no one rolls, both players lose a "core temperature" level and must cross off one of the three "heart warmth" hearts.

* Players then separate, find a new partner, and approach a judge again.

* Play continues for as long (roughly) as it takes for all players to meet up with every other player. If you're playing in a very large group and this isn't possible, set a time limit for half an hour.

* Announce the end of the game and have players turn in their cards. The host will announce the winner.

Winning

The player who has the most points (earned by breaking hearts) AND finds a true love or loves wins the game.

—contributed by Charley Miller (see page 80).

▶▶ **HOST TIP**

Let's say you are hosting a party for family (or attending a party for family) and you want to announce some big news, like you and your sweetie are engaged or expecting a baby. Rather than awkwardly clambering on a chair to get everyone's attention and then shouting the news across the cocktail hour, consider a more playful approach. Write a note saying, "Bob and I are engaged. Pass it on," and pass it discreetly to your neighbor under the table during dinner. Or whisper the news in a game of Telephone around the dinner table.

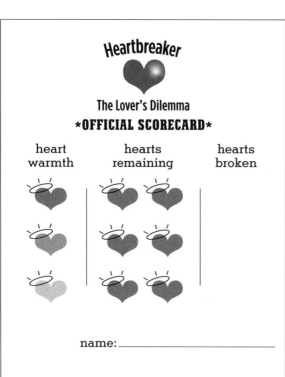

Heartbreaker

The Lover's Dilemma
OFFICIAL SCORECARD

heart warmth	hearts remaining	hearts broken

name: _____

Object of the Game:
The player who breaks the most hearts AND finds their true love wins the game.

The Lover's Dilemma:
Throughout the game, you can approach another player in front of a judge. There you will have two options:

1. <u>roll the dice</u> to find out if the other player is your true love (1 in 6 chance; no penalty for non-match).
2. <u>don't roll the dice</u> to break the other player's heart.

The Lover's Matrix:

	You: <u>True Love</u>	You: <u>Break Heart</u>
Opponent: <u>True Love</u>	When both dice are rolled: if they show the same number, then players are a true love match.	When you don't roll: opponent loses a heart, you get a point.
Opponent: <u>Break Heart</u>	When opponent doesn't roll: you lose a heart, opponent gets a point.	When no one rolls: both players lose a heart warmth level.

 If a player has all six hearts broken, she's eliminated.

 If a player loses his three heart warmth hearts, he is out of the game for seven minutes.

Valentine's Story Slam

Everyone knows that Valentine's Day can be really awful. Certainly it's not *always* awful—sometimes you're in a relationship with the perfect guy or gal, and you're far enough in that you're not anxious about blowing your nose in front of each other . . . but you're not *so* far in that Valentine's Day is just another night of DVDs and takeout. But how often does that happen? Point is, the chances of blissful happiness on any given February 14 are slim. Fortunately, the number of stories and poems that have been written about thwarted love, unrequited love, and love gone comically wrong are infinite and always entertaining. No matter how awful your worst date, someone else's was worse.

Here's where a Story Slam or poetry slam comes in handy. What's a Story Slam, you might ask? Well, it's an evening of competitive storytelling. Participants prepare a story on a particular theme—in this case, "the date from hell" or "she done me wrong"—and then tell the story to the audience. At the end, the assembled group votes for the best story or poem.

PLAYERS: 4–50 (no more than six storytellers; the rest can be audience).

The Game Plan

✖ For an at-home, noncompetitive Valentine's Day party, ask three of your most creative and funny friends to write a short story on the theme of the "worst date ever," to be read at a party on Valentine's Day. (You could invite *all* your guests to write something, but storytelling isn't everyone's forte; most people prefer to listen.) The stories should be short enough to be read in less than ten minutes.

✖ A perfect warm-up to a Valentine's Day slam are Valentine's Day haiku, for which the romantic-advice site BreakupGirl .net has long been sponsoring a yearly contest. Haiku are a form of Japanese poetry in which a deep universal truth is conveyed in three lines; the first line has five syllables, the second line has seven syllables, and the third line has five syllables. Haiku is a particularly succinct way to crystallize the moment when a romance turns sour—such as:

He corrected her
order. "Two gins and tonic."
Soon they would break up. —AMANDA GERSH

Or expressing the wistfulness of mistakes made:

So now you like girls?
I should not have taken you
to the Home Depot. —ASHER HUNG

✖ As everyone arrives, provide index cards and pens so guests can write their own haiku. (Those who are shy about their poetry skills can work in teams or sit the game out entirely—after all, "audience member" is the most important role in any kind of performance.) Give guests a half hour or so of mingling and poetry-composing and then ask them to hand in their haiku and take a seat. The host or hostess, who's also the emcee for the evening, will welcome everyone and, as a "first act" for the evening, read aloud the haiku she has collected. Here's another great one from BreakupGirl:

He looked fat, how fat,
like depressed fat or stressed fat?
Please, not happy fat. —DAPHNE UVILLER

✖ After everyone's had a chance to digest the poetic bon mots, take a moment to freshen drinks and then present the three main storytellers. The performance should take less than half an hour, leaving ample time for guests to mingle and maybe even meet someone new—someone they might want to go on a *good* date with. At the end, guests can vote on the best story, and you can award a prize—like a box of heart-shaped candies—or you can leave the game as a noncompetitive evening of fellowship and entertainment.

>>**STEALTH STRATEGY**
Download podcasts of the Moth Story Slam from iTunes to get an idea of what works and what doesn't in storytelling.

Variation

Have everyone at the party (everyone who wants to participate, that is) jot down their worst-date story on an index card; the size of the card will necessarily keep the stories short. Put all the stories in a hat and pass it around. At random, people pull out a story and read it aloud. After they're all read, guests vote for the best worst-date story. The winner gets dinner for two at a local romantic restaurant.

MARCH

Mardi Gras Costume Party and King Cake

Mardi Gras, the end of the festive season of Carnival, is the Tuesday before Ash Wednesday, which marks the beginning of Lent. It sometimes falls in February and sometimes in March, but whenever it comes, it's a much-needed party at the tail end of winter. Mardi Gras, or "Fat Tuesday," is the last blowout bash before the somber period of abstinence and denial that characterizes Lent. (If you've ever given up French fries or chocolate from Mardi Gras to Easter, you know how long those days can be.)

PLAYERS: 20–200

THE GEAR: Ingredients for the cake (opposite page), costumes, and booze!

The hallmarks of a Mardi Gras party are music, a parade, costumes, and food. If you're in New Orleans, you certainly don't need any help finding the festivities on Fat Tuesday, but for those of us in more northern, straight-laced climes, an at-home party is probably the only way to go. The host or hostess of the party is responsible for baking the "king cake," a round cake decorated with colored sugars. A small plastic baby (perhaps signifying the baby Jesus) is baked into the cake and the cake is cut into slices. Whoever is lucky enough to get the baby is King or Queen

PARTY RECIPE

Mardi Gras King Cake

SERVES ABOUT 20

FOR THE CAKE

2 packets active dry yeast	2 teaspoons salt
1/2 cup granulated sugar	1 teaspoon nutmeg
1 1/2 sticks unsalted butter, melted	1 teaspoon lemon zest
1 cup warm milk	vegetable oil, for greasing the bowl
5 large egg yolks, at room temperature	1 1-inch plastic baby Jesus doll (or a nut, like a pecan half)
4 1/2 cups bleached all-purpose flour	

FOR THE ICING

1 1/2 tablespoons butter, melted	1/2 teaspoon vanilla extract
2 cups confectioner's sugar, sifted	1/4 teaspoon salt
3 tablespoons milk, at room temperature	Purple, green, and gold food coloring

1. Combine the yeast and the sugar in the bowl of a stand mixer fitted with a beater blade. Add the melted butter and warm milk and beat at low speed for about a minute. With the mixer running, add the egg yolks and then beat for another minute at medium-low speed. Add the flour, salt, nutmeg, and lemon zest and beat until everything is mixed. Increase the speed to high and beat until the dough pulls away from the sides of the bowl.

2. Lightly oil a bowl with the vegetable oil. Using your hands, remove the dough from the mixer and form it into a smooth ball. Drop the dough in the bowl and turn it to oil all sides. Cover with plastic wrap and set aside in a warm place until it doubles in size, about two hours.

3. Line a cookie sheet with parchment paper.

4. Turn the dough out onto a lightly floured work surface and punch down until it's reduced in size by about half. Using your fingers, pat it out into a long roll. Twist the roll and form a ring, pinching the ends together. Insert the plastic doll from the bottom so that it is hidden by the dough. Slide onto the cookie sheet. Cover the ring with plastic wrap or a clean kitchen towel and place in a warm, draft-free place. Let the dough rise again until doubled in size, about 45 minutes.

5. Preheat the oven to 375°F.

6. Bake until golden brown, 25 to 30 minutes. Let cool completely.

Icing: Combine the ingredients and stir until smooth. Divide into three bowls and add a different food coloring to each. With a spatula, spread the icing, alternating colors, over the top of the cake.

Note: Alert your guests that the doll is in the cake so they can be mindful of this choking hazard.

Adapted from gumbopages.com.

for the day. Most importantly, this person is responsible for throwing the next party—so serving a king cake ensures that the good times will continue to roll.

As not many people in the United States have access to the traditional masks—or would even care to wear them—costumes have become more of a free-for-all. To encourage guests to assemble terrific get-ups, announce a competition for the best two costumes (one woman and one man) elected by secret ballot. For more themes for costume parties, check out the suggestions for Halloween parties on page 192.

Guests vote for best costume. No matter what, prizes make a party more fun. A few ideas for the costume winners:

- a Dr. John album

- a cookbook of traditional New Orleans food

- tickets to a jazz concert in your area

- Mardi Gras beads

- a skeleton charm for a charm bracelet

- a can of evaporated milk; attach a beignet recipe with a pretty ribbon

Have a Ball

Mardi Gras parties are costume parties—and frequently they're masked balls. The revels around Carnival (the period beginning on January 6 and ending with Lent) and Mardi Gras are designed to lower inhibitions (there's lots of alcohol, and since partygoers are masked, they are more likely to do more daring things . . .). The costumes traditionally were from a set of Venetian masks that revelers wear during Carnival.

MARCH/APRIL
Passover Trivia Quiz

A seder sometimes feels like a long obstacle course to the meal . . . and then, once you begin to eat, you're so hungry that you can't stop yourself from stuffing an entire leg of lamb in your mouth. And then, the food coma. So games played at a seder have to be mellow—like a nice, quiet trivia quiz, opposite page.

ANSWERS

1, c Congregation Mikve Israel was first established in 1651 in Curaçao, Netherlands Antilles.

2, a While traveling with a Major-League all-star team to Tokyo in the mid-1930s, Berg reportedly secretly took photographs later used in bombing raids. In 1943 he began working for the OSS.

3, b Earp and Masterston believed that "calm deliberation" will always win out over speed.

4, c Nisan (March–April, or Passover time) begins the civil calendar, the time when the first crops were harvested. The beginning of Elul, the month preceding the High Holidays, is the new year for tithing animals, a form of charity. Tu B'Shevat, the fifteenth day of Shevat, is the new year for trees.

5, a Shidukh encompasses the idea of peace and tranquility in a marital match.

6, c Although Fortas and Frankfurter were early Jewish appointees to the Supreme Court, Brandeis was the first. A crusader for social justice, he had become known as "the people's lawyer."

7, b In a true love story, Isidor Straus and his wife Ida were passengers on the *Titanic*. Ida was given a chance to board a lifeboat, but refused to be separated from her husband, and both drowned.

8, c *Fiddler on the Roof* was based on Sholem Aleichem's *Tevye and His Daughters*.

9, a According to Nimoy's autobiography, the priestly blessing performed by the Kohanim had fascinated him as a child.

10, False. In 1972, Sally Jane Priesand was ordained at the Plum Street Temple in Cincinnati. In 1935, Regina Jonas was the first female rabbi ordained in the world, in Berlin, Germany.

PASSOVER TRIVIA QUIZ

1. The oldest active Jewish congregation in the Americas is located in:
   a) New York City
   b) Santiago, Chile
   c) Curacao, Netherlands Antilles

2. Moe Berg, a Major-League baseball player for the Chicago White Sox, Cleveland Indians, Washington Senators, and Boston Red Sox, also enjoyed a career as
   a) a spy
   b) a rodeo clown
   c) a WWII fighter pilot

3. Jim Levy, a nineteenth-century Irish-Jewish gunslinger, was celebrated by the likes of Wyatt Earp and Bat Masterson for what quality?
   a) his quick draw
   b) his calm demeanor
   c) his obsessively well-cared-for guns

4. Besides Rosh Hashanah, there are how many other New Year celebrations?
   a) one
   b) two
   c) three

5. The Hebrew word *shidukh,* which means "marital match," has the Aramaic equivalent of *sheket,* which means what?
   a) quiet
   b) soul mate
   c) destiny

6. Who was the first Jew to be appointed to the U.S. Supreme Court?
   a. Abe Fortas
   b. Felix Frankfurter
   c. Louis Brandeis

7. How did Isidor Straus, one of the founders of Macy's, die?
   a. He was shot in the Battle of Gettysburg.
   b. He went down with the *Titanic.*
   c. He fell off a float in the Macy's parade.

8. Who wrote the original story upon which the musical *Fiddler on the Roof* was based?
   a. Isaac Bashevis Singer
   b. Dostoevsky
   c. Sholem Aleichem

9. Leonard Nimoy, who played Spock on *Star Trek,* based his famous Vulcan salute on what Jewish blessing?
   a. the priestly blessing of the Kohanim
   b. the blessing for the dwelling, performed during Sukkot
   c. the blessing for the donning of the *tallit* and the *tefillin*

10. True/False: The first female rabbi in the United States was ordained in 1985.

||||||||||||||||||||||||||||||||||||||||||||||||||||||||||||||||||||||||

Easter Egg Haggle

The absolutely most fun Easter Egg Hunt is a variation on Haggle (see page 136 for the "real" rules for Haggle, which you'll play with colored index cards rather than eggs). Invented by the late Sid Sackson, a renowned game designer, Haggle is an information-trading game. It relies on building on the information you have, wheedling information away from other people, and hopefully also preventing them from gleaning what you know.

Easter Egg Haggle is ideally played after a major Easter egg–dyeing session—let's say you spend the Saturday of Easter weekend having a kids' egg-dyeing party and use the eggs for an adults' Easter Egg Haggle party the night before the Sunday hunt.

PLAYERS: 15 (fewer if you are willing to amend the secret information), plus a nonplaying host/moderator. If you have more than 15 people, players may play in teams of two.

THE GEAR: 150 dyed eggs, 15 baskets, slips of paper, 15 envelopes, pens.

Objective

Players are given a basket of eggs at the outset, and they must haggle with the other players for the most valuable basket of eggs by the end of a certain time. What each egg (and combination of eggs) is worth, however, is unknown to the players at the beginning of the game—they must read their secret information sheets and trade with others to find out more.

Preparation

✄ You'll need twice as many Easter eggs of each color (yellow, blue, red, orange, and green) as there are players in the game. So for a game of fifteen people, the host needs thirty eggs of each color, or a total of 150 eggs. If dyeing such a large quantity of eggs is daunting, plastic eggs may be used instead—you can get a dozen for about $5 from Amazon or big-box stores.

✄ An Easter basket for each player or team.

✄ Information sheets: There are fifteen pieces of secret information (see sidebar, opposite page); the host must print or copy *two* slips of paper for each piece of secret information, for a total of *thirty* "secret information sheets."

✄ Before your guests arrive, mix up the eggs and place ten assorted eggs in each basket along with an envelope containing two "secret information sheets." (Make sure that duplicates are not placed in an envelope; each player should have two different pieces of secret information.) Have pens and paper available in case players want to make notes.

The Game Plan

As your guests arrive, hand them a basket. They then have the rest of the evening to "haggle," trading secret information sheets and eggs, to try to achieve the most valuable basket of eggs. As players obtain information, they'll want to gather other pieces of information and maybe acquire more of one color egg and dispose of another.

Scoring

At an appointed hour, say, midnight, the game is over. Players set their baskets in front of them for scoring, first taking out and setting aside any eggs they don't wish to count. Only thirteen eggs will count. The host then reads out the basic point values of each of the eggs (which can be deduced from the first three pieces of secret information):

yellow=1, blue = 2, red = 3, orange = 4, and green = 5. Players come up with a preliminary tally. Then the host reads out the rest of the information sheets, and players adjust their totals accordingly.

Winning

Highest score wins. Award the winner a top-of-the-line omelet pan.

Secret Information

1. Orange eggs have a basic value of 4 and are equal to the point value of one red egg plus one yellow egg.

2. Green eggs have the highest basic value and are equal to a red egg and a blue egg.

3. Blue eggs have a basic value twice that of yellow and half that of orange.

4. If a player has more than three green eggs, all of his green eggs lose their value.

5. A player can only score as many orange eggs as he has blue eggs.

6. If a player has five or more blue eggs, 10 points are deducted from every other player's score.

7. A set of three red eggs protects you from someone's set of five blue eggs.

8. The player with the most yellow eggs gets a bonus of the number of eggs squared (for example, if the most yellow eggs are five, the bonus is 25). If two or more players tie for yellow, they are eliminated and the bonus goes to the next highest.

9. At the end of the game, if a player hands in a basket containing seven or more eggs of the same color, he automatically loses.

10. Each set of five different colors gives a bonus of 10 points.

11. If a "pyramid" is handed in with no other eggs, the value of the hand is doubled. A pyramid consists of four eggs of one color, three eggs of a second color, two eggs of a third color, and one egg of a fourth color.

12. The player with the most red eggs doubles their value. In case of a tie, no player collects the extra value.

13. Each set of two yellow eggs doubles the value of one green egg.

14. Each set of three blue eggs quadruples the value of one orange egg.

15. No more than 13 eggs in a basket can be scored. If a player hands in a basket with, say, 15 eggs, the moderator will shut his eyes and remove two at random.

"Reverse" Easter Egg Hunt

This is a little like the garden-gnome subplot in the film *Amélie*. Remember how Amélie teases her father by sending photos of his garden gnome in exotic locations from around the world? Well, in this Easter egg hunt, rather than hiding the eggs in the garden, why don't you have your guests hide their eggs in oddball places around the neighborhood and document all the places the eggs have been?

PLAYERS: 8–50

THE GEAR: A digital camera and one Easter egg per team.

Preparation

Create a list of locations in your area where an Easter egg would be incongruous, like in the display at Dunkin' Donuts, on the dispatcher's desk at the local police precinct, or tucked in a bale of hay at the stables—anywhere a brightly colored egg would stand out as a cheerful, silly addition.

The Game Plan

Divide your guests into small teams of two to six players each (any larger means that the group will have trouble moving easily through the town or city). Give each team a list of about five locales, keeping them about even in terms of level of difficulty and distance covered.

Players then have to place their egg in each of the places on the list and photograph their "installations."

First group back with a complete set of photos wins. Have a computer set up to create a slideshow of the photographs. Award the winners a copy of *Bitter with Baggage Seeks Same,* a collection of photographs of chicks in compromising positions.

PARTY RECIPE

Angel Biscuits

MAKES 20 BISCUITS

2 tablespoons warm water	2 sticks unsalted butter, cold
2 teaspoons yeast	2 cups buttermilk
¼ cup of sugar plus one pinch of sugar	1 large beaten egg + 1 tablespoon water for an egg wash
5 cups all-purpose self-rising flour, sifted	

1. In a small bowl, mix together warm water, yeast, and the pinch of sugar. Let sit for about five minutes, or until the yeast expands into a spongy mass.

2. In a separate bowl, combine the sugar and flour. Cut in butter and mix with two knives until the dough resembles small peas. Add buttermilk and mix; then add the yeast mixture and stir. Scrape the dough onto a floury surface and knead until you have a round moist mass (the less you handle the dough the better, so knead only a few times). Plop the dough back into the bowl, cover with plastic wrap, and refrigerate overnight.

3. In the morning, preheat the oven to 400°F. Set the dough on a floury surface and knead, again. With a rolling pin or a clean, empty wine bottle, roll to about ⅓ of an inch thick. Cut rounds of biscuit with a cookie cutter or a glass and place on greased cookie sheets. Brush the tops with the egg wash. Bake 11 to 12 minutes or until golden brown. Serve warm.

Easter Keg Hunt

PLAYERS: 20–100

THE GEAR: Beer in kegs, hidden around town.

Easter brunches usually feature mimosas, but after church and the family meal, you might need a nice big glass of beer. With a few like-minded pals, organize a Scavenger Hunt that will get people running around your town looking for clues. You can either organize a kind of pub crawl, in which kegs are hidden in various locations around your city and players get points (and beers!) for finding each one, or you can do a more standard Puzzle Scavenger Hunt in which players are rewarded with one keg and a party at the very end. See page 326 for more info on setting up a great Scavenger Hunt.

MAY/JUNE

This Is Your Life Trivia

Celebrating Mother's and Father's Day can feel like going through the motions: the brunch, the golf sweater, the last-minute 1-800-Flowers. Oh, and in this day and age, paying attention to all the mothers and fathers in your life (the mother, stepmother, mother-in-law, stepmother-in-law, your sister who's just had her first baby . . .) can be overwhelming. This Is Your Life Trivia makes a game out of that big brunch or dinner or party—and you can have multiple honorees.

PLAYERS: As many as are at your brunch or dinner.

Preparation

Gather reference books or websites from as far back as the year your parent was born; in addition, interview various family members, especially those of your parents' generation.

The Game Plan

Use the information to make up trivia questions for the guest of honor (and others). Pepper in family-specific trivia, like what people did for their first dates or what Great-Grandpa Joe really thought of *Brown v. Board of Education*. Some questions might be:

- What song was the number-one Billboard hit the year Mom met Dad?

- What was the bestselling car the year Mom graduated from college?

- Where did Mom and Dad meet?

- In the first presidential election after they were married, who did Mom vote for?

- What food did Mom make for a picnic that Dad said was the best he'd ever had?

- What was the name of the church where Mom and Dad were married?

- When Mom was a little girl, what did she want to be when she grew up?

- What was Dad's job the first year after he and Mom were married?

Award a point for each correct answer (obviously, the guest(s) of honor will have a much better chance of getting the questions right). The conversation sparked should be the real treat—like when your five-year-old niece asks Grandma to tell her what it was that she made for that picnic with Grandpa, and Grandma explains a delicacy called angel biscuits.

‖‖‖

Human Battleships

From the name, you may have surmised that Human Battleships is not a game for the faint of heart. Remember the Milton Bradley board game with tiny gray plastic boats, where you'd sit strategizing in the comfort of your kitchen to sink your opponent's battleships? Substitute you for the boat, and now we're cooking with oil, pal. We're taking this battle outside. We're talking balloon bombs and intricate subterfuge. Your clothes will get wet. Your best-laid plans will go rapidly awry. Bring your A-game. No sissies allowed.

PLAYERS: 4–30, depending on the length of your windbreak.

THE GEAR: An opaque beach windbreak (a large cloth meant to block the wind; in a pinch you can use a large cloth tied to two poles). 3–5 water balloons per person.

Preparation

Set up the windbreak on a less-trafficked area of a beach or park and fill your water balloons. Enlist help for these tasks.

The Game Plan

✖ Divide your players into two even teams— you'll need as many people on each team as can hide behind the windbreak.

✖ Give each player her water balloons. Each team seats their members on one side of the windbreak. Players may sit anywhere as long as they are not visible to the other team. Once seated, either cross-legged or kneeling, they may not move. If you have players who will not play "on their honor," appoint a referee to watch from the sidelines.

✖ Teams take turns throwing "bombs" over the windbreak. One player, from a seated position, tosses his bomb over the windbreak with the aim of hitting an opponent on the head. If he hits—and the other team must be honest—then the thrower's side may toss another balloon. If he misses, then the other side gets a throw. No dodging is allowed.

✖ When one team has used up all its bombs, the team with the most wet heads loses.

▶▶ IF YOU LIKE THIS GAME . . . check out strange-games .blogspot.com, the source for this game, Yoga Ball Jousting (page 75), and Bubble Wrap Kung Fu (page 76).

Competitive Picnicking

Ah, picnics. They conjure images of genteel conversation as picnickers lounge by a babbling brook, tucking into wicker hampers chock-full of cold chicken, thermoses of iced tea, and wedges of cake. Perhaps, if the conversation gets a little *too* animated, a benevolent governess might raise her gaze from a sketchbook and cast a reproving glance at the merrymakers. In other words, one rarely thinks of a massive, raucous game of Go Fish, in which players roll the dice, swipe one another's Chips Ahoy, and in general wage a war to procure all the edibles for themselves.

Fortunately for those who like their genteel activities to be a little more, well, cutthroat, along comes Competitive Picnicking. Players young and old will roll a die and try to assemble the best "hand," or picnic basket, before any other player can, thus winning the game. It's an activity that's fun for children, as it doesn't require a lot of strategizing—just remembering what other players have asked for and received. And even if a kid loses his Rice Krispie Treat during the course of the game, reassure him that all food items will be returned to their original owners before lunch. This will keep the child who will eat only PB&J from freaking out when he loses his sandwich with a roll of the die.

PLAYERS: 5–50, plus a nonplaying moderator. Each player plays for himself—there are no teams, though parents may assist players too small to manage by themselves.

THE GEAR: Each player will pack a complete lunch, chosen from the "food list" below: one sandwich, one beverage, one salad, one side, and one dessert, plus a bag or a picnic basket. The moderator must bring a six-sided die and as many photocopies of the "picnics," or the winning combinations (see "Winning Combo Picnics," page 186) as there are players. Optional: The moderator may also bring any food items that other players are not bringing (see notes on page 187). Picnic blankets and lawn chairs, as needed.

Preparation

About a week ahead of time, the moderator will e-mail the food list, above, to the players and instruct them to bring a complete lunch to the party, with one item from each

Food List

Each player chooses one item from each category and packs a complete lunch.

- *Sandwiches:* Turkey, Ham, Tuna, Cheese, Peanut Butter and Jelly

- *Beverages:* Iced Tea, Apple Juice, Orange Juice, Lemonade, Soda

- *Salads:* Garden Salad, Chef Salad, Spinach Salad, Potato Salad, Macaroni Salad

- *Sides:* Chips, Apple, Granola Bar, Pickles, Carrots

- *Desserts:* Brownie, Lemon Bar, Rice Krispie Treat, Cookie, Cupcake

category, concealed in a bag or picnic basket.

Let them know that at the party, players will be rolling the die and swapping food items, with the goal of assembling a specific winning combination, or "picnic." These picnics will be revealed at the party.

Players should not tell other players what they are bringing.

Winning Combo Picnics:

- **All-American:** Turkey, Lemonade, Potato Salad, Apple, Brownie

- **School Lunch:** PB&J, Apple Juice, Garden Salad, Carrots, Rice Krispie Treat

- **Crunchy Lunch:** Cheese, Orange Juice, Spinach Salad, Granola Bar, Cookie

- **Old-Fashioned:** Ham, Soda, Macaroni Salad, Pickles, Lemon Bar

- **Cosmopolitan:** Tuna, Iced Tea, Chef Salad, Chips, Cupcake

---

The Game Plan

- When players arrive, have everyone sit in a circle. Each player should have a complete lunch concealed in a bag or a basket.

- The moderator will distribute the list of winning picnic combinations, above. Tell players that the first player to assemble a Combo Picnic will win.

- Any players too young to read may be assisted by parents or may play as a team with a parent.

- The youngest player begins and rolls the die.

  - If she rolls a 1, she may ask any other player for any kind of sandwich.
  - If she rolls a 2, she may ask any other player for any kind of beverage.
  - If she rolls a 3, she may ask any other player for any kind of salad.
  - If she rolls a 4, she may ask any other player for any kind of side.
  - If she rolls a 5, she may ask any other player for any kind of dessert.
  - If she rolls a 6, ants have attacked the picnic! And she may ask any other player for any food item at all.

Possible Outcomes		
• = Sandwich		•••• = Side
•• = Beverage		••••• = Dessert
••• = Salad		••• ••• = Ants!

Example: If little Susie rolls a one, she may say to her cousin John, "John, do you have a ham sandwich?" If John does have a ham sandwich, he must surrender it to Susie.

The player to the left of Susie then takes a turn rolling the die and asking for a food item, and so on around the circle.

Go around the circle once. If, at the end of the first circuit, a player has assembled a complete picnic, that player is the winner! If not, the game continues for another circuit, and so on.

As soon as a winner is declared, the food items are returned to their original owners—unless two players want to trade their items for real—and everyone eats! The first-place winner gets a prize, like an inexpensive jai alai set or a kickball for an after-lunch game. (Have a bunch of token prizes on hand as well, like sparklers, stickers, or wind-up toys, to soothe any small ruffled feathers of runners-up.)

Notes for the Moderator

It is possible that someone, just through random luck, will have a complete picnic upon arriving (the equivalent of being dealt four of a kind in Go Fish). Since this would mean a very short game, all players must play at least one circuit before a winner is declared. If someone wins fairly early in the game, the moderator may decide to keep the game going to establish second and third place.

It also may happen that it's impossible to assemble one or more of the picnics—because no one brings, say, pickles or a lemon bar. This is less likely with a big party, but if the moderator would like to prevent this, she may ask the players in advance what foods they are bringing and "fill in" what they are *not* bringing—so if no one is bringing a spinach salad or a cupcake dessert, she can bring those items in her basket to make sure that players are playing with a "full deck." In this case, she can't play because she knows what everyone is bringing, but other players may ask *her* for items from her picnic basket.

The moderator may adjust the menu options to fit the party. If, for example, many guests are vegetarian, substitute veggie options for the meat sandwiches.

—contributed by Michael Dory, Adam Simon, and Scott Varland, cofounders of Socialbomb, and Daniel Soltis, an interaction designer at Tinker.it! For more about these guys, check out socialbomb.com and tinker.it.

JULY

Taste of America

The Fourth of July is already pretty great. There's beer, hot dogs, fireworks—what the hell else do you need? I'll tell you: something to eat other than hot dogs. So turn your Fourth into a potluck game with some culinary history thrown in.

A week or so before the party, ask your guests to bring an unusual dish that reflects an American regional culinary culture. If your guests are actually *from* that region, all the better. So someone from Maine might bring a dish featuring lobsters (we hope), a guest from New Orleans might fry up some beignets, a native Brooklynite might introduce you to gefilte fish. But it's not mandatory that you bring something from your native region—if you're a New Yorker and you want to make a *cassoulet,* by all means, hit it.

At a party in Gainesville, Florida, I was sure that one dish was jambalaya—it had the meat, the rice, the sausage—and it was heavenly. But I was wrong: The man who brought it was from St. Augustine, Florida, and was descended from the Majorcan Spaniards who had settled the area. He explained that the dish was a *perleau,* not jambalaya (a similar dish from Cajun country). Perleau (not the only name or spelling), on the other hand, is native to Florida. Marjorie Kinnan Rawlings, a chronicler of Florida life, writes about it in *Cross Creek Cookery:* "The *pilau* has traveled a long way to backwoods Florida from its sources in Turkey and adjacent countries, where it is the *pilaf.* It seems likely that the Moors took it to Spain and the Spaniards to Florida. William Bartram found it there on his travels and spelled it 'pillo.' We pronounce the word 'pur-loo.' It is any dish of meat and rice cooked together."

PLAYERS: 4–100

The Game Plan

When your guests arrive, set out the food on a long table. Don't identify the dishes, and ask the individual chefs to keep quiet as well (some of the foods, of course, may be obvious, but many will not). Ask your guests to sample the offerings and to write down the name of the dish and the ingredients. After everyone's eaten their fill and jotted down their guesses, the chefs should identify their dishes and reveal what's in them. (You might ask each chef to bring copies of her recipe to hand out to other guests as take-home favors.)

Winning

Give guests a point for every dish they identified correctly. The guest with the most points wins a copy of a cookbook on a traditional American cuisine.

▶▶ HOST TIP

Round out your dinner table with more examples of the regional melting pot. Ask guests to bring (or you can order ahead of time off the Internet) beverages, snacks, or single items that are regional specialties—Del's Lemonade or coffee milk from Rhode Island, Moxie soda from Maine, blue crabs from Maryland, etc.

AUGUST

Capture the (Waterlogged) Flag

August is a challenging month for gaming. There aren't any major holidays, all your pals are on vacation, and if you're stuck in an urban area you're probably living at the air-conditioned movie theater. If you are fortunate enough to be at the shore, you're probably pretty focused on nothing but keeping sand out of your bathing suit and making sure your lemonade's topped off.

But let's just pretend you get a burst of energy. Not enough to go for a jog, but maybe enough to manage a bellyflop on an inflatable raft. Welcome to Capture the (Waterlogged) Flag. A camp standby, Capture the Flag endures because of its adaptability. The object is simple: to grab the other team's flag and bring it to your side. In the aquatic version, the playing field is water and running is replaced by swimming, paddling, or sailing. If you're playing in a lake or an ocean, teams can paddle around on rafts or inner tubes, or swim; if you're in a pool you might want to forgo the inflatable devices lest the playing field becomes too crammed.

PLAYERS: 6–50, plus nonplaying lifeguards (1 for every 10 people).

THE GEAR: Two lightweight buoys and rope. Beach balls or towels on rafts to act as "flags," plus beach balls for tagging. Inflatable rafts, inner tubes, or small boats (rowboats, Sunfish, canoes, etc). Appropriate safety gear, like life jackets.

Preparation

- Divide into two teams of three or more people each; give each team a flag.

- Delineate territory for each team: String the rope between the two buoys to make a rough centerline, or use a rope to divide the pool in half.

- "Jail" should be in the shallows or in an area at the side of the pool. Mark off this area with rope and buoys.

The Game Plan

- Give each team five minutes to place a flag in its territory. Flags should be attached to buoys or otherwise secured in some fashion so they don't float out to sea. The flag must be visible and no further than the agreed-upon distance from the centerline. (If you're in a very large body of water, like a bay, decide how far from the centerline each team may place its flag.)

- At the end of the five minutes, start the game.

- Some members of each team will attempt to row, swim, or paddle across the centerline, capture the enemy flag, and race back without being tagged by the other side. If you are swimming or paddling on an inflatable raft, tagging means touching the other person or his raft. If you are playing in canoes or other boats, it means tossing a beach ball at your opponent's boat and making contact with the hull or a person. (This will prevent unpleasant ramming of watercraft.)

- Other team members will try to intercept and tag any opposing players who are in their territory. Anyone tagged in foreign territory is "captured" and put in "jail."

- Rescue captured teammates by sneaking across the centerline to the jail, tagging jailed teammates to free them, then racing back across the border with said rescued pals. Prisoners must arrive safely in their own territory before they can be truly free; if an opposing player tags them en route from the jail to their own side, they must go back to jail.

Variation

Captured players must stay in jail for a set period of time (two minutes, for example—players are on their honor to count, "One Mississippi, two Mississippi," etc., until two minutes have passed) and then may return untagged to their side to resume play.

> **▶▶STEALTH STRATEGY ◀**
>
> Send one of your *slower* players across the border to pretend to make a dash for the enemy's flag. Once this decoy has successfully drawn out the other team's players, deploy your *fastest* player. With luck, your opponents' most aggressive players will be distracted by the decoy, giving the second swimmer a clear shot at the flag.

Winning

Win by capturing the enemy flag and carrying it back to your side of the border.

NOTE: You must play this game with at least one lifeguard present, who should have a clear view of the whole playing area.

SEPTEMBER

Priest of the Parish

Labor Day weekends are a prime time for family reunions, and so you'll need big games to keep the troops occupied. If, like my family, you usually convene at a state park for a cookout, you can finally play those games that need a lot of space. Priest of the Parish is appropriate for all ages, requires 50 to 150 people, and is a nice change from the standard three-legged races and whistle-with-a-cracker-in-your-mouth contests. It seems that this game has evolved from a popular eighteenth-century shipboard diversion—those sailors needed *something* to keep them amused on long sea voyages.

PLAYERS: 50–150, plus a moderator or "Gossiper."

THE GEAR: A chair for each player (folding camping chairs or benches will do), timer.

Preparation

Ask everyone who wants to play to find a chair, or a bench that holds three to five. Arrange the chairs in rows of five. Half of the chairs should face the other half, so you will have two banks of chairs, one bank facing the other bank.

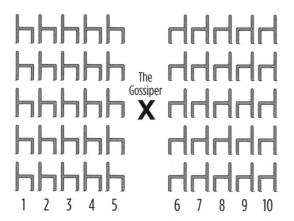

The Game Plan

✖ Divide players into teams of five. Each team takes a row. The first row is Team 1, the second row is Team 2, and so on. It doesn't matter which team is Team 1—you can go from back to front or front to back.

✖ The moderator will set a time limit for the game—ten minutes is a good start.

✖ The moderator (or Gossiper) stands in the middle of the two banks of chairs and announces, in a loud, clear voice: "The priest of the parish has lost his considering cap. Some say this, and some say that, but I say it was team number X." (The Gossiper may say any team's number; let's say she said, "I say it was Team 3.")

✖ Team 3 stands up all at once; they (*in unison*) and the Gossiper then have a conversation that goes like this:

Team 3: (in unison) "Who, me, sir? Couldn't be, sir!"
Gossiper: "Then who, sir?"
Team 3: (in unison) "Team 4, sir!"
At this point, Team 4 stands all at once and says, in unison, "Who, me, sir? Couldn't be, sir!"
Gossiper: "Then who, sir?"
Team 4: (in unison) "Team 1, sir!"

✖ You can see the difficulty—a team has to decide which other team number they are going to call out *while* having the conversation with the Gossiper—which means they have to communicate with hand signals as soon as they stand up—or decide ahead of time which number they're going to use.

✖ The game continues like this until one of the following happens: A team doesn't stand up together, a team speaks out of unison, a team calls out its own number, or the wrong team stands up. When one of these things happens, the team that made the mistake goes to the bottom row of chairs (in our example, row 10), and all of the teams that were below them move up a row (so the team that was in row 10 now goes to row 9, row 9 goes to row 8, and so on). Note that the team numbers will then change—if Team 3 messes up and moves to row 10, its new name is Team 10. If *two* teams make a mistake at the same time— like the wrong team stands *and* only half the members of the right team stand—the Gossiper will send them both to the end, deciding arbitrarily which one will be row 10 and which will be row 9.

✖ The whole process starts again with the Gossiper talking to a team.

Winning
The team that is Team 1 when the time is up is the winner. The winning team is responsible for fetching ice cream or another treat for everyone else.

OCTOBER
Competitive Pumpkin Carving

Sure, pumpkin carving is fun. But it's so, you know, mellow. What if it were competitive? A contest? My husband, when in architecture school, hosted annual pumpkin-carving contests for the other students. He then invited the professors and other architects to come in and participate in a critique. (Architecture students are regularly subjected to reviews, in which their work is constructively savaged by people working in the field.) One year, Jesse Reiser, a New York–based architect of the firm Reiser & Umemoto, was invited to critique the pumpkins.

He awarded second place to a pumpkin carved in the traditional manner (eyes, nose, mouth perfectly symmetrical and expertly carved) and first place to a pumpkin that had been cut clean through, horizontally, into about twenty slices, and then restacked so that the layers were slightly offset. The result was a Cubist, postmodern kind of pumpkin—a Picasso pumpkin.

Mr. Reiser's comments on the two winning pumpkins were these: "The traditional pumpkin [the second-place pumpkin] uses the knife as a means of representation— the cuts in the facade of the pumpkin are basically illustrations on the surface, forming mouth, eyes, nose. The winning pumpkin uses modernist methodology, a simple series of horizontal cuts, essentially 'layering' the pumpkin, using the material of the pumpkin itself in a non-representational context, revealing the underlying 'pumpkinness' of the object in question."

So maybe you're not an architect, and you certainly don't have to use such big words when you're judging the contest. It's still pretty darn fun.

PLAYERS: 4–50

THE GEAR: Pumpkins (one pumpkin per two or three people, plus an extra or two), sharp knives, pencils or markers, newspapers, candles (optional).

The Game Plan
Have your guests help contribute categories for judging pumpkins. Divide your guests into teams of two or three people each and give them thirty minutes to design and carve a pumpkin or jack-o'-lantern. When the time's up, set the pumpkins or jack-o'-lanterns on

display and have everyone vote (or appoint noncarving judges ahead of time) for most beautiful, most bizarre, most like an evil dictator, most like a Looney Toons character (Bugs Bunny dressed as a lady with a flower behind his ear?), best effort (or worst, least recognizable as a face), best portrait of someone in the room, truly scariest, most like George Burns, most like a sand dune at sunset . . .

If you're with a particularly artsy crowd, you can give awards based on the pumpkins' proximity to various art movements: most postmodern, most Cubist, most Renaissance, and so on. Have a few prizes on hand, like a coffee-table book on a particular art movement, a pocket knife, or a fresh-baked pumpkin pie.

PARTY RECIPE

Toasted Pumpkin Seeds

A great snack to serve after the carving contest—get everyone to donate their pumpkin seeds and they will be rewarded with a tasty treat.   YIELD: 2 CUPS

INGREDIENTS

2 cups raw whole pumpkin seeds	Salt, to taste
2–3 teaspoons melted butter	

1. Preheat oven to 300°F.

2. Wash seeds well in a strainer, removing any pulp. Dry. Toss seeds in a bowl with the butter and salt. Spread the seeds in a single layer on a baking sheet and bake for about 45 minutes or until golden brown. Stir occasionally.

Halloween Ball

Children get to dress up all the time, even when it's not Halloween. If they feel like being Wonder Woman, out come the cape and the boots. If Harry Potter seems particularly alluring one day, they dust off the round spectacles and the stuffed owl. For grown-ups, we get one shot a year: Halloween. It's the one holiday in which we can celebrate our alter egos—or what we *wish* were our alter egos: Jessica Rabbit, Lance Armstrong, Frida Kahlo. Dressing up as a superhero or a political figure lets us explore parts of ourselves usually kept under wraps. And when you pretend to be someone else, inhibitions are lowered. *You* might not sneak a cigarette behind the garage and then make out with James Dean, but Rizzo from *Grease* would.

PLAYERS: 10–200

THE GEAR: Costumes, food and drink, prizes, decorations.

The Game Plan

The best Halloween parties have themes—it narrows the options and staunches the "oh god, what should I wear?" panic. Actually, it allows guests to be *more* creative—because the guidelines themselves spark ideas. If the theme is the 1970s, for example, bell-bottoms and Richard Nixon spring to mind. A couple of weeks ahead of time, send out an invite to your pals with the theme and the rules.

Choose a theme and throw your guests a few ideas for costumes:

- Time Warp: Come as your favorite character from another era. Joan of Arc, Dwight D. Eisenhower, Jesus, Daisy Buchanan.

- Through the Looking Glass: Pick your favorite character from *Alice in Wonderland*—Cheshire Cat, the Queen of Hearts, the Mad Hatter, Alice. There are certain to be a few enterprising folks who go off the beaten path and craft a "Drink Me" bottle costume.

- Invasion and Conquest: Think conquistadors, Genghis Khan, Lewis and Clark, and Pocahontas.

- TV Show-Off: Tony Soprano, the cast of *Lost,* any of the *Family Guy* family (Stewie!), the *Big Love* clan, Captain Stubing and Gopher, anyone?

- *Saturday Night Live*: Characters from the show—Keenan Thompson's Virginiaca or the "What's Up with That?" guy, classic curiosities like Pat or the Will Ferrell/Cheri Oteri cheerleaders—the possibilities are endless.

You get the drill. Introduce a theme, then offer some rules to up the ante and make sure no one finks out and shows up in a hoodie and jeans and tries the ol' "I'm the Unabomber" cop-out. Rule #1: No costume, no entry, no points. Rule #2: Showing up in costume (show everyone a little love), +4 points.

Ask your guests to submit their own auxiliary rules to you via e-mail or Facebook before the event and distribute these to all attendees. On arrival, all guests/players will have a comprehensive list of rules on which you and your posse have collectively agreed.

Use sticky notes, or go bananas and make score sheets (see below) to award points to players. At the end of the night, the most laureled player wins. Give prizes for second and third place if you're feeling generous. What's the prize? Why, no one, no matter his age, has ever turned up his nose at this treat—a plastic jack-o'-lantern full of candy.

Halloween Ball Score Sheet

Best Literal Representation of the Theme: +10

Jane

Best Abstract Representation of the Theme: +8

Robert

Most Creative Costume: +6

Ruth

Best Use of Tin Foil: +2

Jorge

Best Use of Pipe Cleaners: +2

Cal

Most Hilarious Costume: +3

Jorge

Darkest or Weirdest Costume: +2

Cal

Misinterpretation of Theme: -2

Susan

NOVEMBER

Grateful Guessing

Play Grateful Guessing around the table, as everyone's enjoying their pumpkin pie with whipped cream on top. (Or, if you're like my Aunt Martha, you're enjoying your brandy with brandy on top.)

PLAYERS: Everyone at your Thanksgiving dinner.

THE GEAR: Paper, pencils.

The Game Plan

* Pass out paper and pencils, and ask each person to jot down three things they're grateful for, on separate slips of paper. The "gratitudes" can be as sincere or lighthearted—I'm thankful to have a job when the economy's gone to hell, I'm thankful for my Nintendo Wii (clearly Dad), I'm thankful that brining the bird actually worked (clearly Mom), I'm thankful that the family gathering hasn't devolved into fisticuffs yet (wild card, could be anyone, probably you)—as your guests see fit. Certainly in a given year one might feel grateful for profound blessings as well as small pleasures.

▶▶ **HOST TIP**

If you want to completely eliminate the handwriting identification factor, have guests type out their "gratitudes" in advance.

* The object is twofold. Technically, you want to stump your family members, and so your gratitudes should be somewhat obscure. (If a slip of paper reads "I'm thankful for my Legos," you can be pretty sure it's little Johnny. But if someone writes "I'm thankful

that what I thought was a polyp was actually a quarter I'd swallowed," well—there's just no telling, is there?) But you also want to spark conversation with your family, and so sincere, nonobscure statements have their place.

* Put all the slips of paper in a hat and take turns pulling them out and reading them. The person who reads the slip of paper announces her best guess as to who wrote it, with justification—which is what's funny ("I think Ruth is thankful for this year's excellent holiday movies because I know she likes seeing Hugh Jackman with his shirt off"). She also writes down her guess on the slip of paper and keeps it in front of her. She then passes the hat to the next player, who draws a slip, reads it out loud, and makes a guess.

* When the hat is empty, everyone reveals which gratitudes he or she wrote.

Winning

The player with the most correct guesses wins (there can be more than one winner), but as mentioned above, the conversation is the real treat.

Variation

Gratitude Fictionary. Players take turns being the Reader. The Reader writes down something she is genuinely grateful for. The other players write down a made-up something for which the Reader is grateful. All the players pass their slips to the Reader, who reads them aloud (making sure, first, that she can decipher everyone's handwriting). Everyone then guesses which item is the one the Reader wrote. The Reader then reveals which one is hers. Players get a point if they were correct; they also get a point if someone votes for their "fake" gratitude. The Reader wins a point if no one votes for her true gratitude.

Inheritance Game

NEW GAME!

Ah, dividing the estate. Who gets what when the patriarch or matriarch shuffles off this mortal coil has been the subject of movies, plays, books—and the bitterest of family feuds. Who hasn't heard of a grandmother inviting the kids and grandkids to affix sticky notes to the backs of the household items they want to claim upon her death . . . and then the inevitable squabbling when two kids tag the same Precious Moments figurine? Well, the Inheritance Game taps into that mindset, but with the smallest of stakes—just ten cents.

PLAYERS: As many as are at your family dinner.

THE GEAR: Ten pennies for each player.

The Game Plan

Each player places ten pennies to the right of his or her Thanksgiving dinner plate (different objects and quantities can be substituted). Over the course of the meal, players try to steal their neighbors' pennies. If a player is caught stealing, she must give back the penny as well as a penny from her own pile. You can only be caught by the person whose penny you are trying to steal. Players may only attempt to steal one penny at a time. The player with the most pennies at the end of the evening is the winner.

While the game may sound simplistic, it leads to a list of hilarious gotchas as you encourage your uncle to wave a cigar and pontificate. By the time he's finished his the-country's-going-to-hell-in-a-handbasket speech, the kids have stolen all of his pennies.

—contributed by Sam Lavigne, a San Francisco–based game designer and a founder of SFZero.org, a collaborative-production game company.

NOVEMBER/DECEMBER

Name-Boggle Poetry

PLAYERS: Everyone at your holiday dinner.

THE GEAR: Paper, pencils.

Another creative game for the holiday dinner table; like the others, this one can include children. Write down all the first and last names of the people who will be at dinner and make a copy for each guest. Give guests a set amount of time, say, fifteen minutes, to create anagrams out of the names and create a poem from the anagrams. If you'd like, you can give the guests access to a computer and an anagram generator, or you can do this yourself ahead of time and supply the list of anagrams. This allows your guests to dedicate themselves to writing the poems. The poems do not necessarily have to be good poems: Doggerel couplets are always funny and take the pressure off the nonwriterly members of the family to churn out masterpieces.

Holiday Trivia

PLAYERS: As many as are in your family.

Before your family members arrive for the big meal (or before you set out for Grandma's house), write or print out holiday-related and family-holiday-related trivia questions on slips of paper. For example, What is the name of the eighth reindeer? What did the Pilgrims really eat on their first Thanksgiving? What is a traditional Christmas gift in Holland? What happened in 2002 that changed the extended Anderson family's Christmas plans? What was an Anderson "first" last Thanksgiving? With which kitchen implement did Mom drench herself three years ago? What ingredient did Billy forget when making pumpkin pie last year? What "big news" did Stan and Katie announce in 2007? Create three to five times as many trivia questions as there will be guests.

After dinner, put all the slips in a hat. Randomly select a guest to go first; have her draw one. If she answers correctly, she gets a point. If not, it goes back in the hat for another player. Regardless of whether she answers the question correctly, the hat passes to the next player. Continue until the hat is empty; the player with the most correct answers wins.

Variation

Try this at family reunions or at wedding-anniversary parties, but with trivia related to the family or couple of honor.

Family Jeopardy!

PLAYERS: Everyone at your family dinner. The host will be the Quizmaster.

THE GEAR: Index cards, pen

Jeopardy!, the long-running quiz show, has a twist: The answers are in the form of questions. When giving their answers, players must preface the statement with a "What was . . . " or "Who was . . . ," in order to make their answer a question. For example, if the statement is "A famous American traitor during the Revolutionary War," the contestant might reply, "Who was Benedict Arnold?"

You, as the Quizmaster, will make up five categories relevant to your group (kids, vacations, family lore, etc.) and create *Jeopardy!*-style questions (in the form of statements) and answers (in the form of questions) for each category. Write the questions and answers on index cards and place them facedown under each category heading. Have players take turns choosing a category. You'll pick up the index card and read the "question" ("This person was Jeff's first girlfriend at summer camp"), and the player must give an answer in the form of a question: "Who is Linda?" If the player is correct, he holds on to the card (to be counted later as a point) and plays again. If he's wrong, the next player gets a turn with that question. When all the cards are gone, the player with the most cards wins.

That's the Way It Was

You know how sometimes, in late December, when you're watching the year-end round-ups—who died, what TV shows started or ended, what countries we invaded—you find yourself saying, "That was only this year? I thought it was ages ago!" Sometimes it seems that last summer is so distant it might as well be the 1930s.

The nostalgically titled, Cronkite-esque *That's the Way It Was* tests your knowledge of recent and ancient history. It's a great game to play after a Christmas or Hanukkah dinner or on New Year's Eve, when thoughts turn to events of the past year, the last decade, the last century.

PLAYERS: As many people as are at your holiday dinner. You will be the Quizmaster.

THE GEAR: Paper, pens.

Preparation

To help you come up with challenging questions, consult a few copies of magazines or websites that round up the notable historic events. The events could all be from, say, the twentieth century (the Armistice, the *Titanic,* the Miracle Mets!), all from the 1950s (Eisenhower defeats Stevenson—for the second time! The Checkers speech! Buddy Holly's plane crash!), or all from very, very recent history. Write or print out fifteen to thirty notable events from a given time period. To keep things interesting, mix comedy with tragedy, sports with politics, war with peace.

The Game Plan

When your guests are enjoying their coffee or wassail after dinner, distribute pens and a piece of scrap paper per person. You, as the Quizmaster, will read out the events (not in chronological order) one at a time. Ask guests to jot down the event and their best guess as to the day, month, and year of the event on their piece of scrap paper. Certainly, very few people will get the exact day right for any given event, with the possible exception of easy ones like when the United States went off the gold standard (October 1, 1971—*everyone knows that one!*), but the closer the guess, the better chance at winning.

When all of the events have been read, reveal the exact dates of the events. The person who's closest wins the point. Everyone keeps their own score (scout's honor), and the one with the highest number of points wins. Everyone will learn something they didn't know and will be surprised by some of the answers (the Polo Grounds were torn down in 1964? Wow! I thought it was 1965!). Everyone is bound to be embarrassed here and there (nope, the *Titanic* didn't sink in 1974), so mix in some really easy ones with the harder ones, and keep that eggnog bowl circulating.

Variation

For a festive holiday party, repurpose a Monopoly or Chutes and Ladders board, use chocolate candies as game pieces, and turn the quiz into a race. Read out the questions one by one, and as the correct answers are revealed, the person with the closest answer moves forward three spaces. First one around the board wins. You can call this variation "Christmas Off the Gold Standard," "New Year's Hangover," or "Gradual Turn of Events."

Baby Shower Games

Baby showers serve a purpose: New parents need stuff, stuff is expensive, ergo: shower. It's nice to see friends and family, sure, but at heart, the event is about buying a gift, showing up, and nibbling on grapes and cheese while the mother-to-be struggles to not look freaked out by the breast pump. Hostesses have *tried* to make baby showers more fun with games—like the one where you melt chocolate in a diaper and force guests to taste it—but these kind of poop-oriented hijinks have a tendency to fall flat, especially at co-ed showers. Below are six games that will keep your guests amused while rattles are opened and Diaper Genies assembled.

Baby Taboo

Ever wish baby showers were a little less about, well, babies? Baby Taboo is a mellow, counterintuitive game that continues throughout the party in a low-key way. The taboo word is (you guessed it) "baby." (It's not that easy—just try going to a baby shower and not saying "baby!") The rules are simple: Everyone is given a string of colorful Mardi Gras beads when they arrive. If someone says "baby," they have to give their beads to the person who nailed them. At the end of the party the person wearing the most beads wins a prize, like a nice big bottle of Scotch.

Baby Promises

Sure, your family and friends are all gung-ho now, while the kid is still in utero and relatively quiet. But what about when you need a night off, say, four or five years from now? Hah! Baby Promises will extract pledges from loved ones that they will spend time with the little one beyond the first birthday. It's a simple activity that should invoke a lot of guilt later on—the best kind of game! Everyone writes down something he or she promises to do with the baby as the tyke grows up. The promises are placed in a hat and read aloud; each person has to guess (either on paper or out loud) who promised what. The guest with the most correct answers wins a prize, like a set of sharp knives. The expectant parents get to keep the chits for the baby, who is the actual "winner" of the game. Down the road he can look up at that long-lost uncle and say "Hey! You owe me a movie!"

A few examples of promises:

- I promise to take my nephew to a Padres game.
- I promise to teach my niece how to fly-fish.
- I promise to show my godchild how to throw a football like Brett Favre.
- I promise not to force my grandchild to watch old Brett Favre highlights.

▸▸STEALTH STRATEGY ◂

When you are writing your baby promises, *don't* write "my nephew" or "my grandchild," or everyone will know who wrote it. The hostess, who is reading the promises out loud, should just substitute "the baby."

Baby Words

Each guest writes down every baby-related word they can think of in a minute and a half. The person with the most words or most unique words wins. You have two options for scoring:

1. Everyone declares how many words they thought of and then reads them out loud (letting the group decide if they are really baby-related).

   or

2. Players share their answers Boggle-style: People read off their lists of words; if someone else also has that word, it doesn't count. The latter takes a little longer, but is more fun because it forces people to be creative.

Examples from a recent game: glider, bib, dribble, rattle, tantrum.

Baby Bingo

Played while the mom-to-be opens her presents. Hand out blank bingo cards to all the guests before opening presents. Each guest composes a list of baby items, listing one in each square of the card. As presents are opened, guests get to mark them off on their card. When someone fills in a row, she shouts "Bingo!" The winner gets a sushi dinner for two. Great for young and old alike,

the game gives guests something to do other than staring down the mom-to-be while she wrestles with the hemp baby sling.

Distract the Parents

Baby showers can get boring because it's all baby, baby, baby! Here's a simple game played among guests, unbeknownst to the parents, in order to keep things varied. Each player has one and only one opportunity during the course of the party to distract one or both of the baby's parents, who are focused on one thing only—baby stuff. Examples of distractions might include, "Oh, look! The azaleas are blooming early this year! Come see!" or "Suzanne, you simply must come see what your dog Jasper is up to in the study!" or "Sidney, is this really a complete set of *Architectural Record* magazines?" The other guests observe the attempted distraction; one guest, armed with a stopwatch, is in charge of timing the interaction.

Sink the Onesie

Wad or wrap onesies into little balls, set up a diaper pail like a basketball hoop, and take turns shooting the onesies into the basket. The winner gets a prize, and the parents get the onesies. If it's too easy, keep pushing the distance between hoop and shooter (just like in real basketball!).

Chapter Eleven

GAMES FOR GAMBLERS & BLUFFERS

One of the most fun aspects of games is pretending to be someone else. And sometimes, you're pretending to be a big fat liar. Lying and seeing if you can get away with it, in real life, might be called "betrayal." Lying and seeing if you can get away with it, in games, is called "bluffing." As a compulsively honest person, I really dig bluffing games because the whole point is to see if you can deliver a whopper with a straight face. You get to test out your own internal lie detector—do you *really* know if your mother is yanking your chain or not? And just to up the ante, most bluffing games force you to put a price tag on your nerve—in Rat-Fink or I Doubt It, for example, calling someone else's bluff can be risky and will cost you points if you're wrong. So not only do you have to mind your own face when you're bluffing, you have to be confident in your ability to read other people's "tells" as well.

In most gambling games, there's a strong element of math and observation—the game will go your way more often than not if you're able to figure probability. So knowing that most gamblers and bluffers are also running calculations behind their smooth, butter-wouldn't-melt-in-their-mouth talkers, we've included a few games that involve your powers of math (Arithmetic Croquet) and observation (Eleusis Express).

Gambling and bluffing are entrenched in our language and culture—there are probably more gambling terms and metaphors than there are even for sports: to *roll the dice, have a beef with someone, crap out*. Games of chance are thrilling—leaving fate up to the gods gives gamblers a rush that can't be matched in everyday life. The uncertain outcome of every round or throw of the dice is the very essence of games in general—despite your best efforts, your superior brain, and your careful calculations, luck must be on your side.

So good luck!

Liar's Dice

If you like poker, you'll want to check out Liar's Dice, which is based on Draw Poker. There are a few ways to play the game; we've identified what we think is the most fun. You bet, you bluff, you lie your head off. The object of the game is to call your opponent's bluff or to convince him to challenge your honest calls.

PLAYERS: 2–4

THE GEAR: 10 poker chips, coins, or candy for each player. Five dice and a dice cup.

The Game Plan

✘ Each player starts with poker chips or other counters.

✘ Throw a die to determine who goes first. Highest number wins.

✘ Each player antes one poker chip.

✘ Begin the round with the first player (the "Caller"), shaking five dice in the cup and turning the cup upside down on the table.

✘ Peek at your dice if you are the caller, keeping the results hidden from the other players. Decide whether you want to "stay" (not re-roll) or "draw" (re-roll).

✘ If you choose to draw, you may re-roll any number of dice. You may re-roll twice in one turn. (In order to keep your opponents from seeing the dice you are *not* re-rolling, block them with your hand, or use a shield, like a book, propped upright between players, or a sheet of paper.)

Rank

Poker hands rank in this order:

- five of a kind
- four of a kind
- full house (three of a kind and one pair)
- high straight (2-3-4-5-6)
- low straight (1-2-3-4-5)
- three of a kind
- two pair
- one pair

✘ After three throws (or fewer, if you choose to stay), you must announce your hand as a poker hand. You have to be specific. That is, you can't say, "I have three of a kind." Rather you should say, "I have three fours." You don't have to tell the truth—you can understate or overstate your hand.

✘ The other player (or the player on the caller's left, if playing with more than two people), can accept the call, or if he thinks you're bluffing, can challenge the call, meaning he lifts the cup to reveal the dice.

✘ If you are caught bluffing, you must put a counter in the pot. If yours was an honest call, the challenger puts a counter in the pot.

✘ If a player decides to accept the call, the dice pass to her, and she has up to three tries to make a good poker hand. She then announces her (perhaps imaginary) hand, which must be a higher hand than the previous player purportedly had, even if he was bluffing.

✷ The player to her left (or the other player, if playing with two) now has the choice of accepting the call or calling the bluff.

✷ Begin a new round, with an additional ante, each time a challenge is made. The person who lost the last round becomes the next caller.

Winning

Win the game when you are the only one remaining who has a counter.

Variations

✷ Betting may also be played as in poker, with each player putting his stake in the pot at the beginning of a round and betting on each call with a wager.

✷ You can make some numbers, like 1s, "wild."

▶▶ IF YOU LIKE THIS GAME . . . for a non–numbers-oriented bluffing game, check out Fictionary on page 101, or the board game Malarkey.

|||||||||||||||||||||||||||||||||||||||||||||||||||||||||||||||||||||||||

Dudo

In the toy store, Dudo is known as Perudo, but there's no need to shell out for the commercial version—a few dice and some plastic cups will do just fine. Dudo is sometimes known as Peruvian Liar's Dice, or Liar's Dice of the Andes; it's said to have been taught to the Spanish Conquistadors by the Incas, and it's still popular in South America. The fun in the game lies in challenging a player's bluff by shouting, "Dudo!" (Spanish for *I doubt it*). It's a game of guessing and bluffing for any number of players.

PLAYERS: Any number, though 5 or 6 is ideal.

THE GEAR: Five dice and a dice cup for each player, plus a container to hold (conceal) dice as they are removed from the game.

Objective

To correctly guess (or make a convincing bluff about) the total number of dice on the table that show a specified face value. For example, in a five-player game, a player whose roll includes two 4s might guesstimate that there are a total of six 4s on the table. The game is made more complicated by the fact that 1s can be considered either as aces or can serve as a wild card, meaning they can stand in for any other number.

Special Rules About Aces

Because the ace is high (it beats all other face values) and can also be used to represent any other face value, it is governed by special bidding rules. The first player of a round may not call aces. When bidding, there are two simple formulas for aces, one when calling aces as an increase over another face value, and the second for converting from an ace bid to a different face value. When increasing a bid to aces from any other value, use one-half the quantity of dice previously bid (round up, if necessary). So if the previous call was seven 2s, the ace-bid must be at least ($7 \div 2$) four aces. To convert *from* an ace bid, double the quantity of the call and add one. To advance a call of four aces, the next player must call at least ($4 \times 2 + 1$) nine of another face value, or else call five aces.

The Game Plan

✖ Each player rolls a die; the highest number goes first.

✖ All players at the same time shake their dice cups and upend them, keeping the dice concealed underneath. Each player peeks at his own dice.

✖ The first player announces a call, or his guess, of the number of dice, at a minimum, that have been rolled that show a certain face value. So she may announce "seven twos." A player can call any face value, regardless of whether her roll includes a die of that value.

✖ The next player clockwise has two options:

- He can declare a higher quantity of the same face value ("eight 2s") or he can declare the same or larger quantity of a higher face value ("seven 3s"). Or,

- He can challenge, by saying "Dudo!" As soon as someone challenges, all the players reveal their dice. All the dice that show the declared value (a 2 in our example) or an ace are counted. If the challenger is correct and there are fewer dice than were called, the declaring player loses a die. But if there are at least as many dice as were called, the challenger loses and must surrender a die. Dice that are "lost" are placed in a container where they cannot be seen by the players—part of the challenge of the game is remembering how many dice are in play.

✖ The player who lost a die begins the next round.

✖ Once a player is down to one die, he is *palafico*. The palafico player starts the next round.

✖ In a palafico round, aces are not wild and the player may start by calling 1s if he'd like. Whatever the opening call, the other players may only call a higher quantity of the same number. The number value doesn't change during the round. For example, if the palafico player calls five 4s, the next player must call at least six 4s, the next at least seven 4s, etc.

✖ Once a player loses her last die, she's out of the game.

✖ When there are only two players left, a palafico round is not played, and normal rules apply.

Winning

The last player with a die is the winner.

|||||||||||||||||||||||||||||||||||||||||||||||||||||||||||||||||||||||||||||||||||||

Craps

A descendant of the European game Hazard, Craps was developed by African Americans in New Orleans in the nineteenth century. Its name may come from the slang for French settlers in New Orleans (*Johnny Crapaud*) or it may come from the Old English term for rolling two 1s—*crabs*. In any case, it's a fast-paced, exciting game that doesn't take a lot of skill (beyond memorizing the probability of rolling certain combinations). It's also a rollicking game for a large crowd—Craps is a game best played with as many people as possible.

Part of the fun of playing is the extensive Craps lingo that goes along with the game: "seven come eleven," which makes an appearance in many a blues or country song, or to *crap out,* or to *rattle them bones* (to roll the dice). Sweet-talking the dice is also part of the fun of Craps—"Mama needs a new pair of shoes"—and half the fun of watching a game is listening to the players cajoling the dice into changing the shooter's fortune with a single throw. Once you master the terms, get as many of your pals together as you can, line up some cereal boxes as a backstop, and place your bets.

PLAYERS: 2–50, the more the merrier.

THE GEAR: 2 dice, poker chips or other counters for each player, and, if desired, something to act as a backstop—a wall, a propped-up hardcover book, or a cereal box will do.

Objective

To not *crap out,* or roll dice that add up to a 2, 3, or 12.

The Game Plan

✴ Seat players in a circle, either at a table or on the floor. Agree on a maximum bet.

✴ Choose at random any player to go first (the "Shooter").

✴ The Shooter decides what he wants to bet and puts that number of counters in the center (known as the *boneyard*). Let's say he wants to bet three. He says, "I'll bet three. Who'll *fade* me?" (*Fade* is probably from the French word *faits,* short for "*Les jeux sont faits,*" or "The bets are laid.") In any case, to "fade a bet" means to match all or part of it. A single player can fade, or cover, the whole bet—in our example, bet three. Or more than one player may fade part of it—so one player will cover one and another player will fade two. If the Shooter

can't get his entire bet faded, he can reduce or *drag down* his bet. He may not bet more than the other players are willing to cover. The players who fade the bet place their counters with the Shooter's.

Craps Vocab:

- The **Shooter**: the person rolling the dice
- To **fade a bet**: to match all or part of a Shooter's bet
- The **boneyard**: the center of the playing area, where the dice are rolled
- The **come-out roll**: the initial roll of the dice. It will result in *craps,* a *natural,* or it will *set the point.*
- A **craps** or to **crap out**: rolling dice that add up to 2, 3, or 12
- To **drag down a bet**: to reduce it
- A **natural**: dice that add to 7 or 11, a winning combo for the Shooter
- **Set the point**: an initial roll of 4, 5, 6, 8, 9, or 10. The Shooter will roll again to try to *make his point.*
- To **seven out**: to roll a 7 before making the point
- A **come bet**: a second bet, made after the Shooter rolls a point, that he will make his point
- To **come right**: to win
- To **come wrong**: to lose
- To **shoot the works** or **let it ride**: to bet everything on the last round
- **Side bets**: bets made among other players around the table and between the Shooter and other players

✖ Once the bet is faded, the Shooter shakes the dice in his hand and shoots them onto the boneyard. There are three possible outcomes:

1. If the dice add up to 7 or 11, called a *natural,* the Shooter wins. He takes all the counters on the boneyard (all the bets that have been placed in the center of the playing area). He then can make a new bet and roll again, or he can surrender the dice to the player on his left.

2. If the dice add up to 2, 3, or 12, the Shooter *craps out.* The people who faded the Shooter's bet take double their bets— that is, what they bet plus the shooter's stake. The Shooter can make a new bet and roll again, or he can surrender the dice to the player on his left.

3. If the dice add up to 4, 5, 6, 8, 9, or 10, that number is the Shooter's *point.* Let's

say it's a 4. He can roll again, over and over, until he rolls the same number again, in our example, a 4. If he rolls the 4, he has *made his point* and wins his bet. But: If he rolls a 7 before he makes his point (*sevens out*), he loses and must pass on the dice to the next player.

✖ Players may also make bets among themselves.

Winning

A Shooter wins all the counters when he rolls a natural or makes his point. He holds on to the dice and may bet on a new round if he likes. He loses the dice if he fails to make his point or if he voluntarily decides to stop betting. In that case, the dice pass to the player on his left.

Liar's Poker

This betting and bluffing game requires minimal equipment: paper money. Players use the serial numbers (disregarding the letters) on one-dollar bills to make up a poker hand. It's an excellent game to play at a bar, or while you're waiting for the guest of honor at a surprise party, or when the bride and groom are outside having a squabble before the wedding rehearsal.

PLAYERS: 2–6; 5 or 6 make the best game.

THE GEAR: Five or more one-dollar bills for each player.

Objective

The object of the game is to win each trick by bidding on how many times you think

---

Come Bet

If the Shooter rolls a point, meaning the dice add up to 4, 5, 6, 8, 9, or 10, he may make a *come bet* in addition to his original bet. Players can bet whether the Shooter will *come right,* meaning to win, or *come wrong,* meaning to lose. These bets are calculated as if the next roll were the first roll. For example, if the Shooter rolls a 6, a player may bet that he'll *come right.* If the Shooter then rolls an 11, this has no effect on the original bets (as they can only be won by the Shooter with a 6 or lost with a 7) but does mean that the Shooter wins the come bets, since he effectively rolled a natural on his first roll. If he rolls a 6, he wins the original bets, but the come bets are still undecided, as he'd have to roll a 6 again to win or a 7 to lose.

a certain digit occurs among all the serial numbers on the bills in play.

The Game Plan

✖ Select a dealer. The role of dealer will pass to the left with each game.

✖ Each player antes one dollar, which is placed in the "pot," or some separate space or container. Then each player contributes a one-dollar bill to the center of the table. These bills are placed serial number–side-down. The dealer shuffles the bills together and distributes one bill to each player.

✖ All players study their bills.

✖ The person to the dealer's left opens the game. He may either bid or pass. A bid is a declaration of the number of times a specific digit occurs among the serial numbers of all the bills in play. If he passes, he may reenter the bidding at a later point, provided it's his turn.

✖ Bidding generally opens with a pair. For example, a bid could be stated as "I bid a pair of 5s."

✖ The player to the opener's left either passes or bids *over* the opener. So, if the opener bids a pair of 5s, the next bidder's lowest progressive bid must be two 6s (or a higher pair, if he desires), or three of something. The numbers rank from 1 (low) to 0 (considered to be a 10 or an ace). When a player bids and all the other players pass, he, as the highest bidder, gets the bid.

> **▶▶STEALTH STRATEGY**
>
> Conceal your serial number from the other players by folding the bill in such a way that only you can see the numbers.

✖ When this happens, serial numbers are exposed, and the final bidder counts the numbers that appear on the bills.

Winning

If the player who bids highest makes his bid, he is the winner and collects the dollar bills in play from each player. If he fails to make his bid, he must pay each player a dollar.

Variation

Players do not contribute to a "pot." At each player's turn, he may either increase the bid, or challenge the previous bid. He cannot pass. Any player, regardless of whose turn it is, may challenge the current bid. (You may not challenge a prior bid.) If the challenge is successful (the numbers on the bills fall short of the bid) each player pays the challenger a dollar. If the challenge is unsuccessful, the challenger pays each player a dollar.

Rat-Fink

Also known as **Spoons,** Rat-Fink is a high-spirited game of bluffing, stealth, and wild scrambling. It's the kind of game you might play on a rainy day at summer camp, or around the kitchen table with your cousins at your grandparents' house. While it seems, on first glance, to just be a raucous kids'

game (and it can be), it's also an exercise in reading your fellow players' faces—and deciding when to trust your gut to call their bluff.

PLAYERS: 5–8

THE GEAR: A deck of cards and a bunch of teaspoons (one fewer than the number of players in the game).

Objective

A game consists of several rounds of play. Each round will have one loser, who earns a letter from the words *Rat-Fink*. The objective is to avoid losing seven rounds (getting the seven letters that spell out Rat-Fink, which is what you are when you lose).

The Game Plan

* Seat players in a circle, either around a table or on the floor.

* From the deck, take out four of a kind for each player. For example, in a six-person game, four 2s, four 3s, four 4s, four 5s, four 6s, and four 7s would be used. The rest of the cards are set aside.

* Place the teaspoons in the center of the playing area. For a six-person game, you'd put five teaspoons in the center of the table or floor.

* Shuffle the cards, cut, and deal them facedown. Every player should have four cards facedown in front of him. They may not look at their cards until . . .

* the dealer shouts "NOW."

* As the dealer shouts "Now," players pick up their cards and assemble them into melds, the object being to get four of a kind.

* The dealer then shouts "pass to your right," and each player passes one card—presumably the card that is least valuable to his hand.

* This passing on command continues at a rapid pace until one of the players holds (or bluffs that he holds) four of a kind.

* When this happens, one of the players takes one of the center spoons—either openly and aggressively or as surreptitiously as possible.

* Once one person has taken a spoon, it is a signal to the others to grab a spoon as quickly as possible. As there is one spoon fewer than the number of players, one player will be out of luck.

* This spoonless player has lost the round and is given a letter—R. The next time she loses, she gets an A, and so on. If she loses, she still continues to play.

* Bluffing: Rat-Fink contains an element of bluffing. The first person to take a spoon (automatically the winner of the round) is not compelled to show his hand unless someone challenges him. So he may or may not have four of a kind. If no one challenges him, he gets away with his bluff.

* However, he can be challenged by any player at any time, even those who reach for a spoon, and then must display his hand. If he does have four of a kind, the player who challenges is penalized by getting two more letters. If he doesn't have four of a kind, he is penalized two letters.

Winning

Play continues until only one person is left who hasn't lost seven rounds. This person is the winner.

Blind Man's Bluff Poker

aka Indian Poker or Forehead Stud

PLAYERS: 4–12

THE GEAR: A deck of cards.

Also known by other, less enlightened, names, this is a game in which only one card is dealt, facedown, to each player. Without looking at the card, each player places it face-side-out on her forehead. (Some players manage to make it stick there without holding it.) Players can see everyone's card but his or her own. A round of betting follows—the first bet is placed by the player to the left of the dealer. You are betting that your card, sight unseen, is higher than anyone else's, so you must try to determine from the bets and/or the expressions on faces whether your card is worth betting on. Once everyone has placed their bets, players reveal their cards. The person with the highest-value card wins the pot. In subsequent rounds the deal shifts to the left.

I Doubt It

Also known as Bullshit if you run with a saltier crowd, I Doubt It is the *ne plus ultra* of bluffing games. It's *all* bluffing. The object is to get rid of all your cards. You lay down what you say are aces, or threes, or whatever—and it's up to you to keep a straight face if you're lying. Every player must bluff at some point in order to get rid of his cards, so keep your eye out for telltale signs: the downcast gaze, the averted eye, the carefully controlled voice. Of course, the best players will trick you into challenging them when they're *not* bluffing, to your detriment. You may remember I Doubt It from rainy days at summer camp or lounging around the pool after a vigorous swim and a heavy lunch.

PLAYERS: 3–12

THE GEAR: For five or fewer players, use a 52-card deck. For six or more, use two decks shuffled together. Aces are high.

Objective

To be the first to get rid of all your cards.

The Game Plan

- Deal all the cards, one at a time, starting on the dealer's left. It doesn't matter if some players have one more card than others.

- Players pick up their cards.

- The player to the dealer's left starts the game.

- Play starts with aces. If playing with a single deck, the player lays down from one to four cards, facedown, claiming that all of them are aces. If he lays down four cards, he would say "four aces," regardless of whether the cards are in fact aces. He is not compelled to tell the truth. If playing with a double deck, players may lay down one to eight cards.

- Any other player may then exclaim, "I doubt it!" or "Bullshit!"

- If the player's statement was true—that is, that he really *was* laying down four aces, the doubter must then take those four cards into his hand. As the object of the game is to get rid of your cards, you want to be careful who you challenge.

✖ If the player's statement *wasn't* true—he wasn't laying down four aces—he must take *all* the cards on the table into his own hand.

✖ When an announcement goes unchallenged—that is, no one called out, "I doubt it," the cards remain face down on the table until someone else is forced to pick them up (by being caught in a bluff).

✖ When the first player's turn ends (challenged or unchallenged), the next player lays down kings. The announcement of the number of kings will be challenged or not, and then the player to his left must lay down queens. Play proceeds down through the deck, until a player announces twos, and then the next player starts with aces again.

> **▶▶STEALTH STRATEGY**◀
> Count ahead. If you know you are going to be responsible for laying down, say, fives, don't use any fives in a bluff call—save your fives for that turn—especially for your last turn.

Buzz

PLAYERS: 2–20

Buzz is an excellent game for testing your mental-math flexibility—and for teaching children about multiples. In sequence, players count off, substituting the word *buzz* for five and every multiple of five: one, two, three, four, *buzz,* six, seven, eight, nine, *buzz,* eleven . . . etc. Anyone who slips up and says the number instead of *buzz* is out. You must stay alert and concentrate on what's coming up—so this isn't the game to play while driving or texting. For variety, choose any other number, say, seven and its multiples, to be replaced by *fizz.* So, one, two, three, four, *buzz,* six, *fizz,* eight, nine, *buzz,* eleven . . . Fifty-seven is represented as "buzzity-fizz" and seventy-five is "fizzity-buzz."

The game continues until every player but one has been eliminated.

Baseball Bingo

My husband came up with this game as a way to parody baseball obsessives—of which he is one—and also as a way to include the nonfan friends for a sports-watching party. The game works best for baseball, because 90 percent of the telecast is everything happening *between* the plays—shots of the dugout or a guy waiting at first base. You can adjust it for any sport; however, it's best for sports with a lot of players.

PLAYERS: 2–10

THE GEAR: Paper, pencil, a few dollars per player, a preselected baseball game.

The Game Plan
✖ Before the game begins, have guests come up with predictions on what might happen: who'll spit, drop a fly ball, trip, flip down his shades, cross himself, hitch his crotch,

be caught playing cards in the dugout, blow a bubble, etc.—you can have as many predictions as your group can create. Then have each guest "adopt" a player of his choosing. Write the predictions horizontally across the top of the page in a row—as many as will fit on a page—and the players/guests in a vertical column along the left-hand side. Either photocopy this sheet or ask each guest to copy it.

✠ Guests ante up a small amount of money—no more than a few dollars each.

✠ As the game progresses, guests will closely watch their adopted players. Each time a player fulfills one of the predictions—David Wright takes off his cap, for example—his box gets a check.

Winning

At the end of the game, the guest/player with the most checks wins the pot.

Braves Versus Mets

	Argues with umpire	Spits	Takes off cap	Grabs crotch	Waves to crowd
Fran = Bobby Cox	✔	✔			
Ken = Chipper Jones	✔	✔	✔✔		✔
Leigh = José Reyes		✔		✔	
Jen = David Wright		✔✔✔	✔	✔	
Mark = Jason Heyward		✔✔			✔

Brain Teasers

PLAYERS: 4–20

THE GEAR: For the host, paper, pen, a book of brain teasers—visual puzzles, math problems, logic problems, any kind of mind puzzles. Index cards, paper, pencils.

Using a book of brain teasers and logic puzzles (see sidebar, below, or type "brain teasers" into Google), write down a bunch of questions and solutions on index cards. When your guests arrive, give them each a pencil and paper. Have one player read out a question. The rest of the players race to figure out the solution. If the first person to call out an answer is correct, he gets a point. If he's wrong, he loses a point. (So negative scores are possible.)

The next card is drawn by another player and read aloud to the group. Continue drawing and reading until the cards are all gone. The player with the most points wins. For a less rambunctious crowd, print out the

Check Out These Books for Ideas:

- *Brain Teasers: 211 Logic Puzzles, Lateral Thinking Games, Mazes, Crosswords, and IQ Tests to Exercise Your Mind and Keep You Sharp 'til You're 100*

- *Logic Puzzles to Bend Your Brain*

- *The Total Brain Workout*

- *My Best Mathematical and Logic Puzzles*

- *The Big Book of Brain Games*

questions and divide the players into teams. Let the teams work on groups of ten puzzles at a time within a certain time frame, say fifteen minutes. The team with the most correct answers at the end of the time wins.

A Few Ideas to Get You Started

Question 1: A professor of antiquities has just returned from a six-month trip to the Middle East. In one of her recent blog posts, she said the highlight of the trip was seeing many of the ancient artifacts first hand; for example, several mummies and tapestries dating as far back as 200 B.C., coins dated 46 B.C., and weapons made of metal from approximately 500 B.C. What is wrong with the professor's claim?
    Answer: *Coins were never dated "B.C."*

Question 2: Mike Peters was surprised to see his window slide open and two strangers climb inside. What transpired next could only be described as a despicable act of thievery. Mike watched as the two thieves systematically began to remove his home's priceless Persian carpets, artwork, and jewelry. Having stripped the room, the thieves climbed back out the window. Mike went back to what he had been doing before the thieves arrived and soon he'd forgotten about the entire incident. Why wouldn't Mike have tried to stop the thieves or at the very least have called the police after they had left?
    Answer: *Mike Peters is a six-month-old baby.*

Question 3: What is a five-letter word whose pronunciation isn't changed by removing four of the letters?
    Answer: *Queue.*

—These came from the great site mindtrapgames.com. Check it out for more puzzles and brain teasers.

Arithmetic Croquet

This two-person mental-math game was invented by Lewis Carroll in 1872. As you know, the actual game of croquet is played on a lawn by hitting balls across the ground with mallets (see page 348). The players construct a course beforehand consisting of wire hoops through which each player needs to hit her ball in order. The first player to hit her ball through the hoops in the proper order and then hit the wooden peg at the end of the course is the winner.

Arithmetic Croquet can be easily played without any equipment (e.g., sitting on a beach or taking a walk). It is loosely based on an imaginary croquet course laid out along the number line. The object of the game is to get through the "hoops" and then hit the "winning peg." There is a hoop at each multiple of ten (ten, twenty . . .) and the winning peg at 100. The position of each player's imaginary ball is represented by a number. Play proceeds from left to right increasing along the number line toward 100. The first time you play you'll probably feel like you have no idea what you're doing, but you'll get the hang of it.

PLAYERS: 2

The Game Plan

✸ The first player names a number from one to eight.

✸ The second player does the same.

✸ Each turn, a player must name a new, higher number. The new number may not be more than eight higher than the number the player named on his previous turn.

✴ The amount by which a player increases his number from one turn to the next is known as a "step."

Barring: A player is *barred* from taking a step that is equal to the most recent step his opponent took, nor may he take a step that is equal to the difference between his opponent's last step and nine. So, if a player takes a step of six—by going, for example, from seven to thirteen—his opponent may not take a step of either six or three on the next turn. He loses the power to bar his opponent when he is at a number between ninety and one hundred, unless his opponent is also between ninety and one hundred.

Hoops: The numbers ten, twenty, thirty, and so on (multiples of ten) are called "hoops." There are *two ways* to go through hoops:

■ To "take" a hoop, a player must go from a number below it to one the same distance above it. For example, a player may go from seventeen to twenty-three (because seventeen is three less than twenty and twenty-three is three more than twenty). To go from seventeen to any other number above twenty causes the player to "miss the hoop."

■ In order to bar his opponent from taking a step of a certain size, a player may "miss" a hoop by deliberately playing beyond it without following the above rules, but then he *must* move backward on his next turn to go to any number below the hoop. If he misses the same hoop twice, he loses the game.

■ A player may also go through a hoop by "playing into it" in two turns. In the first

turn, she would play from seventeen to twenty, and then on the next turn from twenty to twenty-three.

■ If a player "plays into a hoop" in this manner, *he temporarily* (for that turn only) *loses the power to bar his opponent* from taking a step of the same size or a step of nine minus the same size.

Trapping an opponent in a hoop: A player can get temporarily stuck in a hoop if his opponent takes a step of a size that bars the player from using the number he needs to get out of the hoop. This is possible because when a player plays into a hoop, he temporarily loses the power to bar his opponent. If Player A "plays into a hoop" by going from 17 to 20, on his next turn he will need to "play out of the hoop" by going from 20 to 23. Player B knows this and will take a step of three—going from 15 to 18 to block Player A from playing out of the hoop. If this happens, the player loses his turn and must wait for the opponent to take a step of a size that will allow him to move. If a step of a certain size will keep the opponent stuck in a hoop, a player may not take such a step more than once in a row—but he may alternately take steps equal to that size and the difference between that size and 9 in order to cause the opponent to lose more than one turn. For example, if a player has taken a step from 27 to 30, the other can trap him by taking steps of 3, 6, 3, 6, etc.

Winning

The winner is the first player to get to 100. The 100 "winning peg" may, like each hoop, be missed once; but missing it twice loses the game.

Secret Signals

Slightly physical and a little bit goofy, Secret Signals is also practice in decoding signals, rapidly playing, and discarding cards while keeping an eye on your opponents' movements. It is definitely silly, and may not be for people who like more intellectually challenging games. But it's perfect for when you've had a few glasses of wine and are ready to laugh and have a good time. All ages can play, too, as long as they're able to understand the rules and give the signal unobtrusively and at the appropriate time.

PLAYERS: 4–8, divided into teams of 2, plus a non-playing dealer.

THE GEAR: A deck of cards.

Objective

The goal of the game is for one player to obtain a four of a kind (all four 3s, jacks, aces, or whatever—called a *set*), at which point he gives his team member their agreed-upon secret signal and the team member says "Game" out loud, thus netting their team one point.

▸▸ **HOST TIP**
Do not play this game with brand-new cards, as they will get banged up.

The Game Plan

✖ Divide players into teams of two. Team members should briefly step into another room and decide on a secret signal before sitting down for the game. Seat team members opposite each other.

✖ The dealer deals four cards facedown to each player and then four cards faceup on the middle of the table. Players pick up their cards and arrange them into sets.

✖ The dealer counts to three and says "Go!"—at which point the cards on the table are free for anyone to grab. As a player takes a card from the table, he must immediately replace it with a discard from his hand. A player should only have four cards in his hand at any time (except for the moment between picking up and discarding). A player can repeat this picking up and discarding as many times as he wants during the round.

Secret Signals

- Each player on the team has to use the same signal (meaning Player A can't use tugging on the ear while Player B uses coughing).

- Signals can't be verbal—they must be visual or aural.

- Signals must be performed where others can see them (you may not nudge someone under the table).

- Subtle signs are usually better than blatant ones because they're harder to guess. Good signals include:

  — tapping the top of your cards with your finger
  — switching cards from one hand to the other
  — fanning cards vs. closing them
  — flaring your nostrils
  — spinning your earring or your ring
  — biting your lip

- Decoy signals are not allowed (e.g., blatantly tugging your ear just before using your real signal).

- When nobody wants the cards left on the table, the dealer clears those cards. These cards are now out of play.

- The dealer deals four new cards on the table and again says "Go!" This continues until someone collects a set of four and her teammate calls "Game."

  NOTE: The player who collected the set cannot call "Game"—only her teammate can, after receiving the secret signal.

- The other team gets one attempt, beginning with the player to the right of the person who shouted "Game," to guess the winning team's signal. If they get it right, the winning team loses the point and it goes to the "guessers" instead. If they don't guess the signal, the winning team keeps the point.

- Play until one team has 5 points.

- If a player calls "Game," the dealer will check his teammate's cards. If his teammate does *not* have a set (all four of one number), the team loses a point.

- If another team's guess is pretty close to, but not exactly, what the winning team's signal is, then the winners have to ask the guessers to be more specific (e.g., if the guess is *something to do with the hands* and your signal is to *gather all the cards into one hand,* then ask the guessers to be more specific). The guess has to be exactly right.

- A team cannot change signals unless and until their sign has been correctly guessed by another team.

Strategy

Try to remember what cards your partner and the other teams are picking up and seem to be collecting. If you think your partner is collecting fours and you have one in your hand, pick up a random card so you can discard your four and your partner can pick it up. Or, if you think a player on another team is collecting nines, don't discard yours until absolutely necessary.

Keep your eyes open for secret signals between the other teams so that you can guess it after they call "Game."

Also try to remember which cards are out of play so that you don't get stuck waiting for your last five when it was put out of play at the end of the first round.

Make sure your signal isn't something you'll do unconsciously (like tucking your hair behind your ear) or your partner might call "Game" before you have a set.

Make sure you watch your partner for the signal! Many times another team will win because a teammate was too busy watching the other teams for signals while his own partner was desperately trying to get his attention. In order to win the round, you have to call "Game"—even if your partner has had a set for ages. If another team gets a set and calls "Game" first, the round is over and the other team gets the point. Unless, of course, you guess their signal.

Eleusis Express 👓

A card game of inductive reasoning in which the players make up secret rules, Eleusis was invented by Robert Abbot in 1956. His game is a little too complicated to go into here, but fortunately, John Golden, a mathematics professor, has developed this simplified version. It's a social game of observation and reasoning that can be as simple or as complicated as players choose.

PLAYERS: 3–8. Probably best with 4 or 5.

THE GEAR: At least two decks of cards, shuffled together. If the stock runs out, you can (a) shuffle in another deck or (b) declare the round over at that point.

The Terrain

A large playing area—because the "board" can get quite large, Eleusis is usually played on the floor. All plays are made to a central layout (on a table or on the floor) that grows as the game progresses. The layout consists of a horizontal "mainline" of *correct* cards—those cards that follow the secret rule. Below the mainline are vertical "sidelines" of *incorrect* cards—those that did not follow the rule.

The Deal

Choose a dealer at random. The dealer won't play a hand this round; he will make up a "secret rule" which governs the order in which cards may be played. If your group is

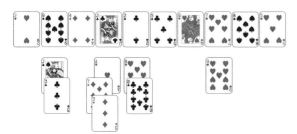

Sample game demonstrating Easy Rule #4

playing for the first time, the dealer should pick a rule from *Samples of Easy Secret Rules* (see following page). Say he picks Rule #4; he writes it down, showing no one else, then deals twelve cards to the other players. The rest of the cards are set aside as a stock.

The Game Plan

⚐ The dealer turns over the top card of the stock and puts it on the table. This will be the start of the mainline.

⚐ Starting with the player to the dealer's left, a player puts one card on the table.

⚐ The dealer says whether it's correct or not. If correct, it goes to the right of the last card on the mainline. If incorrect, it goes below the last card (it either starts a sideline or it adds to a sideline). The player who makes an incorrect play must draw one card from the deck, so his hand will remain the same size. A player who makes a correct play does not draw a card, so his hand is reduced by one.

⚐ **Guessing the Rule:** If a player lays down a correct card, he may try to guess the Rule. The dealer then says whether the player is right or wrong. If he is wrong, he draws a card and the game continues. If he is right, the round ends.

⚐ **Declaring "No Play":** A player may also say "No play," declaring that he does not have any correct cards to lay down. If so, he must show his hand to everyone and the dealer says whether the player is right or not, but he could be "right" for the wrong reason.

- If the player is right—he really could not have played—he sets any card in the sideline. He may then try to guess the rule. If it was the player's last card, he *must* try to guess the rule. If he's correct, the round is over. If he's incorrect, he draws a card.

- If the player is wrong—he could have played—the dealer chooses one correct card from the player's hand and puts it on the layout to the right of the last mainline card. The player must then draw one card from the stock.

Scoring

If a player correctly guesses the rule, or if one player gets rid of all his cards, the hand comes to an end. The scores are then recorded. Each player scores 12 points, minus 1 point for each card left in his hand. If a player correctly guessed the rule, he is given a 6-point bonus. If a player got rid of all his cards, he is given a 3-point bonus. The dealer scores the same as the highest-scoring player in the round.

Winning

Once everyone's had a chance to be the dealer, add up the scores for the hands and declare the winner. The designer notes that people usually play without points—just trying to guess the rule is fun enough.

SAMPLES OF EASY SECRET RULES:

1. If the last card was red, play a black card. If the last card was black, play a red card. In all these rules, "last card" refers to the last card accepted on the mainline or, if no card has yet been accepted, it refers to the "starter" card.

2. If the last card was a spade, play a heart; if the last card was a heart, play a diamond; if last was a diamond, play a club; and if last was a club, play a spade.

3. The cards on the mainline must follow this pattern: three red cards, then three black, then three red, then three black, etc.

4. If the last card is an odd-numbered card, play an even-numbered card; if the last is even, play an odd. When numbers are involved, ace is 1 (odd), jack is 11 (odd), queen is 12 (even), and king is 13 (odd).

5. If the last card is among the cards ace to 7, play a card 8 to king. If last is among 8 to king, play ace to 7.

6. The card played must be the same suit or the same number as the last card.

SAMPLES OF HARD SECRET RULES:

1. If the last card is an odd-numbered card, play a red card. If the last card is even, play a black card.

2. Play a card with a number that is 1, 2, or 3 higher than the number of the last card. The numbers can "turn the corner."

3. If the last card is black, play a card with a number that is equal to or lower than the number of the last card. If the last card is red, play a card equal to or higher than the last card.

Only the dealer may see these samples, as then it would be too easy to guess the rule. But as dealers get the hang of the game, they will make up their own rules for each new game. A rule should allow for several cards to be played at any given time, but not too many. "The next card must be one higher" is too restrictive. "The next card must be a different suit" is too permissive. Avoid exceptions or wild cards, like "face cards are always right" or "an ace can be high or low." And remember: Whatever rule you come up with, it will always be harder than you think.

Chapter Twelve

TRIVIA GAMES

Trivia games, in the form of television and radio shows, have been a major part of American entertainment for decades. But trivia games *really* burst into the national consciousness when Trivial Pursuit was introduced in 1981; tens of millions of copies have been sold since. In other words: If you've been a human being on this earth in the last 30 years, you've probably played a trivia game.

There's a reason they endure: Trivia games offer a certain satisfaction to those with capacious memories for useless facts—to people who are good at them, the games are proof of their intelligence. (To those who aren't good at trivia, the games are just an indicator of a capacious memory for useless facts.) But however you feel about trivia games, they're everywhere: The game shows *Who Wants to Be a Millionaire* and *Jeopardy!* have enthralled the nation (and the world) for years; Facebook has dozens if not hundreds of trivia groups; and a whole new generation of trivia board games has been born in the last ten years.

Trivia pub quizzes have recently revived the game—they add a sense of purpose and focus to boozing that people really haven't had since Prohibition. They're also great date-bait: You can show off your smarts to the cutie across the room. They let you access the deep recesses of your brain for odd facts you never knew you knew, let alone remembered. At one trivia game, the question presented to my team was "Also known as Chinese knotting, this craft is widely practiced by children making pot holders at summer camp." For some reason the word *lanyard* lodged itself in my brain, blocking out all other possible answers. We hemmed and hawed for at least ten minutes until the other team,

exasperated, said, "Look, if you don't know it, it's not the kind of thing that's going to pop into your—"

"Macramé!" I shouted. And that's the sweet kismet of trivia games.

The key thing to keep in mind when writing or compiling a trivia game is *variety*. No one wants to sit through four hours of baseball arcana, and trivia about classic rock can get tedious awfully fast. Particularly if you're playing a general trivia game, that is, one without a theme, you want to give everyone a shot at correctly answering a few questions. So mix it up, and let's get started.

Check out these books for a wealth of trivia questions:

- *The Big Book of American Trivia*
- *Do You Know? Ultimate Trivia Book*
- *The Bathroom Trivia Book*
- *The Best Trivia Book Ever!!!*
- *Ken Jennings's Trivia Almanac*
- *5,087 Trivia Questions and Answers*

How to Prepare for a Trivia Night

The best number of players for a trivia night is six to twenty people in teams of two to six. Motivate your guests with a few silly prizes or gift cards for the winners.

Trivia nights are best played in *sets*—but how many questions per set, and how many sets total, depends on your guests' attention spans (and *your* stamina for compiling questions). I suggest five sets of ten questions each, following the guidelines below, with a blank answer sheet for each set. Each set should have a theme and ideally should play to different strengths: one set of sports questions, one of art history, etc. Consider what will jazz your guests and choose accordingly.

Compiling the questions: You can use Trivial Pursuit, a kids' encyclopedia, your own head, a trivia book (see sidebar, left), or an online trivia site such as pubquizusa.com, funtrivia .com, legendstrivia.com, sporcle.com, and trivia .com. Your answer sheets can be multiple-choice (create two wrong answers to go with each correct answer) or fill-in-the-blank.

You want questions that can be answered by 40 to 80 percent of the players. Random, really hard trivia questions that no one can answer aren't that much fun.

The Sets

Not all sets need to be structured this way, but this is a good jumping-off point if you've never hosted a trivia night before.

First set: Begin with ten standard trivia questions. The moderator calls out the questions and teams mark the answers on their sheets. The round should have a theme: baseball; famous Marys; classic rock; types of birds; world currency.

Second set: Try some audio questions— Name That Tune, for example, in which you play a snippet of a well-known song or clip from a famous film, and teams must guess the name. (Meg Ryan's orgasm scene in *When Harry Met Sally* comes to mind, or Carol Kane's "Mith? Mith?" "Yeth?" in *The Muppet Movie*.) Scroll through your music library or search through IMDB.com for ideas. I stumped someone with this revolting audio clip from the 1985 teen movie *Weird Science:* "How about a nice greasy pork sandwich, served in a dirty ashtray?"

Third set: Create visual questions, printed out ahead of time. For example, before the party:

✖ Google a bunch of maps from your area, delete identifying road names, town names, etc., print them out, and have teams write in the name of a highlighted landmark.

✖ Find an online map of any given area—it can be as big as the Balkans or as small as the five boroughs of New York City. Delete any identifying text, print them out, and have teams identify the location.

✖ Provide extremely close-up photographs of everyday objects or body parts and have players identify what they are. If you take a very close-up photo of a soda can tab or the tines of a fork, the images will be abstract enough to stump people.

Fourth set: This one, like the third set, is also a handout (unlike the first two sets, which are called "call-out" rounds). This can be anagrams—How many words can you make from *Madonna Louise Ciccone?*—or logic puzzles.

Fifth set: End with another round of standard trivia questions, but with a twist: Teams have the option of betting some or all of their accrued points on the final question of the night. This allows teams that are far behind to pull off a surprise upset and win the whole game.

Multiple-Choice Trivia Game

The simplest way to host a trivia evening is with plain old multiple-choice trivia questions. Before the guests arrive, create a few dozen trivia questions from an encyclopedia and/or the Web (see pages 220–221 for inspiration), or grab a pack of Trivial Pursuit cards. Be sure to choose questions from a variety of topics. A good resource for questions is high-school textbooks. (Do *you* remember who John Brown was? How about how to find the area of a sphere?) If you're playing with kids, check out *Are You Smarter Than a Fifth Grader?* on fox.com or scholastic.com for sample multiple-choice questions. (If creating the multiple-choice answers seems like too much effort, forgo the answer choices and just have teams answer the questions.)

PLAYERS: 4–20, plus a nonplaying moderator.

The Game Plan

When your guests arrive, divide the group into teams of two to six players each. Read out the first question to Team A. Give them a moment to confer and debate and then offer their "final answer." If they're right, the team gets a point. If they're wrong, Team B gets a shot. Regardless, play alternates: Getting an answer right does not mean that a team gets to go again.

Possible themes for trivia games:
- Quotes from TV and movies
- Current celebrity gossip
- Current political gossip
- Urban legends, superstitions, and myths
- The ancient Roman empire
- The 1980s in general (politics, art, music, movies, etc.)
- Sorcery and witchcraft
- English language terminology
- Abnormal psych/mental illness/psychopathology trivia

Trivia Betting

Trivia games can be difficult for those of us who don't know, well, anything. They can expose embarrassing gaps in our educations, in our knowledge of current events, in being *au courant* with pop culture. They make us wonder what the hell we were doing during all those years of school. Doodling? Lining our lips? Playing games like Fantasy Football?

But let's say that, despite our lack of knowledge of, like, *stuff*, we have a *deep understanding* of people. (This is how I comfort myself, anyway.) We have intuition, sensitivity, the ability to look into the human heart and predict others' actions. Well, Trivia Betting plays to those strengths. You gain points for, yes, correctly choosing an answer—but you also gain points for correctly predicting how *other* people are going to answer. So you use your knowledge of the other players (or your intuition, if you've only just met the other players) to anticipate how they're going to answer, and profit from that.

PLAYERS: 6–15

THE GEAR: A trivia book or homemade trivia multiple-choice questions (see pages 220–221 for sources), sheets of paper or notepads, and pens.

The Game Plan

✖ Distribute a sheet of paper and a pen to each player and put a stack of multiple-choice trivia questions or a trivia book in the center of the playing area.

✖ Players take turns being the "Guesser." The Guesser selects a multiple-choice question at random from a trivia card or book. Have the Guesser, without looking, put his finger down on a question. This will prevent players from examining the available trivia questions and choosing only those they know how to answer.

✖ The Guesser reads the question and the answer choices aloud and takes a moment to ponder how he will answer it. While he's pondering, the other players write down (keeping their papers out of the view of others) what they think the Guesser will answer (a, b, c, etc.).

✖ Then the Guesser chooses an answer and says it aloud. He then looks up the correct answer and reads it out.

✖ The Guesser gets a point if he gets the correct answer. Players who correctly predicted what the Guesser would choose—whether the Guesser chose rightly or not—get a point as well.

Winning

Play to an agreed-upon number of points, say ten. The first person to reach ten wins a year's subscription to *The Onion*.

▶▶ **IF YOU LIKE THIS GAME . . . check out Wits and Wagers, available at toy and book stores.**

Trivia Fictionary

Trivia Fictionary is more about bluffing than trivia, which makes it a good game for folks who don't keep 20,000 arcane facts at their fingertips. As in Fictionary (see page 101), there will be one correct answer and many incorrect ones. The goal of the game is to simultaneously make up an answer that is believable enough to trick other players to vote for it *and* to determine which of the read-aloud answers are true.

PLAYERS: 4–10

THE GEAR: A pack of Trivial Pursuit cards, slips of paper, pens.

AMP IT UP

If you'd like to get to know your friends' personal and intimate peccadilloes a little better, see if they're up for this "naughty" version: At the beginning of the game, ask each player to make up five or so personal questions with multiple-choice answers. For example: "If you had to choose a part of the opposite sex's body to fetishize, what would it be? A: the feet B: the neck C: the buttocks D: the hair." Put all the questions and answer choices in a hat. (Alert the players, when they're writing their questions, that they may end up answering questions they themselves wrote.) When the Guesser draws a question, he must choose an answer from a, b, c, or d, and the other players will bet on how they think he will answer. If you didn't know about Greg's foot fetish before, you will now.

The Game Plan

- Players take turns being the Reader. To start, the Reader draws a card from the Trivial Pursuit pack and chooses an answer from it (e.g., *Seven, Nova Scotia, The Brady Bunch, Ted Williams, 923,* etc.). He reads this answer—but not the question—aloud.

- Each player must now imagine a question for this answer. Players will write down their made-up questions on slips of paper and pass them to the Reader, who will check to make sure he can decipher everyone's handwriting. (In the event that clarification is needed, a player can whisper in the Reader's ear.) The Reader will write down the real question.

- Then, the Reader will read, in no particular order, all of the questions passed to him, as well as the "real" question. He should take care not to stumble over anyone's writing, as that's a dead giveaway that he's reading a made-up answer. (Unless, of course, he's bluffing.)

- Players will then say, one by one (starting with the player to the left of the Reader), which question they think is the "real" question. If you'd like to eliminate answers influencing others, players may write down their guesses and initials and pass them to the Reader to tally.

- Players win a point for a) guessing the real question and/or b) having another player guess that their fake question was the real one. The Reader gets a point only if no one guesses the real question.

- For the next round, the Reader will be the person sitting to the left of the previous Reader. Continue until everyone has had a chance to be the Reader. Highest score wins.

Trivia Bee

A trivia bee is like a spelling bee—and is great because of its simplicity: Get a question wrong and you're eliminated. If you're playing in a car, you'll need to do a little advance prep and print out questions and answers.

PLAYERS: 3–20

THE GEAR: 100 slips of paper or index cards, each with a trivia question written or printed on them.

The Game Plan

Have everyone stand in a line, as for a spelling bee, or, more casually, seat everyone in a circle. Pose a question to the first player. If she answers correctly, she stays in the game. If not, she's out. Pose a question to the next player, and so on. Continue playing until only one contestant is left—award that player a copy of the DVD *Spellbound,* a wonderful documentary about spelling bees.

In a recent game, we kept the questions confined to the single theme of urban legends, hoaxes, and myths. (Check out snopes.com, a great resource for urban legend questions.) We played a two-part bee—first, players had to "fill in the blank," and second, players had to say whether the story was true or an urban legend. Players could be eliminated for getting either part of the question wrong.

This is the question that put me out of the game: "Prospective gang members are or were being initiated by killing the drivers of cars who __." I answered "Flash their high beams at them!" (Which was correct!)

Then I said, yes, it was a true story, not an urban legend. Which was the wrong answer and eliminated me from the game in the third round. Sob. I heard it in the '90s and I'd always thought it was true.

Hometown Quiz

PLAYERS: 3–50

THE GEAR: Paper, pencils, a book or website about your state.

A game for people who grew up in the same area—so it's great fun for a large family or a reunion of childhood friends (though people *new* to an area, like students arriving for a grad program, might also enjoy the game as a way to learn about their new stomping grounds).

Ahead of time, jot down fifty facts about your hometown and state. Then turn the facts into a quiz: What's the state flower? The nickname? If you're so inclined, research your state's old and oddball laws and include a few in the bunch. Did you know that in 1897 the Indiana General Assembly proposed that "pi" be defined as 3? (Math *would* be so much easier!) Or that "professional" fortune-telling is illegal in North Carolina? Amateur divining—as long as it takes place in a school or a church—is fine.

Print out each question on a slip of paper and put them in a hat.

Have players take turns reading the questions out loud; each player jots down what she thinks is the correct answer. (If you like, and have the time, you can create

a multiple-choice "quiz.") At the end, the person with the most correct answers wins.

Tabloid Trivia

PLAYERS: 4–20

THE GEAR: Supermarket tabloids, gossip newspapers, websites, paper, hat.

Using the supermarket checkout-line newspapers as source material, create short, one- or two-sentence celebrity stories from the patently false articles in the tabloids—that the father of Britney Spears's children is really Bill Clinton; that Michael Jackson kept a vial of monkey glands around his neck at all times; that Dolly Parton, in her youth, was a Nazi skinhead. Find a bunch of weird-but-true facts about celebrities as well: Check out the biography section in the bookstore, weirdnews.about.com, or even Wikipedia for sources. For example, did you know that Amy Smart sanitized the stripper poles when filming the sequel to *Crank*? Or that Cary Grant used LSD for therapeutic purposes?

Write or print these short stories on slips of paper; mark on the paper whether the story is true or false. Put all the papers in a hat. Have players pull out a question and ask the others whether they think it's true or false. Each person who guesses correctly gets a point.

Variation
You can also play this game as a variation on Fictionary: The host compiles a bunch

of true-but-weird stories about celebs ahead of time. The Reader pulls out the real story, reveals the name of the celebrity, and all the guests write down a fake story relating to that person. See pages 100–101 for how to score Fictionary.

PARTY RECIPE

Guacamole

Trivia quizzes often go with beer; and no snack goes better with beer than guac and chips. SERVES 4

INGREDIENTS

2 ripe avocados	black pepper
½ red onion, chopped fine	1–2 serrano chilies, stems and seeds removed, chopped fine
1 tablespoon fresh lime juice	½ tomato, chopped
½ teaspoon salt	

1. Scoop out avocado from the peel, discard the pit, and mash in a bowl. Add the chopped onion, lime juice, salt, and pepper, and mash again.

2. Gradually add the chilies, tasting as you go, to desired degree of spiciness. NOTE: Be careful handling the peppers: Wash your hands after handling with a degreaser detergent to remove the oil, and do not touch your eyes or any other sensitive parts of your body for several hours afterward.

3. Just before serving, add the chopped tomato to the guacamole and mix. Serve with tortilla chips and the best beer you can afford.

Current Events Trivia

Ever heard the NPR quiz show *Wait Wait . . . Don't Tell Me*? It's a trivia contest based on the week's news—with the twist that the panelists also make up fake news stories to try to trick the contestants. (In this way it's a little like Dictionary, but longer, more involved, and more absurd.) A home game of Current Events Trivia in which you and your guests will make up trivia questions on the week's news will be much simpler. Each guest is responsible for creating a few questions for others to answer. Below is a sample game in four rounds—it's for the hardiest of trivia buffs. If that's too demanding for your gang, just limit the game to two rounds.

PLAYERS: 4–8. The game below is for 6, plus a scorekeeping moderator. You can play with as few as 3 people, plus an optional scorekeeping moderator.

THE GEAR: Paper and pencil for keeping score; an optional bell for ringing when questions are answered correctly. Even more optional: a gong for when questions are answered incorrectly.

Preparation

Some prep work is required for all; you will be asking two guests to write fake news stories and all guests to find three trivia questions each.

✴ About a week before the party, ask two guests to each create a *fake* news story—

something ridiculous and outlandish but still faintly plausible; each of these stories should be about two or three paragraphs long. You, the host/moderator, will find a real news story that is ridiculous and outlandish but still *real*. E-mail a third guest your real news story and let her know that she will be asked to read it aloud during the game. *These three guests should not tell other guests that they have been charged with this mission.* These fake news stories, along with your real story, will be used in Part Three of the game.

✖ In addition, instruct all your guests to write three trivia questions: one basic question based on any event in the week's news, one question based on a *quote* from the week's news, and one multiple-choice question based on something historical—an event, a person, an institution, etc. Players should allow their imaginations free rein on this one.

NOTE: For inspiration, turn your dial to npr .org/waitwait to hear the real deal and to get some sample questions.

The Game Plan

The game is played in four rounds. After each question, the answer is revealed, so players will know immediately if they got the question right or wrong. Each correct question counts for one point. The moderator will keep track of the scores.

Round One: Quotes from the News Each player must read her "quote from the week's news" aloud to another player, pretending to be that voice in the news, and then follow up with a short explanation. The question is always "Who said this quote?" or some variation thereof.

The other player must guess who said it and what it is about. If the guesser gets it right, she gets a point.

Sample question: "You should have seen him, going town to town, country to country, Energizer Bunny here. It killed me." That's former President George H. W. Bush describing his newest pal, who apparently just keeps going and going, despite heart surgery in 2004. Who is Poppy Bush's Energizer Bunny?

Answer: Bill Clinton. Former Presidents Bush and Clinton launched a joint effort across partisan lines to raise money for victims of the Indian Ocean tsunami in 2005, and they've been getting along famously ever since.

Round Two: Questions about the Week's News Each player poses her question to another player. This should *not* be the same pairing as in Round One: Make sure that you vary who is receiving which question from whom, just in case a certain guest has made all his questions fiendishly hard or comically easy.

These questions should be standard answer-the-question questions about the week's news.

Sample question: This week, an umpire at a high school baseball game in Iowa threw *who* out of the game?

Answer: All the fans.

Round Three: Current Events Fictionary Inform your guests that three stories from the week's news will now be read aloud—but only one of them is real. (These stories are usually on a theme, but you may dispense with that if the added restriction is daunting.) Have your three guests (two of whom will have written their own stories and one of whom will be in possession of the real story that you e-mailed to her) read the stories aloud. These panelists should pull out their best acting chops to convince the listeners that their story is the real one, as any listener who votes for a panelist's story earns the panelist a point.

The other three players write down which story they think is real. After everyone has written their answers, reveal the answer.

Everyone who chooses the real story gets a point. A panelist, including the panelist reading the real story, gets a point if a listener chooses his story.

Round Four: Multiple-Choice Trivia Each player now presents her historical multiple-choice question to another player. (On the show, these are questions on a theme, and usually historical, like Supreme Court history, Cary Grant's dressing-room peccadilloes, Second Amendment trivia, etc.) The questions are usually interesting *and* wacky.

Sample question: The Indians, the Cubs, and the Red Sox are now official baseball team names, but they used to be informal nicknames, often given by sportswriters. Which of these was a real nickname applied to the team now known as the Cincinnati Reds?

a. The Porkopolitans
b. The Flower Boys
c. The Chiaroscuros

Answer: The Porkopolitans. Back in the 1880s, the team was owned by a meatpacker. By the way, because of anti-Communist concerns in the 1950s, the Reds were briefly known as the Redlegs.

And that's it! Tally up the scores and announce the champion. An inexpensive prize may be awarded to the winner, like the *Wait Wait . . . Don't Tell Me!* audiobook, or she can just bask in the glow of her current events superiority.

> **STEALTH STRATEGY**
>
> Peruse science newspapers, magazines, and blogs—these always make good fodder for interesting questions.

HOST TIP

For maximum enjoyment, ask the guests who wrote the questions to have a little explanation ready.

Six Degrees of Kevin Bacon

This game is what you might call a meme. No one knows where it started, no one knows why they know what it is, or why Kevin Bacon is the centerpiece. Wikipedia claims that three college students created the game in 1994, but who knows? Wikipedia's been wrong before. I've known about it since the '90s.

PLAYERS: 2–10

The premise is simple: Name an actor or actress and try to connect that person to Kevin Bacon in as few links as possible. So if you said "Elizabeth McGovern," she can be linked to KB with one degree of separation. (They starred together in *She's Having a Baby*.) But if you named, say, Leonardo DiCaprio, he'd have two degrees of separation. (DiCaprio was in *The Quick and the Dead* with Sharon Stone, who was in *He Said, She Said* with Kevin Bacon.) If you want to practice online, go to oracleofbacon.org.

This game can go on for a pretty long time, so it's great if you're trying to stay awake while driving across Pennsylvania or one of the square states.

Winning

Six Degrees is noncompetitive, but if you'd like to eliminate people when they're stumped, you can crown the last person standing the winner.

AMP IT UP

Don't forget *Jeopardy!*, the TV show that's been running since 1964. Any trivia game can be played *Jeopardy!*-style—just give the answers instead of the questions, and contestants have to frame their answers in the form of a question. So the host might say, "The inventor of the theremin," and the contestant might answer, "Who was Leon Theremin?"

Quizlinks!

NEW GAME!

Quizlinks consists of four sets of four questions and should take about twenty minutes plus grading time. The goal of the game is not just to answer the questions but also, from the answers, to find the link for each set, and then the link, or the common theme, that connects the four sets.

PLAYERS: Teams typically consist of 2 to 6 people, but the size of the crowd is up to you.

THE GEAR: A copy of the questions and answers for the Quizmaster—i.e., you (see the following page). An answer sheet for each team. See Appendix, page 371, for an answer sheet you can copy.

The Game Plan

The Quizmaster reads the questions one by one, usually with about a ten-second pause between each question, so that teams can discuss the answer before they write it down. All teams note their answers on the answer sheet. Tell folks they can figure out the links at the end, after all the questions are read.

After all sixteen questions have been read, give teams about five minutes to figure out all the links. After the five minutes are up, teams turn in their answer sheets for grading— whether they've figured out the links or not. Each numbered question is worth five points, each lettered link is worth 10 points, and the final Quizlink at the bottom is worth a big 20 points. The team with the highest number of points at the end wins.

—contributed by Alisa Stewart of PubQuiz USA. For more about Alisa and to check out more of her quizzes, go to pubquizusa.com.

QUIZLINKS!

1. This rap album contains previously unreleased music recorded by Tupac Shakur before his death in 1996. Produced by Eminem, it was released on December 14, 2004, and is very reminiscent of Eminem's style. **A:** *Loyal to the Game*

2. Type III is a military classification of this, which can protect against 7.62 mm Full Metal Jacketed (FMJ) bullets. **A:** body armor

3. In chess, these two terms refer to the coordinate axes of the 8 x 8 square chess board. **A:** rank and file

4. This Mel Gibson movie introduced the world to the character of Mad Max. **A:** *The Road Warrior*

Link A: *Loyal+Armor+Rank+Warrior* = Knight

5. This torturous custom was started in the Teng dynasty on young females and lasted more than 1,000 years, finally being discontinued in the early twentieth century. **A:** foot binding

6. This off-Broadway show became a rock musical film in 2001 and featured a transsexual punk rock "girl" from East Berlin touring the United States with her rock band. **A:** *Hedwig & the Angry Inch*

7. This device, usually considered a children's toy, consists of a pole with a T-bar handle at one end and is used for hopping up and down. **A:** pogo stick

8. This Shakespeare comedy/tragedy centers around the fate of Claudio, who is sentenced to death by the moralistic Lord Angelo for impregnating his girlfriend Juliet out of wedlock. Claudio's chaste sister Isabella begs Lord Angelo to have mercy on her brother, and ironically, the lascivious Angelo will only let Claudio go if Isabella has sex with him. **A:** *Measure for Measure*

Link B: *Foot + Inch + Stick + Measure* = Ruler

9. This type of torture seemed necessary to use on terrorists to make 'em talk, according to Dick Cheney. **A:** water boarding

10. This '70s ABC TV spin-off starred Lindsay Wagner as a tennis professional nearly killed in a skydiving accident and rebuilt by Oscar Goldman. **A:** *The Bionic Woman*

11. This dangled over the head of a Greek figure by a single horsehair, which today epitomizes the feeling of impending doom. **A:** The Sword of Damocles

12. This 2003 Clint Eastwood film that starred Sean Penn garnered two Academy Awards, winning both in the best actor and best supporting actor categories. **A:** *Mystic River*

Link C: *Water + Woman + Sword + Mystic* = Lady of the Lake

13. In Disney's 1940 feature film *Fantasia*, this role was played by Mickey Mouse. **A:** The Sorcerer's Apprentice

14. The Assistant to the President for National Security Affairs is more commonly known by this title. **A:** National Security Advisor

15. This animated superhero created by Terrytoons studio in 1942 was originally a superpowered housefly. **A:** Mighty Mouse

16. This large London institution was the brainchild of physician, naturalist, and collector Sir Hans Sloane, who died in 1753. He wanted his collection of more than 71,000 objects, library, and herbarium to be preserved intact after his death, so he bequeathed it to King George II for the nation in return for payment of £20,000 to his heirs. **A:** The British Museum

Link D: *Sorcerer + Advisor + Mighty + British* = Merlin

20-Point Link to A-B-C-D: *Knight + Ruler + Lady of the Lake + Merlin* = King Arthur

Chapter Thirteen

A CARD-GAME REFRESHER

Gaming with cards is a very old pleasure. No one knows how or why it all began, but we do know that Asian fortune-telling arrows bore symbols that were later borrowed by Koreans for use on oiled paper playing cards. The ancient Chinese had similar cards, ancestors that resemble our current four-suit, fifty-two–card deck.

The games expert and writer John Scarne notes that the world's oldest known playing card was found in Chinese Turkestan and is believed to be from the eleventh century. In Chinese literature, cards are mentioned as early as the Tang dynasty (A.D. 618–907). We know that playing cards arrived in Europe in the fourteenth century, but we don't know exactly how they got there: They may have been brought by the Arab conquerors in Spain and Sicily, or via the China trade, or via the Crusades. The only certain thing is that card games spread like wildfire; church and governmental authorities objected; and cards have had the whiff of immorality, the occult, and great fun ever since.

Card games are the most elegant of games, as they perfectly blend strategy, psychology, and sociability. While luck plays a role in all games—some more than others—card games tend to favor the alert, the problem solvers, and the mathematically inclined. But even for those players who remember every card played, understand probability, and are not startled when that last ace appears on the last trick, cards still carry enough of a surprise element—the luck of the draw and the play of your opponents—to keep the games fresh. Cards also boast an infinite variety: They range from the simple matching kind (Go Fish) to more complicated partnership games, like Canasta. If you've got a deck, you've got a game. Politically inclined? Oh, Hell can't be beat for its unique blend of cooperation and the sudden double-cross. Enjoy the thrill of the chase? Try the cutthroat pace of Hearts. Need to while away some alone time? There are countless versions of Solitaire to keep you company. You like reading people as well as cards? Poker has enjoyed a massive wave of interest in the last few years with the advent of televised tournaments and online games open to anyone.

There exist literally thousands of card games, and volumes have been written about them. In fact, you can find volumes devoted to a single game, such as bridge or poker. We've selected a few of the most social, well-known games—the kind you might play with your neighbors over a beer and a bowl of chili.

The Skinny on Cards

Before you get that beer and break out the deck, you need to know that some words and slang terms are common to almost all card games. The games are easier to understand if you're familiar with the lingo. For the benefit of everyone in the family, we'll start at the very beginning with a few of the more basic terms.

Suits: Your basic deck of cards is made up of four "families," or suits, which are identified by a symbol. Hearts ♥ and diamonds ♦ are red suits, while spades ♠ and clubs ♣ are black. In the standard fifty-two–card deck, each suit consists of thirteen cards.

Rank or Value: Those thirteen cards each have their own numerical value or status or rank. In most games (there are some exceptions), the ace is the highest-ranked card, followed (in descending order) by the king, queen, jack (these three cards, bearing a picture of the royal member, are known as "face cards"). The nine remaining "number" cards are numbered in sequence from ten down to the lowly two (or "deuce"). Since there are four suits, there will be four aces, four kings, etc.

Wild Cards: Wild cards add variety to standard card games, but they also introduce an additional level of luck and uncertainty (excitement), and many serious card players avoid games that use them. Any card can be used as a wild card, but the most common are the deuce (sometimes all deuces, sometimes deuces of one color), the jack (sometimes all jacks, sometimes one-eyed jacks), and the joker. (Most decks come with two jokers; they are in addition to the fifty-two playing cards, and they have no suit or rank.) Before the cards are dealt, the dealer must name the card or cards that will be wild for that game. A player holding a wild card has the privilege of deciding the suit and/or rank that the card will represent, regardless of what is printed on the card. Because a wild card can become any card, based on the player's needs and strategy, it is a very valuable card.

Trump: In some games, one of the suits will be ranked higher than the other three. Any card in the trump suit will outrank the cards in the other three suits. If, for example, clubs are trump, the deuce of clubs outranks the ace of hearts, diamonds, or spades. In some games, players bid for the right to determine the trump suit, while in others it's decided by the turn of a card.

The Deal: Virtually all card games begin by dealing a specified number of cards to all players, beginning with the player to the left of the dealer and proceeding in a clockwise direction (so the dealer is dealt last). Most games require that the cards be dealt one at a time for as many times as it takes around the table, but for some games (like Euchre) the rules call for more than one card at a time. In almost all games, the action (bidding, betting, playing a card, etc.) begins with the player to the dealer's left and proceeds in a clockwise direction, in sequence from one player to the next.

Who Deals? In many games, it doesn't really matter who deals out the cards. But in some games—Poker and Pitch, to name just two—the dealer enjoys some advantages. In Poker, for example, the dealer's playing is informed by what all the players before him do, and how they do it. In Pitch, the dealer has the final bid, and in some cases can override anyone else's bid.

So to prevent brawls and bad feelings, it's best to have some random and impartial means of determining who deals. Here are the most common solutions:

✖ **First Ace Deals:** Any player shuffles the cards and deals out one card to each player, in turn, around the table. The first player to be dealt an ace becomes the dealer. If no ace appears on the first round, additional rounds are dealt until an ace appears. (Aces aren't magic—any card can be designated as the determiner.)

✖ **Pick a Card:** Place the deck facedown on the table and fan the cards out a bit. Each player draws one card at random from the deck. The highest ranking card drawn (or lowest—you decide beforehand) identifies the dealer.

Once the dealer has shuffled, she sets the pack facedown in front of the player to her right. That player, with one hand, lifts off approximately the top half of the deck—called *cutting the deck*—and sets that half facedown on the table beside the bottom half. The dealer picks up the bottom half, sets it on top, picks up the whole deck, and deals. Cutting the deck is a ritual of etiquette intended to reduce the chances that someone has arranged the cards in a particular order for the purposes of cheating.

The deal, in most games, moves to the player at the left of the dealer after a hand is completed, thus insuring that all players have a turn at dealing.

Keeping Score

Check out the Appendix for some versatile score cards.

A Word About the Rules

Card games behave like language: They change and evolve over time. Card players modify the "grammar" of games; they develop local "accents." They transform Whist into Contract Bridge and Rummy into Canasta. They introduce variations to make a game simpler or more challenging, or faster-paced, or to fill in gaps in memory.

You may sit down to play an old familiar game your grandfather taught you, only to find that someone else's grandfather taught a slightly different version. I've played games in which I was the only nonfamily member at the table, and discovered that this family had developed their own "house" rules.

So don't be surprised if there's at least one game in this chapter that prompts an outcry of "That's not the way this game is played!"

What I have tried to describe here are rules that are commonly accepted—basic rules. You may argue about what is orthodoxy and what is variation, but the differences in question are usually like local accents. They may alter some of your playing strategy, but they probably won't change the grammar or your understanding of the language of the game.

If you tend to be a purist who speaks only the Queen's English, you're welcome to bypass the bastardization suffered by some card games. But if you don't mind deciding for yourself which variations can add to your pleasure, then embrace the diversity—as long as all players agree on the rules before the cards are dealt, anything's game.

||||||||||||||||||||||||||||||||||||||||||||||||||||||||||||||||||||

Go Fish

A simple matching game for children, Go Fish is an excellent way to familiarize your kids with numbers and suits, and a good opportunity to teach them the honor system. For adults it will get dull fast, unless you turn it into a drinking game or otherwise raise the stakes a bit.

PLAYERS: 2–5

THE GEAR: A standard deck of 52 cards.

Objective
To get the most sets of four of a kind (all four cards of the same rank).

The Deal
Deal seven cards to each player if there are two players; with more than two players, deal five cards to each player. Set the remaining cards facedown in the middle of the playing area to form a stock—known in this game as the "ocean" or "pool." Players should arrange the cards in their hands by values—all the sevens together, all the aces together, etc.

The Game Plan
- The player to the left of the dealer begins. Let's call her Sally.

- Sally asks any other player for their cards of a certain rank. For example, Sally might ask Steve, "Steve, do you have any threes?" Players can't ask for cards they aren't holding.

- Steve must then hand over all cards of that rank. If the call was successful, Sally has another turn.

- If Steve does *not* have the requested cards, he tells Sally, "Go fish." This means the player must choose one card from the pool of cards at the center.

- Sally then draws a card from the pool, and the turn passes to the player on her left.

Variation
Some children play that as long as a player is successful—if she draws a card she needs from the pool—her turn continues. More often than not, though, when a player "goes fish," she will *not* get the card she was asking for, and the turn passes to another player.

- When a player collects four of the same cards of a given rank, they form a *book,* and the cards are placed faceup on the table.

- A player who makes a book earns an extra turn.

- The game is not over when a player runs out of cards. That player simply draws a card from the ocean, and the turn passes to the next player in the rotation.

Winning
When the ocean is empty, the player who has made the most books wins.

||||||||||||||||||||||||||||||||||||||||||||||||||||||||||||||||||||

Old Maid

O ld Maid, Queen of Spades, or Chase the Ace is a children's card game for two to eight players. It takes its name from an old term for an unmarried, elderly woman. Old Maid is an "avoidance" game—you don't so much try to win as you try not to lose.

PLAYERS: 2–8

THE GEAR: A standard deck of 52 cards, with the queen of spades removed.

Objective

Players must put together pairs of cards of the same rank (two fives, two kings, etc.). Because one queen is missing, there is always a queen that can't be paired. The player who is left with the unmatched card is "stuck with the Old Maid" and loses.

The Game Plan

✳ Choose a dealer at random; in subsequent games the dealer will shift to the left.

✳ The dealer deals all of the cards to the players. Some players may have more cards than others; this is acceptable.

✳ Players look at their cards and discard any pairs they have (e.g., two kings, two sevens, etc.) faceup. If you have three of a kind, you can only discard two of them.

✳ Beginning with the dealer, each player takes turns offering his hand facedown for the person on his left to select a card and add it to her hand. (A player is allowed to shuffle his hand before offering it to the player on his left.)

✳ This player then looks at the cards in her hand to see if the selected card can make a pair. If so, the pair is discarded face-up with the others.

✳ The player who just took a card then offers her hand facedown to the person to her left, and so on.

Winning

Eventually one player will be left with the lone queen and is the "Old Maid," or loser.

Variation

Discard a single card from the deck facedown so players cannot know which card is the Old Maid.

Oh, Hell

Also known as **Up the River,** Oh Pshaw, Blackout, and variations with other, naughtier names, Oh, Hell is an easy-to-learn trick-taking game. The object is to take exactly the number of tricks bid, no more, no less. It's been around since the 1930s, and it's Bill Clinton's favorite game. The name comes from the utterances heard when the game is not going your way—Oh, Hell is one of the milder ones.

PLAYERS: 3–7; **4 players is best.**

THE GEAR: A standard deck of 52 cards; aces are high.

Objective

Each player bids the number of tricks he thinks he will take from each hand; the object is to take *exactly* that many—no more and no fewer. If you miss your bid, either over or under, points are deducted from your score.

Sequence of Hands

The game consists of a series of hands, or deals. For the first hand of the game, each player receives one card. For the second hand, each player receives two cards. The third hand, three cards, and so on until the end of the game.

The number of hands in the game varies according to the number of players:

- Three players, fifteen hands
- Four players, thirteen hands
- Five players, ten hands
- Six players, eight hands
- Seven players, seven hands

The Game Plan

✖ Appoint one player to be the scorekeeper. Divide a score sheet into columns, one for each player. You can copy the blank scoresheet on page 239 or 374.

✖ The cards are shuffled and cut, and the dealer deals the cards singly until everyone has the appropriate number of cards for the hand being played. (As mentioned above, one card for the first hand of the game, two cards for the second hand, and so on.)

✖ The next card is turned faceup. The suit of this card is the trump suit for the hand. The trump suit beats any of the other three suits played in that hand. (In the last hand of the game, there is no trump suit, so no card is turned up.)

✖ The remaining cards are set aside and not used in that hand.

Bidding

✖ The bidding in each hand begins with the player to the left of the dealer, then continues clockwise, back around to the dealer, who bids last.

✖ Each bid represents the number of tricks the player will try to take in that hand. Everyone must bid—it is not possible to

Card Vocab

A **trick:** Card games like Bridge, Hearts, Euchre—and Oh, Hell—are divided into rounds in which each player plays one card. A single round of one card from each player is called a *trick.* The person who puts down the first card *leads the trick;* and each player in turn, starting with the player to the left of the lead, contributes a card to the trick. In practically all games, players are required to "follow suit," which means they must play a card in the same suit as the card that was led. If a player doesn't have any cards in that suit, he either discards ("sloughs") by contributing any unwanted card, or in games that have a trump suit, he may try to win the trick by playing a trump. The winner of the trick can be determined once every player has set down a card. The player who contributed the highest-ranking trump card, or if no trump was played, the highest-ranking card of the suit that was led, *wins the trick.* That player collects those cards and sets them facedown in front of himself. Usually the winner of a trick leads the next.

pass, but you can bid zero, in which case your object is to take no tricks at all. In the first hand, a player may bid zero or one. In the second hand, the bids may range from zero to two, and so on.

✖ The scorekeeper notes down the bids. Players may ask the scorekeeper to read back the bids at any time.

✖ A bid may be changed only if the next player to the left has not yet bid.

✖ Here comes the sticky part. The total of the bids for the hand cannot be equal to the number of tricks available. In other words, if four cards are dealt (so there are four tricks for the taking), the sum of the players' bids can be greater than four or less than four, but it cannot equal four. Right away you can see at least one Oh, Hell coming—it's guaranteed that someone will go bust. You also might recognize the Dealer's Dilemma: if there are, let's say, five players in a four-trick hand, and each of the first four players bids to take one trick, the dealer is now required to bid at least one (the sum of the bids cannot be four), even if his hand is a hopeless four deuces. But suppose one of the four players instead bids zero or two (bringing the total to either three or five); then the dealer is off the hook, and can safely bid zero.

Play

- The play begins with the player to the dealer's left, who leads the first trick.

- The lead may be any suit (including trump). Play follows clockwise.

- Each player must follow the suit led, if he can. If not, he may play any other card in his hand, including trump.

- The player who has played the highest trump card, or if no trump was played, the highest card of the suit led, wins the trick.

- The player who wins the trick places the cards facedown in front of her and lays

the next one she takes crosswise against it, so that the number of tricks taken may be easily counted by all players at the table.

- That player then leads the next trick. Continue until all tricks for that hand have been played and won.

Scoring

- A player who wins the exact number of tricks bid scores 10 plus the number of tricks bid (10 points for zero tricks, 11 for one trick, 12 for two tricks, etc.) Players who take more or fewer tricks than they bid— also known as *busting*—score nothing.

- Gather the cards, shuffle well, and start a new hand.

Winning

When all hands have been played (thirteen hands for four people) the scorekeeper totals the scores. The person with the most points is the winner. The scorekeeper should announce the scores of each player at the end of each hand so players can challenge if a scoring error is made.

Variation

If you'd like a longer game, you can play the hands starting at one, going up to the maximum number (fifteen for three people, thirteen for four, etc.) and then back down again to one.

▸▸ **HOST TIP**
Alternating between two packs of cards will make the game go faster, as one player can shuffle the pack that was just used while another player deals from a fresh deck.

SCORE CARD			
Player ❶	Player ❷	Player ❸	Player ❹

Hearts

Hearts is a trick-taking game in which the objective is to avoid winning tricks containing hearts or the trick that contains the queen of spades. (In fact, the game that most of us know as "Hearts" is really a version called "Black Lady," named for that dreaded card.) It is a perfect dorm-room game, or porch-sitting game—and it's got built-in suspense: The scream of terror when the queen of spades is dropped is always good for a laugh.

PLAYERS: 3–6, but 4 is best.

THE GEAR: A standard deck of 52 cards; aces are high.

Objective

Lowest score wins this game, so the object is to avoid scoring points. Each heart you take counts as 1 point; the queen of spades counts as 13 points. The game ends when someone reaches 100 points.

The Deal

Shuffle and deal all the cards. All players receive the same number of cards; any leftovers are placed facedown in the center of the table. (This pile is called the "kitty," or "widow," or "blind.") With three players, each gets seventeen cards, and there is one card in the kitty. With four players, each gets thirteen cards, and there is no kitty. With five players, each gets ten cards, and there are two cards in the kitty, and with six players, each gets eight cards, and there are four cards in the kitty.

The Game Plan

✖ The person who holds the two of clubs must lead it for the first trick. (If no one holds the two of clubs, which means it's in the kitty, the player holding the three of clubs leads.)

✖ Moving in clockwise order, each player must play a card of the suit that was led (clubs, for the first trick). If a player does not have a club, any card may be played, with one restriction—you cannot play a heart or the queen of spades on the first trick. The person who plays the highest club wins the first trick, and also wins the cards in the kitty. That player, and only that player, can look at the kitty cards. The player then collects the cards in the trick plus the kitty and places them facedown before him. (When there are six players, the winner of the first trick takes only one of the cards from the kitty; the winner of the second trick takes one card from the kitty, and the third and fourth winners take the last two cards from the kitty.)

✖ The winner of the trick leads the next trick. Excepting hearts and the queen of spades, any card can be led for the second trick.

✖ For this and all subsequent tricks, players must follow suit if possible. A player who cannot follow suit may play any card, including a heart or the queen of spades.

✖ The highest card of the suit that was led takes the trick. (There is no trump suit in Hearts.)

✖ It is illegal to lead a heart until *after* a heart has been played in a previous trick (called "breaking hearts") unless your hand contains nothing *but* hearts.

✖ Continue until all cards have been played.

Scoring

Players receive 1 point for every heart they take. The person who takes the queen of spades gets 13 points. But remember that low score wins, so these are penalty points. However, if you are dealt a hand with lots of hearts and/or lots of high cards, you have an option, and it's usually a longshot. If you can manage to take *all* the hearts *and* the queen of spades, (which is known as "shooting the moon"), you can add 26 points to everyone else's score. (For a blank scorecard, see page 373.)

The cards you need to "shoot the moon"

Winning

The game is over when someone reaches or goes over 100 points. The winner is the player with the lowest score at this point.

Variations

✖ Many people play Hearts with no kitty. If you are playing with three players, simply remove the two of clubs; if you're playing with five players, remove the two of clubs and the two of spades; if you're playing with six players, remove all four twos. Set these cards aside; they are not used in the game. Shuffle and deal an even number of cards to the players.

✘ After the deal, but before play begins, players exchange cards with one another. For the first deal, each player passes three cards, facedown, to the player on her left. Each player then picks up the three cards passed from the player on her right. The next deal, cards pass to the right; the *next* deal, players exchange cards with the player across from them. The next deal is a "hold hand"—no cards are exchanged. The deal after that begins the cycle again. If you are playing with five or six players, pass two cards instead of three.

✘ Some people play that the jack of diamonds reduces your score by 10 points, so players try to take the jack of diamonds. If a player manages to take all the hearts *and* the queen of spades *and* the jack of diamonds ("shooting the universe") he would score –36 points.

Gin Rummy

There are many, many flavors of Rummy, which in the 1930s and 1940s was probably the most popular game in America. In some variations of the game, like 500 Rummy (also known as Michigan Rummy), the emphasis is on scoring by *melding*. In games like Gin Rummy, the emphasis is on scoring by *going out* (ending the hand). Most variations can be played and enjoyed by everyone in the family, and by modifying the scoring rules, most can be made appealing to even the serious gambler.

I played Gin Rummy with my grandfather on the back porch when I was a child, and we killed a lot of time on plane and train trips when we traveled together when I was a teenager. We played for a penny a point.

Success in Gin is based entirely on observation—you must be keenly aware of what your opponent is taking and discarding. If you really want to disconcert the other player, abandon strategy entirely. You probably won't win, but the look of bafflement when you randomly take up and discard is almost worth it.

Card Vocab

A **meld:** In all Rummy games, the players try to get cards that can be matched into *runs* or *sets*. In 500 Rummy, the matched cards can be *melded* (laid in front of the player) and contribute to the player's score. In Gin Rummy, the player keeps the matched sets in hand until someone either goes "Gin" or "knocks." The matched sets have no point value; only the unmatched cards count.

A *run* or a *sequence* consists of three or more cards of the same suit in consecutive order, such as ♠4, ♠5, ♠6 or ♣8, ♣9, ♣10, ♣J.

A *set* is three or four cards of the same rank, such as ♣7, ♠7, ♦7.

A card can belong to only one combination at a time—players cannot use the same card as part of both a set of equal cards and a sequence of consecutive cards.

Note that in Gin Rummy the ace is always low, so A-2-3 is a valid sequence but A-K-Q is not. Some versions of Rummy, like 500 Rummy, allow the ace to be either high or low (players' choice).

PLAYERS: 2

THE GEAR: A standard deck of 52 cards; aces are low.

Rank of Cards

The unmatched cards have values as follows:
- Face cards (K,Q,J): 10 points
- Ace: 1 point
- Number cards are worth their face value.

Objective

To accumulate points by either going "Gin" or by "knocking." To go Gin, a hand must contain nothing but sets and runs—every card is part of a set or a run. A person can knock without waiting until all his cards are in sets or runs—some cards may be in sets or runs, but some are unmatched (or "deadwood"). To knock, the point value of the unmatched cards must be 10 or less. There is a bonus for going Gin, so unless you have a very good knocking hand within the first four or five turns, it may pay to hold out for Gin. Players also receive bonus points for each hand won, whether Gin or knock.

The Deal

Deal alternates. Each player is dealt ten cards. The twenty-first card is turned faceup to start the discard pile, and the remainder of the deck is placed facedown beside it to form the stock. The players look at and sort their cards.

The Game Plan

The First Turn: The nondealer has the option to pick up the turned card or to refuse it. If she does not want it, she says "pass," and the dealer now has the same option. If *he* doesn't want it, the nondealer draws the top card from the stock pile. The player who has taken a card completes the play by discarding one card from the hand. A normal turn consists of two parts:

The Draw: You must begin by taking one card from either the top of the stock pile or the top of the discard pile, and adding it to your hand. The discard pile is faceup—what you see is what you get. The stock is facedown, so you can't see the card until after you have committed yourself to take it. If you draw from the stock, you add the card to your hand without showing it to the other player.

The Discard: To complete your turn, discard one card from your hand and place it faceup on top of the discard pile. Taking the top discard and putting the same card back is not allowed—if you take a card from the discard pile, you must discard a different card.

Ending the Hand: When a player draws a card that allows her to arrange all ten of her cards into sets or runs, she has Gin. She makes her final discard facedown and says, "Gin!" (usually triumphantly) when this happens. She then lays down her cards faceup, arranged in sets and runs (so her opponent can verify the defeat), and the hand is over.

However, a player does not have to wait until she has Gin. She may *knock* as long as the total value of her unmatched cards is less than ten. (See above for point values of cards.) Traditionally, the player literally knocks on the table as she does this, but she may just choose to make her final discard facedown.

She then lays down her cards face-up, arranged in sets and runs, with the unmatched cards off to the side. The other player does the same, and tries to "lay off" as much of *his* deadwood as he can onto the knocker's melds. In other words, if the knocker has three sevens, the other player may tuck his lone seven in with the knocker's three sevens in order to reduce his point value. If a player goes Gin, or knocks with no unmatched cards, the other player may not lay off any cards.

An example of a "Gin" hand

Scoring

✖ Each player sets aside his or her melds—these are out of play and do not count toward the score.

✖ A Gin hand (no deadwood) scores 25 points plus the value of the opponent's deadwood. (The opponent cannot lay off deadwood against a Gin hand.)

✖ When someone knocks, compare the point count of the deadwood after the opponent has laid off his unmatched cards; if the knocker's deadwood has a lower point value than the opponent's deadwood, the knocker scores the difference. If the opponent has an *equal or lower* value of deadwood, the opponent scores the difference between the two plus a bonus of 25. This is called "undercut" or "underknock."

✖ In each hand, only one player scores. A running tally is kept, with the score of each hand entered on a separate line (so it's easy to see the number of hands a player has won).

Winning

The first player to reach 100 wins the game and gets a bonus of 100 points.

✖ Then each player gets a bonus of 25 for each hand won during the game.

✖ If the winner has won every hand in the game, this is called a "shutout," a "whitewash," a "skunk". . . it's bad (for the loser). The winner's score, including the bonus of 100, is doubled.

✖ If you are playing for money, you tally up the difference in points. If the difference between the two players' scores is 100 and you are playing for a penny a point, the winner will get one dollar.

500 Rummy

I f **Gin Rummy can be described** as the game played in airplanes, club cars, and country-club grill rooms, then 500 Rummy is the game played on kitchen tables. While a hand of Gin can be played in a short time in a small space, the game of 500 encourages you to cover as much territory as possible by melding (a specific assortment of cards), and to forget about time. It's an excellent rainy-day absorber for kids as well as adults.

PLAYERS: Best with 2–4 players, but can be played with up to 8.

THE GEAR: A standard deck of 52 cards, plus paper and pencil for scoring. If more than 4 are playing, use two decks shuffled together (104 cards).

Rank of Cards

Face cards (K, Q, J) are worth 10. Number cards are worth spot value (a two = 2, three = 3, etc.). Aces may be played as either a high or low card. When melded as three or four of a kind in a set, or as part of a high run, aces are worth 15 points (A-K-Q of the same suit adds up to 35 points, and A-A-A is worth 45). When melded as a low card, they are worth 1 (A-2-3 of the same suit counts as 6 points). If you are caught with aces in your hand (you haven't laid them down as meld) when an opponent goes out, each ace scores as 15 points against you.

Objective

In each hand, the primary objective is to score as many points as possible by forming melds. Going out (see "Stealth Strategy" on page 245) is a secondary, tactical, objective. The first player to meld 500 points wins.

The Deal

Cards are dealt one at a time, starting with the player to the dealer's left. When two are playing, each gets thirteen cards. If there are more than two, each player gets seven cards. The remaining cards (the stock) are placed facedown in the center of the playing area. The top card is turned over and placed faceup next to the stock, becoming the start of the discard pile.

Card Vocab

The stock: The undealt cards, usually facedown in a pile, that are available for future use.

The Game Plan

Starting with the player to the left of the dealer, each player's turn consists of

1. **Taking a Card:** either from the stock or from the discard pile. A player may draw one card, the top card, from the stock. If there are several cards in the discard pile, a player may look through them to determine if there is a card he wishes to pick up. If he chooses to pick up a discard, he must also pick up any and all discards that are on top of the card he wants (i.e., if he wants the bottom card in the pile, he must pick up the entire pile).

2. **Melding:** (See sidebar, page 241, for definition.) A player can lay down meld during his turn. He cannot meld during someone else's turn. *If a card is taken from the stock* and the player has meld, he may lay it down if he wishes. He is not required to meld; he may prefer to wait if, for example, he has a sequence of 9-10-jack and hopes his opponent may discard an 8 or a queen. A player may add cards to anyone's meld, but he keeps these laid-off cards with his own meld for easy scoring at the end of the game. (So if an opponent melds 8-9-10 and you hold the 7 or jack of the same suit, you can place your 7 or jack in front of you and declare that you are extending the run. A player with the 6 or queen could continue the extension, and so on. Also, you may add the fourth card to complete an opponent's three-card set.) Once a card is declared as an extension of an opponent's meld it cannot be used in any other meld. When a *card is taken from the discard pile,* that card must be used in a meld to be laid down immediately. If more than one card

Each hand is a balancing act between melding (which encourages holding onto cards that can be made into high-scoring melds) and minimizing the damage should someone else go out by holding as few high-count cards as possible. In the early part of the game, the best strategy is either to maximize your chances for melding (which usually means picking up a pile of cards from the discards) or going out quickly (hoping to catch opponents with lots of points in their hands). In later stages, it's best to reduce the number of points held in your hand, and/or play to go out.

is taken from the discard pile, it is the bottom-most card that must be used in a meld immediately. Any discards that were picked up along with that card must remain on the table until the meld has been played, to show that the bottom-most card is used. (So the player must hold at least one card of the meld before he picks up from the discards.)

3. **Discarding:** Place the card faceup on the discard pile so it's shifted slightly to the right of the previous discard. The suit and value of all discards should be visible at a glance. The hand ends when a player gets rid of all the cards in his hand by melding (with or without discarding), or when there are no cards left in the stock. If, after the last discard, the next player is able to draw from the discard pile and meld, play can continue until a player is unable to draw and meld (or chooses not to).

Scoring

When play ends, each player adds up the point count of his melds on the table and subtracts the point count of the cards in his hand. All cards in the hand are counted, regardless of whether they could have been melded or not. It is possible to end up with a negative score for the hand. There are no bonuses for going out. Each player's score is entered, and a running tally is kept. The first player to reach 500 wins. If more than one player reaches 500 on the same hand, the highest score wins.

Canasta

Canasta, a member of the Rummy family, arrived in the United States in the late '40s by way of Uruguay and Argentina. The game sparked a fad in the early '50s that was unmatched until the poker craze of the early 2000s. It's a social game for two couples; as in bridge, you must rely on your partner's skill, as well as your own. My mother, a rather competitive gal, calls this family of card games the "marriage-busters."

PLAYERS: 4, in teams of two. Seat partners across from each other. Elect one person to be the scorekeeper and furnish that person with paper and pencil.

THE GEAR: Two standard decks of 52 cards, plus 4 jokers, shuffled together, for a deck of 108 cards. The jokers and the twos are wild cards and may "stand in" for any other card in a meld.

Objective

To score 5,000 points before your opponents do by melding your cards into *canastas,* or seven of a kind. A canasta is known as *natural* when it has no wild cards, and *mixed* when it does. A natural canasta is worth more than a mixed canasta.

The Deal

A player, chosen at random, deals one card to each player. Low card becomes the dealer. In subsequent games the deal passes to the left. Deal eleven cards to each player. The next card is turned faceup to start a discard pile. The remainder of the cards are turned facedown to form the stock. If the faceup card is a red three or a wild card (a joker or a two), another card is turned faceup on the discard pile. Players take a moment to look at and organize their hands by rank—placing all the fours together, all the fives, etc. Sequences and suits do not matter.

A meld (in Canasta):

* A meld is three or more cards of the same rank. The goal is to get as many *canastas,* or melds of seven cards, as possible.

* A meld must have at least two natural cards (meaning not wild) and no more than three wild cards.

* A team can't make more than one meld of cards of the same rank—after a player has made one meld, all other cards of the same rank that he or his partner holds must be "laid off," or added on to, the original meld.

* Players may not lay off on their opponents' melds.

Special Cards

* **Jokers** and **twos** are wild.

* **Black threes** are unmeldable, except in the final turn when a player "goes out." In that case, the player may lay down a set of three or four black threes. If a player discards a black three, the next player *must* draw from the stock, and may not take from the discard pile. In this fashion, it is possible to "block" the discard pile for one player's turn.

* **Red threes,** also known as "bonus cards," are also never melded but are laid down one at a time for bonus points. If a player holds a red three in his original hand, he must, on his first turn, lay it faceup on the table and draw another card from the stock. (This is in addition to, not a replacement for, his regular draw.) Similarly, if a player draws a red three from the stock, he must lay it faceup on the table and draw a replacement. If a player gets a red three by taking the discard pile (which is only possible the first time the pack is taken), he must lay the card on the table but *cannot,* in this case, replace the card.

The Game Plan

* The player to the left of the dealer begins. He has two choices:

1. Draw a card from the stock. He may then meld it if he can and wants to. The first, or "initial," meld or melds must be worth at least 50 points. (See the chart on the opposite page for "opening melds.") He can reach 50 points by laying off as many or as few melds as will suffice.

2. Pick up the whole discard pile, *if* the upcard matches with two natural cards already in his hand to form a meld. Before taking the upcard, the player must lay down the cards to be melded with it. (This is to prove that the player does indeed have those two natural cards in hand.) Again, the meld or melds have to total 50 points. He then picks up the entire discard pile and makes any possible melds, and then discards one card.

A player may not take the discard pile until he has laid down an opening meld worth 50 points or more. Wild cards may not be used in opening melds.

- The procedure for the second player is the same as for the first.
- For the third and fourth players (the partners of the first and second players): If the partner has not melded any cards, the rules are the same as above. If the partner *has* melded, however, two new rules come into play:

1. The player can pick up the discard pile if he holds only *one* natural card that matches the upcard, plus one wild card. The upcard can't be matched with two wild cards.
2. The player may pick up the discard pile when the upcard can be added to either his or his partner's melds.

NOTE: A team's melds can be consolidated in front of either partner.

FROZEN PILE

A player can *freeze* the discard pile by discarding a wild card. To pick up the frozen pile, a player must match the top card with a natural pair. A player can't pick up the discard pile in order to play off the upcard on an existing meld.

BLACK THREES

A black three, known as a "stop card," on the discard pile will make the pile inaccessible to the next player. The discard pile may only be picked up if a player can meld the top card, and black threes can only be melded on going out (which isn't going to happen if a player is picking up the discard pile). So the black three blocks the next player from picking up the discard pile, but as soon as that player discards, the pile will again be accessible.

Ending the Game

- A player "goes out" or "melds out" when he gets rid of the last card in his hand. At this point he may meld three or four black threes. It's not necessary to make a final discard. A player asks his partner, "May I

Point Values

CARD VALUES	
Joker	50
Ace and two	20
K, Q, J, ten, nine, eight	10
seven, six, five, four, black three	5

BONUS POINTS	
For going out unconcealed	100
For going out concealed	200
For each red three	100
For each natural canasta	500
For each mixed canasta	300

OPENING MELDS

The first meld made by a team in a deal must meet a minimum score.

Previous Score	Requirement
Minus	15
0–1,495	50
1,500–2,995	90
3,000 or more	120

If it is the first deal of the night, the minimum requirement is 50.

go out?" and the partner will reply "yes" or "no." (This is the only table talk allowed.) The player must abide by what his partner says. A team may not go out until they have made at least one canasta.

✖ Natural canastas are topped off with a red card; mixed canastas are topped off with a black card. A canasta may not have more than three wild cards.

✖ If the stockpile runs out and the last card is a red three, the game ends. If it is anything but a red three, the players take turns picking up the top card in the discard pile (if it can be melded and if the pile is unfrozen). When no more discards can be used, the game is over.

✖ If a player can lay down her opening meld and meld out in the same turn, this is called going out *concealed* and earns 200 points.

Scoring

✖ First, each side figures out its basic score from the bonus points section in the chart on page 247.

✖ If one side has all four red threes, their total value is doubled. (So, 800 instead of 400.)

✖ If one side has no meld at all, their red threes count as a minus.

✖ To the basic score, each team adds the total point value of all its melded cards. Then the team subtracts the point value of all the unmelded cards in the hands of both team members.

✖ The first team to reach 5,000 wins.

Poker
Texas Hold 'Em

Poker, spurred by the televised World Series of Poker, as well as a plethora of online poker gaming sites, has seen a surge of interest unlike any since the Canasta craze of the early 1950s. Dozens of poker variations exist; Texas Hold 'Em is popular both in casinos and living rooms and so it's a good one to start with.

PLAYERS: 2–10, best for 5–8.

THE GEAR: A standard deck of 52 cards; poker chips or other counters.

Objective

To win the pot with the best hand, using the two cards in one's hand as well as the five community cards to create a five-card poker hand.

The Game Plan

✖ Two cards are dealt, one at a time, facedown, to each player.

✖ Betting goes clockwise, starting to the left of the dealer.

✖ The first two players to the left of the dealer must make blind bets; that is, without looking at their cards. This functions as a kind of ante.

✖ Each player, in turn, must either match ("call" in poker terminology) or raise the previous bet, or fold. The betting round ends when all players have either matched the previous bet or folded. If every player

Rank of Poker Hands

Straight flush: five cards in sequence, all of the same suit.

Four of a Kind: four cards of one rank, and an unmatched card of another rank.

Full House: three matching cards of one rank, and two matching cards of another rank.

A Flush: five cards of the same suit, not in sequence.

A Straight: five cards in sequence but in more than one suit.

Three of a Kind: three cards of the same rank, plus two unmatched cards.

Two Pairs: two cards of the same rank, plus two cards of another rank, with an unmatched card.

One Pair: any two cards of the same rank.

High Card: If you are comparing hands that do not fit into any of the above categories (no pairs, etc.), then the hand with the highest-ranking card wins.

Tie-Breakers

If the winning hand is a *straight* or a *flush* or a *straight flush* or simply a *high card* hand, and more than one player holds that kind of hand, here's how to determine the winner: The hand with the highest-ranking card wins (an ace-high flush beats a king-high flush; the other four cards don't count.) If the highest-ranking cards are of equal rank, then the rank of the second-highest card determines the winner (ace-ten beats ace-nine, and the remaining three cards are ignored). If the second-highest cards are equal, compare the third highest, and continue the progression until the comparison yields a winner. It would be unusual for all five cards to parallel each other (unless you're playing with wild cards), but if all five are of equal rank, split the pot evenly between the winners.

For *four of a kind,* the higher-ranking foursome wins.

For a *full house* or *three of a kind,* compare the set of three; the higher-ranking triplets win.

For *two pairs,* the highest-ranking pair wins. If the high-ranking pairs are of equal rank, then the rank of the second pair determines the winner. If the second pairs are also of equal rank, then compare the rank of the fifth, unmatched card. (A pair of aces with a pair of threes beats aces and deuces; a pair of aces with a pair of tens and an unmatched three beats aces and tens with a deuce.)

except one folds, the remaining player collects the pot.

How much can you bet? Betting rules should be agreed upon before the game begins. Players in a friendly game of poker (although that may be an oxymoron) usually set minimums and maximums on the amount a player can bet or raise, and maybe a maximum on the number of raises allowed during a round of betting. Only hardened gamblers and the foolhardy play "No Limit" poker, where you can bet your house, if you still have one.

✖ After the first round of betting, the dealer deals three faceup cards to the center of the table. These are known as the *flop.* They are the first of five cards that are known as *community cards.*

✖ Players may consider these community cards their own when mentally arranging their hand.

✖ Another round of betting commences.

✖ A fourth community card, called the *turn,* is dealt faceup to the center of the table, and a third round of betting begins.

✖ Then the last common card, called the *river,* is dealt and is followed by the last round of betting.

Winning
The winner is the best five-card poker hand using any combination of the player's two cards and the five flop cards.

Seven Up

Seven Up is a member of the "All Fours" family of card games, which originated at least three hundred years ago in England. All Fours refers to the four points that players try to score: *high, low, jack,* and *game.* Seven Up arrived in the United States in colonial times and is also known as High-Low-Jack and Old Sledge. The objective is to be the first player or team to score seven points.

PLAYERS: 2–4. Four may play in partnerships of two.

THE GEAR: A standard deck of 52 cards; aces are high.

The Game Plan
✖ The dealer deals six cards, three at a time, to each player. No player except the dealer and the player to his left may look at his cards until the trump has been decided upon.

✖ He then turns up the next card as a proposed trump suit.

✖ The player to the dealer's left has two options: either to say, "I stand," meaning he accepts the faceup card as trump and play begins, or to say, "I beg," meaning the decision is passed to the dealer.

✖ If the decision is passed to the dealer, the dealer may say "Take it," meaning that the dealer accepts the faceup card as trump, and the player to the left scores 1 point for "gift."

✖ Or the dealer may say "Refuse," meaning that the dealer does not accept the faceup card as trump. If this happens, the dealer must *run the cards,* that is, deal three more cards to each player, and turn another card faceup as a proposed trump. (If the new faceup card is of the same suit, the dealer discards it, runs the cards again, and turns another faceup card, and so on until the faceup card is a new suit.) That suit then becomes trump. If a jack is turned for the new suit, the dealer scores 1. If the dealer runs through the pack before a new suit is declared for trump, all the cards are gathered, shuffled, and redealt by the same dealer.

- Once trump has been declared, players discard enough cards to bring their hands to six cards each.

- The player to the dealer's left leads any card.

- Players must follow suit or play a trump. In other words, a player can play a trump even if he is able to follow suit.

- A trick is won by the highest trump in it, or, if there is no trump, by the highest card of the suit led.

- The winner of each trick leads the next.

Scoring

There are a maximum of 4 points in each hand. Players get points for:

- **High:** 1 point for the player or team who was dealt the highest trump in the hand.

- **Low:** 1 point for the player or team who was dealt the lowest trump in play, regardless of who took it in a trick.

- **Jack:** 1 point for the player or team who took the jack of the trump suit in a trick.

- **The Game:** 1 point for the player who has the highest card values in the tricks they took. Calculate the total value of your cards as follows:

  - Each ten: 10
  - Each ace: 4
  - Each king: 3
  - Each queen: 2
  - Each jack: 1

(For a blank scorecard, see page 375.)

NOTE: If there is only one trump in play, it counts as 2 points, as it is both the high trump and the low one. If that one trump in play is the jack, it counts as 3 points. The 1 point for game is not counted if there is a tie for highest score.

Winning

The first player or team to get to 7 points wins. If both players or teams reach 7 in the same hand, the points are scored in order to determine the winner: First count high; then low; then jack; then game. The player or team who reaches 7 first wins. If the dealer only needs 1 point to win and he turns over a jack on the next deal, he wins. If the dealer's left-hand opponent has 6 points and begs, the dealer would be wise to refuse the trump suit, as this would give the left-hand opponent one point for "gift," ending the game.

||||||||||||||||||||||||||||||||||||||||||||||||||||||||||||||||||||||||||||||

Pitch

Some games seem as if they were made to be played with a beer in hand. Euchre and Pinochle are two of them. Pitch is another. Pitch, or Set-Back, as it is sometimes called, is another of the All Fours family of games that came to America from England in the eighteenth century. It is an every-man-for-himself trick-taking game in which each hand, and the game itself, can be played in a relatively short period of time.

PLAYERS: **3–5, best for 4.**

THE GEAR: **A standard deck of 52 cards.**

Objective

Each hand offers a maximum of four points (high, low, jack, and game). Players bid for the right to name trump. Scoring is cumulative, and the first player to reach 11 (some play to 9 or 21) wins.

The Deal

Starting at the dealer's left, cards are dealt three at a time to each player until all have six cards. The remaining cards are set aside and are not used.

The Bidding

Once the cards are dealt, the player to the dealer's left starts the bidding by either announcing the number of points he intends to take (the minimum bid is two, maximum is four), or by passing. Each player, in turn, has one opportunity to bid or pass. Each bid must be an increase over the bid made by a previous player. Traditionally, when a player bids four, he announces his bid silently, by leading out (pitching) a card in the suit he is declaring as trump. If none of the players bids, the cards are reshuffled and the same person deals again.

The Game Plan

The player who wins the bid starts the play by pitching a card of the suit he is naming as trump. Each player must follow suit or, lacking any trump, must slough. The trick is won by the highest trump card that is played to that trick. The winner of the trick leads to the next trick, and all players must follow suit, if possible. If trump is led, a player without trump must slough. If a non-trump suit is led, a player without that suit must trump, or lacking any trump, must slough. Play continues until all six cards have been played.

> ### Card Vocab
> **To slough:** To play a card that is not the suit led or the trump suit; to discard an unwanted card.

Scoring

One point is scored for each of the following:

- **High:** the highest trump card played in the hand, scored by the player who wins it in a trick (i.e. the player to whom it was dealt).
- **Low:** the lowest trump card played in the hand, scored by the player who wins it in a trick.
- **Jack:** the jack (if present) of the trump suit, scored by the player who wins it in a trick.
- **The Game:** the sum total of the "game point" cards in the tricks taken by a player. Calculate the total value of your cards as follows:
  - Each ten: 10
  - Each ace: 4
  - Each king: 3
  - Each queen: 2
  - Each jack: 1

NOTE: If two players tie for the game point, no point is awarded. If there is only one trump present in the entire hand (an improbable but theoretically possible scenario), it would score as two points (it is both high and low). If that one trump is the jack, it would score as three points.

The player who names trump must take at least the number of points bid. If he falls short, his score is reduced by the amount of the bid (negative scores are possible). If he makes his bid, he also scores any points he makes beyond his bid. The other players score whatever points they take during the hand.

The first player to reach 11 wins. If two players reach 11 in the same hand, and one of them is the bidder, the bidder wins regardless of who has the highest score.

Blackjack

Blackjack, also known as 21, is the most popular casino table game in the world. It dates from at least the 1700s in France, where it was called Vingt-et-Un. The name *Blackjack* came about when, in order to gain publicity, some casinos offered a special bet: A hand that contained the ace of spades plus either the jack of clubs or the jack of spades would pay ten-to-one odds on the player's bet. Blackjack popularity endures simply because casino gamblers believe it to be one of the few games they can actually win. If the dealer is using more than one deck, however, counting cards becomes difficult—so even if you're consistently winning at home, you're not necessarily going to win in Vegas.

Rules vary from casino to casino and even from home game to home game. The game described here is a social at-home version.

PLAYERS: 2–7

THE GEAR: A standard deck of 52 cards, or two decks of 52 shuffled together, plus one joker. Poker chips or other counters.

Objective

Each player is on his own, playing against the dealer. Both you and the dealer are trying to draw cards totaling exactly 21, or to get as close as possible to 21 without going over. Each face card is worth 10; each ace is worth either 11 or 1, player's option, depending on which works to the player's best advantage. Number cards are at face value. If you make 21 with only two cards (an ace plus a face card or a 10) you have Blackjack.

The Deal

After the cards have been shuffled and cut, the dealer covers the bottom of the pack with a "dead" card—a card that is excluded from play during the course of that deal. In the game of Blackjack, this is called "burning" a card. The "burn" card may be either a joker or any card from deuce to nine. (Aces, tens, and face cards cannot be used because they are needed as components of a Blackjack.)

To determine the "burn" card (if the joker isn't used), the dealer turns the top card of the deck and shows it to all players. If it is any card from deuce to nine (or if a joker is used), it is placed face-to-face with the card at the bottom of the pack. Now only the backs of cards show at both top and bottom of the deck.

If the turn card is an ace, ten, or face card, the entire deck is reshuffled, and the process is repeated until a suitable card is turned. (Variation: return the ace, ten, or face card to the deck, random placement, and turn another card. If a suitable card fails to show up after three tries, re-shuffle the deck and repeat.)

There are at least two reasons for covering the bottom card in the deck. First, a decent Blackjack player has a general sense of those cards that have already been played and those that are still available. If the dealer's opponents could catch a glimpse of the bottom card, it could offer some advantage. (How helpful might it be to know that the last ace won't appear until the last card?)

Second, the "burn" card acts as a placeholder, or marker, to separate "live" cards from "dead" ones. After each hand, the dealer collects the used cards and places them on the bottom of the deck, after the "burn" card, and facing the same direction as the "burn" card.

The Game Plan

* The dealer sets the minimum and maximum bets and may change those at will between hands.

* Players place a bet, in full view, before any cards are dealt. All bets are against the dealer.

* The dealer deals one card, facedown, to each player, beginning with the player on his left. He then deals one card to himself, faceup.

* The dealer deals a second card to each player, including himself, facedown.

* If the dealer's first card is an ace or a card worth 10 points, he looks at his facedown card (the "hole" card). If he has a natural Blackjack (a face card or a ten, plus an ace), the dealer shows his cards, and automatically wins. The other players then show their cards. If a player also has a natural, his bet is returned (he doesn't win

anything, but he doesn't lose either). All other players lose their bets.

* If the dealer does not have a natural, he leaves his hole card facedown and play commences with the player to the dealer's left. Players' cards remain facedown until it's been determined that they have either won or lost.

* If a player has Blackjack, he shows his cards and is paid double by the dealer. Many friendly home games (noncasino) are played with a house rule that says a Blackjack also wins the deal. A player who has Blackjack has the option to assume the role of dealer, or leave the deal with the current dealer. Since odds usually favor the dealer, many players look forward to dealing. (Another option for changing the deal is to have a dealer deal five hands, and then pass the deal to the left.)

* The dealer offers each player in turn the opportunity to take additional cards to try to improve his hand. A player looks at his cards and may either *stand*—meaning he does not want any other cards—or he may say "I draw" or "hit me," indicating that the dealer should deal him another card.

A player who asks for a "hit" receives one card, faceup. He then decides to either stand or receive another hit. He may do this as often as he likes, but once he says "I stand," he may draw no additional cards, and the dealer moves on to the next player. Remember, the goal is to get as close to 21 as possible without going over.

* If his point count goes over 21, he must announce this immediately, saying "I bust." If a player busts, he turns his cards faceup, the dealer collects his bet, and his cards are placed faceup at the bottom of the deck.

✗ When every player except the dealer has either stood or busted, the dealer turns up his facedown card. (If every player busts he simply discards his cards and begins the next hand.)

✗ The dealer decides whether to stand or draw. In most casinos, the dealer is required to stand if his first two cards total 15 or more.

✗ If the dealer busts, he pays each player who has stood.

✗ If he stands on less than 21, the players turn over their cards. The dealer wins the bets of players who tie his count or have a lower count. He pays each player having a higher count.

Players' Options

✗ **Doubling Down:** In her turn, after looking at her two cards, a player can *double down*. This means she turns two cards faceup, and doubles the bet. She then draws one more card, facedown. (Sometimes doubling down is permitted only when the first two cards total 10 or 11.)

✗ **Splitting Pairs:** If a player's first two cards are a pair, they may be *split*—meaning she plays them as two different hands, each carrying the value of the original bet. She turns the two cards faceup, and the dealer deals one card to the hand on the player's right; the player plays this hand as above. Once she's finished—either stood or busted—she is dealt another faceup card to the hand on her left, which she plays as above.

Continuing Play

After each bet is settled, the player gives her cards to the dealer, who places them faceup at the bottom of the pack. When the faceup cards are reached, the pack is shuffled and play begins again as described above.

Euchre

Possibly a descendent of the Spanish game Triomphe, Euchre is a trick-taking game, probably introduced to America by the French in Louisiana. Euchre is actually a very large family of games; some variations allow for five to seven players, but the standard game (described below) is a four-person partnership game.

PLAYERS: 4

THE GEAR: A standard deck of 52 cards from which the twos, threes, fours, fives, and sixes have been removed to make a 32-card deck. (Some players also remove the sevens and eights to make a 24-card deck.)

Objective

To win at least three of the five tricks.

Card Ranking

✗ Euchre has a unique way of ranking the trump suit. The jack of the trump suit is the highest-ranking card. Next comes the jack of the same color as the trump suit (so the two highest-ranking trumps are either both red jacks or both black jacks). The remainder of the trump suit has "normal" ranking, as in ace, king, queen, ten, nine, eight, seven. For example, if hearts are trump, the rank of trumps would be: jack ♥, jack ♦, ace ♥, king ♥, queen ♥, 10 ♥, 9 ♥, 8 ♥, 7 ♥. Since the jack of diamonds is now part of the trump suit, the diamond suit no longer has a jack, and the diamond ten follows the queen. The other suits retain their ranks.

- The jack of trumps is called the *right bower*, and the jack of the same color suit is known as the *left bower*.

The Game Plan

- The dealer deals five facedown cards to each player, two at a time and then three at a time, or vice versa.

- The twenty-first card is turned faceup as a proposed trump.

- Starting with the player on the dealer's left, each player has the right to accept the upturned card as trump, or pass. The opponents of the dealer will say, "I order it up," if they wish to accept the suit as trump. The partner of the dealer accepts by saying, "I assist." The dealer either says, "I take it up," or simply takes the card into his own hand and discards a card. Regardless of who decides to make the upturned card trump, that card belongs to the dealer, and he has the right to exchange it for any card in his hand. Traditionally, the dealer simply places his discard facedown under the deck, and leaves the upturned card on the table so everyone can see it until it is played.

- If all players pass—including the dealer—by saying, "I turn it down," the dealer places the upturned card facedown.

- Now each player, starting with the player on the dealer's left, has the option of declaring the trump suit or passing. The suit that was just rejected cannot be named as trump. If all four players pass in this second round, there is no play; the cards are collected, and the next player in turn deals.

- The player who fixes the trump suit, either by accepting the upturned card or by declaring the trump suit, is known as the "maker." Euchre is a partnership game, but the maker has the option of playing alone, without the benefit of her partner's cards. There is no change in scoring if the maker takes three or four tricks, but if the maker takes all five tricks on her own, the score for that hand is doubled. If the maker wishes to go it alone, she says, "I play alone," and her partner sets his cards facedown and does not play that hand; the game is now two against one. The player to the left of the dealer leads, regardless of who the maker is. (In a two- or three-player game, the player to the left of the maker leads.)

- There are five tricks. A player must follow suit to a lead if he's able. If he is unable to follow suit, he may play any card. A trick is won by the highest trump in it, or, if there is no trump, by the highest card of the suit led.

- The winner of one trick leads the next. A player lays his or her tricks facedown, overlapping, so that other players can count the number of tricks.

Scoring

- The maker's side scores 1 point for winning three or four tricks, or 2 points for winning all five tricks (called "march"). If the maker's side does not win three or more tricks, they have been *euchred*. The maker's opponents score 2 for euchre. If the maker is playing alone, she scores 1 point for three or four tricks and 4 for march. (For a blank scorecard, see page 375.)

- The first side to reach an agreed-upon number (usually five, but sometimes seven or ten) wins.

Casino

Sometimes spelled **Cassino,** this card game is at least two hundred years old and may descend from the Italian game Scopa or from French gambling games of the fifteenth century. It experienced a surge of popularity during the early part of the twentieth century, but was supplanted by the Gin Rummy craze of the 1930s. It's a game that's appropriate for children who can count to ten, but also contains enough room for subtle strategy, maneuvering, and mathematical skill to appeal to adults. It's simple in principle, but many expert card players believe it's one of the hardest games to play well.

PLAYERS: 2, with a variation for 3.

THE GEAR: A standard deck of 52 cards. Aces count as 1, twos count as 2, threes count as 3, and so on. Face cards do not have a point value. Suits do not matter.

Objective

To get to 21 points by collecting the ten of diamonds (called "big casino"), the two of spades ("little casino"), aces, and as many spades and as many cards as possible. (See "Scoring" on page 259.)

The Deal

✖ The dealer deals two cards to her opponent(s), lays two cards faceup in the center of the table, and deals two cards to herself. She then repeats the process so each player has four cards and there are four cards in the center of the table. The dealer sets the rest of the deck facedown to her left.

✖ After these four cards are played out, the dealer gives four more cards to each player, two at a time, but does not set any more in the center of the table. These new hands are played out, and four more cards are dealt to each player, and so on. Six deals will exhaust the pack. Before the sixth deal, the dealer must say "Last." There is no scoring until the pack is exhausted.

The Game Plan

✖ The nondealer begins. Each player, in turn, must play one card from her hand. Each player may *capture, build,* or *trail* with each card. Trailing means that a player simply lays one card faceup on the table.

✖ A player's primary goal is to pick up, or capture, cards from the table. Trailing and building is a preliminary to capturing. When cards are captured, the player places them facedown in front of him.

✖ Capturing can be done in the following ways:

  ▪ *Pairing:* Pairing is the simplest way to capture cards. A card from your hand can be used to take a card (or cards) of the same rank from the table. For example, if you have an ace in your hand, you can pick up all the aces that are on the table. However, you may take *only one* face card at a time: A jack can be paired with a jack, a queen with a queen, and so on, *unless* there are three of a particular face card on the table and you have the fourth. So, if you have a king in your hand, you can pick up one king or you may pick up three kings, but you aren't allowed to pick up two kings.

  ▪ *Combining:* A player can capture any pair or group of cards on the table whose numerical value adds up to the numerical value of a card in his hand. For example:

If you have a nine in your hand, you could capture a two, three, and four from the table. Or, if you have a ten in your hand, and on the table lie three tens, an ace, a six, and a three, you may capture all three tens (pairing) and the ace, six, and three (combining). If you clear the board in a single turn, you earn a *sweep*.

- All captured cards, including the card you used to capture them with, are placed facedown in a pile in front of you. Sweeps are marked by turning one card faceup in the pile.

✖ **Building:** A player may leave one of her cards on the table and announce that she is *building* to a certain numerical value. For example, if a two and a six are on the table, and Player A has a nine and an ace in his hand, he may gather the two and the six together and put the ace on top of them and announce that he is *building to nine,* intending to take all three cards with his nine on his next turn. This is called a *single build*.

  - Any player may then change that build. If Player B holds an ace and a ten in his hand, he can place his ace with the two, six, and ace on the table and announce that he is *building to ten*. This grouping may now be taken only by a ten.
  - Any player can "steal" an opponent's build if he also has a card of the same value as the build. So if Player A also holds a ten, he may take the build that Player B changed.
  - A player can't use a card that's already on the table to change the number value of a single build; he has to play a new card from his hand.
  - A single build may be changed to a *multiple build* by duplicating the single-build value with other cards. For example,

if there is a six, a three, and a two on the table, and you hold a seven and a nine, you can bring the three table cards together and lay your seven on top, and announce that you are building nines. You have two sets of cards totaling nine—a multiple build. An opponent can't add a card to change the value of a multiple build, but the build can be taken by an opponent who has the right card. Only a single build can be increased.

- Once a player has started a build, on his next turn, he may not trail. He must capture the build, turn a single build into a multiple build, or add to a multiple build.
- **Example:** A player has built eight on his previous turn and has two eights in his hand. He sets one on his single build of eight, making it a multiple eight ready to be captured with his remaining eight on his next turn.
- **Example:** A player has a single build of ten. There is a six on the table. In addition to holding a ten, he holds a four. He can add his four to the six, call "ten," and add those cards to his build pile of ten, intending to take it with the ten in his hand on his next turn (unless he can make another ten build or an opponent takes the build with a ten from *her* hand).
- **Example:** A player has placed a five from her hand on top of another five on the table, and called "fives" (a multiple build). Her opponent can't take these two cards with a ten.

Ending the Game

When the deck is exhausted, the last player to capture any cards also takes any remaining cards on the table.

Scoring

Players get points for the following:

- **Each Ace:** 1 point
- **Two of Spades** (called the little casino): 1 point
- **Ten of Diamonds** (called the big casino): 2 points
- **Capturing the Majority of the Spades:** 1 point
- **Capturing the Majority of the Cards** (known as "cards"): 3 points
- **Capturing All the Cards on the Table in One Hand in Any Single Turn** (known as a "sweep"): 1 point

Variation for Three Players

The dealer deals four cards to each player, and four to the table only in the first round. The player to the dealer's left plays first. The rest of the rules are the same as in two-hand Casino.

Winning

Generally, players will play to twenty-one. If at any point during a hand a player believes he has reached twenty-one, he may stop the game and count the cards. If he's correct, he wins; if he's wrong, he loses.

Pinochle

Pinochle, a trick-taking game for two or four players, descends from the French game of Bezique. "Pinochle" is actually the name of a whole family of games, but for a good introduction, check out the basic game for two players, below. A favorite game among major-league baseball players, Pinochle might be a good introduction to the world of cards for a young friend who's baseball-crazy.

PLAYERS: 2

THE GEAR: A Pinochle deck consists of eight aces, kings, queens, jacks, tens, and nines. You can buy a special deck, or just use two standard decks of cards with the twos through eights taken out. Paper and pencil for scorekeeping.

Rank of Cards

A-10-K-Q-J-9. Note that the ten is the second-highest card in a suit. When two identical cards are played in the same trick, the first one played ranks higher.

> **▶▶STEALTH STRATEGY ◀**
>
> For players new to Pinochle, the card ranking is weird. Try chanting "A-10-K" together to remember that the ten is the second-highest card. Order the cards in your hand A-10-K-Q-J-9 to make sure you remember the rank.

Objective

To be the first player to reach 1,000 points by forming melds. There are three categories of melds: sequences, groups, and pinochle.

SEQUENCES

- A-10-K-Q-J of the trump suit (aka a *flush*) 150 points
- K-Q of trump suit (aka a *royal marriage*) 40 points
- K-Q of a nontrump suit (aka a *marriage*) 20 points

GROUPS

- Four aces of four different suits (called *100 aces*): 100 points
- Four kings of four different suits (called *80 kings*): 80 points
- Four queens of four different suits (called *60 queens*): 60 points
- Four jacks of four different suits (called *40 jacks*): 40 points

PINOCHLE

- The queen of spades and the jack of diamonds (called *pinochle*): 40 points
- The 9 of the trump suit (called the *dix*): 10 points

You may use a single card in more than one meld, as long as the melds are in different categories. So the queen of spades can be used for a marriage, pinochle, and 60 queens, because these melds are from different categories. But you can't use the queen in a flush as well as a marriage, as those are both from the "sequences" category.

The Deal

Deal twelve cards to each player, four at a time. The next (twenty-fifth) card is turned faceup; that suit is trump. If this card is a nine (in Pinochle lingo, this is the "dix," pronounced "deece"), the dealer scores 10 points. The rest of the pack is set facedown as the stock. The dealer sets the trump card under the stock, but visible, so the players can remember what trump is.

The Game Plan

The game is played in two stages:

The first stage, which lasts as long as there are cards left in the stock:

- The nondealer leads any card.

- The other player may play any card of any suit she wishes. She may follow suit, play a trump card, or discard a card she doesn't want (called *sloughing*).

- The highest trump wins the trick; if no trumps are played, the highest card of the suit led takes the trick. If two identical cards are played, the first played beats the second.

- A trick is set facedown in front of the player who took it.

   The winner of the trick is now entitled to meld, if she can and if she chooses to. (She is not obliged to meld.) She is limited to one meld per trick won. As she melds, she announces the point value to be recorded.

- After each trick, the winner, and then her opponent, draws a card from the stock.

- The winner of a trick leads the next.

   A card that has been melded is still considered part of the hand, and can be played on any trick.

- Tricks won in this first stage are set aside and have no value. In this stage, players score points by melding. (See opposite page.)

- After the first trick is taken, but before the draw, the dealer, if she's holding the dix, can swap it for the turned-up trump card. Thus, the dealer not only gets a higher trump card, but also scores 10 points for the dix. This can be done along with any other meld. When the second dix comes up, it may be laid faceup on the table in the same turn with another meld, and that player scores ten points.

   Play continues until the stock is exhausted. The winner of the last trick takes the last stock card, and the loser takes the upcard.

Melding

A player may lay down a meld *only* immediately after winning a trick. The player lays the meld faceup in front of herself and announces the score. A player can only score one meld in a turn (with the exception of the dix), even if the cards he uses for that meld can be used in another scoring combination. Melded cards can be used later to make another meld of a different category. A new meld made this way must be made on a new turn and must have the addition of at least one card from the player's hand. For example, a player can meld a royal marriage and score 40 points, and then later add the A-J-10 and score 150 for the flush. But a player may not meld a flush and then score separately for the royal marriage contained in the flush—a player has to lay down at least one new card from his hand. If the card from his hand would make two new melds, the player may only score for one of them.

Endgame

After twelve tricks have been taken, the endgame begins.

✄ The players pick up the melds they have laid down and add them to the cards in their hands, so each player again has twelve cards.

✄ The second stage of play now begins. The winner of the last trick in the first stage leads the first trick in the second.

✄ The rules for the endgame change slightly. Now players must follow suit if they can. If they can't, they must play a trump. If a trump is led, the other player must play a higher trump if she can. Tricks are won as in the first stage.

✄ No player may meld in this stage of the game.

✄ Once all cards have been played the game ends.

Scoring

Score the melds during play. After the endgame, add up the players' scores of the cards they have taken in tricks during the second stage.

✄ Winner of last trick = 10 points
✄ Cards scored toward game:
  ▪ Each ace = 11 points
  ▪ Each 10 = 10 points
  ▪ Each king = 4 points
  ▪ Each queen = 3 points
  ▪ Each jack = 2 points

Add together the scores for the melding and the trick-taking stages.

Winning

The first player to get to 1,000 wins. If a player *thinks* he has reached 1,000, he may say so. Play ends and the cards are examined. If he's right, he wins—even if the other player has a higher score. If he's wrong, he loses. If both players pass 1,000 points on the same deal, play continues until 1,250. If the same happens again, play continues until 1,500, and so on in increments of 250.

‖‖‖

Four-Handed Pinochle

Four-handed Pinochle can be played as a cutthroat game, with every man for himself, or as a partnership game. In either version of the game, players bid for the right to select the trump suit. Players score points in two stages, first by melding, and then by taking tricks during the play. Meld values and card values are the same as in the two-handed version of the game.

PLAYERS: 4

THE GEAR: A Pinochle deck consists of eight aces, kings, queens, jacks, tens, and nines. You can buy a special deck, or just use two standard decks of cards with the twos through eights taken out. Paper and pencil for scorekeeping.

The Deal

Each player is dealt twelve cards, four at a time.

Bidding

✖ Bidding starts with the player to the dealer's left. Players try to estimate the number of points (melds plus tricks) that they can make with the hand they hold. In a partnership game, you may count on your partner for some support, but it's a guess as to how much of a contribution your partner can make.

✖ There is no minimum bid. Bidding is in multiples of 10, and each player's bid must be at least 10 points higher than the previous high bid. A player may pass (no bid) but he cannot reenter the bidding during that hand. Bidding continues around the table until all players but one have passed. That player has won the right to name any suit he pleases as trump.

Melding

Once the high bidder names trump, all players lay down their melds in front of them, and each player's total is recorded on

the score sheet. In a partnership, each player melds on his own, but the two scores are combined into a partnership score. When the melds have been recorded, the players pick up their cards and return them to their hands.

The Game Plan

✖ The winning bidder leads with any card he chooses. Each player, in turn, must play a card of the same suit. If a player can't follow suit, he must play a trump. If he has no trump, he may slough. The highest trump wins the trick, or if trump wasn't played to the trick, the highest card of the suit led wins the trick. If two cards are tied for highest, the first card played wins the trick.

✖ Anytime trump is led, each player must play a higher-ranking trump than the previous card. When a player has a higher-ranking trump than the card led, he must play it, and each succeeding player must, if able, beat the highest card that has been played to the trick. If a nontrump suit has been led, and two or more players are unable to follow suit (which means they must play a trump) they are not required to over-trump a previous card.

✖ The winner of a trick leads the next. In a partnership, winning tricks are usually collected by one partner. Play continues until all cards have been played.

Scoring

✖ Once play is completed, each player counts his points. The bidder's point count (meld plus tricks) must at least equal his bid. If the point count is less than his bid, he scores no points for tricks, he loses the points from his meld, and the amount of his bid is deducted from his score.

* Other players get credit for points scored. A player must win at least one trick to score his melds; a player who fails to take a trick during play loses the entire value of his meld. In partners, one player must take a trick in order to preserve the value of the team's meld.

Winning

The first to reach 1,000 points wins the game.

‖‖

Solitaire
aka Klondike or Patience

Solitaire, obviously, is a game played alone, and is terrific for passing twenty minutes at lunchtime or for playing online during a boring conference call. These days most people play Solitaire on their computers, but the real feel of cards slipping through your hands can be a balm when your fingers need a break from the mouse.

THE GEAR: A standard deck of 52 cards.

Objective

To build four foundation piles, one of each suit. Each pile will be in sequence by rank, starting with the ace (played as the low card) and proceeding, one card at a time, up to the king. To accomplish this, you must move all the cards from the tableau and the stock into the appropriate foundation pile.

The Deal

Lay down a horizontal row of seven cards, dealing from left to right, with the first (leftmost) card turned faceup, and the remaining six facedown. Now put one card faceup on top of the second pile, then one facedown on each of the piles to its right. Then start with the third pile—one card faceup and the rest facedown and so on, until the last pile on the right receives one card, faceup. That pile will contain seven cards, six down and one up.

Set the remaining cards aside, facedown, to form the stock from which you'll draw cards. Leave room above the row, because you'll be moving cards into this space to form sequences, called "foundation piles."

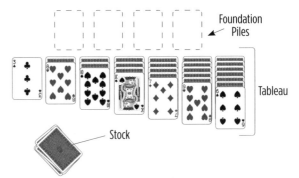

The Game Plan

* Start the game by moving any aces showing to the space above the tableau to start a foundation pile. Turn over the card that was beneath the ace. If there is a two of the same suit as the ace anywhere in the tableau, you may place the two on the ace and turn over the card that was beneath the two. (In the diagram on the next page, the player's next move might be to move the two of diamonds on top of the ace of diamonds.) If the three of the same suit is visible, you may place it on the two in the foundation pile and turn up the card where the three used to be. This process will be used throughout the game to build sequences for all four suits. An exposed ace must be played to start a

foundation, but if other cards of the same suit come up, you may not want to play them right away (see below).

✘ When there are no more faceup cards to transfer, you're ready for the challenging part—arranging the tableau in columns, in descending order and in alternating color. For example, if your exposed cards include the ten of clubs, the nine of hearts and the eight of spades, you can move the nine to overlap the ten, and the eight to overlap the nine to make a column. You then can turn over the cards that were covered by the nine and the eight, so you will have two new up-cards.

✘ Up-cards are the only cards that can be moved, and the challenge is to expose (turn over) all your down-cards so they can be transferred to a foundation pile. If an up-card is next in the sequence of a foundation pile, but also could be built upon using a card from another pile, and moving that card would allow you to expose a down-card, you may decide not to play to the foundation and instead move around the cards in the tableau.

✘ On each turn, look for opportunities to expose down-cards in the tableau or to add to a foundation. In each play you may:

- Move cards from one tableau pile to another. All faceup cards in the column must move as a unit. If you have a column of ten, nine, eight, seven, you may move all four cards to overlap a jack. You cannot move the seven by itself. If you move an entire column and create an empty space, the space can only be filled with a king or a column headed by a king.
- Take a card from the stock and add it to the tableau or the foundation. If the stock card can't be played, place the card faceup on the discard pile. You may draw another card from the stock.
- Use the top card from the discard pile to add to a column or foundation.

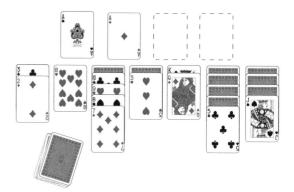

Winning

If you are able to make four piles of ascending cards in the same suit and color, you have won. If you find yourself flipping over the discard pile into the stock pile over and over again and don't see any moves, you have lost.

This is not an easy game on your ego, because it's tough to beat. Longtime players are usually content to count the number of cards in foundation piles, happy to beat their previous total. They become absolutely giddy if all cards move to foundations.

These variations can make the game more player-friendly.

Variations

✖ Build the tableau by dealing seven cards facedown, then seven more down-cards on top of the first row, and finally seven cards faceup on top of them. Play is the same as above, except that when you reach an impasse (no moves available), you deal seven cards from the stock onto the piles. When you reach the last three cards, they go on the first three piles.

✖ When there are no more cards in the stock, shuffle the discards and use them as new stock. Do this as many times as you wish.

✖ A space created by moving a column may be filled with any card or column. The rule still applies for moving all faceup cards as a unit.

Spades

If you thrill at the prospect of Hearts or Oh, Hell, you'll love Spades. It's a four-person bidding and trick-taking game, but unlike Oh, Hell, every hand is thirteen tricks. The partnership aspect and bidding process makes Spades a little more complicated than Hearts, but still simple enough and entertaining for players just getting the hang of card-counting and probability. And if your team is really lagging in the scoring, Spades allows for a kind of "Hail Mary": You and your partner can each bid *blind nil*—which basically means crossing your fingers and praying—and rack up 400

points if the gamble pays off. Plus it's a partnership game, so there's always someone to shore you up . . . or blame if things go awry.

NOTE: There are so many versions and variations of this game that it is hard to tell what is "standard" and what is a variation. What follows is as close to a "standard" as I can get, with some variations thrown in.

PLAYERS: 4, in teams of 2. Spades is sometimes played as a three-, four-, or five-player "cutthroat" (every man for himself) game, with the same playing rules as for the partnership game.

THE GEAR: A standard deck of 52 cards; aces are high. Spades are always trump. Paper and pencil for scoring.

Objective

To take the number of tricks you have bid and to be the first team to reach 500 points.

The Deal

Dealer deals thirteen cards to each player, one at a time. In a three-player game, the two of clubs is removed from the deck, and each player is dealt seventeen cards. With five players, both red deuces are removed, and the players each receive ten cards.

Bidding

✖ The game begins with a round of bidding, starting with the player to the left of the dealer. Each player indicates the number of tricks he intends to take by bidding any number from zero (no tricks) to thirteen (all of the tricks). That number, plus his partner's bid, represents the number of tricks the team must take in the hand. So if Joe bids 1, Anne bids 3, Sally bids 2, and

Frank bids 5, Joe and Sally together must take at least three tricks, and Anne and Frank must take at least 8. The total of all the bids does not have to equal the total number of tricks to be played in the hand. (In one variation of the game, the total of the bids must *not* add up to thirteen—the total must be either greater or fewer than thirteen; this prohibition guarantees that someone will fail.) Each player must make a bid (a "no bid" is not acceptable), and bids do not have to be higher than the previous player's bid. In an alternative variation of bidding, partners may place a single bid to indicate the number of tricks they intend to take as a team. Before placing their bids, partners can discuss their potential in a general way ("I think I can take four tricks and maybe eight"), but cannot discuss specifics ("I have almost no face cards, but I'm short in a red suit").

✖ The following bids are rewarded with a bonus when the bidder is successful, and a penalty when not. In each case, there is a separate accounting for the partner's bid and tricks, after which the scores of the two partners are combined to arrive at the team score. See the section on scoring, page 267, for specifics.

✖ *Bidding Nil:* Bidding zero (no tricks) is called *bidding nil.* Both partners may bid nil (called *double nil*). If both succeed in taking no tricks, each scores the bonus; if they fail, each earns the penalty. If one is successful and the other fails, they cancel each other, and no points are added or subtracted.

✖ *Bidding Blind:* If a player feels adventurous, blessed, or just plain lucky, she may place a bid before she looks at her cards. The maximum allowable blind bid is seven.

✖ *Bidding Blind Nil:* A player may, *before* he looks at his cards, bid "blind nil." In most games, this bid is permitted only when the team is at least 100 points behind in the score.

✖ *Bidding Double Blind Nil:* Both partners may bid blind nil (called, surprisingly, double blind nil). If both are successful, the team earns a bonus, and if both fail, they incur a penalty. If one is successful and the other fails, they cancel each other, and no points are added or subtracted.

✖ *Passing:* When a player bids nil or blind nil, he can exchange two (some play three) cards with his partner. After the bidding is over, he takes two cards from his hand and passes them facedown to his partner. Before looking at those cards, the partner passes two cards from her hand, and then picks up the cards her partner has passed.

✖ If *both* partners bid nil or blind nil, they do not exchange cards.

The Game Plan

✖ The player to the dealer's left leads. She may lead any card except a spade. Spades may not be led until either (a) spades are "broken," which means that someone has trumped on a previous trick (a player who was unable to follow suit elected to play a spade on the trick) or (b) a player has no cards in her hand *except* spades.

✖ Players must follow suit if they can. A trick is won by the highest trump in it, or if there are no trumps, by the highest card of the suit led. A trick is set facedown in front of the player who won it. As subsequent tricks are won, the player must place those tricks in such a way that any player may count the number of tricks taken. The number of tricks cannot be disguised or misrepresented. (See page 238 for a diagram of how to stack your tricks in front of you.) The winner of a trick leads the next trick, and play continues until all cards have been played.

Scoring

Once all thirteen tricks have been played, the game is scored by comparing the number of tricks taken vs. the number of tricks bid. (For a blank scorecard, see page 375.)

✖ Each trick that you *bid* for is worth 10 points.

✖ If you succeed in taking at least the number of tricks you bid, score 10 for each trick that you bid. Additional tricks (or *overtricks*) count as 1 point each. A team that bids four, but then takes seven tricks, would score 4 x 10 = 40, plus 3 x 1 = 3, for a total of 43 points. If you fall short of your bid, you lose points equal to your bid times ten, and you score nothing for your tricks. A team that bids seven but takes only four tricks would have 70 points subtracted from their score (so negative scores are possible).

✖ If a player bids nil and succeeds in taking no tricks, the team scores a bonus of 100 points. If that player takes any tricks, the team is penalized 100 points. Those overtricks do not count toward her partner's score, but they do count as bags (see sidebar) for the team. Her partner's score is calculated separately, and then is combined with the nil bidder's score to arrive at the team score.

✖ If both players bid nil and they both succeed, the team wins 200 points (some play that it automatically wins the game),

Optional "Sandbagging" Rule

To discourage players from deliberately and safely underbidding every hand, there is a penalty that is assessed for taking too many overtricks (in the game of Spades, overtricks are called "bags"). A running tally of overtricks is maintained, and each time a team accumulates ten bags, they lose 100 points from their score (upon reaching ten bags, deduct 100 points; upon reaching twenty bags, deduct another 100 points). The tricks you bid are scored in multiples of 10, but overtricks are scored as single digits. Therefore, the right-hand digit of your score represents a running tally of the number of bags a team has accumulated.

but there is a 200-point penalty if both fail. If one succeeds and the other fails, no points are added or subtracted.

✖ If a player bids blind and succeeds in making the bid, the team scores 100 points, but there is a 100-point penalty for falling short of the bid.

✖ If a player bids blind nil, the team wins 200 points if he is successful and incurs a 200-point penalty if he fails.

✖ If both players bid blind nil, the team wins 400 points if successful (some play that it automatically wins the game) but incurs a 400-point penalty if both players fail. If one player succeeds and one fails, no points are added or subtracted.

Winning

The first team to reach 500 points wins. If both teams go over 500 points in the same hand, the higher score wins.

Store

S tore is a fun, fast-paced, and sometimes chaotic game that pretty much anyone can play. Andrew has developed Store into a commercially available game called Anomia, which is more sophisticated but still a ton of fun for both kids and grown-ups.

PLAYERS: 3–7 players, ages eight and up, plus a judge.

THE GEAR: A standard deck of 52 cards.

The Game Plan

- Shuffle a deck of regular playing cards and place it within easy reach of all players.

- Each player then chooses a type of store to be (e.g., pet store, candy store, toy store, etc.). Everyone announces what his or her store is, and all players need to *memorize* what one another's stores are.

- Randomly choose someone to go first. The player draws a card and *quickly* flips it faceup in front of himself for all players to see.

- The next player, in clockwise order, draws a card and also *quickly* flips it over in front of herself. (If it's your turn to draw, and you already have a faceup card in front of you, flip the new card on top of your existing card.)

- Drawing continues until the values on any two players' cards match (a jack and a jack, or a three and a three, etc.). When you match with another player, you must "face-off" with them by naming an item that can be purchased in his store before he can name an item in your store. For example: If I am a pet store and I match with a player who is a candy store, then I could win the face-off by yelling "Snickers" before she says, "Poodle!"

- The first person to blurt out a correct answer wins the face-off. The winner takes the top card on the loser's pile and places it facedown in her separate winning pile.

- Drawing then continues with the next player in the clockwise drawing sequence. Once all the cards in the center pile are gone, the player with the most cards in her winning pile wins the game.

Special Instructions

Card flipping: You must flip your card quickly and keep your hands out of the way of other players' view of your card. If you win a face-off because you have blocked your opponents' view (intentionally or not), you will lose your turn.

No repeats: Once an item in a store is named, it cannot be used to win another face-off by you or any other player!

Speaking at the same time: If both players say their answer at the same time, the person who *finishes* the word first wins. So if you are trying to blurt out a dog breed, it's better to say "Lab" than "Pomeranian." Close calls will be decided by an impartial judge, if there is one monitoring the game, or by the majority. If it is truly a tie, no one wins and the game continues.

—contributed by Andrew Innes, a Boston-based game designer. For more about Andrew and his latest game, Anomia, check out anomiapress.com.

Chapter Fourteen

BRAINY GAMES FOR TWO

Let's say you and your pal arrived at the new *Star Wars* movie a little early. *OK,* way early. You snagged the best seats, sure, but . . . there's half an hour till showtime, people in Ewok costumes have ceased to be interesting, and the popcorn is long gone. So what the hell are you supposed to do now? Read? That's not very social. Chat? You can't bear to hear one more time about how his girlfriend tracks his every move on Facebook—and has for the last three years—and what should he do? This is exactly where Brainy Games for Two comes in.

I know, you're thinking Hangman—booooring. But! There are more strategy games for two than you've ever dreamed of . . . there may well be an infinite number. This chapter includes some oldies but goodies—like Mancala and Nine Men's Morris (and when I say "oldie," I'm not kidding: archeologists have discovered Nine Men's Morris boards from 1300 B.C.; stone Mancala boards dating from roughly the same period make that game another contender for the World's Oldest Pastime. For both, game boards were carved into temples or pyramids). Note to game designers: If you want your game to last for centuries, carve the playing area in stone, preferably on some structure that's going to be around a while, and keep the playing pieces simple: pebbles or beans. Another feature of enduring games is their malleability—they can be adjusted for level of expertise.

You'll also find the *newest* generation of strategy games for two—games invented in just the last few years. Decipher, Depth Charge, and Coup d'Etat are all opportunities to test your powers of deduction. Best of all, the game boards and playing pieces for these three games are all things you probably already have around the house: cards, coins, and paper. These games combine elements that are totally new (spies, coups, code breaking) with elements of the familiar (cards, battleships, and secret information).

In other words, games for two go way beyond Tic-Tac-Toe. We've collected the best—the most fun, the most strategy-oriented—to really stretch your reasoning, logic, foresight, and territory-capturing skills. Plus, they're all fairly quick games, ranging from five to twenty minutes, so they're perfect for the odd moment when there's not enough time to do anything more involved. Here are a couple of examples: Demolition Tic-Tac-Toe is perfect to play on the sly with a colleague during an especially tedious meeting. On a first date, get right down to brass tacks with a round of Coup d'Etat before the appetizers arrive. If your date doesn't go for it, cut the evening short. Who wants to be romantically involved with someone who doesn't like Brainy Games for Two?

Expanda-Toe

If you're over eight years old, Tic-Tac-Toe can be a little dull. Expanda-Toe is a far more challenging way to occupy a few minutes with a friend. And if you're in academia, take a clue from the master: Thi Nguyen, the fellow who created this game, finds it a great way to occupy himself and a colleague in the back of a lecture hall while a professor is droning on and on.

Like basic Tic-Tac-Toe, you have to play both offensively and defensively—to plan where you want to go while blocking your opponent's path at the same time. But the board doesn't remain static: It constantly expands and players must be able to visualize options that don't even exist yet. Every play you make lets your opponent draw a new square and put his mark in it—which will in turn let you do the same. Expanda-Toe is best for players with strong visual imaginations.

THE GEAR: 2 pencils, a sheet of paper.

The Game Plan
Draw a standard three-by-three Tic-Tac-Toe board. Play is the same as standard Tic-Tac-

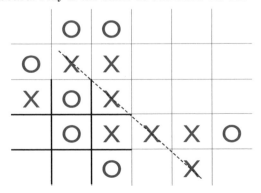

Toe, with one addition: You may play in a square *outside* the board, provided that your play is orthogonally (horizontally or vertically, not diagonally) adjacent to at least one previously played mark, either yours or your opponent's.

Winning
A player who draws four Xs or Os in a row—either horizontally, vertically, or diagonally—wins.

> **AMP IT UP**
> Many pen-and-paper games can be played outside by real human beings. Try Tic-Tac-Toe with real people as the Xs and Os, or snap down some chalk lines and play chess with real-life knights and pawns.

Demolition Tic-Tac-Toe

Demolition Tic-Tac-Toe starts with the basics of Expanda-Toe. It feels a little more like Chess or Go, with threats, counter-threats, and weirdness.

The Game Plan
Add the following twist to Expanda-Toe (left): If your marks orthogonally (horizontally or vertically, but not diagonally) surround your opponent's mark on three sides, you may, on your turn, instead of placing a new mark, choose to *demolish* that surrounded square. That means the square is blacked out and is permanently out of the game.

Once a demolition occurs, check to see if all off-grid plays are connected via orthogonal connections to the original grid. (The

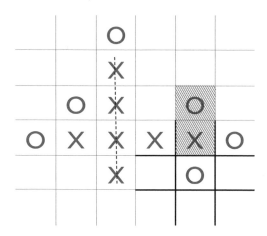

connection can make as many right turns as it needs.) Any marks that have been disconnected are immediately demolished (blacked out).

Winning

The first player to get four squares in a row, either horizontally, diagonally, or vertically, wins.

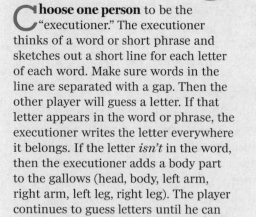

Hangman

Choose one person to be the "executioner." The executioner thinks of a word or short phrase and sketches out a short line for each letter of each word. Make sure words in the line are separated with a gap. Then the other player will guess a letter. If that letter appears in the word or phrase, the executioner writes the letter everywhere it belongs. If the letter *isn't* in the word, then the executioner adds a body part to the gallows (head, body, left arm, right arm, left leg, right leg). The player continues to guess letters until he can either guess the word or phrase (he wins) or until all six body parts are on the gallows (he loses). The executioner wins if the full body is hanging from the gallows.

Sprouts

This game, invented in 1960 by John H. Conway and M. S. Paterson, seems quite simple. But depending on how many dots you initially start with, the game can become very complicated, mathematically. It's ideal for filling a few moments with a friend over coffee.

THE GEAR: Paper, pencil.

Objective

To block the other player from drawing a line.

The Game Plan

✖ Start the game by drawing any number of dots on a sheet of paper. Our example has three dots, but you may play with as many as you wish.

✖ The first player takes a turn by joining two of the dots and marking a new dot in the middle of the line. Alternately, the line may start and end on the same spot.

✖ There are two rules: Players may not draw a line that crosses another line, and a dot may not have more than three lines leading to or from it. For example, in the game below, dots A and B cannot be used any more because they already have three lines. Dots A and B are "dead."

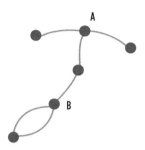

Winning

Players take turns until one player runs out of moves. The last person to draw a line is the winner.

▶▶ IF YOU LIKE THIS GAME . . . check out Word Logic on page 106 or 25 Letters on page 98.

||||||||||||||||||||||||||||||||||||||||||||||||||||||||||||||||||||||||

Coup d'Etat

Designed by Scott DeMers, Coup d'Etat is a game that pits your memory and powers of deduction against those of your opponent. Here's how Scott describes the game: "DespotLand has forever been a rival to your country. As the leader of EnlightenedRealm, the time has come to replace DespotLand's ruler with someone more agreeable to you. Of course, your rival may be attempting the same thing against you.

"The goal of Coup d'Etat is to overthrow your enemy. You must deduce where he is hiding and assassinate or turn the populace against him by locating important supporters of a coup among the citizens of his country."

THE GEAR: A standard deck of 52 cards and ten coins of two denominations (five nickels and five dimes, for example).

Separate the following cards from the deck: ace through seven in all suits; a black eight, jack, queen, and king; and a red eight, jack, queen, and king. The remaining cards are not used.

CARD EXPLANATIONS

King: your alter ego; the leader of your country.

Queen: your wife. A potential ally to the coup plotters.

Jack: your son. Another potential ally to the coup plotters.

Ace: an assassin who can remove people who oppose you.

Cards two through eight: the population of the country who can influence the success of a coup.

EXPLANATION OF THE COINS

Each player uses one coin type.

Heads represent spies that travel into the other player's country to identify supporters for a coup and move around your own country to block the other player's spies.

Tails represent supporters of a coup and may not move.

Preparation

One player takes the black cards and the other player takes the red cards. Each player then secretly places the cards facedown in a grid six wide and three deep in front of them. Card placement is subject to these limitations:

✖ The queen must be directly adjacent or diagonal to the king.

✖ The jack must be directly adjacent or diagonal to the queen.

✻ The top "wide" edge of the player's grid should align with the top wide edge of the other player's grid. The entire playing board will be a six-by-six grid of cards. Each player's "country" is the eighteen cards nearest him, with an imaginary border in between.

> **▸▸STEALTH STRATEGY**
>
> Set up your country in a way that will be least expected by your opponent. The further back you place your jack and queen, the longer it should take to locate your king.

When the map is built, each player then places five heads-up coins, representing spies, on any of the six cards on the bottom edge of their country. (The "bottom" edge is the edge closest to the player and furthest from the border.) Each card may only contain one spy. When done, one card in the bottom row should be open; the other five should contain coins. (See diagram below.) Later in the game, coins may be flipped over, tails up, to form supporters.

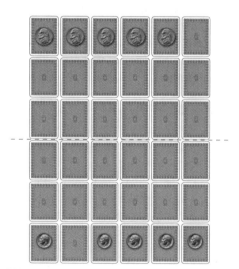

Possible starting configuration for Coup d'Etat

The Game Plan

The red player moves first. A player *must* move one, and only one, spy each turn one space in any direction—horizontally, vertically, or diagonally:

✻ A spy may land on a player's own card or his opponent's card.

✻ Only spies may move. Supporters may never move. (See "Create a Supporter," below, to learn how to turn spies into supporters.)

✻ A spy may not land on a card containing another spy or supporter, regardless of who owns the spy or supporter.

✻ A player may look at *any* card, either his own or his opponent's, on which he has a spy or supporter at any time (usually upon landing on a card for the first time). Otherwise players may not look at a card, regardless of which country contains the card. A good memory is rewarded in this game: If you can recall where you placed your cards at the beginning of the game, you'll be able to strategize more efficiently.

After a player has moved, landed on a card, and looked at that card, he *may* do one, and only one, of the following:

1. CREATE A SUPPORTER

✻ If a spy is on a number card or the jack or queen in the other player's country, the player may make that card a "supporter."

✻ The spy coin is flipped over (heads down) to represent a supporter. The person represented by the card is now supporting a coup.

✻ A supporter may not move or change back to a spy.

✻ The supporter card remains facedown, but,

as mentioned above, the person who landed on it may look at it at any time.

2. ASSASSINATION ATTEMPT

✖ If a spy is on an ace card in the other player's country, the player may declare an assassination attempt by flipping the card faceup (to prove it is an ace).

✖ That player then selects any card on the board for assassination (no matter if the card is empty or has a spy or supporter on it). That card is flipped over.

✖ If the selected card is a king, the game ends immediately.

✖ If the selected card is not a king, then the selected card and any spy or supporter of either player on the card is permanently removed from the game. No spy may enter the space again.

✖ The spy remains on the ace card and may be moved normally next turn. The ace card remains faceup for the remainder of the game and may be entered normally, but it may not be used for an assassination attempt again, nor may the ace be made into a coup supporter.

Winning

There are two ways to win Coup d'Etat:

✖ If a player assassinates the other player's king, he wins; or

✖ If a player can prove that she has twenty-five influence points in the other player's country during her turn. The first player to declare and prove the necessary influence wins.

A player's influence is calculated by adding the value of all cards on which he has

supporters, but not spies, in the other player's country. The values are as follows:

- **Queen:** 9 points
- **Jack:** 9 points
- **Ace:** 0 points
- **Eight:** 8 points
- **Seven:** 7 points

and so on.

If a player declares influence, the cards of her opponent on which she has supporters are flipped faceup. If she cannot prove necessary influence, then the cards are flipped back facedown and play continues.

If neither player can complete either of the above tasks, the game is a draw. (Though technically possible, a draw is highly unlikely.)

Decipher

Can you crack the code in time? Designed by Zach and Amanda Greenvoss, a husband-and-wife design team, Decipher is the perfect game for sprawling on the living room floor on a rainy day. You must figure out your opponent's hidden code before they figure out yours. It requires logic, deduction, and strategic cardplay.

THE GEAR: **A standard deck of 52 cards; six counters (e.g., pennies), paper and pencil for note-taking.**

Preparation

✖ Shuffle the deck and deal three cards facedown in a row in front of each player. Each player may examine her cards, but the cards must remain secret from the opposing player. Leave enough space between the two rows of cards for two additional rows of cards.

✖ Next, deal six cards to each player. These represent the player's starting hand, and should be kept secret. Set aside the rest of the deck as a stockpile.

✖ Finally, give three pennies to each player.

✖ A player's facedown cards represent her hidden code (which will not change during the game). It is this code that the opponent is trying to guess. The cards that will be played directly in front of these cards are called the Decipher cards: These are played by the opposing player from her hand.

The Game Plan

Flip a coin to determine the starting player. Each player's turn has two phases: Player places one to three Decipher cards, and Opponent evaluates his hidden cards.

1. PLAY DECIPHER CARDS

✖ Each turn a player must place one, two, or three cards from her hand into the Decipher card piles directly in front of her opponent's hidden cards.

✖ In the first turn, the player must play three cards, and these cards will be laid on the three empty spaces in front of her opponent's hidden cards. (After the player's first turn, these Decipher cards will cover some or all of the already-played faceup cards.) The player must start at the far left column and indicate if she will place a card there or not. (Before placing a card on a pile, she is allowed to look through her previously played Decipher cards in that pile, to remember what cards she's already played.) Once she has played a card onto that pile, or indicated that she is not going to play a card and moved to the next column, she may not look through this column's cards again until her next turn.

✖ After placing these Decipher cards, the player must draw cards from the stock to keep her hand at six cards.

2. EVALUATE HIDDEN CARDS

✖ After the cards have been played, the non-active player must "evaluate" his hidden cards against the active player's three faceup Decipher cards. This will give the active player information about her opponent's "secret code." Players must be honest when evaluating their cards.

✖ This evaluation is done on a column-by-column basis. The first hidden card is compared to the Decipher card in the same column (without revealing the hidden card). If the faceup card matches the hidden card's suit or number or both, the non-active player must place one penny on top of his hidden card. This indicates the active player has scored a "hit" and is closer to deciphering the code. This process is repeated for each of the hidden cards. In the diagram on the following page, you can see that Player B has indicated that his

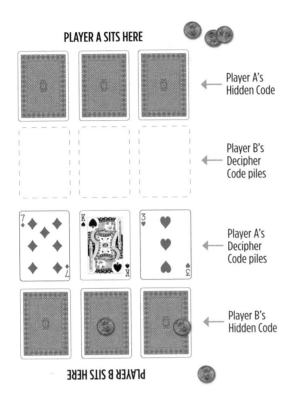

PLAYER A SITS HERE

← Player A's Hidden Code

← Player B's Decipher Code piles

← Player A's Decipher Code piles

← Player B's Hidden Code

PLAYER B SITS HERE

right-hand card is either a three or a heart; that his middle card is either a king or a spade; and that his left-hand card is neither a seven nor a diamond.

⤬ Once each column has been evaluated, and the pennies have been placed on the hidden cards, the active player's turn is over. Note that the pennies remain on the hidden cards until the Decipher card in front of them changes. This way players can always see how many "hits" they have with the currently active Decipher cards.

While the pennies indicate a player is getting closer, they will never actually reveal the exact card. Only through careful card selection and deduction will a player figure out what each hidden card is.

The Endgame

At the beginning of a player's turn (before she plays any cards), a player may declare she is going to "break the code." This immediately ends the game, and both players must now guess their opponent's hidden cards.

Starting with the active player, each player guesses what each hidden card is. This is done on a column-by-column basis, much like playing the Decipher cards.

NOTE: A player may look through her previously played Decipher cards for the current column she is guessing, before making her guess. Once she moves to the next column, she may not look through any other column of cards. This rule must be strictly enforced to ensure players do not simply count cards.

The closer players are to the correct hidden card, the more points they receive:

⤬ Correct suit: 1 point

⤬ Correct card value: 2 points

⤬ Correct suit and value (exact match): 3 points

Thus, in a perfect game a player could receive nine points if she correctly guessed each of the opponent's hidden cards' suits and values.

After the current player has made her guesses and received the appropriate points, the other player does the same.

Winning

⤬ The player with the most points wins.

⤬ If the deck is exhausted before a player declares they are going to "break the code," the players may continue to play their hands until someone has no cards remaining. At that point, the active player must end the game and begin guessing.

The L Game

The L Game was designed by Edward de Bono, an expert on lateral thinking. On his website, de Bono explains that he loves games but doesn't like to concentrate on a large number of pieces (as in chess). He set out to design a simple game that could, in theory, be played forever. The L Game was the result. Well, it *seems* like a simple game—but there are more than 18,000 positions on the board. There are fifteen basic winning positions. It's a great game for a plane or train trip.

THE GEAR: A board of four-by-four squares; two L-shaped pieces whose short end will cover two squares and whose long end will cover three (see diagram, below); two tokens (coins will do) that will fit inside one square.

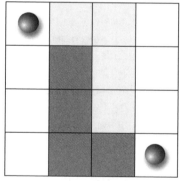

Starting position

The Game Plan

* Randomly decide who goes first. Set up the board in the starting position, above. (For a blank board, see page 376.) Play alternates between the two players.

(For a blank board, see page 376.)

* On each turn, a player picks up her L-piece and sets it somewhere on the board—anywhere it can cover four empty squares. At least one of the squares must be different than the four squares just vacated. (In other words, you can't just pick up your piece and set it back down in exactly the same place.) The piece may be turned around or over.

* The player may then move either one of the tokens to cover an empty square. A token allows a player to block single squares from her opponent. The player does not *have* to move a token, however—she may leave them where they are, if she chooses.

Winning

A player wins when the other player has no place to move his L piece.

Dots and Boxes

Dots and Boxes is a paper-and-pencil territory-capturing game. You're trying to gain ground by connecting dots to make boxes.

THE GEAR: Paper, pencil.

The Game Plan

* Make a grid of four dots by four dots for sixteen dots total (see the blank grid, on the next page).

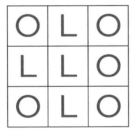

- ✖ Randomly decide who goes first.

- ✖ Each player, in turn, will draw a line, either vertical or horizontal, between two dots. You must draw a line when it's your turn; no passing allowed.

- ✖ If a player finishes off the fourth side of a box, she has "captured" that box and writes her initial in it.

- ✖ When all the dots are connected, the game is over. The player who has captured the most squares is the winner. (See completed game board, right.)

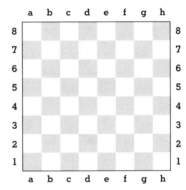

O is the winner here

AMP IT UP
Once the four-by-four grid gets boring, make it bigger—five-by-five, etc.

Depth Charge

Designed by David E. Whitcher, Depth Charge is a deduction game with a naval theme: "It's time once more for naval exercises on Lake Ashtapada* to test what the new crewmen have learned

about using sonar. They will be split into two teams, Red and Black, who will set three targets to represent mines for each other to find. The first team to find the other's mines wins the trophy; the other will be scrubbing toilets."

Ashtapada is Sanskrit for an eight-by-eight board or any game played on it.

THE GEAR: A chess or checkers board with the vertical columns labeled A through H and the horizontal rows labeled 1 through 8.

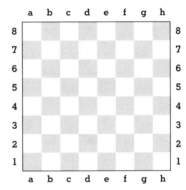

2 pawns or checkers, in different colors, to represent ships. Red and black are described in these rules.

1 marker (penny, button, etc.) to mark Depth / Sounding Charge location (optional).

2 Depth Charge record sheets (which you can photocopy from page 281).

2 screens for each player to hide their record sheets (hardcover books work well, or just hold the record sheets on your lap under the table).

2 pencils.

Preparation

- ✖ Give each player a Depth Charge record sheet, a ship, a screen, and a pencil.

- Set the board on the table with the black and red players placing their ships in opposite corners, as shown on the record sheets.

- On their record sheets, each player secretly marks the locations of three target mines with the letter *M* in the sea of his or her color: The red player will place mines in the Red Sea and the black player in the Black Sea. The shaded diagonal between the seas is off-limits for mine placement.

The Game Plan

The youngest player goes first. On a player's turn she must do exactly one of the three following actions.

1. Move her ship: Move her boat one, two, or three spaces in a straight line along a row or column (never diagonally) as long as it is not through her opponent's ship. If she moves over an opponent's mine, her ship is destroyed and she loses. She may freely move over or stop in the location of one of her own mines.

2. Drop a Sounding Charge: Call out one of the eight spaces immediately surrounding her ship (e.g., "F6" or "B4"), marking it on her sheet for easy reference and setting the marker on the board. Her opponent will report the "ping" times of each of his remaining mines. (See "reporting," right.) She should note the ping times on her record sheet for easy reference.

3. Drop a Depth Charge to destroy a mine: Played just like a sounding charge, but no ping report is made. If dropped on an opponent's mine, the opponent will say so and the mine is marked as destroyed. Because the exercise is about accuracy, players are allowed only one miss. If a

player drops a depth charge twice and misses twice, she loses the game.

Reporting

When a player announces where she is dropping a sounding charge, her opponent must report the "ping times" of his remaining mines, according to the following:

- If a mine is directly in line along any row, column, or diagonal from the space where the sounding charge was dropped, count the number of spaces to the mine, not including the space where the sounding charge was dropped.

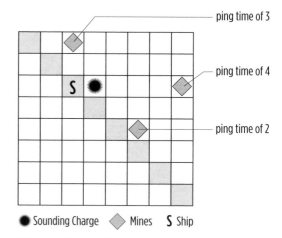

ping time of 3

ping time of 4

ping time of 2

● Sounding Charge ◆ Mines S Ship

Diagram for sounding charge

- If a mine is not directly in line from the space where the sounding charge was dropped, count the number of spaces it takes to reach the column the mine is in, and then add the number of spaces it takes to reach the mine from that row.

  Mines are not reported if the sounding charge was dropped in the space occupied by the mine, nor if another enemy mine lies directly in line between it and the sounding charge.

DEPTH CHARGE RECORD SHEET

							red starts here
					red sea		
	black sea						
black starts here							

= Off limits for mine placement

Winning

There are three ways to win. A player wins if:

1. She locates and destroys all three of her opponent's mines; or

2. her opponent moves onto one of her mines; or

3. her opponent misses blowing up one of her mines for the second time with a depth charge.

▶▶ **IF YOU LIKE THIS GAME . . . you can find more of David's great games, including a new, souped-up version of Depth Charge, on pyromythgames.com.**

Footsteps

Footsteps is a psychological game that requires a bit of mind reading and bluff. It's a great little "appetizer" game—play while you're sipping an aperitif and munching on salted peanuts.

THE GEAR: Paper, pencils, a coin to use as a token.

The Game Plan

Trace the coin seven times, making a horizontal line of circles. Place a vertical slash through the center circle. One side of the line belongs to one player (the leftmost three circles, for example, for Player A, and the rightmost three circles for Player B).

✴ Place the coin on the center circle. The object of the game is to get the coin on your opponent's end circle.

✴ Each player begins with 50 points.

✴ On each turn, both players jot down the number of points they wish to "spend." This can be any number from 1 to 50.

✴ The two players then reveal their numbers to each other. The player with the larger number moves the token one space into his opponent's territory. If the numbers are the same, the coin stays in the center.

✴ Both players deduct the amount they had jotted down from their totals (on the first turn, they will be deducting from 50).

✴ Players again write down how many points they wish to spend, and so on.

Winning

If one player uses up all his points, the other player wins. If one player advances the coin to the far end of her opponent's territory, she wins. If both players run out of points, the game is a draw.

▶▶**STEALTH STRATEGY** ◀

Try to win each turn by as small a margin as possible— one point is ideal. If you bet too large, too soon, you'll quickly run out of points.

Battleships

Originally known as **Salvo,** Battleships is a pen-and-paper game that seems like a war game, but is really a test of players' deductive reasoning skills.

THE GEAR: 2 pieces of graph paper with two grids, ten squares by ten squares. (For blank grids, see page 377.)

Objective
To sink your opponent's four ships.

Preparation
* Each player draws two ten-by-ten grids on a single sheet of paper. Label the grids "my ships" and "enemy ships" to avoid confusion. Mark the horizontal rows 1 through 10 and the vertical columns A through J. You will now be able to identify any individual box by its coordinates—A-1, for example, or E-9.

* Each player has a fleet of four ships. One is a battleship (B) that is five squares long; a cruiser (C) that is four squares long; and two destroyers (D) that are each two squares long.

* Each player then decides where to place his four ships; the ships are marked by

writing in the appropriate spaces. The ships must all be placed in straight lines either horizontally or vertically, but not diagonally. The other grid is blank and will be used to keep track of your opponent's fleet.

The Game Plan
* Players sit opposite each other with a screen or a hardcover book between them so they can't see each other's grids.

* Flip a coin to see who goes first.

* Players take turns firing salvos at each other. A shot is taken by calling out the coordinates of a space on the ten-by-ten grid. The first round will be a salvo of seven shots.

* The number of shots is determined by the number and types of ships a player has remaining. The battleship is worth three shots; the cruiser is worth two shots; the two destroyers are worth one shot each. So in the first round, each player has seven shots.

My Ships

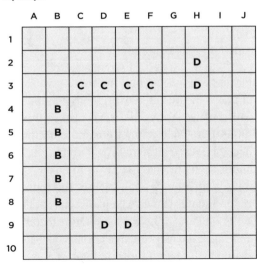

Enemy Ships

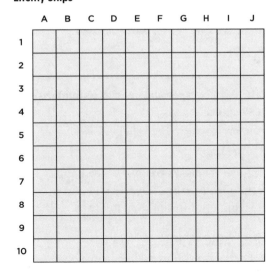

✼ As a player calls out coordinates, he marks them on his "enemy ships" grid so he will know where he has fired. The seven squares of the first salvo are marked with a 1, the second salvo will be marked with a 2, and so on. The opponent also marks the shots on her own grid. The opponent then announces what damage has been done. She doesn't announce the coordinates of the square, she only names the type of ship hit and the number of hits it received. For example: "Three hits: one on a battleship and two on a cruiser."

✼ Once all the squares of a ship have been hit, the ship is sunk and the player identifies the coordinates of the sunken ship. Her ability to fire shots is now reduced: If her battleship was sunk, three shots are removed from each salvo; if her cruiser was downed, two shots are reduced from each salvo; a sunken destroyer removes one.

Winning

The player who sinks all his opponent's ships is the winner.

Poker Squares

THE GEAR: Paper and pencils; a standard deck of 52 cards.

Objective

To form the best possible poker hands orthogonally—that is, vertically and horizontally, but not diagonally.

The Game Plan

✼ Each player draws a five-by-five grid to form twenty-five squares. (For a blank grid, see page 372.) This grid should be shielded from one's opponent.

✼ Shuffle the cards and set them facedown on the table. One player will draw the top card and announce the rank and suit; for example, the "seven of hearts." All players must write this card, noted as 7H, in one square before the next card is drawn. They can't later change the location of the square.

✼ The next player then draws a card and calls out the rank and suit. Players again write it into a blank square. S = spades, H = hearts, C = clubs, D = diamonds.

✼ After twenty-five cards have been drawn, players tally up their poker hands, using the chart below.

Straight flush (five cards in sequence in the same suit)	30
Four of a kind (any four cards of the same rank)	16
Straight (five cards in sequence but not of the same suit)	12
Full house (three of a kind and a pair)	10
Three of a kind (three cards of the same rank)	6
Flush (five cards all of the same suit)	5
Two pairs (two cards of any one rank and two cards of another rank)	3
One pair (two cards of any one rank)	1

✼ Players will quickly find their own style of play: One player may prefer to go for a conservative strategy—e.g., securing a flush rather than trying something more daring, like going for a straight. The fact that the hands aren't ranked exactly as in poker reflects the unique challenges of this game. Poker Squares can also be played as a Solitaire game—just turn the cards over, one by one, and mark the card in your grid—and is also available in several free online programs.

Winning

Highest score, determined by placement and chart, below, wins.

Winning Poker Squares Hand

JD	10D	2D	5D	4D	**flush** = 5 points
JH	QC	2S	5S	4S	
KH	QH	2H	5C	7C	
KD	8H	QS	4C	AD	
KS	AH	9D	9S	9C	**3 of a kind** = 6 points

full house = 10 points	pair = 1 point	3 of a kind = 6 points	3 of a kind = 6 points	pair = 1 point

TOTAL = 35 points

|||||||||||||||||||||||||||||||||||||||||||||||||||||||||||||||||||||||||||||

Nine Men's Morris

Nine Men's Morris may be the oldest game in the world—a Nine Men's Morris board is cut into the temple at Kurna, Egypt, and is presumed to date from around 1300 B.C. Ovid references the game more than a thousand years later, and Shakespeare refers to it in *A Midsummer Night's Dream*. The word *Morris* is a corruption of the word *merels,* from the Latin *merellus,* a counter. The board is three concentric squares with twenty-four points of intersection. Pieces are placed on the corners and on the points of intersection; there are twenty-four playable points.

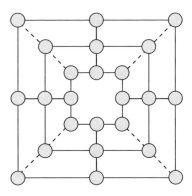

THE GEAR: A board, which can be sketched on paper, like the one above. Eighteen playing pieces of two different colors; nine pieces for each player. You can use chessmen, checkers, or even two different denominations of coins.

Objective

To make "mills"—vertical or horizontal lines of three in a row—of one's own men. When a player makes a mill, he takes one of his opponent's men off the board.

The Game Plan

- The board is empty at the beginning of the game. (For a blank board, see page 378.) Toss a coin to decide who will go first.

- Play is in phases. In the first phase, players take turns placing their pieces, one at a time, on the board on points of intersection. If a player forms a mill, he takes any opponent's piece that is *not* part of a mill off the board. If all the opponent's pieces are in mills, he may take any piece.

- When all the men are in play (minus any that have been captured), the second phase starts: Play continues alternately, but in each turn a player moves one piece along a line to an adjacent point. In this phase as well, if a player forms a mill, he may remove one of his opponent's pieces that is *not* part of a mill. If all the opponent's pieces are in mills, he may take any piece from the board.

✺ It is permissible and even desirable for a player to break his own mill by moving a piece out of it and then, in a subsequent turn, moving it back again, thus forming a new mill and removing another enemy piece.

✺ If, on a turn, a player is stalemated (can't move), the other player continues to play until the stalemate is relieved.

✺ When a player has only three pieces left, the third phase begins. The player with three pieces may move anywhere on the board, not just to adjacent points. The capturing rule is still in effect.

Winning

The game is over when one player is reduced to two men or when a player has no legal moves. The other player is the winner.

Variations

Five Men's Morris: Draw just two concentric squares and give each player five playing pieces. Play is as in standard Nine Men's Morris.

Twelve Men's Morris: The board is the same as in Nine Men's Morris, except that the diagonals are connected as well as the midpoints. Players, who have twelve playing pieces each, may move along the diagonals.

Labyrinth

Called **Pathfinder,** this pen-and-pencil maze game was commercially available in the 1970s. Thanks to David Pritchard's wonderful *Brain Games: The World's Best Games for Two*, we can retrieve it here. It's not unlike Battleships.

THE GEAR: Pencil and paper, preferably graph paper.

The Game Plan

✺ Each player draws two six-by-six grids on a single piece of paper; the vertical columns are labeled A through F and the horizontal rows are labeled 1 through 6. (For blank grids, see page 377.) Label one grid "mine" and the other grid with your opponent's name. It will be used to note information about your opponent's labyrinth as you get it.

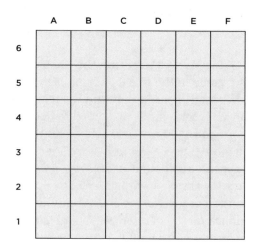

✺ Each player marks one square with an S for "start" and one square with an F for "finish"

on his or her own grid. These can be placed anywhere. At the start of the game, the opponent's grid is blank.

✖ Then each player creates a maze from start to finish. (The paper should be shielded from the opponent.) This is done by darkening the sides of the squares to form "walls." No more than three walls may be linked continuously, whether in a straight line or in a step-up pattern. So it must be possible, traveling either vertically or horizontally, to reach every square on the grid.

Sample Labyrinth game

✖ The number of walls that can be made should be agreed upon beforehand. Start with twenty and then experiment with more or fewer after your first game.

✖ Both players announce the coordinates of their start and finish squares and note their opponent's start and finish squares on the blank grid.

✖ Randomly choose who starts; play alternates. Each turn has two parts:

■ First, a player asks if a wall exists between two squares. For example: "B5/C5?" meaning "Is there a wall between B5 and C5?" The other player must answer truthfully.

■ Then, the same player asks if he can move either one square, two squares, or three squares. For example, a very conservative move would be "Move B5 to C5?" because he already knows he can do it. The opponent would answer "yes" and the player would move, charting his move on his opponent's grid. The player can also attempt a longer, riskier move: "Move B5-C5-D5-D4?" gambling that those four spaces aren't blocked by a wall. The opponent would answer "no," because there is a wall between C5 and D5. The asking player would not move and the turn ends.

NOTE: When asking if you can move (the second part of your turn), you must name each square you will be moving through, as there is frequently more than one way of getting from one square to another.

✖ The other player takes a turn.

✖ As a player gleans information, he should fill in walls on his opponent's blank grid.

✖ Play continues, with these two questions being answered in order in each turn.

Winning

A player wins when he arrives at the other's finish.

||||||||||||||||||||||||||||||||||||||||||||||||||||||||||||||||||||||||

Reversi

Marketed under the commercial name *Othello,* Reversi has been around for about 125 years, though there is some dispute about who actually invented it. It's an abstract strategy game and, while buying an Othello set has the advantage of aesthetics, it is not necessary to play the game.

THE GEAR: A chessboard or checkerboard; the colors of the squares have no significance. You may also draw a board of eight-by-eight squares on a piece of paper.

Thirty-two playing pieces for each player. A store-bought Othello set will have pieces that are white on one side and black on the other; each player is assigned a color. When a piece is "captured," it is turned over, revealing the other color, and thus belongs to the other player. You can make your own playing pieces by affixing a bit of colored tape to one side of coins, or even using heads and tails (although a clear color difference makes the layout of the board easier to grasp at a glance). If you want to get creative, collect some black pebbles and paint or put white tape on one side of each stone. Or cut disks from cardboard and paint one side a bright color. I will refer to the two sides as *black* **and** *white,* **but you can use any two colors you like.**

Objective

To have the most pieces of your color showing at the end of the game, when the board is entirely covered with playing pieces.

The Game Plan

✖ Flip a coin to determine who goes first. Let's say this player is white.

✖ For the first four turns, in turn, beginning with white, players place a piece on one of the center four squares of the board until those four squares are filled. (See the diagram, below, for a possible starting position.) The board is now ready for play.

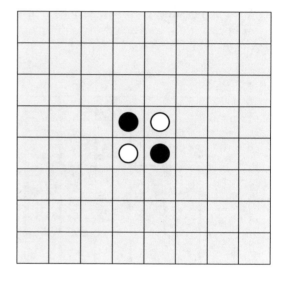

✖ Play alternates, beginning with white. A player places a piece on a square, in any direction, adjacent to one occupied by his opponent's piece.

✖ Any enemy pieces directly between this piece and another of the player's own color, either vertically, horizontally, or diagonally, are captured and turned over to show the capturing player's color.

✖ In other words, in the first move: White must place a piece on a vacant square next to a black piece such that the black piece is trapped between two white pieces in a straight line (either vertically, horizontally, or diagonally). In the first move, white has a choice of four possible moves. The trapped black piece is turned over and becomes a white piece. Play continues in this way until the board is full or there is no legal play for either player.

✖ Each player's objective is to place pieces on the opposite sides of an opponent's man—or on an unbroken *line* of an opponent's men— thereby capturing the intervening piece or pieces.

✖ Pieces may change owners several times in a game.

✖ If you cannot make a capture, you miss a turn.

✖ Only pieces captured by a player's move are turned over—there are no passive captures.

✖ More than one man may be captured in a single play, even on more than one line. So if by playing a single piece you can capture some of your opponent's men on a vertical line as well as a diagonal or horizontal line, go for it!

✖ The more pieces are on the board, the more observant you have to be, because more and more combinations open up.

Winning

When all the squares of the board are covered, or when it is not possible for either player to move, the player with the most of their color showing wins.

> **▶▶STEALTH STRATEGY ◀**
> The corner squares are the strongest; if you occupy a corner square, you have an anchor in three directions.

Mancala

Mancala is a family of games that are found across Africa and parts of the Middle East and Asia. It's another contestant for the world's oldest game: It was played in Egypt more than 3,000 years ago, and stone boards have been found at Thebes, Memphis, and Luxor. The equipment is very basic: It can be played by scraping holes in the ground and using shells for counters. In our beginner's version, below, you can assemble a board yourself using jar lids and beans.

THE GEAR: Twelve small containers and two large containers. Use jar lids, saucers, or even circles drawn on a piece of a paper. The two larger containers can be small bowls or larger saucers or circles.

Forty-eight counters (for a beginners' game). Once you've got the hang of it, you can increase the number of counters to seventy-two. Counters can be dried beans, beads, or coins.

Objective

To get as many counters as possible into your scoring pit (your big container).

The Game Plan

Set up two parallel rows of six small containers. These containers are called *pits*. One line belongs to Player A, and one line belongs to Player B. At the end of the two lines, on Player A's right, place the larger container, known as a *scoring pit* or Mancala. Player B's scoring pit goes at the other end, to his right.

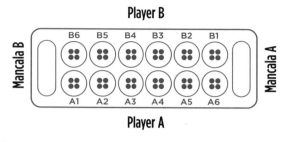

- Place four counters in each of the twelve small pits.

- Randomly decide who goes first.

- Each player, on his turn, picks up all four counters in any one of his small pits and *sows* them, or distributes them, one in each pit starting with the next pit to the right and proceeding counterclockwise. He distributes these counters, one at a time, into his own pits, his opponent's pits, and his own scoring pit, but skips his opponent's scoring pit.

- If the player's last counter lands in his own scoring pit, he gets another turn.

- If the player's last counter lands in an empty pit on his own side, he captures all his opponent's counters in the opposite pit and puts them and his own counter into his own scoring pit.

- The game finishes when the player whose move it is has no counters left to sow.

- The player who *does* have counters left puts them into his own scoring pit.

Winning

Each player tallies his counters. Whoever has the most counters in his scoring pit wins.

Chapter Fifteen

GAMES FOR A WEEKEND AWAY

Monday through Friday can drag—the commute, the meetings, the irascible boss. And if your life is like the rest of ours, not much of the week is spent *playing*. Maybe, if we're lucky, we manage a poker night once a month or a round of Monopoly with the kids before bed.

So when Friday evening rolls around, we're ready for a change of scene. Sometimes this just means turning off the phone and hanging out at home, but sometimes it means a bona fide minivacation, a whole weekend away. An escape. When we're *really* fortunate, we manage to flee the gritty, stinky confines of town for fresh, cooling draughts of country air. And once we've had a chance to catch our breath, to pour a glass of wine, well . . . of course we'll want to play a few games.

This chapter covers those games that take a little while. They're for folks with a decent attention span (though many can be played in and around other activities, and some can be started and stopped as the participants wish). They let you build a long-term strategy over the course of two days (or, in one bout of Forbidden Words, over a few *years*). Spending a couple of days on a leisurely activity—whether it's knitting or building a model train or playing a card game—is luxurious. A long, empty weekend with nothing planned but recreation hearkens back to a time when work didn't intrude seven days a week, when whole summers were reserved for riding bikes and building tree houses.

I'm reminded of Jane Austen's society in her novels, in which groups of young people spend days planning games, charades, and balls. In *Emma,* for example, the young ladies encourage the gentlemen of the neighborhood to compose riddles in the form of poems (called "conundrums"); the challenge continues over the course of several weeks. In Louisa May Alcott's *Little Women,* the girls present a play on Christmas Eve—an English tradition called pantomime. These little plays usually are performed over the holidays, but as a pantomime needs a few days for creation and rehearsal, we've included it here in the weekend games. Presumably, a panto can do double duty as a weekend game and a holiday game: Take a couple of days to write and rehearse, and then perform the show during your winter festivities.

Certainly not every weekend away means games: Sometimes you just want to ski or sunbathe or do whatever it is you went away for. But more than one vacation has been ruined by foul weather—you wished you'd packed a sweatshirt, you've drunk enough tea to sink a ship, and you've watched all the DVDs—so we've also included some standard parlor games at the end of this chapter, just to round out the weekend. There are games in this chapter for every type of interest: Card sharps will like 9-5-2; treasure seekers will want to try Geocaching; theatrical types will put on a play. Let's get started.

Wink Murder

Wink Murder is best played in and around other activities and can stretch over the course of several days. Put slips of paper (one for each guest) in a hat; make sure that one slip of paper is marked with an X and the rest are blank. The person who draws the X is the "Killer"; his objective is to eliminate the other players by discreetly winking at them. Once a player has been winked at, or killed, she must wait a few minutes and then announce her demise—either with an informative, "Guys, I'm dead," or, for the more theatrical among us, by staging a histrionic expiration. Wink Murder may be played over hours or days—and sometimes guests forget they're in the middle of a game. I was once playing at a housewarming party in Providence, and a cute guy approached me in the kitchen, smiling. I smiled back at him—and he winked. Oh, well—I got him back later in another round. Live by the wink, die by the wink.

Usually, the Killer is chosen by picking a name out of a hat or drawing straws, so no one knows who the Killer is. But you can mix it up by having a nonplaying host assign the role of Killer to a guest, and as the weekend progresses, players can (privately, to the host) make a guess as to the identity of the Killer. If they're wrong, they're dead. If they're right, they win. So Jane might go to Simon, the host for the weekend, and say, "Jason and Marla walked to the clam shack by themselves this afternoon, and later that evening Marla was dead—so I accuse Jason." If Jason is not the Killer, Jane is eliminated from the game, and she must not tell the rest of the group that

she's out. If Jason *is* the Killer, Jane wins and the host will announce the winner to the rest of the group. The winner gets to be the moderator for the next game. At the end of the weekend, all the winners have to buy dinner at the local clam shack.

PLAYERS: 6–30

THE GEAR: Paper, pencil, a hat.

Best Long-Form Board Games, for a Rainy Day at the Beach

- **Diplomacy:** A game of negotiation and warfare set in the years prior to World War I. Best for 6 to 7 players ages 12 and older.

- **The Settlers of Catan:** Players compete to build settlements, roads, and cities on the island of Catan, trying to be the first to establish a viable civilization. Best for 4 players ages 10 and older.

- **Axis and Allies:** A war game set in World War II; players compete to win battles and gain territory. Best for 2 to 5 players ages 12 and up.

9-5-2

A card game that can last an entire day, 9-5-2 is a trick-taking game for three and only three players, a rarity in the world of cards. It's the perfect activity when you've got a long stretch of time, two buddies, and some cold wine.

PLAYERS: 3

THE GEAR: A standard deck of 52 cards, paper, pencil.

Objective

To take more tricks than the required nine for the dealer, five for the player to the dealer's left, and two for the player to the dealer's right.

The Deal

Choose a dealer by cutting the deck; low card deals. The dealer deals sixteen cards to each player and sets aside four cards as a kitty. Aces are high.

The Game Plan

- Choose a number to play to, say, 10, which will take about an hour. Playing to 50 will pass a rainy day.
- Players arrange their cards in sequence, in suits. The dealer announces what's trump based on the strongest suit in his hand.
- The dealer then adds the four cards from the kitty to his hand and discards four unwanted cards from his hand.
- The player to dealer's left leads *any card to the first trick*. Others must follow suit if they have it; a player holding no card of the suit led may play any card. Each trick is won by the highest trump it contains, or if there are no trumps in it, by the highest card of the suit led.
- The winner of the trick gathers the cards and sets them facedown in front of him so that the number of tricks he's taken (as the game progresses) is easily countable by everyone at the table. He leads the next trick.

Show your tricks.

- No player may peek at the cards after they have been taken.
- Play continues until all the cards have been played and taken—sixteen tricks in all. Of these sixteen tricks, nine must be taken by the dealer, five must be taken by the player to the dealer's left, and two must be taken by the player to the dealer's right. This is called *book;* no points are awarded for making book.
- For each trick *over* book, a player gets 1 point. For each trick *under* book, a player loses 1 point. (So negative scores are possible.) A cumulative score for each player is kept on paper as the rounds are played. But wait! It gets worse: If a player takes fewer than the required tricks ("underbooks"), he is punished.
- In the next hand, before trump is declared, the player who overbooked gets to *hit* the player (or players) who underbooked. This means that for each trick over book, the winner will hit the loser with the lowest card she has in a suit and in return will get back the highest in the suit that he has.
- For example: In the first hand, Sally, the dealer, takes nine tricks; Alice, the second player, takes seven tricks; and Fred, the third player, takes no tricks. This means that Alice overbooked by two and Fred underbooked by two, and so Fred must be

punished. In the second hand, before trump is declared, Alice gives Fred the three of hearts and the four of spades. Fred hands over his ace of hearts and jack of spades. The cards exchanged can, but do not have to, be all in one suit. If the card Alice gives to Fred ends up being the highest he has of that suit—let's say Alice gives him the ten of diamonds and Fred has no higher diamonds—he simply returns that card to her, indicating that he has no higher cards of that suit.

✖ If one player is punishing two other players, she gives them each their cards before they return their cards. If two players are punishing one, the player with the higher target for the *hand about to be played* trades first.

> **▶▶STEALTH STRATEGY**
>
> If you're hitting the dealer, pass cards in several suits, if you can, so he doesn't know what your weak suit is.

Tableaux

Tableaux is a guessing game that combines elements of playacting and long-dormant directorial skills. Each team creates a "tableau" of a particular word (preferably a three-syllable word) for the other team to guess. The game appears in both *Vanity Fair* and *Jane Eyre*.

PLAYERS: 8–40

The Game Plan

Randomly divide your players into teams of at least four players. Teams go into different rooms. Each team generates a list of three or four three-syllable words, and creates a series of tableaux from the different syllables of the word. For example, if the word is *attenuate,* the first player might point to his wrist, encouraging players to guess "at." The second player might hold up ten fingers, the third might point at the audience to indicate "you," and the fourth player might mime eating. These poses are all held simultaneously and in a line; the first person from the other team to shout out the word gets the point. So you are both cooperating with your teammates (to make the tableaux) and competing against them (to guess the other team's tableaux).

A Few Ideas to Get You Started . . .

- idolize (i doll eyes)
- urinate (your in ate)
- masticate (mass tick ate)
- Tennessee (ten i see)
- peony (pee on knee)
- ingratiate (in gray she ate)
- neighborhood (neigh bore hood)
- trampoline (tramp oh lean)
- Germany (germ man knee)
- pantyhose (pan tee hose)
- telegraph (tell leg graph)
- fiancée (fee on say)
- acrobat (act row bat)
- romantic (row man tick)
- adultery (add dull tree)

Winning

Play three rounds; the person with the highest score at the end wins a prize, like a basket of beach essentials—sunscreen, a broad-brimmed hat, bottled water, and a paperback novel.

▶▶ **IF YOU LIKE THIS GAME . . . check out other Victorian Parlor Games on page 153.**

||||||||||||||||||||||||||||||||||||||||||||||||||||||||||||||||||||||||||||||||||||

Make Your Own Pantomime

Pantomimes, or pantos, are a traditional English family entertainment usually performed at Christmas time. Writers borrow the narrative from a fable or fairy tale; the plot usually features a theme of good battling evil (with good, of course, always prevailing). Men's roles are frequently acted by women and vice versa, though this is not mandatory. Pantos usually include singing and dancing, slapstick, double entendres, and ribald jokes (intended to go over the heads of any children in the audience). The style of play, employing improvisation, melodrama, and physical comedy, has its roots in the Middle Ages and is a direct descendant of the commedia dell'arte.

Making a traditional panto is no small undertaking—the group has to write the words and the jokes, and construct costumes and sets, but you can make it as big or as little a deal as you want. (Remember that you're not mounting a production at the Met.) Pantos are supposed to be more than a little rough around the edges, and if your set is corrugated cardboard and your hair is a mop

of yellow yarn, all the better. And if you think it's far too much effort to write and direct a whole play over a weekend, keep in mind the plots already exist ("Little Red Riding Hood," "Jack and the Beanstalk") and the songs are usually well-known melodies, like "I've Been Working on the Railroad" or "Yankee Doodle," for which you'll compose your own silly lyrics. If you're apprehensive about your comedy-writing skills, grab a copy of a joke book from the library and crib liberally. Two words to keep in mind for the script: *rough draft.* Try to write the script quickly and leave plenty of room for improvisation.

PLAYERS: 2–40

Preparation

Advance Collaboration: Putting on a panto is best done with a group of like-minded friends, of course—the sort with show tunes on their iPods and Ticketmaster on speed dial. So either plan to invite these types along on your weekend away, or identify the fellow theater geeks within the gang once the guest list is set. You'll need to divvy up the work, so a few weeks before the event, e-mail your group and ask who wants to put their skills to use in putting on a little play. Some people are great at making up little rhyming ditties; others will like nothing more than

> **▶▶STEALTH STRATEGY**
>
> For more detailed help, check out *Pantomime: A Practical Guide,* available from Amazon. Amazon's U.K. site has a wider selection of make-your-own-panto books than the American store—a quick search turns up *The Pantomime Book* and *The Friars Club Encyclopedia of Jokes.*

to assemble costumes from thrift shops or Halloween stores; still others will love to slop paint on muslin backdrops (or make digital slides for a backdrop). Assign a person to head up each of the "teams" of two or three for costumes, sets, music, and script.

The Script: If *you're* in charge of the script, first find a co-writer—many of the greatest comic writers worked in teams. As for the plot, well, the secret of pantos is that it doesn't matter which story you choose. Choose a well-known children's story and adapt it for your particular group of friends and family—add in-jokes or TV show dialogue. A very popular pantomime is "Cinderella," which you could adapt by mixing in the sound track from *A Charlie Brown Christmas* and dialogue from *The Partridge Family.* Select the characters you want to include: Cinderella, the prince, the father, the fairy

godmother, the stepmother, and the two evil stepsisters are musts, of course. Pantomimes usually have animal characters, so cast the mice that are Cinderella's footmen, too.

As you're writing and assembling your script, e-mail your fellow troupe members and keep them up-to-date on the roles that will need to be filled. Ask who's up for treading the boards and assign roles. If you have a party guest who likes to be in the spotlight and is unhappy if he's not, make him the narrator! If your party is small, consider double-casting the roles: A stepsister can double as the fairy godmother, for example, or draft the resident dog for a nonspeaking part (does this sound like a shambles? That's really the point!).

The Jokes: The story lines are just the foundation of the piece—the real fun is in the subplots (think topical political satire

How to Make a Backdrop

Equipment
Measuring tape, muslin, fabric paint (available at craft stores), wooden dowling or PVC pipe the length of the fabric.

Directions
- Measure the length and height of the space where you plan to hang the backdrop. Add several inches to your dimensions—a little extra is critical in the event of mistakes.

- Sketch out your design on paper. This can be as simple or as complicated as you like: a single tree can indicate the forest; a fireplace will let the audience know we're now in grandma's house.

- Cut the fabric based on your measurements. Using your design as a

guide, paint the fabric with your scenes, leaving several inches at the top unpainted. Let dry.

- Turn under the top of the fabric about two inches and sew or safety-pin to create a sleeve through which to pass the rod.

- Depending on your space, you may either hang the backdrop from the ceiling, using ceiling hooks and twine or plastic ties threaded through slits in the fabric, or affix the rod to a wall with two or three hooks. If you can't nail or drill into the ceiling or walls, the rod can be propped between two stand-alone coat racks.

- **Shortcut:** If you don't want to fool with paint or fabric, an easy, fantastic backdrop can be had by projecting slides on a wall.

or just random, silly, comical tangents), the jokes, and the cross-dressing. When you're writing the jokes, imagine a drummer doing the classic bah-dum-bah-dum after a set-up; nuance is not really the goal here. A book of jokes, like *Jokelopedia: The Biggest, Best, Silliest, Dumbest Joke Book Ever,* or *777 Great Clean Jokes,* or *The Pretty Good Joke Book* can come in handy as well.

In a 2008 panto at the Old Vic, written by the actor and writer Stephen Fry, the jokes were plentiful and ribald:

- Buttons, referring to an ugly stepsister: "Is she ugly? Let's just say that the local Peeping Tom came along and begged her to close her curtains."

- Cinderella, after a dream in which she meets the Prince at dawn as the rooster is crowing: "Oh, your Royal Highness, what an urgent, insistent cock."

The Songs: For the music, which is an integral part of pantomime, instruct your songwriters to start with well-known tunes—"Material Girl," "Billie Jean," "Take Me Out to the Ballgame," etc., and create new lyrics. (This may sound like an arduous undertaking, but believe me, there are some folks who *love* to compose doggerel. When you're preparing, find a couple of these people for the music team.) By using well-known melodies, the songwriters can encourage the audience to sing along by having the lyrics written on big pieces of posterboard. It may help to have the narrator double as the musical director and lead the songs. Some appropriate instruments for live musical accompaniment: ukeleles, kazoos, washboards.

Costumes and Set: For pantos in America, choose some political figures or celebrities—Sarah Palin, Paris Hilton, Rihanna, Barack Obama—and assemble the appropriate costumes. A little stuffed dog and a blonde wig immediately indicates that a stepsister is Paris Hilton, for example. I'm sure that a pop star or a well-known woman in politics will spring to mind when you're designing the costumes for the stepmother; the father can be a well-meaning but clueless political figure or celebrity.

Sets for pantomimes can be as simple as one or two backdrops, painted to indicate locations. In "Little Red Riding Hood," for example, you might have one backdrop painted as a forest and another as the grandmother's house. The actors can travel from one place on the stage to another, or you can appoint "stagehands" to slide the backdrops across the stage as the actors pretend to walk from one place to another.

The Play Plan

Once your guests arrive for the weekend, it's time to assemble the set, have a brief rehearsal, and prepare for the Saturday night opening. If you've managed to get the scripts

AMP IT UP

Slapsticks—or the sticks that make a loud cracking sound when slapped together—are classic tools in physical comedy. They're what makes the loud crack when one of the Three Stooges smacks another. They're typically made of two thin boards fastened together at the base to form a handle. For a quick at-home version: Saw a wooden yardstick in half, and bind the pieces loosely together at one end with some duct tape. Test it by slapping it against your palm. It should make a loud "crack." It'll come in handy for any scenes in which a husband is being henpecked by his wife, or for Ralph Kramden/Ed Norton-type disputes, or for when the villain is just being villainous.

to the actors in advance—great, they'll know what to do. If not, they can just bone up on their lines before the play. It's fine to tape scripts to various pieces of the set or to the backs of props, and allow plenty of room for improv. Make the panto the centerpiece of your weekend: Reserve a separate room (the kitchen, the living room, the den, the porch) for the play. To fill out your audience, invite the neighborhood children for the theatrics— kids are usually cheerful critics, especially if you have a liberal hand with the candy and ice cream at intermission. Launch a few icebreaker games, liberally dispense booze, and after the turkey dinner, the big game, or the opening of presents, have your guests assemble in the "theater," where the hijinks will unfold.

1,000 Blank White Cards

You make up the rules as you go along, a bit like in Nomic (see page 148). But unlike Nomic, you get to draw. And frankly, the drawing is the best part: The illustrations and the points/penalties give the game life, not the actual winning or losing.

Created by Nathan McQuillen, 1,000 Blank White Cards is a little tough to explain, since there aren't any starting rules, and the rules you *do* create can be as complicated or as silly as the crowd wishes. No one "wins" or "loses" in the traditional sense. Have you ever seen the Drew Carey version of *Whose Line Is It Anyway?* where he says that, say, Colin wins 28 points for the best impersonation of

Madame Chiang Kai-shek? Same thing. It's completely subjective, which is a large part of why it's funny.

1,000 Blank White Cards is a game that's best learned by playing. Either you'll love the freedom and total randomness that comes with playing a game that is unfettered by rules—or you'll hate the fact that you can't get your head around what the heck you're supposed to be doing. People's response to this is usually very revealing. The cards you create are slightly reminiscent of the Monopoly cards ("You did such and such—go directly to jail," or "You are surprised by such and such—collect $200"): Their instructions will either add or deduct points from your score. To get an idea of what good cards look like, search flickr.com for "1,000 Blank White Cards" or "1KBWC."

PLAYERS: 6–25. 8 is ideal.

THE GEAR: Pencil, a stack of blank cards (you don't need 1,000 to begin with). Unlined index cards are fine; cut them in half if you're super-frugal.

Creating the Deck

✹ Give each player five blank cards and a little time to draw on them. Allow anywhere from ten minutes to half an hour for each person to create an initial hand of five cards.

✹ A card must consist of a title or instruction at the top, an illustration in the middle, and the points gained or lost at the bottom. (If the card is an instruction, like "Jump up and down" or "Fetch me a beer," you may choose to omit the points gained or lost.) See the illustrations on the next page for some examples.

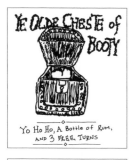

The Game Plan

Set the remaining stack of blank white cards in the middle of the playing area; each player will start with the initial set of cards he created. Make sure everyone has kept a pencil, in order to generate more cards as the game progresses. Elect a scorekeeper and equip her with a paper and pencil. Choose someone who's somewhat alert for this task.

✗ Play starts at the scorekeeper's left.

✗ In a turn, a player may play a card to any other player, or to the whole table (so that everyone is affected), or to himself. The cards should be set in plain view, whether they're in front of a player or in the middle, so everyone can see. Cards with lasting effects, such as awarding points or changing the game's rules, are kept on the table to remind players. Cards with no lasting effects, or cards whose points or instructions have been nullified by newer, later cards, are placed in a discard pile. As players play one of their

already-drawn cards, they will then take a blank card from the center and draw a new rule on it. In this fashion, each player always has five cards in his hand.

✗ Play continues until there are no cards left in the middle and no one can play. The winner is the player with the highest score of total points at the end of the game—though in most games the points don't actually matter; the pleasure of the game is in making silly rules and funny drawings. Since you're drawing new cards to offset anyone's advantage, if a player is ahead by, say, a million points, another player can simply draw a card that says "Your stimulus package failed. Lose 2 million points." The game can, in theory, go on indefinitely—especially if one of the cards has an instruction like "Shuffle the discard pile into the blank-cards pile."

✗ At the end of the game, save some of the best cards for use in the next game.

Thanks to Nathan McQuillen and Chloe Lopez for their cards and to Stewart King for explaining the game.

Murder Mystery Games

A **weekend in the country makes** one think of English manors, butlers, filmy dresses . . . and murder and plotting and nefarious doings. In short, every mystery story on PBS for the last twenty years. Of course, a couple of days in a mountain lodge or ski cabin is the perfect time to watch a murder mystery movie, but it's also the perfect time to *play* a murder mystery game—one in which the guests take on the roles of the characters in the mystery, a body is found, clues are given, and players try to discover "who done it."

There are quite a few online companies from which you can buy a mystery package, complete with a background story, a setup (the murder!), character descriptions for each player, and clues to be distributed at particular points in the game. For example, Host Party, an online company that sells mystery games for about $30 each, offers a story called "Death Before Dinner," set in an English Regency country manor.

The game, illustrated with pictures straight from a Jane Austen novel, kicks off the mystery with a gruesome murder:

"It had been planned as an intimate dinner party for eight. Lady Fanny's guest list was small, but all were members of society: Hon. and Mrs. Charles Ruskin, the Duke and Duchess of Wollingford, Captain and Mrs. Middleton, and Lady Fanny and her husband Baron Ruskin. Fanny had planned for everything . . . except for the discovery of a very dead body just before she, her husband, and her guests were about to sit down for dinner. Traditionally, it's always the butler who did it. It can't be the butler this time—he's the one who's dead!"

PLAYERS: 8–20

THE GEAR: A downloaded set of roles and secret clues from a murder mystery website.

The Game Plan
Check out the summaries at the various sites for mysteries (check out thegamesbible .com for suggestions)—or, if you're feeling

ambitious, use a mystery novel or a play, like Agatha Christie's *Ten Little Indians,* to write your own game. Games are organized by the size of your party and by theme—so decide if you'd like to have a night on a New Orleans riverboat, or in a Southern antebellum mansion, or on a ranch in the Wild West. Download the host's instructions, clues, the character summaries, and the solution.

✦ Before the weekend, e-mail your guests their roles so they can assemble their costumes and "get into character"—for example, "Death Before Dinner's" Hon. Charles Ruskin, the heir to the throne and a bit of a ladies' man, walks with a slight limp. You will also e-mail a secret piece of information to each guest—a different piece of information for each player—that will give the characters information about themselves. This might be a piece of backstory, like "You have secretly hated Lady Bennington ever since she stole your fiancé twenty years ago," or a clue as to who might be the killer: "Three weeks ago you spied Colonel Adams arguing vehemently with the deceased behind the stables." This information isn't meant to be shared with the group. (Everyone has secrets at this country-house gathering.)

✦ After all players arrive for the weekend and you're serving drinks, you'll hand out the first round of clues concealed in envelopes. Each guest gets a new clue each round different from everyone else's; some are designated as clues to be concealed, and some are designated as clues to be revealed.

✦ During the game, which can last for anywhere from two hours to the whole weekend, guests will socialize and interact, asking questions of the other guests to try to glean information from them while keeping their own information close to the vest. (The clues will give guests hints as to what kinds of questions to ask the other characters, and as suspicions are aroused, players will be inspired to ask their *own* probing questions.) Players may not lie outright, but they do *try* to keep their secret clues hidden.

✶ As the game progresses, players gather more and more information about one another's characters and sort through fact and fiction to narrow in on the murderer.

✶ At the end of the evening or weekend, invite your guests to announce their suspects and why. Then reveal the real killer in the way that's specified in the game materials.

For a selection of companies that sell online murder mystery games, go to thegamesbible .com.

Geocaching

PLAYERS: 1–50

THE GEAR: A handheld GPS device and an Internet connection; Garmin seems to be the device of choice for Geocachers. You'll also need sturdy socks and shoes and a bottle of water.

Geocaching, or exploring with a GPS device, is a game of hiding and seeking treasure. All players, from beginning to expert, start with geocaching.com, the central information hub for all matters relating to the game. A player hides a *cache*, or a small treasure (usually a trinket and a notebook), and posts the GPS coordinates

of the cache on the site—sometimes with a written clue to the whereabouts.

Other players then trek out to find the treasure—hiking over hill and dale, or meandering down side streets in far-flung cities. Once a player finds the cache, he signs the notebook, replaces the cache, and goes on his merry way. Some Geocachers have buttons or coins manufactured and printed with a unique stamp; they leave these in the caches and take others. The general rule is that if you take something, you should leave something of equal or greater value. Other players, of course, will also find the cache over the course of weeks, months, or even years—some caches have been in place since the inception of the game in the year 2000.

If you want to try Geocaching on a weekend away when you're up for exploring some new territory, type in the zip code on geocaching .com, download the GPS coordinates, and go in search of the hidden treasure. Geocachers hide caches literally all around the world, so wherever you are, there likely will be a cache waiting to be found. What could be better on an autumn weekend in Vermont or a summer Sunday in Charleston?

I tagged along with a Portland, Oregon native, Jon, who was Geocaching in Central Park, New York. He'd downloaded the coordinates to his handheld GPS before we set out, and he told me that the clue was "look up." We briskly covered about a quarter mile through wooded paths until we arrived at a wooden pagoda overlooking the lake. A group of rambunctious children were hanging out inside, so we took a seat and waited for them to scram. (The non-Geocaching public are known as "muggles," and any muggles who might steal a cache must be waited out.) Once they left, we climbed onto the railing and crossbars of the pagoda and craned our necks. Tucked into a corner of the rafters was a small Tupperware container. Jon, taller than me, fished it out. We each signed the log book—a small spiral-bound notebook—and examined the trinkets earlier Geocachers had left inside.

After we replaced the cache, we sat for a moment and watched the couples rowing on the lake. It was a spot I'd never seen before, despite decades in New York. For Jon, it was a sight he might have missed if he'd relied on the standard New York tourist guides. "What I like about Geocaching," he told me, "is that it's provided a way to see places that I wouldn't have had a reason to visit. This is true even for my hometown."

Weekend-Long Forbidden Words

NEW GAME!

Players choose a short list of words that they must not say for the entire weekend. If a player uses one of the forbidden words, he loses a point and the person to whom he is speaking gains a point. (This has to be zero-sum, i.e., you lose as many points as other people gain; otherwise it opens it up for "I'll say *grapefruit* if you say *peculiar*" deals.)

The goal is to have a relatively normal weekend—lolling by the pool, walking in the woods, grilling on the patio—while strenuously avoiding saying certain verboten words. The evasive strategies—as well as offensive maneuvers to try to get other players to say the forbidden words—will imbue the whole weekend with subtle strategizing and acute paranoia. Members of the party will prompt the others to say the words—let's say two of the forbidden words are *house* and *nice*:

"So, what do you think of the place, pretty great, eh?"

"It's really nice," or "Such a beautiful house" . . .

. . . would net a point for the first speaker and lose a point for the second speaker.

The Game Plan

At the start of the weekend, compile (as a group) a list of five to ten banned words, some common, some rare. For example:

- ✖ *paper*
- ✖ *house*
- ✖ *nice*
- ✖ *milk*
- ✖ *peculiar*
- ✖ *grapefruit*
- ✖ *hopscotch*
- ✖ *hallelujah*

The hostess writes them down and posts the list on the fridge, so guests can periodically refresh their memories (though they could

Optional But Great Rule

If there's a forbidden word that nobody's said at all over the weekend, that word remains in play indefinitely. You are no longer allowed to say it while you're with any of the friends who were on the trip; if you do, you lose, and you have to write to everyone who was there and inform them of this. That word then leaves play. It took Holly *two and a half years* to get someone to say *hopscotch*.

also just ask someone else—in the hopes of tricking that person into saying the words.)

Over the weekend, *nobody is allowed to use these words.* If a person says a forbidden word, the player who points it out gains a point and the player who said the word loses a point.

The trouble with—and the beauty of—this game is that you potentially spend the entire weekend feeling rather suspicious, not quite sure whether to trust that anyone means what they're saying and wondering if they're just trying to lead you toward an answer that uses one of the banned words.

> **▶▶STEALTH STRATEGY◀**
>
> A rousing chorus of "It's Raining Men" will often trick people into an accidental "hallelujah."

Winning

Each player should keep track of how many points he has; at the end of the weekend, the person with the most points wins.

Variation

This is kind of a cross between Assassins and Forbidden Words. Ahead of time, the host writes on index cards the name of a guest and a word. (The words should not be super common—obviously not *and* or *I,* but not absurdly difficult. So *polka,* or *wall,* or *mouse,* or *capable* are okay, but not *lagniappe,* or *obstreperous,* or *caterwaul.*) When everyone arrives, the host gives each person a card with another guest's name on it (taking care that no two people have each other) and a word he needs to prompt that person to say. If the person says the forbidden word, he is eliminated, and the player who made him say it takes his card and takes on his "mission." Eventually, the game will get down to two people who must engage in a very careful conversation. The first one to slip up is the runner-up and the remaining player is the victor.

—Holly Gramazio is a game designer based in London. For more about Holly and her projects, check out severalbees.com.

||||||||||||||||||||||||||||||||||||||||||||||||||||||||||||||||

Classic Beach House Games

Charades and Pictionary are loads of fun no matter where you are. But if you're at the shore, why not make use of the random collection of books and magazines that are surely littering the shelves of your summer rental? Perusing those books can raise questions about the tenants who came before you: Did the guy reading *Rich Dad, Poor Dad* finally make his fortune? Was the torn-out recipe in the 1986 *Ladies' Home Journal* any good? How many Barbara Taylor Bradford books can a person read on one vacation, anyway?

So maybe you don't really want to read the material lying around—you probably brought your own books anyway—but they *can* serve a purpose: Launch a game of Charades or Pictionary with your housemates one rainy afternoon—with the only rule being that players can only act out or draw words pulled from books or magazines around the house. Limiting the phrases and titles that players generate creates a theme for the game that makes the party more focused and fun anyway.

THE GEAR: 2 sketch pads or a bunch of reasonably large pieces of paper, pencils, timer, and an easel or two (optional).

The Game Plan

Beach House Charades and Pictionary are played pretty much the same way as the standard versions of those games (see pages 37 and 113), with one exception: In the clue-generating phase, teams generate their clues using only the books and magazines that were in the house when you arrived. Pile ten or so books and magazines on the coffee table in the playing area. Teams must write their clues using these books and magazines as reference. For a variation in scoring, stipulate that guests can earn an extra point by naming the source along with guessing the clue. (So a player who correctly guesses the acted-out clue "erect nipple" can earn another point for guessing that it came from the Jude Deveraux romance novel.)

The following games are great to play over the course of a weekend:

NOMIC, *page 148*

Nomic is the quintessential long-form game. (Some online games, in fact, have been running for years.) Nomic is meant to mimic the legislative experience, so you start out with a bunch of rules, some mutable and some immutable, and then you propose amendments to the rules and the group votes to change them or not. This process is the whole game; the fun is in what rules you make (everyone has to employ a silly walk for the rest of the weekend; anyone who is under the age of eighteen must provide a constant supply of snacks to the adults until sundown . . .) and the behind-the-scenes arm-twisting to get the votes for your proposals.

MAFIA, *page 132*

Depending on the size of your group and how long it takes the bad guys to deliberate, Mafia could go on for a couple of days. To adjust Mafia to be weekend-long, have the "day and night" cycles run for as long as the Mafia need to plan a hit and the Villagers need to retaliate. The Mayor will indicate to everyone when decisions have been made. As the game isn't played in the same room at the same time, players will have to confer at odd moments—like when they're putting the laundry in the dryer or running out for more beer.

PSYCHIATRIST, *page 60*

One guest, called the Psychiatrist, is asked to leave the room while the others (the patients) decide on a pattern with which they will answer questions—perhaps each player must bite his lip or otherwise manifest some kind of tic as he answers, or as if he has some "extreme right-wing syndrome," or as if he were a particular person—"Ronald Reagan syndrome." The Psychiatrist must diagnose the patients' ailment by asking questions, from the very banal: "What's your favorite color?" to the introspective: "What is one thing you wish you'd done differently with your life?" The object is to observe the common pattern in the way patients answer. Players can go about their activities as usual—making lunches, inflating rafts, hosing down the deck—but whenever they're asked a direct question by the Psychiatrist, they must answer using the agreed-upon pattern. The game continues until the Psychiatrist has guessed the "ailment."

ASSASSIN, *page 317*

You can compress Assassin into a weekend-length game. Secretly assign each player the name of another player, taking care that no two players are assigned to each other. Your guests will then stalk each other. You "kill" your prey by getting him alone—in the car, in the blueberry patch, on the floating dock in the middle of the lake. You quietly tell your target that he is now "dead," and his target becomes your new prey. (Players should keep the hostess informed of each development so she can moderate any disputes and clear up any confusion.) When there are two people left alive, the game is over and those players are declared the winners.

Assassin adds an element of strategy and intrigue to ordinary weekend-away activities: You'll think twice about sitting in the kitchen shucking corn if your sister might assassinate you while she's clarifying butter.

SITUATION PUZZLES, *aka Murder Mystery Puzzles, page 122*

Situation Puzzles, also known as lateral-thinking puzzles, don't have to be played or solved in one sitting—so players can go about their other activities and ask questions as they crop up.

To start, the host thinks of a situation in which someone dies in some way that seems implausible or unlikely or baffling and informs his audience of this scenario. The audience can ask yes-or-no questions any time over the weekend, in and around other activities and conversations, until they come up with the explanation.

For examples of puzzles, see pages 122–124.

Chapter Sixteen

IMPROMPTU GAMES

Any game that's launched without the knowledge of one of the players (and can be played anywhere, anytime, with no gear) is an impromptu game. They don't make much sense and don't take any skill to play—which makes them perfect for revving up a boring conversation, a car trip, or just a walk down the street. Another advantage: If you're the one who thought of playing the game, you're probably going to win. The best known is probably Punch-Buggy—in which you punch someone whenever you see a VW Beetle and say "Punch-buggy [color of Beetle]." This game has existed for decades; others seem to have evolved more recently. Impromptu games are generally played by the young—college students, twentysomethings, even high-schoolers. Something about the total randomness—or maybe the aspect of ganging up on people—appeals to the younger set.

Not It

PLAYERS: 2–20

Let's say you want to get out of doing something—like pull the car around when it's raining, or take out the garbage, or shove the dog's medication down his throat. Well, if you're "Not It," you're in the clear. You don't have to do it. It's like the Fifth Amendment. "Not It" can*not* be argued with.

Not It generally comes about when a pal wistfully says something like, "Wouldn't it be nice if someone would go get a pizza?" or, "Gee, I guess the dog is going to die soon if someone doesn't give him his medication." And then whoever doesn't want to do the chore places her finger vertically alongside her nose. The last person to do this is It and must do the task.

Variation

Altitude. If you don't want to do the chore, hit the floor. The last person standing is on the hook.

Not OK

PLAYERS: 2–20

Anyone, at any time, may make a hand gesture that looks like an upside-down OK sign (thumb and forefinger in a ring, other fingers extended). The object is to catch another player looking at your hand while it's in this position. Your hand must be below your waist to count. The victim—the person you catch looking at your hand—gets punched.

Punch-Buggy

PLAYERS: 2, the puncher and the punchee.

The 1960s saw the introduction of the Volkswagen Beetle—a symbol of the regeneration of Germany, a masterpiece of auto design, and the impetus for a game that has startled and injured siblings and playmates for the last fifty years. The game is generally played on long road trips, but can be launched anywhere cars are visible, which is to say, anywhere but outer space.

If, when in the car, or ambling down the street, or sipping a latte at an outdoor café, you should happen to spot a Volkswagen Beetle (either parked or moving) you must punch your (hopefully playful) companion lightly in the upper arm and say, "Punch-buggy [color]." So, if you see a blue Beetle, you would say, while punching, "Punch-buggy blue."

Winning

If you manage to do this before the other person does it to you, you've won. Be prepared for retribution.

Variation

Chop-a-Croc. Whenever you see a pair of Crocs shoes, you karate-chop your partner and state the color of the shoe. So, you'd karate-chop and scream "Chop-a-Croc orange!" if you saw a pair of orange Crocs.

El Dorado Omega Johnson

PLAYERS: 2–6

On a long road trip, be the first person to call out a freeway exit sign and stick one of your fellow passenger's last names to the end of it. That person must then have a child and give the child those first and middle names. For example, in Florida, you might yell "El Dorado Omega Johnson!" and so your friend Dave Johnson would have to name his kid El Dorado Omega.

What?

PLAYERS: 2–20

What? is possibly the most nonsensical of the impromptu games. Yes, it's even more nonsensical than the others. The person launching the game deliberately mumbles or slurs his words, trying to get the other person to say "What?" So, in the middle of a conversation—or not, it can be launched after a long, sleepy silence in the car, for example—drop your voice, mumble, or slur your words, with the intention of getting your partner to say "What?" If he does, you've won. If he's onto you—or just polite—and says "Pardon?" or "Sorry?" or "Say that again?" you've lost.

Jinx

PLAYERS: 2

If you and a friend say the same thing at the same time, the first person to shout "Jinx!" or, alternatively, "Jinx! You owe me a Coke!" wins. The other player *must* buy the winner a Coke.

▶▶ IF YOU LIKE THIS GAME . . . in Season Two of *The Office,* Pam jinxes Jim. In their version, the loser may not speak until a Coke has been purchased and presented to the winner. Unfortunately, the soda machine is sold out. Watch the episode "Drug Testing" for the full hilarity.

Head Splinter

PLAYERS: 2–10

Slang for a song that gets stuck in your head, Head Splinter is a cruel game, we'll tell you right off the bat. It's as insidious as mind control, as tenacious as the Asian long-horned beetle, and as numbing as a crack to the funny bone. In short, one player quietly hums or sings a terribly annoying song; say, "Jesus Christ Superstar" from the musical *Jesus Christ Superstar.* If that person—the instigator, let's call him Joe—hears any other of his company singing, humming, or whistling that song within the next twenty-four hours, he's won. If another player realizes what he's doing, she can say something like, "Don't try to get that piece of crap song stuck in my head,

Joe," and *she's* won. If she finds herself singing it sometime later, however, she's lost. Really, this is a game where everyone loses.

The Game

PLAYERS: 2–20

I hesitated to include the Game in my book, for the reason that it's not *really* a game. But enough people mentioned it to me that I thought, well, why not? The premise is both simple and baffling: We are all always playing the Game, at all times. But if you think about the Game, you've lost. And you must announce that you've lost: "I just lost the Game." So really, there's no way to win. You can only be the last one to lose.

Get Down, Mr. President

PLAYERS: 3–10

A rather roughhouse-y game, Get Down, Mr. President, as with many other impromptu games, punishes the player who is the last to notice that the group is playing a game. This person becomes Mr. President and is rewarded by being thrown to the ground.

While going about the day, shopping at the mall, strolling through the quad, or whatever, someone will discreetly touch his ear (just as the Secret Service press their earpieces).

When someone else sees this, he too should touch his ear. When everybody but one person has touched his ear, they have all become the Secret Service. The last person to notice becomes Mr. President. The Secret Service yells "Get down, Mr. President!" and tackles the President.

I've Always Thought BBQ Panda Cubs Would Be Delicious

PLAYERS: 3–5

Choose a member of your party to be the mark. (This person should not *know* she's the mark—so your group is essentially ganging up on one unsuspecting member of the crowd.) Come up with a sentence that the mark would never say—like "I've always thought BBQ panda cubs would be delicious." Over the next few hours (or days) try to get the mark to say all the words in the sentence, not necessarily in order.

▶▶ IF YOU LIKE THIS GAME . . . watch a bout online at thegamesbible.com.

Chapter Seventeen

OUTDOOR GAMES

When you were a child, you'd run around for *hours* without getting tired; nowadays you jog to the corner and have to stop to catch your breath. Why is this? Well, younger heart and lungs, more flexible joints, yeah, yeah, sure. But also—and this is huge—*you were having fun.* You weren't thinking about calories burned or miles covered or how tendons really aren't that elastic. You were focused on unfreezing your teammates, or taunting Marco Polo, or capturing that damn flag. You were running and jumping and shrieking until your mother made you stop for a PB&J and a glass of lemonade . . . and then you staged a jailbreak, busted out your compatriots, and tagged every single member of the no-good O'Shaughnessy clan from down the block.

Big games are exhilarating. They trigger the same adrenaline rush that team sports do, but the games are more playful than athletic—and it's the playfulness that we adults are looking to recapture. A whole new crop of young game designers and artists has tapped into this nostalgia by designing activities and contests that contain elements of both sports and theater— like Wiffle Hurling, in which costumed contestants play the traditional Irish sport of hurling with Wiffle bats and balls. Other designers and artists have run large-scale games on the city streets, like Human Chess (played on the grid of New York's Lower East Side) or urban scavenger hunts like Midnight Madness (twenty-four-hour puzzle hunts that ran yearly in San Francisco and New York, respectively, until the early 2000s). These large-scale events hearken back to the neighborhood-wide games we played as kids—circling the block on bikes and dashing through backyards until dusk.

Of course, not everyone has the time or inclination to produce citywide, or even neighborhood-wide, games (which frequently require permits and organizers with experience in running large outdoor events). But just getting outdoors and enjoying an afternoon of play—whether it's dashing through fresh-mown grass in No-Equipment Baseball, kicking though a pile of leaves on a Hash Run, or knocking a ball through a wicket in Croquet—is well within most everyone's ability. Many of these games will keep you fit: The resurgence of childhood games (Capture the Flag, Kickball, Manhunt) may be replacing spinning classes and hot yoga as thirtysomethings struggle to keep their beer guts in check. So plan a few of these for your family reunion, or your college alumni weekend, or even just a pickup game in the park or at the beach. You'll be surprised at how many of these games come back to you—and you'll be psyched to learn about a bunch of new ones, too. Get ready to "come out and play!"

Capture the Flag

A camp standby, Capture the Flag is a perennial favorite because of its simplicity and malleability. The object is simple: to grab the other team's flag and bring it back to your side. The basic game is oodles of fun, but if you play a few rounds and feel like trying something different, amp it up with variations. Try playing with water guns, paint guns, GPS devices, maps, bikes, compasses—or change the boundaries and make a whole city or forest your playing field.

PLAYERS: 6–100, the more the better.

THE GEAR: Two bright pieces of fabric to act as flags; old T-shirts will do. Compasses or GPS devices for the variations.

Objective
To capture the other team's flag and defend your own.

Preparation
- Divide into two teams of three or more people each; give each team a flag.

- Mark off a playing field. The size of this playing field depends on the number and stamina of players: If you have a very big group—or a very *fit* group—you might use a six-by-six–block square in an urban area or an entire city park. Others might want to limit the terrain to a smaller clearing in a park or a school athletic field. Streets, chalk lines, trails, creeks, and fences all make good borders. Delineate a clear centerline between the two teams' territories using clothesline, a chalk line or natural boundaries. (Make sure this centerline is apparent to all players at the start of the game, as once a player is in the other team's territory, he can be tagged, and you don't want the fun to devolve into arguments about whether or not someone was over the line.) Each team should mark off a roughly 10-by-10-foot jail within its territory. Clothesline or tape on the ground, or a few items to mark the corners of a square, will do fine.

- Decide how far from the centerline each team may hide its flag—50 yards is a good rule of thumb; you can adjust this proportionally according to the size of your playing field.

- Decide whether you want to allow "guarding" of the jail and flag. In general, it's more fun to *not* have a guard—so each team must agree not to lurk within 20 feet of its flag and jail.

The Game Plan
- Give each team five minutes to hide a flag in its territory. The flag must be visible—i.e., not buried under a rock or tucked in a hole—and no further than the agreed-upon distance from the centerline. At the end of the five minutes, start the game.

- Some members of your team will try to sneak across the centerline, find and capture the enemy flag, and race back without being tagged by the other side.

- Other members of your team will try to intercept and tag any opposing players who are in your territory.

- You can capture enemy players by tagging them while they are on your side of the border. Put captured enemy players in "jail."

- Rescue captured teammates by sneaking across the centerline, finding the jail, tagging your teammates, then racing back across the centerline without being tagged.

- If someone tries to free *your* prisoners, recapture players by tagging them again before they reach the centerline.

Winning

Win by capturing the enemy flag and carrying it back to your side of the border.

▸▸STEALTH STRATEGY

Send one of your *slower* players across the border to pretend to make a dash for the enemy's flag. Once this decoy has successfully drawn out the other team's players, deploy your *fastest* player. With luck, your opponents' most aggressive players will be distracted by the decoy, giving the second runner a clear shot at the flag.

Variation

Captured players must stay in jail for a set period of time (two minutes, for example) and then may return unmolested to their side to resume play.

Variation

Use a compass or GPS device: Each team hides its flag and then gives the other team the bearings or GPS coordinates. Each team must find the other team's flag using that information—of course, without being tagged. For even more fun, use water guns: Instead of being tagged, players must be shot with a water gun.

Jesse James

Jesse James is essentially a very large-scale variation on Capture the Flag, but you try to capture people as well as flags. The highest-value people are the two captains—the captain of one team is Jesse James and the captain of the other is Frank James (Jesse's brother and partner in crime). So, even if you don't manage to snag the other team's flag, it's still possible to win, provided you capture enough of the other team's players. It's played over a large area, like a park or a part of a college campus, but without defined territories for each team. No one is ever "out" in Jesse James, either—the other team gains points if you're captured (i.e., your waistband "flag" is snagged), but you're then allowed to reenter the fray. An excellent game for amusing large numbers of people for an hour or two, Jesse James is perfect for, say, your next college reunion weekend.

PLAYERS: 50–200; plus a neutral scorekeeper.

THE GEAR: Rags, T-shirts, pillowcases, or other fabric in two colors.

Specifically, you'll need:

A big flag for each team—a T-shirt or a pillowcase will do—in that team's color.

Several handkerchief-size flags for each player in that team's color.

A bandanna-size flag for Jesse James (the captain of one team) in that team's color, plus an extra.

A bandanna-size flag for Frank James (the captain of the other team) in that team's color, plus an extra.

Pen, paper, and a watch for the scorekeeper.

The Terrain

Ideally, the topography is varied, with trees, glades, rocks—you know, places to hide and ambush. Make sure the boundaries are crystal clear (14th Street *including* 14th Street? From the edge of the cornfield to the brook *including* the brook? These are the questions that can spark large-scale squabbles rather than merry hijinks).

The Game Plan

☒ Divide into two teams and assign each team a color.

☒ Select a captain for each team—Frank and Jesse James.

☒ Each player tucks a handkerchief-size flag into his waistband; Frank and Jesse James forgo the waistband flag and wear bandanna-size flags on their heads, do-rag style. Each team gets one big flag.

☒ The remainder of the small waistband flags go to a neutral party, the scorekeeper, who presides over a "No-Man's Land"—just a small marked-off neutral territory somewhere in the middle of the playing area. (The scorekeeper role is good for someone who's not super mobile or doesn't feel like running around: the elderly, the infirm, or the largely pregnant.) This person has three important functions: to dole out more waistband flags to those who have had theirs snatched, to keep score, and to keep track of the time.

☒ Each team has a few minutes at the start of the round to hide the big flag. The hiding places must be within reason: nothing too high or buried in the earth or pinned to a moving vehicle, for example. An ideal place would be in a visible but slightly hard-to-access spot, like draped over a large rock.

☒ Decide on a time limit for the game—a half hour is fine; an hour if your players have major-league stamina.

☒ Start the clock.

☒ The object is to capture the other team's large flag *and* as many of their smaller flags as possible. Frank and Jesse roam with posses of body guards; foot soldiers dash about looking for flags; everyone tries to capture other flags and hold on to their own.

☒ Captured flags should be given to the scorekeeper in No-Man's Land. She will collect them, mark down the points, and redistribute them as needed.

☒ If your waistband flag is snagged, you must walk, not run, to No-Man's Land to retrieve a new flag from the scorekeeper. No one is ever "out."

PARTY RECIPE

Lemonade

You'll need to refresh the troops and the outlaws after a rousing game of Jesse James. SERVES 8

INGREDIENTS

3 cups sugar	Fresh mint leaves
3 cups water (for the simple syrup)	3 cups fresh lemon juice
	9 to 12 cups cold water

1. Make a simple syrup by heating the sugar and water in a small saucepan until the sugar is dissolved completely. Add the mint leaves. Steep for a few minutes.

2. Add the juice and the sugar water to a gallon-size pitcher or jug. Gradually add the cold water, stirring and tasting as you go. Refrigerate. If the lemonade is too sweet, add a little more straight lemon juice.

To serve, pour over ice and add thinly sliced lemons.

✖ If a team's big flag is captured, the game ends immediately and the points are tallied.

Winning

At the end of the appointed time, tally up the number of flags each team has captured. The other team's flag counts for 50, Frank and Jesse's "bandannas" are worth 25, and each small waistband flag will net you 3. The highest number wins.

▶▶ **IF YOU LIKE THIS GAME . . . check out Sardines (page 67), which can also be played outdoors.**

||||||||||||||||||||||||||||||||||||||||||||||||||||||||||||||||||||||||||||||||||

Manhunt

Manhunt is another name for Zombie Tag, which begins with one "It," and as It tags other players, those players also become Its. This means that if It is aggressive with his tagging, soon an *army* of people will be chasing you. Manhunt is played over a large area, or at least one city block. Ideal topography includes places to hide and enough space to roam.

PLAYERS: 5–100, the more the better.

THE GEAR: Brightly colored armbands, if you're playing in a city among nonplaying civilians, and a timer.

Objective

For the Manhunter (It), to tag as many people as possible. For everyone else, to avoid being tagged.

The Game Plan

✖ One person is the Manhunter, or It. The rest of the players are Fugitives.

✖ Establish a playing area with clear exterior boundaries.

✖ Appoint a timekeeper, and set a time limit for play, say fifteen or thirty minutes— longer if your players are very fit.

✖ At the start of play, the Manhunter covers her eyes for two minutes. The Fugitives take this opportunity to hide or at least to put some distance between themselves and the Manhunter.

✖ When the two minutes have ended, the Manhunter begins a search for the Fugitives.

✖ If a Manhunter tags a Fugitive, the Fugitive also becomes a Manhunter and tries to tag other Fugitives. You never know who's been converted, so you'd best stay away from everyone.

Winning

At the end of play, all Fugitives who are still Fugitives win. If there are no Fugitives left, no one wins. There is no way for the Manhunter to win, so always select a new Manhunter for each round. Typically, a group might play one or two rounds and then adjourn to a bar for beers.

Travel Advisory

Check out sfzero.org for "Journey to the End of the Night," a kind of tag played periodically in different cities. If you're in Toronto, check out that city's large-scale urban bouts of Manhunt: manhunt-toronto.com.

Assassin

Assassin is what is known as "lifestyle-invading," which means you play it over a course of days or weeks while you go about your regular daily activities—with no break. You can hunt or be hunted at any hour of the day or night—every player is both a stalker and a stalkee. You play on your own—there are no teams, and players aren't in the same location with other players at any time—except for the moments of assassination. It's often played on school campuses—Curtis Sittenfeld details a bout of Assassin in her novel *Prep*.

At the start of the game (which is usually a predetermined time announced by e-mail), you will receive, via e-mail, a photograph and some vital details (home address, work address) of your prey. Someone else will receive your information. Players must "assassinate" their prey—either by tagging them, shooting them with a water gun, or simply cornering them—while trying to avoid the same. You'll become wildly paranoid. It is not a game for the faint of heart.

NOTE: Assassin requires a very organized moderator to gather the photographs and vital information and to determine who is hunting whom at the beginning of the game.

PLAYERS: 5–50, and a non-playing moderator. There is no upper limit to the number of players, but more than fifty might be difficult to organize.

THE GEAR: Water guns, Nerf guns, cardboard swords, or some other means of eliminating players (see the following page for options).

Objective
To be the last player left "alive."

Preparation
Preparation for the moderator is substantial.

✷ You, as the moderator, will identify a group of friends who wish to play. (Usually the moderator and a few friends send out an e-mail to their contact lists, ask who's up for a bout of Assassin, and then compile a list of players.)

✷ Collect photographs, as well as the home and work addresses, of each player.

✷ Give each player the name, photograph, and addresses of another player—his target—taking care that no two players are stalking each other.

✷ Set a time limit for the game—anywhere from a few days to a few weeks—or have it be open-ended (see "Winning").

✷ Decide on a start day and time and e-mail it to the players; e.g., "The game will begin at 7 A.M. Monday morning." If there's an end day and time, let the players know that as well.

✷ Provide a phone number for players to call in their "hits" to the moderator. The moderator will keep track of who is stalking whom as players acquire new targets.

✷ Designate "safe zones" in which targets may not be eliminated. (Safe zones are generally inside workplaces, religious services, classrooms, toilets, etc.)

✗ Choose one method of elimination. Some options:

- Shooting the target with a water or Nerf gun.
- Touching the target with a cardboard sword, a plastic spoon, or some other object.
- Touching the target's exposed skin with a magic marker, leaving a mark.
- Grabbing some item (which all players must wear at all times when not in a safe zone) of the target's, like a clothespin pinned to a belt.
- Simply tagging the target.

▶▶HOST TIP

Streetwars.net, a group that runs these games around the country, screens out "overzealous freaks" by requiring ID and having all players pick up the photographs and addresses of their targets in person. If you're launching a game with people you don't know, you might want to be similarly cautious.

The Game Plan

At the start of play, say, high noon on a certain date, players will commence trying to track down their prey and eliminate them using one of the methods described. Once someone has been eliminated (disputes between two players are heard and ruled upon by the moderator), he must pass on the photograph and details of his prey to his assassin. The assassin calls in the hit to the moderator and begins stalking this new prey.

Winning

If the game is open-ended—i.e., there's no specified time limit—then the game will continue until one person is left alive; this person is the winner. If there is a time limit, say, three days or three weeks, then the players who are still alive at the end are declared the winners. Of course, the latter version may have only one winner as well, and may end earlier than the agreed-upon time if one player is particularly successful at eliminating his targets.

Horse

Horse is a basketball game in which players try not to accrue the five letters in the word *horse*. For two players: Player 1 shoots from anywhere on the court. If she makes the shot, Player 2 must duplicate the same shot from the same position. If Player 2 misses, he receives the first "letter" from the word *horse* (so he's used up one of his five chances). However, if Player 1 misses her original shot, Player 2 can shoot from anywhere on the court and, hopefully, force Player 1 to duplicate his shot. A player is knocked out of the game once he has enough letters to spell out the word *horse*.

Yukigassen

or, the Ancient Japanese Art of Snowball Fighting

Remember waking up early on snowy mornings and spinning the dial for the school-closures announcements? Remember the thrill of gleefully chasing your brother through the house when your school was named (and the frisson of pity for those schools overlooked)? Remember your mother screaming that if you didn't go outside and play *right now,* she'd sell you to the farmer down the road as a tiny, still-malleable slave? No? Maybe that was just my family. Anyway, the point is: snowball fights are mad fun. So dust off the moon boots and get ready to bury your nearest and dearest.

Of course, a plain ol' snowball fight is fine, but maybe you crave order, rules, point systems, diagrams—in short, more *precision* for your winter battle. Well, you're in luck! Whenever you want something to be just a little more precise—let's say *your* tea ceremony is dunking a bag of orange pekoe in an old Earth Day mug—you can count on the Japanese to make it a thing of specific, codified steps. If you're going to play Yukigassen, a highly organized Japanese snowball fight, you're going to need uniforms, helmets, containers for making snow bricks, a snowball-making machine, flags, a measuring tape, and a willingness to commit hara-kiri on behalf of your team.*

You don't have to commit hara-kiri. You also don't really need any of these tools—you can modify the rules to fit your particular circumstances.

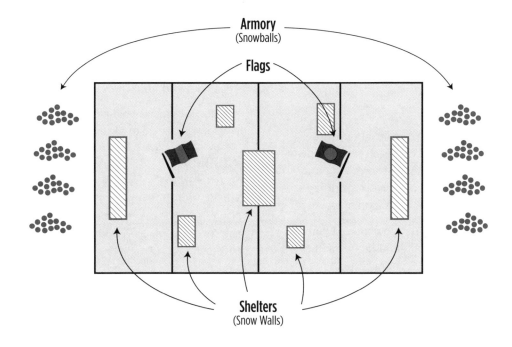

Armory
(Snowballs)

Flags

Shelters
(Snow Walls)

PLAYERS: 17. Two teams of seven players, plus a nonplaying captain for each team and a referee.

THE GEAR: Warm, waterproof clothes in a color scheme to tell the teams apart, two flags, and a snowball maker. The Japanese have a special mold that makes dozens of perfectly spherical snowballs at once. You will have to use your hands or a snowball mold from Amazon or L.L.Bean.

Containers, such as small rectangular trash cans, for building snow walls. (You can also buy a snow-block maker from L.L.Bean for about $13.)

Objective

To snag your opponents' flag and defend your own flag.

The Terrain

A level playing field 130 feet by 33 feet. You may change the dimensions according to your own particular circumstances.

Preparation

* Divide the playing field in quarters with a center line. (See the diagram on the previous page.)

* Erect shelters or snow walls about three feet high, at intervals on each team's side of the court. You may change the sizing and the intervals of the snow walls, but they must be the same for each side of the field.

* Each team creates 270 snowballs. If you don't have an army of child laborers, just make an even number for each team, or change the rules so that teams can make snowballs during the heat of battle.

* Each team plants its flag in its territory, the closer to the back line the better.

Travel Advisory

There are annual tournaments in Sweden, Finland, Norway, and Japan. For the international rules, check out thegamesbible.com.

The Game Plan

* A game consists of three sets.

* Each set runs for three minutes.

* At the start of play, the seven active players line up on their end line.

* The referee toots her whistle and play begins.

* Only three players may cross the center line at a time. If a player is hit by a snowball, he is out for the duration of the set.

* Use the snow walls for cover. Keep a couple of team members hanging back to toss or roll fresh supplies of ammo to teammates.

* Players may carry only as many snowballs as they can hold in their hands.

* Concealing snowballs on one's person is grounds for disqualification.

Winning

Your team wins the three-minute set when you snatch the enemy's flag; or, if no flag is snatched in three minutes, by the team with the most players left standing. Best two out of three wins.

Classic Outdoor Kids' Games

These games are great for family reunions, alumni weekends, and general large-scale events:

WHEELBARROW RACE

One player is in plank position; his partner holds his ankles. Together they run for the finish line—one player "running" on his hands, the other holding his legs. First pair there wins.

EGG-IN-THE-SPOON RACE

Players balance an egg in a spoon and run. First person to the finish line with a non-dropped, intact egg wins.

THREE-LEGGED RACE

In pairs, players stand side by side and bind their inside legs together with a belt or strip of cloth. Thus attached, they dash to the finish line. First pair there wins.

BACK-TO-BACK RACE

Pairs hook arms at the elbows while standing back to back and then run. First pair to the finish line wins.

DODGEBALL

Divide players into two teams. One team has one shot to try to hit someone on the other team, thereby eliminating them. If the targeted player catches the ball, the thrower is out. Regardless, the other team now has a chance to throw the ball. First team to eliminate all its opponents wins.

TELEPHONE

One player whispers a sentence—preferably a silly or outrageous sentence—into the ear of a neighbor. The neighbor whispers the sentence to her neighbor, and so on until it goes around a circle. The (now) garbled sentence is compared to the original, to great hilarity.

SIMON SAYS

One player is Simon. He instructs the players to do some action, like "Rub your tummy," prefaced by "Simon says." Players must do that action: rub their tummies. If Simon does *not* preface the command with "Simon says," players should not follow the command. Anyone who messes up is out.

RED LIGHT, GREEN LIGHT

One person is "It" and turns his back on others, who line up at least twenty-five paces behind him. It may call out "Green light!" giving the other players permission to advance. Or It may call out "Red light," and spin around; if It catches anyone moving, that player must go back to the starting line. The first person to touch It wins.

MOTHER, MAY I?

One player is Mother. The rest of the players start about twenty paces away from Mother. One by one, players ask permission to move toward Mother, saying, "Mother, may I take three giant steps [or two baby steps, or whatever] forward?" Mother either grants permission or denies it. The first person to touch Mother wins.

RED ROVER

Two teams stand about twenty feet apart. Players join hands and face the other team. One team calls out, "Red rover, red rover, send [so-and-so] over!" (substituting the name of a player for "so-and-so"). That player must run toward the other team and try to break through their linked hands. If he's successful, he returns to his team; if he's not, he's absorbed into the opposing team. Teams take turns calling out; once one team has absorbed another, the game is over.

SACK RACES

Players step into burlap sacks and clutch the sacks at waist height. At "Go," players hop toward a finish line. First one there wins.

CRACKER-WHISTLING CONTESTS

Contestants pop a cracker in their mouths, chew rapidly, and try to whistle. First one to do so wins.

RELAY RACE

Divide into two teams and then divide the two teams into two sides. The two sides will stand opposite each other single file, separated by a distance of about twenty paces. Each team has a baton; on "Go," the first runner from one side runs to the other side and passes the baton to his teammate; that teammate runs to the other side and passes it off, and so on. The first team to return the baton to the original runner wins.

VARIATIONS ON TAG

- **Freeze Tag:** When you're tagged, you must immediately freeze in position. Another member of your team may unfreeze you with a touch.

- **Flashlight Tag:** On a dark, dark night, arm all your players with flashlights that are turned off. Every player is "It" and tries to tag—by quickly shining his flashlight on another player. If a player is tagged, he's out. The last player standing wins. Alternatively, It can be the only player armed with a flashlight, the flashlight must stay on, and if It "tags" another player by shining the light on him and calling out his name, that player is It.

- **Blob Tag:** Two players link arms and are It. If they tag someone, that person must link arms and become part of It, creating a long, many-headed blob. Only the ends of the blob may tag people, so chasees may run *through* the blob if they think they can make it without the ends catching them.

- **Ghost in the Graveyard:** Must be played at night. Choose a "home base," like a large tree; players touching the tree are "safe." One player is the Ghost. The other players stay on home base, counting "one o'clock, two o'clock," etc., until they get to midnight, while the Ghost hides. Then the other players go in search of the Ghost. The Ghost's job is to leap out and tag someone before he or she can get back to home base. If a player spots the Ghost, he yells "Ghost in the Graveyard!" to alert his fellow players, who all try to get back to home base. If someone is tagged, that person is the new Ghost.

- **Go-Tag:** Players squat in a line. One player is "It" and chases another (the Chasee) in an oval around the crouching players. The Chasee may not reverse direction. But at any point It may touch the back of a crouching player and replace him in his squatting position. The crouching player then becomes It. When the Chasee is finally tagged, she squats at the end of the line. The It that tagged her becomes the new Chasee, and the person at the other end of the line becomes the next It.

Frisbee Golf

Context clue: It's a lot like regular golf, and a thermos of martinis afterward (or during) really can enhance the experience. You stand at a "tee" and toss a disc at a target like a tree or telephone pole and hope to hit it. Repeat eighteen times as you make your way around the course. Frisbee or disc golf courses already exist in many public parks, but you and your friends can make new ones simply by deciding on a series of targets around a park and tees an appropriate distance away. This has the advantage of letting you choose the distance between each tee and target, and so adjust the course to your group's skill level.

I live in Brooklyn, and Prospect Park has a discreetly marked course that took us through parts of the park that I'd never seen before. My friend and I were possibly the worst Frisbee players ever to play the course, so we made it through only about six holes before exhaustion set in. Plus, the course took us past the park's "dog beach," and hurtling Frisbees proved irresistible to the local canines, which slowed our progress. But still, a good, damp, muddy time was had by all.

PLAYERS: 2–4

THE GEAR: A Frisbee for each player, a printout or list of each "hole" for each player, and a pencil to keep score. Frisbee Golf is mellow and cheap, unless you want to order special disc baskets online at discnation.com. If you live in an urban area, be prepared to have them stolen, but the equipment can be worth it if you have a lot of land and want to set up a proper course. Plaid pants are optional.

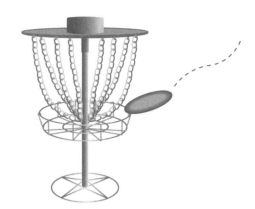

A disc basket

Objective

To complete a course (anywhere from nine to twenty-five "holes") with the fewest number of throws of the disc.

Preparation

Disc golf courses are normally laid out in wooded areas with diverse terrain to provide natural obstacles to the flight of the disc. The holes (usually trees) are marked with disc baskets, paint, or chalk. Type your zip code into the online course directory at pdga.com/course/index.php and see if there's a course in your hometown.

Or, you can map out your own course— thereby controlling how many holes you have the energy to play and the distance between holes. To do this, you'll have to walk around your local park with a map and some chalk, marking each target, noting it down along with the accompanying tee (for example, "Tee from the west corner of the little bridge"). For a beginner game, the tee should be close enough to the hole that an average player would need not more than two or three tosses of the disc to hit the target.

Give each player a copy of the map.

The Game Plan

- Begin the game by "teeing off," or making your first toss toward the first "hole" (a tree or a lamppost). Players go in sequence, so Bob, John, Bob, John . . . (and after Bob hits the target) John, John, John . . . etc. (Poor John.)

- Each consecutive throw is made from where the disc came to rest after the last throw.

- Proceed to each successive hole around the course as a group, so nobody gets left behind.

- Score is determined by counting the number of throws made on each hole and then adding them up at the end. Use the printout of your course map to record the number of throws made by each player at each hole.

Winning

Complete the course with the *lowest* score, and you've won.

▶▶ IF YOU LIKE THIS GAME . . . check out pdga.com for more about disc golf.

> **▶▶STEALTH STRATEGY ◀**
>
> Wear long pants and socks, in case your disc lands in a patch of poison ivy.

Kickball

Kickball was a game for those of us who couldn't hit the side of a barn; who mistook baseballs and tennis balls and squash balls for little whizzing gnats; who shrieked and covered our eyes when a softball sailed in our direction. A kickball is big enough

that you really can't miss, and it makes a satisfying rubbery *bonk* when you make contact.

But there's one important thing about adult Kickball, now, in the second decade of the twenty-first century: Some people treat it as a casual backyard game; other people treat it as a *sport*. Below you will find the rules (remember, *guidelines*) for the casual backyard version. If you're the type who's really, really into the *exact right* way to play—rules, diagrams, what-ifs, etc., check out kickball.com and print out the eleven-page PDF of the official rules.

PLAYERS: 8–30

THE GEAR: Four bases (old T-shirts will do), clothesline or other items to mark foul lines, a big red rubber ball.

Preparation

- Divide into two teams of at least four people each. If you have four on a team, you can play without a catcher.

- Set up three bases and a home plate in a diamond shape using old T-shirts.

- Establish foul lines with clothesline, soda cans, or cones.

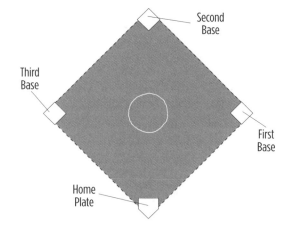

The Game Plan

- The rules are roughly the same as for baseball, except you kick a large soft rubber ball rather than swing at a little hurtling missile.

- Five innings. Three outs per inning.

- The pitcher pitches the ball by rolling it on the ground; it can't be excessively bouncy.

- You tag a runner out by hitting her with the ball or touching the base while holding the ball before she gets there.

- If a player catches the ball before it hits the ground, it's an out (just like a pop fly in baseball).

- Try to have a referee who's not an idiot to settle disputes, because even with casual backyard games there *will* be disputes. (For example: What *is* excessively bouncy?)

Winning

The team with the highest score wins.

Ringoleavio

Ringoleavio is kind of like Capture the Flag but without the flag. You're trying to tag members of the other team, thereby sending them to jail, and to keep any free members of the opposing team from staging a jailbreak.

PLAYERS: 6–50, the more the better.

THE GEAR: T-shirts or backpacks to mark the jail.

Preparation

Outline the boundaries of the game—a small park, a few backyards, a closed-off street—and make them clear to everyone. Designate an area to be the "jail"—either a space with natural boundaries or boundaries made of T-shirts or backpacks. Set a time limit for the game—fifteen to twenty minutes is good to start—and appoint someone to keep an eye on the time.

The Game Plan

One team (the hunters) closes their eyes and counts to thirty. Players on the other team (the hiders) hide themselves within the playing area. After the count is up, the hunters go in search of the hiders. If a hunter can grab and hold (think bear hug) a hider long enough to shout, "Ringoleavio one-two-three!" the hider is captured and must proceed to jail. Teammates may free their imprisoned comrades by dashing within the boundaries of the jail, yelling, "Home free!" and dashing out again—at which point the prisoners will scram as fast as they can.

▶▶ **ETIQUETTE**

"Grab and hold" can mean different things to different people. When in doubt, err on the side of being gentle. And try not to elbow anybody in the throat.

Winning

If the hunters capture all the hiders before time's up, the hunters win. Otherwise, the hiders win. Teams should switch roles and play again.

Variation

You may choose to allow prison guards or not. In some variations, the jail may not be guarded, and lurking in the vicinity will result in the prisoners shrieking, "Babysitting!" If a team is found to be "babysitting," or guarding the jail, the prisoners may go free.

Scavenger Hunts

Wonderfully malleable, Scavenger Hunts can be designed for all ages in any location, and they can be as ordinary or as oddball as you want. In urban settings, Scavenger Hunts provide a new way of looking at the city and interacting with other members of the community. Best of all, Scavenger Hunts can have themes, based on the occasion or your guests' interests. Say your pals are foodies: Send them on a chase for foie gras and caperberries. If your family is crazy about sailing—well, they can't come home until they've photographed a halyard, a bitter end, and a salty dog (either the drink or the sailor). It's also fun to incorporate antics or stunts into the hunt—maybe someone has to turn a cartwheel on the poop deck, for example, or recite a portion of *The Rime of the Ancient Mariner* to a tour group at the seaport.

PLAYERS: 4–30, plus a game designer/host (you).

THE GEAR: Pen and paper, bags if players are gathering actual items, and/or digital cameras if players must photograph sites, objects, or stunts. For some games, players might need cell phones with Internet access or the phone number of a friend stationed at home in front of the computer.

Your game can also be fairly abstract and open to creative interpretation, if you think your group is up for it. For example, snap a picture of a "pretentious hipster," or something equally subjective, like "an example of lax parenting." When the groups reconvene, the debates about what constitutes pretentious hipster or lax parenting are inevitable. (Does a carefully mussed bedhead count? How about a parent crossing the street without holding his child's hand?)

Finally, if your players are different ages, be sure to include some simple clues that the youngest team members can solve. Intergenerational games are a great activity when the whole clan is home for the holidays or gathered for another family event, like a wedding. They keep the attention focused on the (fun) group-task at hand, rather than leaving Junior to his Gameboy or Aunt Rose to poke around your kitchen.

PARTY RECIPE

Lobster Rolls

When the troops return from their scavenging, they're going to be hungry. If lobster meat is on your teams' lists, you can quickly assemble lunch for the whole group.　　　SERVES 4

INGREDIENTS

1 pound lobster meat	4 warm grilled hot dog
½ cup mayonnaise	rolls
Celery, finely chopped	chopped lettuce, for
(optional)	garnish
1 tablespoon lemon juice	melted butter, for dipping

1. Split up the lobster meat into smaller pieces if it's a tail or claw.

2. In a medium bowl, toss the meat very lightly with the mayonnaise. Add celery and lemon juice to taste.

3. Place lobster salad on a warm grilled roll with the chopped lettuce. Serve hot melted butter on the side.

Double or triple the recipe for larger groups, but make sure you have at least a few teams bringing back the lobster meat so the cost is shared among the players.

Objective

To be the first person or team to find all the items on a list. Teams can be as large or small as you like, though more than five people tends to be unwieldy.

Put people who don't know each other well on the same team, so all your friends and family can become acquainted.

Preparation

Before your guests arrive, prepare a list of things they must find or tasks they must do. This *can* be limited to physical objects, but it doesn't *have* to be—you can have your players find a couple kissing, or a policeman scowling, and snap a picture.

You can make the same list for each team, or mix it up so that teams are looking for different things. If the latter, make sure that no team's list is harder or more time-consuming than another's.

Print out a list for each team.

The Game Plan

- Divide your players into teams. Hand each group a sheet of things to find, tasks to perform, or places to photograph. Physical things must be put in a bag and brought back to HQ. Places and tasks must be photographed.

- Make sure everyone has your phone number and you have theirs; set a time limit (everyone back at the HQ by noon) and say, "Go!"

- If you're playing a more abstract game, i.e., players have to snap a picture of "disaffected youth," teammates will have to discuss which pic to submit for judgment and whether what they see "counts":

Does rolling up one's cigs in one's T-shirt sleeve and slouching toward the drugstore mean you're disaffected? How about a Che Guevara hoodie? They must agree on one photo that satisfies that clue and present

Tips for the Game Designer/Host

A few ideas to make the hunt more silly or fun:

- Set a "total point goal"—the first team to reach, say, 25 points, wins. Each task is worth a certain number of points. Assign more points to the outrageous tasks—5 points for dunking a team member in the reflecting pool in Washington, D.C., for example, but only 2 points for posing with a street performer or riding the carousel at the park. So teams who don't want to do crazy things, or get wet, may focus on doing a greater number of the less-outrageous tasks.

- Clump all the tasks and things to find in one neighborhood and make a rule that people may not use private cars—only foot or bicycle or public transport.

- For certain tasks, specify that the entire team must be in the photo, so they will have to interact with strangers or include tasks that involve strangers: getting or giving a piggyback ride to a tourist.

- Ask each team to bring back a few servings of a particular food item—one team must bring sandwiches from a particular deli, another brownies from a particular bakery, a third French lemonade from a gourmet grocery store. Then have a picnic when everyone's reconvened!

it at the end. The host has the final say regarding whether the team has satisfied the requirement and whether to award the point(s)—but in these more abstract games, the host should not be too sticky about what counts. A large part of the fun is the slideshow at the end of the game.

✖ If a team is completely stumped by something on their sheet ("What is *sashimi?*" or "What is the *green monster?*"), or gets lost, they should call the host for help, clarification, and hints.

Winning

In a basic scavenger hunt, the first team back with all the correct items and photos wins—or, if no one finishes, the team who got the most items checked off their list wins. If teams are playing for a total number of points (see "Tips for the Game Designer/Host" on the previous page), the highest number wins.

▶▶ **IF YOU LIKE THIS GAME . . . try your hand at a psychological scavenger hunt: Charles Ate a Goat Testicle in Algeria, which appears on page 22.**

Some Ideas to Get You Started . . .

- Find a particular food-cart vendor and instruct the team to photograph one team member feeding another team member. The Great Urban Race, a company that runs scavenger hunts all around the world, had its players find the "Sugar Cube," a baked-goods food cart in Portland, Oregon, and snap a photo of team members feeding each other a cupcake.

- Have team members find a particular city monument and photograph themselves standing on top of it. If you're in New York, you could have your teams snap a photo of themselves draped on the bull on Broadway near Wall Street, or procure a piece of chocolate from Jacques Torres in Brooklyn's Dumbo neighborhood.

- Have team members find your city's street performers and snap a pic. If you're on a family vacation in Key West, teams have to take a photo of one team member in front of the "human statue" at Mallory Square.

- If your city has an art gallery that displays paintings or sculpture in the window,

players have to find the gallery, pose themselves like the piece of art, and get a passerby to snap a photo.

- Find a wedding party in a park and get a picture.

- Photograph a team member in a Victoria's Secret store.

- Photograph all team members in full Kiss makeup inside Sephora.

- Take five photos of words that rhyme with "bird."

- Find a gourmet grocery store and photograph the most unusual item you can find.

- Photograph a large public clock at a specified time during your event.

- Some suggestions for physical items: a matchbook from a French restaurant, a menu from a Chinese restaurant, a checked-out library book, a sample card spritzed with perfume from a department store.

Urban Bingo

U rban Bingo, a reinvention of the traditional senior-center game of Bingo, turns city elements into Bingo squares. The game board consists of twenty-four objects (or concepts) that can be found in your city, and one free marker in the center.

Each player has his own game board and is playing for himself; however, he wanders about the city in a group of three to seven people. The player is *competing against* these three to seven people. But in order to check off a Bingo square, he must get the corroboration of the group that what he sees satisfies the requirement printed in that square. For example, in a game I played in New York, one of the squares on my board said "juxtaposition of extreme wealth and extreme poverty." I spotted a very down-on-his-luck man crossing in front of a BMW and announced that to the group; they all said, "Yeah, we'll give it to you." It might be tempting to *not* corroborate what someone's seeing (in fact, earlier I had suggested that the presence of a Whole Foods Market in a just-barely gentrified neighborhood would count as a juxtaposition, but several group members disagreed) just to keep them from winning, but keep in mind that if you're too much of a hard-ass, your group members will simply retaliate and not corroborate what you're seeing. So play fair.

PLAYERS: 3–7, plus a game designer/host.

THE GEAR: 3–7 Bingo game boards, created by the game designer/host.

Preparation

Make game boards with text inside each box (see the sample Seattle game board, right, for ideas) or contact David Jimison, the designer, to purchase game boards specific to your city. You will need enough game boards so that each person in a group has his or her own. (If you have a few different groups playing at once, it *is* permissible for players to have the same game boards as players in another group.) So for a game with seven people, you will need seven distinct game boards. For a game of three people, you will need three distinct game boards, and so on.

The Game Plan

➤ When the players arrive, distribute game boards, taking care that no two group members have the same one. Players should not show each other their game boards. Players should ask you, as the game designer/host, to clarify anything that they don't understand.

* Tell everyone that in order to check off a square, all group members must agree that the found object (or example of a concept, like "juxtaposition of extreme wealth and extreme poverty") fulfills the text in a Bingo square. Symbolic objects can count. For instance, a player may spot a picture of the Statue of Liberty in a shop window or on a T-shirt; this can be used instead of seeing the actual monument.

* The group must stay together.

* If you have several groups playing at once, announce that players will meet back at a bar for drinks post-game; make sure everyone has the address.

* Say "Go."

Winning

The first player to mark off five squares in a vertical, diagonal, or horizontal line across their board wins. The center square counts as a free space and counts toward the five. Continue playing for second and third place. Each group will have a winner.

—contributed by David Jimison, a game designer based in New York and Atlanta. For more about David and his projects, check out davidjimison.info and urban-bingo.com.

Puzzle Scavenger Hunt

Regular Scavenger Hunts have you searching for items and checking them off a list. But what if you had to solve a puzzle in order to progress to the next clue? Books like *The Da Vinci Code* and shows like *The Amazing Race* have made these types of scavenger hunts hugely popular—and now you can get into the fun. Participants must solve a puzzle—like unscrambling an anagram—which will give them instructions on where to proceed to next. If you like, teams can be led to a final destination where there will be a picnic or drinks or some other big, fun, finish-line event.

PLAYERS: 10–50, plus a game designer/host.

THE GEAR: Paper, pens, chalk, and any technological resources, like anagram generators, digital cameras, or cell phones, that the game designer/host deems necessary.

Objective

To be the first to solve all the puzzles and cross the finish line.

Preparation

Preparation is substantial. For each clue, you, as the game designer/host, create a puzzle that players must solve in order to move on to the next clue—an anagram, a riddle, a code, a piece of paper that must be folded in a certain way to make a map, crosswords that when completed give instructions, etc. Each clue takes the players to another locale, where they will find another puzzle that will further direct them. (The final puzzle should, when solved, send players to a location, like a bar, that the organizer has set up for a party.) Once you've made up all your puzzles, stash any information you need to stash (such as pinning slips of paper to a supermarket bulletin board, or tucking sticks of chewing gun in the knot of a tree, à la *To Kill A Mockingbird,* or affixing a sticker to the bottom of a jar of anchovies at a particular grocery store). If you're worried about your clues getting stolen or erased, you should post sentries at each clue place. If the information that solves puzzle number seven gets washed away in a spring shower, you'll need to write it again or have a backup plan.

Shortcut

For scavenger hunts that you don't have to organize yourself—or for ideas when you're creating your puzzles—check out ravenchase.com or greaturbanrace.com.

Decide whether you want to offer a certain number of "hints" or "fast-forwards" per team if they're stuck (this will move things along if a team is in a hopeless muddle). While out in the field, teams can call the game designer/host for a hint if they just *can't* figure out a certain clue.

Also decide if you want to allow team members to call nonplaying friends for assistance (to look up something on the Internet, to lend their expert opinion on the Fibonacci sequence, etc.) and decide if you want to limit the number of those calls. In general, allowing players to use any and all tools at their disposal is a good idea and will keep the game moving.

▶▶ **HOST TIP**

Test out all your puzzles on several nonplaying friends ahead of time. This will give you an idea of how long, on average, it takes to solve each one, and help you plan the length of your game. The primary hazard for a Puzzle Scavenger Hunt is making the hunt too long and/or too complicated. Err on the side of brevity and simplicity. You can perfect your technique over time.

The Game Plan

✖ Divide your players into teams of three to five people. (People may play in larger teams if they wish; a large team will have more brainpower but will move more slowly.) Provide the host's phone number for hints or help; get a phone number for each team so you can alert players if the game has been won or if something has gone wrong (like a clue has washed away, a certain part of town is blocked off—anything unexpected that might impact the game).

✖ Distribute the first clue. All teams will do the same clues in the same order, so the game is also a race—and teams must be careful to avoid being followed from location to location by another team. (Warn your teams that this would be unsportsmanlike, anyway.)

✖ Start the game.

✖ Keep in touch with your players by phone—have them call you at each checkpoint, or simply call them on a regular basis. This will minimize teams going off half-cocked—getting on a plane to Schenectady, breaking into the United Nations, etc.—and ensures that everyone is on track and having a good time. Don't be too stingy about giving hints or guidance—it's no fun if one team finishes in fifteen minutes and another is still struggling with the first clue hours later.

Sample clues for a puzzle scavenger hunt:

- Wild blue yonder
- How we know the sun's in the sky
- If you wine her . . .

Which of course translate to:

- Sky
- Light
- Dine her

So the team now knows they must race to the Skylight Diner for their next clue. If not everyone knows where the Skylight Diner is—or has even heard of it—the team might look up the address on their iPhones, call a friend, or even borrow a phone book from a local merchant. Once they get there, they find a message chalked on the sidewalk (or handed to them by a sentry who's standing at the door): *A deb replies, muting it,* which, once they move around a few letters, tells them *Empire State Building.* (Teams should know in advance that anagrams are one type of puzzle that may appear in the game.)

And so on. The clues can be as hard or as easy as you wish.

Winning

The first team to solve all the clues and arrive at the last locale (which will be wherever the last clue directs them to go) wins.

Variation

Town Hunt: Instead of finding places or things, you have to find people (the Hiders) who are hiding in plain sight. The Hiders—there should be about ten—don a distinctive piece of clothing, such as a striped hat, and hide themselves "in plain sight" around town— sitting in a coffee shop, shooting the breeze with a cop, squeezing melons at the fruit stand. The first team to find all the Hiders and get their signatures wins.

Midnight Madness

Midnight Madness was an annual puzzle scavenger hunt that ran in the 1990s and early 2000s in New York City. The game always began at about 10 P.M. on a summer Saturday night and lasted well into the next afternoon. (Many teams or members of teams would drop out over the course of the night, as not everyone has the stamina to play a fifteen- or twenty-hour game that sent players running all over the island of Manhattan and sometimes the outer boroughs as well.)

Teams would organize themselves and sign up. They could be as large or small as the members wished, but usually were between ten and twenty people. Teams chose a color as their name—Team Orange, Team Burnt Umber—and had to have a captain who registered online, in advance, with the organizers. Private cars or taxis were not allowed: bikes and public transport only.

A typical clue: We arrived outside an art gallery in the meatpacking district at about 1 A.M. In the window stood a display of toy soldiers—seven in a row. Each soldier blinked a light in a different pattern: *blink blink blink,* for example, or *blink blink.* We then realized that each soldier had a number: *blink blink* equaled two, *blink blink blink* equaled three, and so on—until we got seven digits. A phone number! We dialed the number, which then told us where to go next.

I stayed in the game until about 4 A.M. that night and then abandoned my teammates for bed. When I phoned them at noon the next day, they were racing across the Brooklyn Bridge for the final clue.

Museum Scavenger Hunt

In case of rain, plan a "backup" hunt inside a museum: i.e., find an example of chiaroscuro, find an example of early Renaissance use of perspective, etc. If you feel like a quick scavenger hunt *right now,* though, this short game, contributed by Watson Adventures, can be played by letting your fingers do the walking—all the way over to the museums' websites. When you think you've got them all figured out, check out the answers, below.

Questions

1. In the Hals of the Metropolitan Museum of Art, whose naughty gesture might make you exclaim, "I never sausage behavior!"?

2. At the Museum of Fine Arts, Boston, search for a gleaming Diana ready for a "stag party." If she stops in front of you, what must you do? (Hungry for more? Order her with fries.)

3. In the American paintings galleries of the National Gallery of Art, find our skinny-dipping namesake. That trace of red indicates he clearly got off on the wrong foot with another swimmer. But which was the ill-fated foot, left or right?

4. Go Dutch in the Art Institute of Chicago. Find a seventh-day celebration made unholy by wicked kin of Glinda and Sabrina. Where on his body might Kermit expect to receive a bite?

5. At the Getty Center in Los Angeles, find a "playa hater" who conducts a test with lemon aid. What is he testing?

6. At the Legion of Honor in San Francisco, a Younger man's painting might remind you of the bitten one at the Art Institute of Chicago—but there are more of them here. Whose kiss must be only partly effective at producing princes? Hint: She almost sounds like she could be a Jackson.

—for more about Watson Adventures' tricky, witty scavenger hunts, check out their website at watsonadventures.com.

Answers

1. In Frans Hals' *Merrymakers at Shrovetide,* Hans Wurst, with a sausage pinned to his hat, makes an obscene gesture.

2. You must drink. *Diana and Stag Automaton,* with the goddess Diana riding a stag, is a drinking game.

3. *Watson and the Shark* shows Watson's left foot, so he lost his *right,* unseen (also suggested by the blood in the water).

4. A hound bites a frog on the *thigh* in *A Witches' Sabbath,* by Dutch painter Cornelis Saftleven.

5. In *The Musicians' Brawl* by Georges de La Tour, a man squirts a lemon into a musician's eyes to test *whether he is blind.* (We're not sure how that works, exactly, but that's what the experts say.)

6. *Latona* is seen with men with frog heads in *Latona and the Frogs,* by David Teniers the Younger.

Fox and Hounds

Fox and Hounds is a chase and tracking game. The hounds pursue the foxes, who flee for their lives. The foxes get a head start—but they must leave a trail, in flour or chalk, for the hounds to follow. In this fashion we mimic ye olde English hunts of yore—but we're hunting people instead of animals. More PETA friendly, anyway.

PLAYERS: 4–50, plus a moderator.

THE GEAR: Whistles, chalk, or small baggies of flour.

Objective
For the hounds to catch the foxes; for the foxes to remain free.

Preparation
✖ About one-fourth of your players will be foxes, so prepare enough baggies of flour—or buy enough whistles—for each fox to have one. If you're playing in an urban area, you might want to go with the whistles or chalk, as antiterrorism squads are made nervous by bags of white powder.

✖ Divide your players into foxes (the chasees) and hounds (the chasers). There should be about three hounds to one fox.

✖ Have the foxes decide ahead of time on a route through the woods or city that can be run in about twenty minutes. They should not tell the hounds what this route is, but they should tell the moderator the finish point, so she can be waiting there.

The Game Plan
✖ Give each fox a bag of flour, a piece of chalk, or a whistle.

✖ Set a time limit—perhaps twenty minutes for the first round; you can increase or decrease depending on the stamina of your players.

✖ Give foxes a one-minute head start.

✖ Foxes must lay flour or a chalk mark, or blow their whistle, every twenty to thirty seconds of their flight.

Travel Advisory
Hash runs began in colonial Malaysia in the late 1930s as a way for drunken Brits to sweat out weekend hangovers. The original players were billeted in the Royal Selangor Club, which was known as "Hash House" after its notoriously bad food; the club was dubbed the "Hash House Harriers."

The runs are usually three to six miles long, over varied terrain. The "hare," or chasee, gets a head start of about fifteen minutes and leaves a trail, usually in chalk or flour, for the "hounds" to follow. The trail is rife with dead ends and false leads; the fastest runners alert the pack to these as they double back. In this fashion, the group more or less stays together to the end. After finding the end of the trail, the group convenes at a local bar, called the "on-in." Weird initiation rituals—like singing special songs and downing cups of beer—ensue. In case you're worried you're not fit enough: If you can jog and walk for three or so miles (there are plenty of opportunities to stop and catch your breath), you'll be fine.

Hash clubs exist in nearly every city in the world. **To find a club:** half-mind.com or gotothehash.net.

⚑ After the initial minute is up, the hounds are released. They must try to tag the foxes, who are trying to finish the route before the hounds can tag them. In other words, the goal for the foxes is to lay the trail and try not to be tagged; the goal for the hounds is to follow the trail and to tag the foxes.

Winning

At the end of the time period, any foxes left untagged win. If all foxes are caught, the hounds win.

Coast Guard and Smugglers

Like Capture the Flag, except you're trying to get things *into* enemy territory instead of *out*. For Coast Guard and Smugglers you'll need a fairly large playing field: a big wooded area, a city park, or a several-block radius in an urban area.

PLAYERS: 10–100, plus two neutral roles: the scorekeeper and the holder of the loot.

THE GEAR: Armbands or different-color T-shirts to differentiate teams, thirty-six slips of paper.

The Game Plan

⚑ Divide the group into two teams, the Smugglers and the Coast Guard. Each team retreats to separate ends of the playing area. The Coast Guard sets up their "country," a ten-by-ten-foot (or larger) space with clear boundaries. The Smugglers set up their

Contraband

On small pieces of paper write out the following for "contraband."

- **Chocolate:** 50 points (ten slips of paper)

- **Sugar:** 75 points (eight slips of paper)

- **Animal Pelts:** 100 points (eight slips of paper)

- **Gunpowder:** 150 points (six slips of paper)

- **Designs for new secret weapon:** 300 points (three slips of paper)

- **Map to buried treasure:** 500 points (one slip of paper)

hideout, which can be smaller—it's used only to hold the loot.

⚑ Select a person to be the scorekeeper, who sits in the Coast Guard's country, and select a person to be holder of the loot, who sits in the Smugglers' headquarters. These are good roles for nonathletic players—the elderly, the pregnant, or the sedentary.

⚑ Distribute the "contraband" slips of paper to the Smugglers. They will hold on to the tiny pieces of paper, which they are going to try to carry into the enemy's (Coast Guard) country.

⚑ Give each team a few minutes to brainstorm and devise a strategy, such as sending out the low-value contraband on slower runners as decoys, and then, when the other team is distracted, sending out the faster players with high-value contraband. Then start the game. The Coast Guard fan out away from their headquarters and try to intercept

Smugglers as they attempt to "smuggle their goods to the border," or cross the boundary into the Coast Guard's country.

* The paper has to be hidden in external clothing layers. When a Smuggler gets tagged he must stand still and permit the Coast Guard a thirty-second search of his person. If the Coast Guard cannot find the contraband within thirty seconds, the Smuggler is free to try to advance again into the headquarters. If the Coast Guard does find the contraband, he takes the piece of paper into his country and gives it to the scorekeeper to be tallied, while the Smuggler returns to *his* headquarters to receive another piece of contraband.

> **▶▶STEALTH STRATEGY**
>
> Send out a runner *without* a piece of contraband. As that runner is being pursued and searched—meaning the Coast Guard is distracted—send out a faster runner with a high-value piece of contraband. Hopefully the Coast Guard will be too occupied with the decoy smuggler to fully pursue the second runner.

* If a Smuggler penetrates inside the Coast Guard's country (crosses the boundary of the space the Coast Guard marked off at the beginning of the game), he gives his goods to the scorekeeper, and is allowed to return swiftly and unmolested to his headquarters to retrieve another piece of contraband.

* The game continues for a set period of time, say twenty minutes. When it ends, goods (points) are totaled. If the Smugglers have managed to sneak in more points than the Coast Guard has managed to find, the Smugglers win. If the Coast Guard

has managed to find and turn in more contraband points than the Smugglers, the Coast Guard wins.

Ace-King-Queen

Also called Chinese Handball, Ace-King-Queen is a street game that relies on reflexes and hand–eye coordination. It's the sort of game you might see street urchins in knickers playing on a Bronx block—think *Billy Bathgate*. It requires even less equipment than regular handball—you don't even need a court, just a wall and a street. You do, of course, need a ball. Remember those small pink rubber balls (sometimes called "pinky balls" or "Spaldeens") made by Spalding? You can get them on Amazon for just a few bucks.

Ace-King-Queen with a pinky ball is a children's game that many people remember fondly—even if they were terrible at the game and were subject to "asses-up." (The loser puts his hands against the wall, spread-eagle position, backside out. The rest of the players then take turns firing their balls at his tush.)

I was not good at handball, but I was also a crier, so I wasn't frequently subjected to asses-up. While everyone likes to win, no one likes to see their opponents sobbing. So if you're playing with a weeper, maybe skip the asses-up.

PLAYERS: 2–6. There is technically no upper limit to the number of players, but a three- to four-player game is ideal.

THE GEAR: A ball—preferably a pink rubber Spalding—and a piece of chalk.

Objective

To avoid getting points by missing the ball or hitting it out of bounds.

Preparation

Play anywhere a wall and a sidewalk meet. Use the boxes that occur naturally in a sidewalk; otherwise chalk boxes that are about four feet square—as many boxes as you have players—in a line along the wall. (See the diagram, below, as a guideline.)

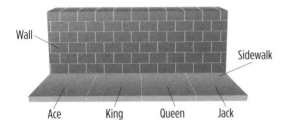

Wall

Sidewalk

Ace   King   Queen   Jack

The Game Plan

- Each player occupies a box. The leftmost player as you face the wall is the Ace, the next player is the King, the next is the Queen, and so on. Each player in line gets the name of the descending card in the deck.

- The Ace serves by bouncing the ball on the ground and then hitting it with his palm against the wall and into the box of either the King, who is on the Ace's right, or the box of any other player.

- That player hits it in the same manner—the ball must bounce once on the ground, and then against the wall, and then into the box of another player. A player may hit the ball against the wall in her own box as many times as she likes, positioning the shot perfectly, before sending it into another player's box.

- When the last player receives the ball, he switches its direction, sending it gradually back up the line to the Ace.

- If a player misses the ball or hits it out of bounds (not in someone's box), he gets a point and moves to the end of the line. Everyone else moves up a box.

- Play is to 11 points.

Winning

The first person to get to 11 loses and is eliminated from the game. The last remaining player wins.

▶▶ **IF YOU LIKE THIS GAME . . . for more information about traditional urban street games, like Four Square and Stoopball, check out streetplay.com.**

‖‖‖

Kick the Can

Kick the Can is the classic neighborhood kids' game. Usually played in adjacent backyards or a cul-de-sac, Kick the Can is a brilliant example of childhood ingenuity: All you need are a bunch of people and a can (or a milk carton, if you're playing in bare feet). As such, it's pretty simple—it had to be something that kids (and adults) of all ages could play with minimal equipment on any kind of terrain. A few different variations of Kick the Can have evolved; below you'll find a bunch of ways to play, and you can adapt them to your group or playing area.

PLAYERS: 4–50

THE GEAR: A can or some other kickable object.

Objective

For "It" to tag as many of the other players as he can; for the other players to remain untagged.

The Game Plan

There are several acceptable ways to play Kick the Can. In most versions, one person is It and the other players are Kickers, who are trying to stay untagged, but there are also a few versions where there is an offensive and a defensive team. To start, set the can in the middle of the playing area. Designate a place for "jail"—like a large tree (players have to touch it to be "home free") or an approximately five-by-five-foot area marked off with backpacks or T-shirts.

Variation 1

One "It"; many Kickers. It covers her eyes and counts to fifty as the rest of the players hide themselves. It then goes in search of the other players and tries to tag them; if a Kicker is tagged, he is sent to jail. If a Kicker manages to kick the can without being tagged, all the Kickers in jail are set free. If all the Kickers are tagged, It wins and a new game begins.

Variation 2

One "It"; many Kickers. It must merely call out the name of the player and where he is hiding—i.e., "Bob! Behind the maple tree!" If Bob is indeed behind the maple tree, he must go to jail. Prisoners can be freed from jail by another member kicking the can without being tagged. (If a player is clearly running for the can, It may not yell "Bob! Running for the can!" as a way of eliminating him before he gets to the can—he must be tagged.)

Variation 3

One "It"; many Kickers. The Kickers hide; It tries to find each person. Once It has spotted someone and called his name, that person and It must race for the can. The first person to step on the can wins the round. The loser becomes It for the second round.

Variation 4

One "It"; many Kickers. Kickers hide; It roams about looking for them, trying not to stray too far from the can. If It spots a Kicker, they must race for the can. If It touches the can with his foot and calls out the person's name, that person must go to jail. If the Kicker beats It to the can, the prisoners are freed.

Variation 5

Two equal teams, Chasers and Kickers. The Chasers try to tag the Kickers; the Kickers try to kick the can. If a Chaser tags a Kicker, the Kicker is either 1) out for the round or 2) sent to jail, to be freed if a teammate tags him. If a Kicker kicks the can, the game is over and the Kickers win.

‖‖‖

Marco Polo

Marco Polo was a twelfth-century Venetian whose explorations of Asia introduced the Orient to Europe. I'm sure he would be proud to know that his name is also the name of a popular swimming-pool game—a version of tag in which "It" must keep his eyes shut. Legend has it that Marco Polo didn't know where he was going when he set out on his adventures—perhaps explaining why the game that bears his name is played with Marco's eyes shut.

PLAYERS: 3–12

Objective

For Marco to tag anyone at all.

The Game Plan

✕ Select one person to be Marco, or "It."

✕ That person closes his eyes and counts to ten, giving the other players adequate time to swim away.

✕ Marco must keep his eyes closed. He locates his prey by shouting "Marco!"; the other players (unless they are underwater) must reply with "Polo!" Marco then tries to tag anyone he can (still with eyes closed); if he succeeds, the tagged person becomes Marco.

Variations

✕ Marco may keep his eyes open when underwater.

✕ Players may get out of the pool, but if Marco shouts, "Mermaid on the rocks!" anyone out of the pool is caught and must be Marco for the next round. If there is more than one person out, Marco chooses who becomes the next Marco.

Winning

The game continues until people get tired and drowning looks like a real possibility.

Jump Rope Rhymes

A long with early- to mid-twentieth-century street games like Ace-King-Queen came other activities traditionally played by girls, like Hopscotch and double Dutch. Remember this jump rope rhyme? The challenge was to keep jumping all the way through the rhyme.

> *Miss Susie had a steamboat,*
> *the steamboat had a bell;*
> *Miss Susie went to heaven,*
> *the steamboat went to*
> *Hello, operator, please give me*
> *   number nine,*
> *and if you disconnect me,*
> *I'll kick you from*
> *Behind the refrigerator, there*
> *   was a piece of glass,*
> *Miss Susie sat upon it, and*
> *   cut her little*
> *Ask me no more questions,*
> *tell me no more lies,*
> *the boys are in the bathroom*
> *   zipping up their*
> *Flies are in the meadow,*
> *the bees are in the park,*
> *Miss Susie and her boyfriend*
> *   are kissing in the*
> *Dark is like a movie,*
> *a movie's like a show,*
> *a show is like a TV screen,*
> *   and that is all*
> *I know, I know my ma*
> *I know, I know my pa*
> *I know I know my sister with*
> *   the eighty acre alligator bra.*

No-Equipment Baseball

NEB, a creation of Stephen Sniderman, is the brilliant combination of tag and baseball; a game in which, like in Alice's tea party, people assume the roles of objects. Unlike real baseball, in which the team playing offense sends out one player—the batter— No-Equipment Baseball uses two people at once—the "ball" and the runner. The runner makes a beeline for first base while the "ball" runs crazily about in the outfield, trying not to get tagged.

PLAYERS: 16–24

THE GEAR: None! That's the whole point!

Objective

To finish five innings with the greatest number of runs.

Preparation

Find a field to play in—either a real baseball diamond or one roughly sketched out with bases and foul lines made of T-shirts or backpacks, plus an outfield boundary.

   Divide into two teams and choose a referee. Flip a coin to see who "bats" first.

The Game Plan

- The defensive team spreads out over the playing field.

- The offensive team divides itself into two lineups: the runners and the balls.

- The runner stands at home plate. The ball enters the playing field from right or left field; this is the beginning of the play. Simultaneously, the runner begins running for first base.

- The ball's objective is to not be tagged before the runner can get to first base; the defensive team's objective is to tag the ball.

- If the ball is tagged before the runner gets to first base, the runner is out.

- If the runner makes it to first and the ball is still not tagged or forced out of bounds, the runner has the choice of whether to run for second or to stay at first.

- If the runner goes for second base and the ball is tagged, the runner is out if he hasn't already reached the base. The defensive players must freeze where they are.

- Once the play is over—either the runner is out or safely on base—another ball and runner take their turn.

- If two runners are running for a base—say, one runner is heading for first and another is heading for second—and the ball is tagged, the frontmost runner is the one that is out.

- If two or more runners are on the same base—which isn't a scenario you'd see in real baseball—when the ball is tagged or forced out of bounds, all but the first runner to reach that base are out. (This is the defense's only way to make a double play.)

- A runner crossing home plate scores a point for her team.

- Three outs means defense and offense switch places.

Winning

Tally up the runs after five innings. If it's a tie, go into extra innings. The team with the most points wins.

▸▸ HOST TIP
A very muddy field will make this game even more fun.

Sharks and Minnows

Sharks and Minnows is a tag game that relies on stealth, silent swimming, and the honor of the shark to keep his eyes closed. It has a lot in common with Red Light, Green Light or Mother, May I, except it's in a pool. And if it's 90 degrees, what's better than a tag game in the pool? Sharks and Minnows can also be a powerful aid for flirting—think about how nice it is to be chased and caught by someone you've set your cap for. Especially if he or she is in a swimsuit and has had a Tom Collins or two . . . but I digress. Below are the rules for Sharks and Minnows.

PLAYERS: 3–12

Objective

For the minnows to get to the other side of the pool without being tagged by the shark.

The Game Plan

- Two sides of the pool are home base. You can orient yourselves either lengthwise or width-wise (you know, "portrait" or "landscape," if the pool were a Microsoft Word doc).

- Choose one shark; the rest of the players are minnows.

- The minnows cling to one side of the pool.

- The shark stands or treads water in the center of the pool, eyes closed, and counts to five.

- As he counts, the minnows swim as fast as they can for the other side—trying to be as quiet as possible.

- As soon as the shark has counted to five, he tries to tag the minnows.

- The shark can only keep his eyes open underwater. If his head's above water, his eyes must be shut.

- If a minnow is tagged, she becomes the shark.

Variation 1

The shark stands out of the water with his back to the pool and the minnows and counts out loud to 20. The minnows must remain in contact with the wall until the shark starts counting. Once a minnow lets go, he must keep swimming to the other side, as silently as possible. If the shark hears a minnow moving, he can turn around, jump in the pool, and try to tag the minnow. If the shark *thinks* he hears something, turns around, and all the minnows are still clinging to the side of the pool, he must take two steps farther away from the edge and start counting again.

Variation 2

Minnows can get out of the pool and try to (quietly) run to the other side. But if the shark yells, "Fish out of water!" any minnow out of the pool is now a shark. If more than one minnow is caught in this way, the shark chooses which one will be the next shark.

Variation 3

The shark picks a category, like colors or breeds of dogs. Each minnow thinks of an example of that category silently and keeps it to himself (this game relies on the minnows' honor). The shark stands or treads water in the center of the pool, eyes closed. He then calls out a color (or a breed of dog, or whatever). Any minnow who is thinking of that color must (silently) try to get to the other side. If the shark hears someone move, he'll try to tag 'em.

Chicken Fights

Best played in a pool, chicken fights are the quintessential hot-weather wrestling match. Put one person on top of another's shoulders. These two are a team. They will struggle to knock off a player perched on another's shoulders. The first person to fall in the water loses the match for her team.

Slip 'n Slide Curling

In curling, a game similar to shuffleboard, teams on ice take turns shoving heavy polished stones toward a target. In Slip 'n Slide Curling, two players hurl themselves down a couple of Slip 'n Slides and see who gets the farthest. Of course, regular curling seems a little more strategy-oriented. But sometimes, when it's 100 degrees, you just want to hurl yourself down a wet piece of plastic, and maybe win a little race. To watch a bout of this game on ice, search YouTube for "Human Curling."

PLAYERS: 2–10

THE GEAR: Two Slip 'n Slides.

Objective

To slide the farthest on the plastic.

Preparation

Lay out the plastic sheets side by side and set a hose at the top of each one. Lay the sheets on an incline, if you have one.

The Game Plan

Establish a starting point at which to run toward the slide. At "Go," get a good running start and fling yourself onto the Slip 'n Slide.

> **▸▸STEALTH STRATEGY**
> Lots of sunscreen will get you good and slippery.

Winning

Whoever gets the farthest wins. If both parties slide to the end, the winner is the slider who arrived first.

Urban Orienteering

Abasic orienteering game and a race, Urban Orienteering uses no tools except a map. You'll get to know your city—or the city you're visiting—in a new and different way. The first part of the game is purely random, with directions decided by many flips of a coin. Speed is important, however, and luck also plays a role—you want to cover as much ground as you can in the first half hour and then find the fastest way back once that half hour is up. Urban Orienteering is best played when you're on vacation and you want to see parts of a city that aren't in the guidebook. After the game is over, you and your pals can retrace your steps to check out the cafés, shops, and sights you happened upon while playing the game.

PLAYERS: 2–20, in teams or individually.

THE GEAR: A map of the city, a coin for each team, pencils.

The Game Plan

✗ Give each team or person a map of the city, a pencil, and a coin.

✗ Synchronize your watches and establish a time for the game, say, half an hour.

✗ Start at an intersection and have each team or person flip a coin to decide the next direction: Heads they go right, tails they go left.

✗ Each team or person will mark the route on their map and continue to the next intersection, where they again flip the coin to determine their next direction, and so on, continually marking the map.

✗ At the end of half an hour, each team or person consults the map and takes the quickest route they can back to headquarters.

Winning

The first team or person back doesn't necessarily win. The winning team or person is the one that covered the greatest distance in the time allowed.

Triathlons and Relay Races

PLAYERS: 10–50, in teams. Optional rule: Each team must have at least one child.

Don't be scared. Homemade triathlons can be as easy or as hard as you like. They can also be as silly as you like. Case in point: I go to a music camp (for adults!) near Woodstock, New York, every summer. And every summer there is a "triathlon." The game is played in teams (so not everyone has to compete in every leg). One person must run across a very wobbly rope bridge without falling in the creek. She then tags the second person, who must canoe across the pond while another teammate in the boat plays a musical instrument. They tag a fourth team member, who must swim from one side of the pond to the dock. A fifth member must clog (dance) on the dock to sixteen bars of music. A sixth member must then catch a fish from the pond. Points are given for style; bribing the judges is encouraged. It's a beautiful thing, like watching a bizarro version of the crew races at Henley.

To launch your own relay or triathlon, first consider the stamina and interests of your guests. Obviously, Great-Aunt Tillie is not going to rollerskate through the neighborhood carrying a tray of malteds. But if your party is large and varied enough, you may wish to have a rollerskating leg that can be filled by the twelve-year-old contestants and a knitting requirement that can be completed by their octogenarian teammates. Use your imagination to create a game that showcases the skills of all your guests.

Fox and Geese

Fox and Geese is a tag game played on a specific playing field—you need an expanse of either fresh snow or an unmarred stretch of beach on which to draw a big wheel. Once you've played a round (and wrecked your formerly pristine playing field) you'll need to draw another one for the next round. If you're far from the beach or a fresh snowfall, you can chalk up the pavement.

PLAYERS: 4–10

The Game Plan

✖ Draw a large wheel with six spokes, either by dragging a stick in the sand, kicking your way through the snow, or drawing it with chalk on pavement.

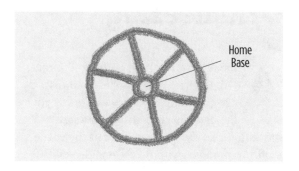

Home Base

✖ Select one person to be the "Fox," or "It." The rest of the players are "Geese." The Fox chases the Geese; players may run only on the edge of the circle or on the spokes. The center of the circle (the hub of the spokes) is "home base," and the Geese are safe from being tagged there. If a player steps off the line, she's out. If two Geese run into each other, they must reverse direction or somehow maneuver around each other without stepping off the line.

✖ There are three ways to end the game: 1) When a Goose is tagged, he becomes the new Fox. 2) Or, he's out, and the last Goose to be tagged is the winner. 3) Or, a tagged Goose becomes a Fox in addition to the original fox (a kind of Zombie Tag), so the number of Foxes grows quickly; in this scenario, the last Goose is the winner.

Counter Squirt

A tag-and-capture game with water guns, Counter Squirt has so many additional elements that the fun goes far beyond just chasing and being chased. The game incorporates elements of role-playing: Each team is trying to capture high-value targets—the Traitor, the Informant, and the Scientist, who are worth certain points. At the same time, teams are also trying to eliminate opponents by shooting them with water guns, and a certain number of hits entitles a player to a more powerful Super Soaker. The game was played on Governor's Island, an abandoned Coast Guard base in the middle of New York Harbor, for an arts festival in 2007. Playing in and around the doorways and alleys of that abandoned town created the feeling of a city under siege. Well, under siege from water guns, anyway.

PLAYERS: 20–30 divided into four or five teams, plus a moderator (you), scorekeeper (your assistant), and three actors willing to be the VIPs: the Scientist, the Informant, and the Traitor. (These actors are not actively "playing"— they can't win the game. They will hide at the outset and probably be captured by the teams hunting for them.) The scorekeeper will be stationed at the game HQ at the center of the playing area.

THE GEAR: Different colored armbands for each team member, plus six or seven extra per team.

Map of the playing area (optional).

A simple water gun for each player, plus six or more high-powered Super Soakers.

Three costumes for the VIPs: A Scientist costume (lab coat), an Informant costume (whatever you think an informant would wear), and a Traitor costume (whatever you think a traitor would wear). The VIPs are not armed.

Paper and pencil for the scorekeeper.

The Terrain

Any large area with plenty of places to hide. A farm or park is ideal, or any place with outbuildings, woods, hills, hay bales, rocky outcroppings, etc.—try to find a playing area with ample places to hide oneself and ambush opponents.

Preparation

- The moderator (you) should scout out the area and select a place as headquarters for yourself and the scorekeeper. Pick three hiding locations: one for the Scientist, one for the Informant, and one for the Traitor. The Scientist is worth the most points, so he should be the furthest away from the HQ.

- If your playing area is very large or has complicated topography, you may want to draw a map for your players.

▶▶ **HOST TIP**
For the sake of economy, ask players to bring their own water guns and borrow the Super Soakers.

Objective

To score the most points in forty-five minutes.

The Game Plan

All the players gather at HQ, where the scorekeeper describes the game, distributes maps (if you have them), and explains how to score points. While the scorekeeper does this, the moderator will take the Scientist, Informant, and Traitor to the hiding locations that he has previously found. For beginner play, the scorekeeper can tell the players where the three VIPs are hidden. For advanced play, players must figure this out on their own, so the moderator should be discreet when escorting the three VIPs to their hiding places.

✖ When the game starts you must try to find the hiding VIPs—the Traitor, the Informant, and the Scientist—who are wearing indicative costumes.

✖ Tag a VIP target by touching his arm (the Traitor is worth 5 points, the Informant is worth 10 points, and the Scientist is worth 15 points) and escort him to HQ without being shot. If you are shot while escorting a VIP and no other of your teammates are immediately available to accompany the VIP, the VIP will simply return to his hiding place.

✖ The VIP must go with you willingly and listen to your commands, as long as they are reasonable. The VIP will ultimately decide what is reasonable—if you tell him to duck, he should duck, but VIPs are not required to climb fences or ford streams.

✖ Once you have escorted the VIP to HQ, your team is awarded its points.

✖ The VIP may then return to his former hiding spot—for a beginner game—or to a different one—for advanced games. He may not be captured on his way back to the hiding spot.

✖ While your team is looking for and escorting VIPs, you will also try to shoot other teams (and of course avoid being shot).

✖ If you shoot another player, she must give you her armband, which you will turn in to HQ for 1 point. Players who have been shot may go to HQ to retrieve a new armband and then reenter the game on the same team.

✖ During the game, you can redeem six armbands for a Super Soaker. (If the scorekeeper runs out of Super Soakers, that's too bad for you. It's an arms race—so try to get them early in the game.)

Winning

The highest score at the end of forty-five minutes wins. The scorekeeper may give score updates throughout the game if players request.

—contributed by Greg Trefry and Mattia Romeo (see page 34)

The Lost Sport of Olympia

The Lost Sport of Olympia was created by Jane McGonigal, a game designer based in San Francisco. It is generally played outdoors, though inside is fine if it's okay to chalk on the floor. In the summer of 2008, teams playing the Lost Sport of Olympia competed against other teams from all around the world. According to Jane, "The ancient Greeks banned it, but we're playing it anyway! Here's the secret legend: The Lost Sport, aka 'the human labyrinth,' was invented 2000 years ago. It was mysteriously banned from the ancient Olympics and only recently rediscovered."

At heart, the game is a race: You chalk a labyrinth on the ground, the players form the walls of the labyrinth, a runner is blindfolded and placed in the center, and you try to see how fast you can get him out. It's an exercise in nonverbal communication, quick reflexes, and teamwork. Below you'll find a three-circuit labyrinth, appropriate for beginners; once you've got the hang of it, you can chalk a larger one for more advanced play. If you want to *see* what the game is all about, search YouTube for "The Lost Sport of Olympia."

PLAYERS: 22–44, plus a timekeeper.

THE GEAR: Chalk, blindfold, stopwatch, diagram of the labyrinth, and a measuring tape.

Objective

For the runner, who is blindfolded, to make it through the labyrinth in as short a time as possible.

Preparation

Chalk a labyrinth on the ground. The dimensions for the three-circuit labyrinth are twelve-by-fourteen feet, or 168 square feet.

The Game Plan

✗ Divide into teams of at least eleven people. Each team has a runner and many wall members (at least ten).

✗ Choose one team to go first.

✗ A team will choose a runner; the other players are "wall" members.

Instructions for wall members:

✗ The wall members stand on the lines of the labyrinth. They will spread their feet wide and hold hands or shoulders to form the wall. They work together to help the blindfolded runner. They shouldn't let the runner knock them over, and they shouldn't let gaps in the wall form.

✗ Wall members may not touch the runner with their hands—the runner will inevitably bump into them and perhaps roll along the wall, but it is illegal for wall members to grab the runner with their hands and direct him.

✖ The runner is blindfolded and put at the center of the labyrinth. When the timekeeper says "Go," the runner will start running to escape the labyrinth.

✖ When they see the runner coming, wall members will *hum*. They will stop humming when the runner passes them. The runner will be guided by the sound of the wall's humming. Wall members may not speak.

✖ Because there probably will not be enough players to form the entire wall at once, as soon as the runner passes a wall member, she should run to make *more* wall, farther toward the outside of the labyrinth. (Wall members do not have to follow the path of the labyrinth—they may step over the chalk lines to get where they need to go before the runner arrives.)

Instructions for the runner:

✖ The runner must escape the labyrinth as fast as he can.

✖ He may not peek, and he may not feel the wall with his hands.

✖ He should try not to get confused and run backward.

Winning

When every team has had a chance to go, compare times—the fastest time wins. Then play again!

—contributed by Jane McGonigal, a game designer who has created and deployed games and missions in more than thirty countries on six continents. For more about Jane and her projects, check out avantgame.com.

PART II: LAWN GAMES

Croquet

There's nothing quite like a spirited game of Croquet on a bright spring day! The smell of the mowed grass, the percussive wooden clacking of the balls, the good-natured humiliation of your best friend . . . it's the perfect mildly athletic activity for a luncheon, garden party, or barbecue.

You may think of Croquet as a genteel sport for blue-blooded WASPs played on manicured New England lawns, but in the late nineteenth-century Croquet was considered immoral—conducive to drinking, gambling, and vice (which it still is!)—and as a consequence was banned in the city of Boston. In recent decades the game has acquired a rather ironic tinge—the thing to do while eating crumpets and taking tea, dressed head to toe in white—but in fact the game requires strategic maneuvering, control, and dexterity. And it doesn't *have* to be played on a manicured lawn. At a rainy May Day party a few years ago, the hostess moved the game inside her rambling farmhouse and jammed the wickets into the old floorboards. The floor was warped and sloped and totally impractical as a Croquet course, which only added to the fun.

There are *many* variations of the game; for an extensive set of American Croquet and International Croquet rules, check out the United States Croquet Association's website at croquetamerica.com.

Croquet used to be played between two teams, but individual (or "cutthroat") Croquet is probably the most popular way to play now. It's essentially the same as team Croquet, but with one ball per player, every man for himself. Below, the basics for a fun, casual, "cutthroat" game.

PLAYERS: 2–6

THE GEAR: Nine wickets, two stakes (the *starting* stake and the *turning* stake), and a ball and matching mallet for each player.

The Terrain

Any grassy area, which can be as flat, bumpy, or hilly as the players wish. The United States Croquet Association specifies 100 by 50 feet, but any largish backyard with short grass will do. Arrange the stakes and wickets in a double-diamond pattern as shown, right, and make sure they are hammered firmly into the ground. You may draw boundaries with chalk, or simply note natural boundaries like trees or rocks.

Objective

To be the first to hit your ball or balls through the wickets and stakes in the correct order (unless you're playing Poison—see Variation on page 351).

The Game Plan

Choose colors. The colors are painted on the Croquet stakes and set the order of play, from top to bottom—or you can simply choose

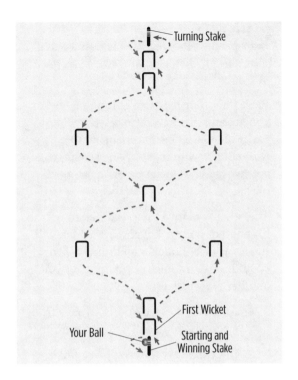

an order at random. The order will remain the same throughout the game. (If a player finishes the game, just skip that color.) You may only hit your color ball with your color mallet.

✖ To begin the game, position the first ball halfway between the starting stake and the first wicket.

✖ Each turn is one stroke. The traditional Croquet stroke is to set your gin and tonic down momentarily and hit the ball from between your legs (not from the side, Tiger Woods–style), but you should do whatever feels comfortable. You may not push, nudge, or scoop the ball—you must hit the ball cleanly in one stroke. If you swing and miss the ball entirely (as often happens, see gin and tonic), your turn ends amid a chorus of gleeful giggles from your opponents.

Variation

Gentler people play that the ball has to go a "mallet's-head" distance; otherwise you get to do it over.

* Each time your ball goes through a wicket, you get another turn (stroke). If you're really on your game and manage to go through *two* wickets with one stroke, you get two chances to get through the next wicket.

* The other way to get two extra strokes is to hit another ball with your ball, which will thwart your opponents and improve your position. You have four options after you hit another player's ball:

    1. You can take two bonus strokes from wherever your ball came to rest.

    2. You can move your ball a mallet's-head's length (about nine inches) in any direction from the ball you hit and take your two bonus strokes from there.

    3. You can set your ball so that it touches the ball you hit and knock them both off in separate directions (this is called "taking Croquet") and then take your second bonus stroke from where your ball lands.

    4. You can set your ball so that it touches the ball you hit, place your foot on top of your own ball, and hit your ball—thus "sending" the other ball somewhere far away and leaving yours in the same place. Then take your second bonus stroke from there.

    NOTE: Bonus strokes aren't cumulative— you may only have a maximum of two bonus strokes at a time.

* You may hit another ball with your ball only once until you clear a wicket or hit the turning stake. If you hit one by mistake, your turn is over and the balls get reset to where they were before the bad shot.

* Going backward through a wicket is permitted to improve your position, but you lose a turn.

Croquet Terms

Roquet: Hitting an opponent's ball with your ball, worth two bonus strokes.

Taking Croquet: Setting your ball so that it touches the ball you hit and then knocking them both off in separate directions.

Sending: Setting your ball so that it touches the ball you hit, placing your foot on top of your own ball and hitting the ball as hard as you can (preferably, without hitting your foot)—thus knocking the opponent's ball as far away as possible (the neighbor's yard, for instance) and leaving yours in the same place. *Sending* your opponent is without a doubt the most joyful (or vexing) part of Croquet!

Running a break: *Roqueting* balls and making consecutive wickets, and so earning bonus strokes, similar to "running the table" in pool. But you may *roquet* another ball only once until you clear a wicket or hit the turning stake.

Dead ball: Once an opponent's ball has been hit, it is "dead"; the ball is not "alive" to you again until you go through a wicket or hit the turning stake.

Ball in hand: Lifting up your ball and moving it somewhere else (options 2, 3, and 4 for your bonus strokes). The second bonus stroke may never be a "ball in hand."

- If a player hits another player's ball through a wicket or a stake, the player whose ball went through the wicket earns the wicket or stake, but doesn't get any extra strokes.

NOTE: Out of Bounds: Any ball that crosses the boundaries may be set back on the playing field three feet (or the length of a mallet) from the point it crossed the boundary.

Winning

The first player to arrive back at the starting stake after going through all the wickets, in the right order, wins. Continue playing to establish second and third place and so on.

Variation

In Poison, the first player to finish a game of cutthroat Croquet becomes "poison"—that is, he stays in the game and tries to eliminate other players by hitting their ball. A poison ball can be eliminated if another poison ball hits it or if it passes through a wicket in any direction.

|||||||||||||||||||||||||||||||||||||||||||||||||||||||||||||||||||

Horseshoes

Horseshoes is thought to have descended from the ancient Greeks' discus throw; it is also similar to the British game of quoits, in which rings are tossed toward a stake. In any case, it's like a million different games in which you toss an object toward a target. Probably brought to the United States by English settlers, the game was for some time derided as "barnyard golf," as it was usually played in rural, or at least grassy, areas. The National Horseshoe Pitchers Association takes its official rules from the game devised during the Civil War: Union soldiers would pass the time pitching mule shoes toward a target. Below is all you need to launch a casual backyard game.

PLAYERS: 2 for singles play or 4 for doubles play.

THE GEAR: 2 horseshoes for each player or team, 2 three-foot stakes.

Preparation

Prepare a horseshoe "pitch," or playing field. A pitch is a long, narrow rectangle, about forty feet long, and can be on grass, sand, or dirt. Pound the stakes into the ground at either end, tilted slightly toward each other. About fourteen inches of the stakes should be above ground.

Objective

To be the first player to score a predetermined number of points—21 is a good number—by tossing *ringers,* or horseshoes that completely surround the stake.

The Game Plan

- Flip a coin to determine which player or team goes first.

- *Singles play:* Standing next to a stake, a player tosses his first horseshoe and then his second horseshoe toward the other stake. Then the other player does the same.

- *Doubles play:* Two players stand at one pitch and their partners stand at the opposite pitch—taking care not to be hit by a flying horseshoe. Once the first two players have tossed and the scores are calculated, their teammates take their turns, tossing back to the original pitch.

- A *ringer* (a horseshoe that completely surrounds the stake) is worth 3 points.

✹ A *leaner,* or a horseshoe that leans against the stake, is worth 1 point. If there aren't any ringers or leaners in a round, the player who threw the horseshoe closest to the stake gains 1 point, and 2 points if both of his horseshoes are closer than his opponent's horseshoes.

NOTE: If you're not sure if a horseshoe is *completely* surrounding the stake, lay a ruler or other straight edge against the two "feet" of the horseshoe. If the ruler doesn't touch the stake, it's a ringer.

Winning

The first player or team to get 21 points wins.

|||||||||||||||||||||||||||||||||||||||||||||||||||||||||||||||||||||

Badminton

Badminton is descended from the ancient game of Shuttlecock, in which a small ball crowned with feathers was kicked back and forth among players—similar to today's game of Hackysack. Shuttlecock plus paddles evolved to become the game of Battledore and Shuttlecock in England, generally played by children, and by the second half of the nineteenth century the game we know as Badminton had taken hold in India and England. Military officers on leave in the 1870s played at the country estate of the Duke of Beaufort; the game takes its name from his estate, Badminton Hall. It's basically a combo of volleyball and tennis played with a feathered birdie. Badminton became an Olympic sport in 1992; to read more about it, check out internationalbadminton.org.

PLAYERS: 2 for singles play or 4 for doubles play.

THE GEAR: A shuttlecock, a Badminton net, and a racquet for each player.

The Terrain

A regulation Badminton court is 44 feet long by 20 feet wide for doubles play and 44 by 17 feet for singles play. For a backyard game, though, set up your net in any grassy, flat area. Draw a "short service line" anywhere from five to nine feet away from the net on either side. For a doubles game, draw a "long service line" two and a half feet in from the back boundary.

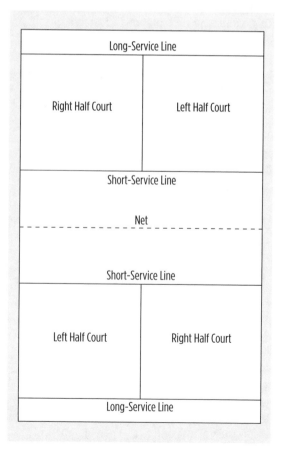

Long-Service Line	
Right Half Court	Left Half Court
Short-Service Line	
Net	
Short-Service Line	
Left Half Court	Right Half Court
Long-Service Line	

Objective
To win rallies by hitting the shuttlecock over the net and onto the ground before the other team can return it. Servers score a point for each rally they win.

The Game Plan
- ✖ Decide on a number to play to—11, 15, or 21 are standard. Toss a coin. The winner of the coin toss may choose her side of the court and whether to serve first or not. The server stands on the right-hand side of her court and serves underhanded to her opponent's right-hand court. The serve has to land past the short-service line and inside the court to be good. In doubles games, a serve can't land past the long-service line.

- ✖ If the serve is good, the opponent will try to hit the shuttlecock back. If the receiver fails to hit the shuttlecock back or if the server wins the rally, the server gains a point and serves again, this time from the left-hand court.

- ✖ If the serve is bad—if she hits it into the net, fails to clear the net, serves into the wrong court, falls short of the short-service line, or goes out of bounds—she loses the serve and no one scores a point.

- ✖ The receiver must stand with both feet in the half court diagonally opposite the server (see diagram). If he doesn't do this, he is at fault, and the server gains a point and serves again.

- ✖ Any player is at fault if he touches the net with his body or racquet, if the shuttlecock touches the ground before he can return it, or if he hits the shuttlecock into the net or out of bounds or if he hits it twice.

- ✖ In any volley, only the serving side can score.

- ✖ A match consists of three games; after each game players will switch sides. The winner of each game serves first in the next game.

Winning
Best two out of three games wins.

Tetherball

The origins of Tetherball are not entirely clear—one gruesome story speculates that the Tatars used to hang the heads of their victims from poles and bat them about. It may be descended from Maypole dances. More likely though, Tetherball, which originally used a volleyball, followed on the heels of that sport's creation in the late nineteenth century. It's a game that's rarely seen outside of playgrounds, gym class, and summer camps, though it did make an appearance as a motif emphasizing the loneliness of the high-school outcast in the film *Napoleon Dynamite*. Tetherball is a refreshing break from more genteel lawn games—after all, sometimes you just want to whack something.

PLAYERS: 2

THE GEAR: A Tetherball set, which consists of a tall, sturdy metal pole, about 8 to 10 feet high, with a rope attached at the top. The rope will have a ball about the size of a volleyball affixed to the bottom. At rest, the ball should be about 2 feet from the ground.

Objective
To wrap the rope entirely around the pole so that the ball touches the pole.

The Game Plan

- The players stand on opposite sides of the pole behind a line that divides the playing field into two distinct territories.

- Tetherball is played in matches of three, five, or seven games each. The loser of each game serves the next.

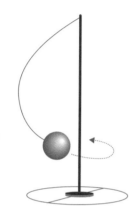

- One player sets the ball in his hand and hits it with his other hand, or throws it up and hits it. His opponent then tries to hit it back. The serving player may hit it again when it comes back around to his side, adding speed and force to the ball as it wraps around the pole.

Violations

There are four violations: a player steps out of bounds; a player catches and then throws the ball; a player hits the rope instead of the ball; or a player hits the ball twice before it's circled the pole or been returned by the opponent.

When a violation occurs, the ball is stopped and returned to the place it was before the violation, with the same number of wraps around the pole. The player who didn't commit the violation then serves the ball.

Winning

When a player hits the ball so that the rope wraps all the way around the pole and the ball touches the pole, that player has won the game.

Variation

Under the basic version of the rules, the server has a tremendous advantage. In this variation, the server must wait until her opponent has hit the ball back *or* the ball has wrapped four times around the pole before she can hit again. This gives the advantage to the receiver.

Bocce

Ball-tossing games have been around since there were human beings and balls to toss. A game similar to Bocce was played throughout the Roman empire and eventually evolved into Lawn Bowling, Ninepin, *Boules,* and Bocce. Bocce has experienced a surge of popularity in the last ten years, and recreational leagues have sprung up all over the country. If you live in an urban area, take a look at meetup.com for other players or just Google "bocce league" and the name of your city. If you have a lawn or a backyard, you have a ready-made Bocce court for an outdoor game. Below you'll find a game plan for a casual, backyard game; if you'd like the official rules of the United States Bocce Federation, check out bocce.com.

Bocce Vocab

I*nside:* The ball that is closest to the pallino is known as the inside ball, so the first ball thrown will automatically be inside.

PLAYERS: 2–8. Two players or two teams of 2–4 players each.

THE GEAR: A Bocce set, consisting of eight large balls in different colors, four per team, and one small target ball called the "pallino." A tape measure (the game can get competitive!).

The Terrain

An official bocce court is 86.5 by 13 feet, but you may adjust the proportions for your backyard. Bocce courts in bars or outdoors are usually a flat surface of hard-packed clay or sand, but for a backyard game, mown grass will work as well. Mark two foul lines at either end, beyond which players may not step when tossing the ball.

Objective

Players try to roll their Bocce balls nearer to the pallino (the target) than their opponents' balls. (Sometimes this means knocking away the opponents' balls.)

The Game Plan

* The winner of a coin toss chooses either a color or to toss the pallino. The other team gets the remaining option.

* The player stands at one end of the court and tosses out the pallino. The pallino must cross the center line.

>>STEALTH STRATEGY

It's an advantage to go last in a Bocce game. A lob without too much spin or bounce is probably the most exact throw, but a bumpy grass court "levels" the playing field and can throw off the best player's game.

* The player who tossed the pallino throws a single ball, trying to get it as close to the pallino as possible. When tossing the ball, a player may not step over the foul line.

* Then, the other team or player tosses one of their balls, trying to get closer to the pallino than the first player's ball. If they succeed, the turn reverts to the first player or team. If they don't succeed, they continue tossing their remaining balls, for a maximum of four throws in a row.

Winning

Once all the balls have been thrown, get out the tape measure. A team or player gets 1 point for every ball that's closer than their opponent's balls, for a maximum of 4 points per game (or "frame"). Only one player or team scores per frame. The team that wins a frame gets to toss out the pallino for the next one. Play as many frames as it takes to reach 12 points; the first player or team to reach that number is the winner.

Foul
Line

Center
Line

Foul
Line

APPENDIX

ID Cards for Ministry of Silence, page 77

To the right, you will find the key to the ID cards, which the moderator, or MC, will need. On the following pages are the twelve ID Cards, which the moderator distributes to the twelve active players.

The MC will have to prepare by reading the instructions on page 79-82 and collect the props. To prepare the cards, photo copy them, cut them out, fold in the middle, and tape the back to the front. The MC describes the cards to the players in the following way:

"Each card has a discrete piece of information and players must barter their bit of info with the other players in order to solve the puzzle."

The key to the cards, right, should be read only by the MC.

Key to the ID Cards, for the MC:

1. One

2. Handcuffs key

3. Thirty-four

4. With ID card #7, player will be able to decipher Target Wears Red Scarf

5. Thirteen

6. Handcuffs key

7. With ID card #4, player will be able to decipher Target Wears Red Scarf

8. 451

9. The order of the digits: 34 451 131. Winner will have to figure out that he must delete duplicate numbers in sequence to get 345-131 for the secret code.

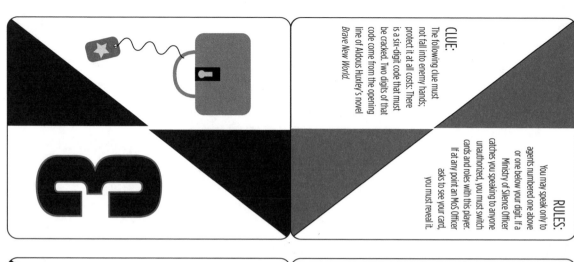

CLUE:

The following clue must not fall into enemy hands; protect it at all costs: There is a six-digit code that must be cracked. Two digits of that code come from the opening line of Aldous Huxley's novel *Brave New World*.

RULES:

You may speak only to agents numbered one above or one below your digit. If a Ministry of Silence Officer catches you speaking to anyone unauthorized, you must switch cards and roles with this player. If at any point an MoS Officer asks to see your card, you must reveal it.

3

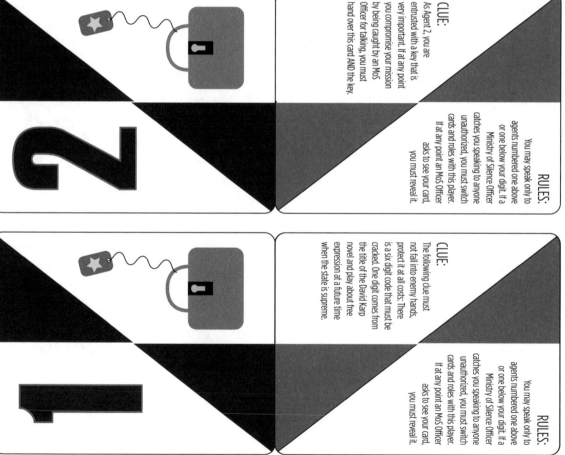

CLUE:

As Agent 2, you are entrusted with a key that is very important. If at any point you compromise your mission by being caught by an MoS Officer for talking, you must hand over this card AND the key.

RULES:

You may speak only to agents numbered one above or one below your digit. If a Ministry of Silence Officer catches you speaking to anyone unauthorized, you must switch cards and roles with this player. If at any point an MoS Officer asks to see your card, you must reveal it.

2

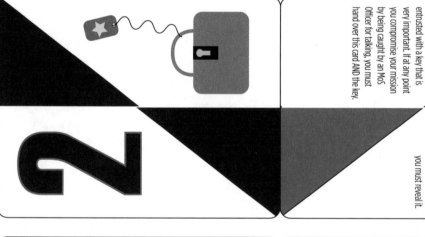

CLUE:

The following clue must not fall into enemy hands; protect it at all costs: There is a six digit code that must be cracked. One digit comes from the title of the David Karp novel and play about free expression at a future time when the state is supreme.

RULES:

You may speak only to agents numbered one above or one below your digit. If a Ministry of Silence Officer catches you speaking to anyone unauthorized, you must switch cards and roles with this player. If at any point an MoS Officer asks to see your card, you must reveal it.

1

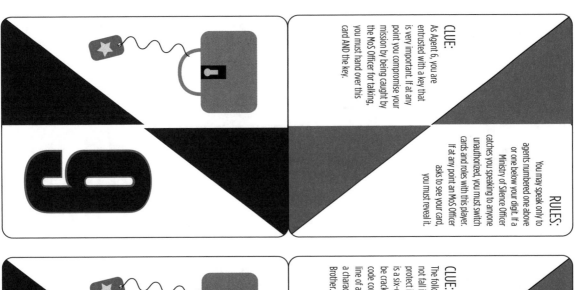

Card 6

CLUE:
As Agent 6, you are entrusted with a key that is very important. If at any point you compromise your mission by being caught by the MoS Officer for talking, you must hand over this card AND the key.

RULES:
You may speak only to agents numbered one above or one below your digit. If a Ministry of Silence Officer catches you speaking to anyone unauthorized, you must switch cards and roles with this player. If at any point an MoS Officer asks to see your card, you must reveal it.

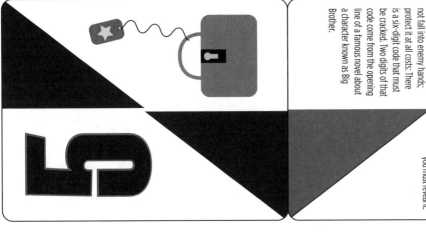

Card 5

CLUE:
The following clue must not fall into enemy hands; protect it at all costs. There is a six-digit code that must be cracked. Two digits of that code come from the opening line of a famous novel about a character known as Big Brother.

RULES:
You may speak only to agents numbered one above or one below your digit. If a Ministry of Silence Officer catches you speaking to anyone unauthorized, you must switch cards and roles with this player. If at any point an MoS Officer asks to see your card, you must reveal it.

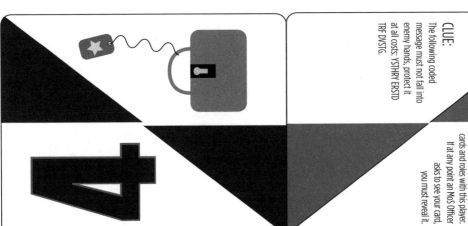

Card 4

CLUE:
The following coded message must not fall into enemy hands; protect it at all costs: YSTHRY ERSTD TRF DVSTG.

RULES:
You may speak only to agents numbered one above or one below your digit. If a Ministry of Silence Officer catches you speaking to anyone unauthorized, you must switch cards and roles with this player. If at any point an MoS Officer asks to see your card, you must reveal it.

Card 6

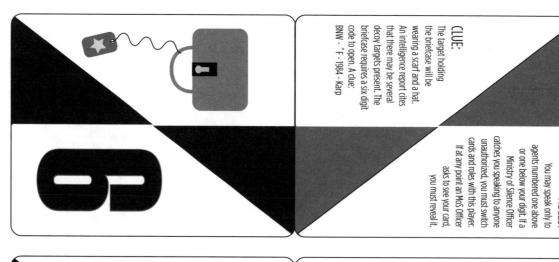

CLUE:
The target holding the briefcase will be wearing a scarf and a hat. An intelligence report cites that there may be several decoy targets present. The briefcase requires a six digit code to open. A clue: BNW - " F - 1984 - Karp

RULES:
You may speak only to agents numbered one above or one below your digit. If a Ministry of Silence Officer catches you speaking to anyone unauthorized, you must switch cards and roles with this player. If at any point an MoS Officer asks to see your card, you must reveal it.

Card 8

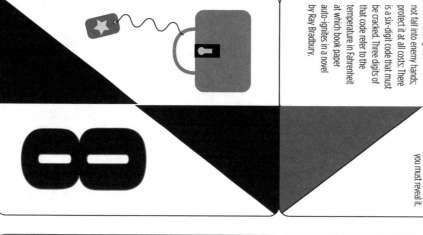

CLUE:
The following clue must not fall into enemy hands; protect it at all costs: There is a six-digit code that must be cracked. Three digits of that code refer to the temperature in Fahrenheit at which book paper auto-ignites in a novel by Ray Bradbury.

RULES:
You may speak only to agents numbered one above or one below your digit. If a Ministry of Silence Officer catches you speaking to anyone unauthorized, you must switch cards and roles with this player. If at any point an MoS Officer asks to see your card, you must reveal it.

Card 7

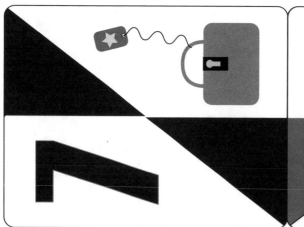

CLUE:
You are entrusted with the following code breaker: For the secret message, find a QWERTY keyboard and shift each letter one space to the left. Safeguard this information and share wisely.

RULES:
You may speak only to agents numbered one above or one below your digit. If a Ministry of Silence Officer catches you speaking to anyone unauthorized, you must switch cards and roles with this player. If at any point an MoS Officer asks to see your card, you must reveal it.

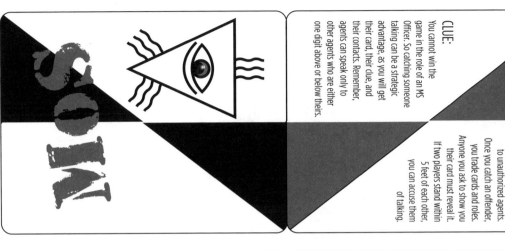

RULES:

You are a Ministry of Silence Officer. Your task is to hunt for offenders who are talking to unauthorized agents. Once you catch an offender, you trade cards and roles. Anyone you ask to show you their card must reveal it. If two players stand within 5 feet of each other, you can accuse them of talking.

CLUE:

You cannot win the game in the role of an MS Officer. So catching someone talking can be a strategic advantage, as you will get their card, their clue, and their contacts. Remember, agents can speak only to other agents who are either one digit above or below theirs.

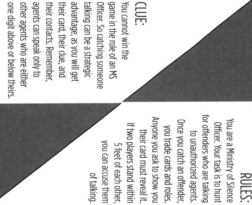

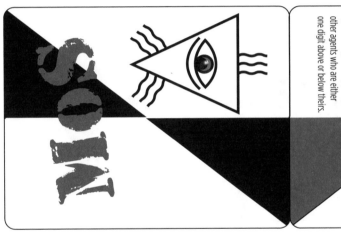

RULES:

You are a Ministry of Silence Officer. Your task is to hunt for offenders who are talking to unauthorized agents. Once you catch an offender, you trade cards and roles. Anyone you ask to show you their card must reveal it. If two players stand within 5 feet of each other, you can accuse them of talking.

CLUE:

You cannot win the game in the role of an MS Officer. So catching someone talking can be a strategic advantage, as you will get their card, their clue, and their contacts. Remember, agents can speak only to other agents who are either one digit above or below theirs.

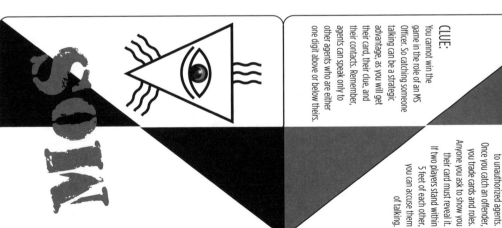

RULES:

You are a Ministry of Silence Officer. Your task is to hunt for offenders who are talking to unauthorized agents. Once you catch an offender, you trade cards and roles. Anyone you ask to show you their card must reveal it. If two players stand within 5 feet of each other, you can accuse them of talking.

CLUE:

You cannot win the game in the role of an MS Officer. So catching someone talking can be a strategic advantage, as you will get their card, their clue, and their contacts. Remember, agents can speak only to other agents who are either one digit above or below theirs.

Letter Cards for Rewordable, page 109

Photocopy and cut out cards.

a	an	at
a	an	ate
a	and	ati
a	ant	b
al	ar	b
all	as	be

ble **ble**	co **co**	der **der**
c **c**	com **com**	e **e**
c **c**	con **con**	e **e**
ca **ca**	d **d**	e **e**
ch **ch**	d **d**	e **e**
ck **ck**	de **de**	ea **ea**

ed	er	f
el	ers	g
ell	es	g
en	ess	h
ent	est	h
er	f	ha

he	ic	ion
he	**ic**	**ion**
her	ies	is
her	**ies**	**is**
i	ill	ist
i	**ill**	**ist**
i	in	it
i	**in**	**it**
i	ine	ive
i	**ine**	**ive**
i	ing	j
i	**ing**	**j**

k	le	man
k	li	me
l	lin	men
l	m	n
l	m	n
la	ma	n

n	ni	ons
na	ns	or
nd	nt	ou
ne	o	ous
nes	o	ow
ng	on	p

p	ra	ro
per	ran	rs
qu	rat	s
r	re	s
r	re	s
r	res	se

sh	tar	ti
st	te	tin
t	ted	tio
t	ter	to
t	th	tra
ta	the	u

u	w	on
un	w	n
v	x	in
v	y	es
ve	y	
ver	z	

Answer Sheet for Quizlinks!, page 229

QUIZLINKS! TEAM NAME: _____

The answers to each group of four serves as clues to a lettered answer. Once you figure out what the answers are cluing you into, put your answer on the lettered line following that group. The clue can be *either* all or part of the answer (for example, if an answer is "Portland, Oregon," the clue could be either Portland or Oregon, or both!).

1. _____

2. _____

3. _____

4. _____

A. *Link to 1–4:* _____

5. _____

6. _____

7. _____

8. _____

B. *Link to 5–8:* _____

9. _____

10. _____

11. _____

12. _____

C. *Link to 9–12:* _____

13. _____

14. _____

15. _____

16. _____

D. *Link to 13–16:* _____

20 Pt. Link for A-B-C-D: _____

Five-by-Five Grid

This grid can be photocopied and used for Psychological Scavenger Hunt, page 24, 25 Letters, page 98, Guggenheim, page 139, and Poker Squares, page 284.

Score Sheet for Bidding Games

Round	PLAYER 1:		PLAYER 2:		PLAYER 3:		PLAYER 4:		PLAYER 5:		PLAYER 6:		PLAYER 7:	
	Bid	Score	Bid	Score	Bid	Score	Bid	Score	Bid	Score	Bid	Score	Bid	Score
TOTAL:														

☞ SCORE CARD ☜

Player ❶	Player ❷	Player ❸	Player ❹

SCORE CARD

Round	Player 1	Player 2	Player 3	Player 4	Player 5	Player 6	Player 7	Player 8
TOTAL:								

Game Board and L-Pieces for The L Game, page 278

Grids for Battleships, page 282

My Ships

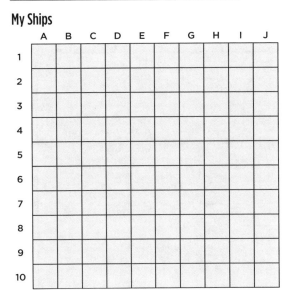

Enemy Ships

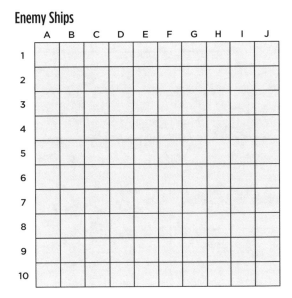

Grids for Labyrinth, page 286

My Labyrinth

Opponent's Labyrinth

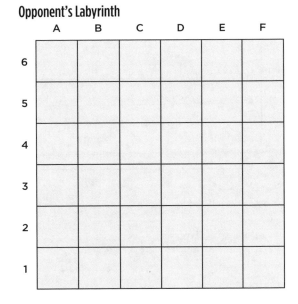

Game Board for Nine Men's Morris, page 285

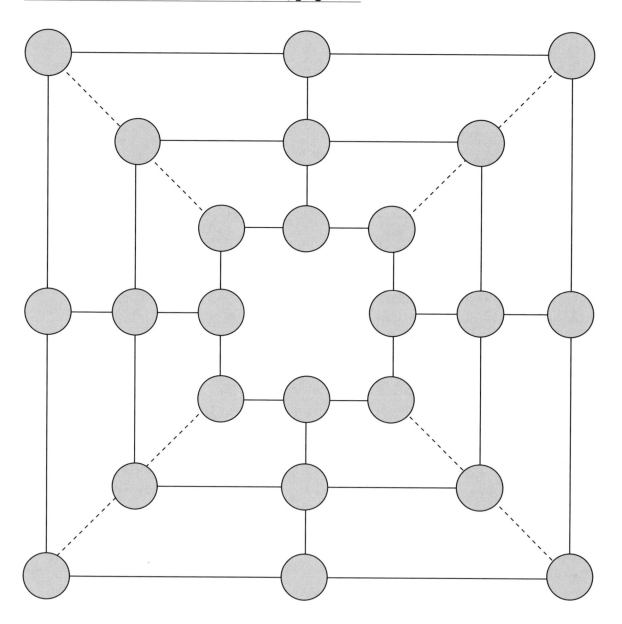

ACKNOWLEDGMENTS

I am deeply grateful for the support, advice, and expertise of Ruth Sullivan, Jennifer Griffin, Melissa Kirsch, and Ralph Titus.

This book would not have been possible without an army of play-testers, readers, game experts, party-throwers, and generally all-around great folks: Robby Weinstein for Jesse James, the IM back-and-forths, and the waiting-room bouts of Reversi; Alexis Juneja, Jennifer Bokus, and Ellie Bronson for pizza, wine, and cards; Lockhart Steele for early-iteration advice; Chris Hacker, Melanie Hoopes, and Stefanie Weiss for draft after draft of support and encouragement; Heather Southwell for finger food, murder mysteries, and the Ethicist game; and Emily and Andrew Bowers, Karen Palmer, David Scott, Pat Penta, Alex Kipp, Greta Schwerner, Charles Puckette, Jen Larson, Jake and Masha Kipp, Ken Ficara, Chris Staffa, Lynn Harris, Will Lashley, Andrew Bielski, the Costellos, Tim Sozen, Kristin Pizzo, Angela Starita, Dave Gochfeld, Mohit Santram, Brad Klein, Scott Atkins, Katherine Slingluff, Andy Stuckey, Danny Passiglia, and Martha Burgess for game testing and explaining, playacting, finger food, and many rounds of Mafia; Katie Giordano and Monica Cooper for baby-wrangling; Josh Steichmann for telling me about El Dorado Omega Johnson; Jessamyn West and Madamina for their thoughts on 1,000 Blank White Cards, Douglas P. Moore and Bob Kroeger for their expertise with Croquet, Eli Zabar for inventing and then giving me the recipe for Jelly-Doughnut Pudding; and Maisie Tivnan for the F-train editorial relay race.

Thanks to the game designers who graciously fielded my endless questions about their games and games in general: Greg Trefry, Mattia Romeo, Will Shortz, Mike Dory, Adam Simon, Charley Miller, Sam Lavigne, Alisa Stewart, Watson Adventures, David Jimison, Thi Nguyen, Scott Varland, Daniel Soltis, John Golden, Zach and Amanda Greenvoss, David E. Whitcher, Holly Gramazio, Scott DeMers, Andrew Innes, Peter Suber, and Jane McGonigal.

And finally, my love and gratitude to Sam for his willingnesss to ride to the rescue over and over again, and to Fran, who makes everything more fun, every day.

GAMES BY CATEGORY*

Athletic Games

- Ace-King-Queen
- Adult Musical Chairs
- Assassin
- Badminton
- Balloon Football
- Capture the Flag
- Capture the (Waterlogged) Flag
- Classic Outdoor Kids' Games
- Coast Guard and Smugglers
- Counter Squirt
- Cushion Dance, The
- Dancing Cheek to Cheek
- Frisbee Golf
- Fox and Geese
- Fox and Hounds
- Geocaching
- Hallway Bowling
- Horse (basketball)
- Human Battleships
- iPod Dance Charades
- Jail
- Jesse James
- Kick the Can
- Kickball
- Limbo Dance Contest
- Lost Sport of Olympia, The
- Manhunt
- Mr. Hit
- No-Equipment Baseball
- Old-Fashioned Dance Party
- Priest of the Parish
- Pussy Wants a Corner
- Ringoleavio
- Slip 'n Slide Curling
- Squeak, Piggy, Squeak
- Tetherball
- Triathlons and Relay Races
- Yoga Ball Jousting
- Yukigassen

Cocktail Party Games

- Acting Rhymes
- Adult Musical Chairs
- Adverbs
- Animal Attraction
- Blackjack
- Bocce
- Brainy Baseball
- Can I Buy You a Drink?
- Character Guessing
- Charles Ate a Goat Testicle in Algeria
- Common Interests
- Craps
- Cringe Party
- Croquet
- Cushion Dance, The
- Dancing Cheek to Cheek
- Divide and Conquer
- Easter Egg Haggle
- Easter Keg Hunt
- Essences
- Euchre
- Exquisite Corpse
- Four-Handed Pinochle
- Frisbee Golf
- Get Down, Mr. President
- Halloween Ball
- Hallway Bowling
- Hearts
- I Doubt It
- I Never
- Jail
- Just a Minute!
- Karaoke
- Knotty Problem, A
- Lap Game, The
- Liar's Dice
- Limbo Dance Contest
- Mafia
- Mardi Gras Costume Party and King Cake
- Match the Match Ad
- Murder Mystery Games
- 9-5-2
- Oh, Hell
- Old-Fashioned Dance Party
- Pass the Orange
- Pictionary Down the Lane
- Pitch
- Poker, Texas Hold 'Em
- Police Lineup
- Prediction Bingo
- Quizlinks!
- Sardines
- Save Yourself
- Secret Signals
- Seven Up
- She's So Fine . . .
- Song Scramble
- Spades
- Tableaux
- Tabloid Trivia
- Trivia Betting
- Trivia Fictionary
- Two Truths and a Lie
- United Nations
- Up Jenkins
- Valentine's Story Slam
- What's Your Line?
- Wink Murder
- You Don't Say . . .
- Your Other Half

*All page numbers appear in the alphabetic index, pp. 386–390.

Family Games

- Ace-King-Queen
- Acting Rhymes
- Alphabet Minute
- Ant and the Cricket, The
- Associations
- Axis and Allies
- Badminton
- Balloon Football or Volleyball
- Baseball Bingo
- Battleship
- Blackjack
- Bocce
- Breakfast Combo
- Buzz
- Capture the Flag
- Capture the (Waterlogged) Flag
- Casino
- Celebrity
- Character Guessing
- Charades
- Classic Outdoor Kids' Games
- Clumps
- Coast Guard and Smugglers
- Common Ground
- Competitive Picnicking
- Competitive Pumpkin Carving
- Consequences
- Crambo, Versions 1 and 2
- Croquet
- Cushion Dance
- Depth Charge
- Dictionary
- Diplomacy
- Dots and Boxes
- Dudo

- El Dorado Omega Johnson
- Exquisite Corpse
- Family Jeopardy
- 500 Rummy
- Footsteps
- Forbidden Words
- Four on the Couch
- Fox and Geese
- Fox and Hounds
- French Rhymes
- Geocaching
- Geography
- Go Fish
- Grateful Guessing
- Great Minds Think Alike
- Group Therapy
- Guess the Proverb
- Guggenheim
- Halloween Ball
- Hallway Bowling
- Happy Days
- Head Splinter
- Hearts
- Holiday Trivia
- Hometown Quiz
- Horseshoes
- Human Battleships
- I Accuse
- I Doubt It
- Idiot's Delight
- Inheritance Game
- iPod Dance Charades
- Jesse James
- Jinx
- Just a Minute!
- Kick the Can
- Kickball
- L Game, The
- Labyrinth
- Literary Rebus

- Lost Sport of Olympia, The
- Make Your Own Pantomime
- Mancala
- Manhunt
- Marco Polo
- Mardi Gras Costume Party and King Cake
- Match Game, The
- Mora
- Mr. Hit
- Multiple-Choice Trivia Game
- Name Game
- Name-Boggle Poetry
- No-Equipment Baseball
- Not It
- Old Maid
- Old-Fashioned Dance Party
- One, Two, Three
- Opposites
- Passover Trivia Quiz
- Password, Versions 1 and 2
- Physical Word Hunt
- Pictionary
- Police Lineup
- Priest of the Parish
- Profiles
- Punch-Buggy
- Pussy Wants a Corner
- Questions R-and-G Style
- Rat-Fink
- Resolutions
- Reversals
- "Reverse" Easter Egg Hunt
- Ringoleavio

- Sardines
- Save Yourself
- Scavenger Hunts
- Secret Signals
- Self-Portrait
- Settlers of Catan
- Sharks and Minnows
- Sight Unseen
- Slip 'n Slide Curling
- Song Scramble
- Spades
- Sprouts
- Sticky-Note Game, The
- Store
- Storyteller, The
- Tableaux
- Taste of America
- Telephone Murder
- Tetherball
- That's the Way It Was
- This Is Your Life Trivia
- Tiered Name Guessing
- Traveling Alphabet
- Triathlons and Relay Races
- Unfortunately . . .
- Urban Bingo
- Urban Orienteering
- Vowels
- What Are They Thinking?
- What?
- Who-Where-What
- Wink Murder
- Would You Rather . . .
- Yankee Gift Swap, *Survivor*-Style, The
- Yukigassen

Games Best Played with Strangers

- Can I Buy You a Drink?
- Charles Ate a Goat Testicle in Algeria
- Consequences
- Dancing Cheek to Cheek
- Divide and Conquer
- Heartbreaker
- Hot Cockles
- I Never
- Lap Game, The
- Match the Match Ad
- Mr. Hit
- Pass the Orange
- Psychological Scavenger Hunt
- Read My Mind
- Shag, Marry, Cliff
- Six-Word Memoir
- Two Truths and a Lie
- Up Jenkins
- What's Your Line?
- Would You Rather . . .

Games for Quiet, Small Groups

- Anagrams
- Associations
- Biography
- Blind Man's Bluff Poker
- Botticelli
- Breakfast Combo
- Canasta
- Chain-Link Music
- Common Ground
- Dots and Boxes
- Eleusis Express
- Epitaph
- Essences
- Expanda-Toe
- Footsteps
- Grateful Guessing
- How Why When Where
- I Never
- Nocturnal Time Completely Lacking Noise
- One, Two, Three
- Opposites
- Shag, Marry, Cliff
- Situation Puzzles
- Solitaire
- Sticky-Note Game
- That's the Way It Was
- Three Bests
- Unfortunately . . .
- Walrus
- Who-Where-What
- Word Links
- Word Logic
- Would You Rather . . .

Games for the Waiting Room

- Arithmetic Croquet
- Band Name, Album Name, or Boat Name?
- Biography
- Botticelli
- Breakfast Combo
- Butterfly or Bumblebee
- Buzz
- Cage Match
- Can You Live With It?
- Character Guessing
- Contact
- Dots and Boxes
- Epitaph
- Expanda-Toe
- Footsteps
- Hangman
- How Why When Where
- Labyrinth
- Liar's Poker
- Mora
- Nocturnal Time Completely Lacking Noise
- Not OK
- One, Two, Three
- Opposites
- Punch-Buggy
- Questions
- Shag, Marry, Cliff
- Six Degrees of Kevin Bacon
- Solitaire
- Sprouts
- Three Best
- Throwing Light
- Traveling Alphabet
- 25 Letters
- Unfortunately . . .
- Walrus
- What Are They Thinking?
- Word Links
- Word Logic
- Would You Rather . . .

Geeky Games

- Ace-King-Queen
- Alphabetical Quotations
- Anagrams
- Arithmetic Croquet
- Art Charades
- Assassin
- Brain Teasers
- Canasta
- Carnelli
- Casino
- Coup d'Etat
- Craps
- Croquet
- Current-Events Trivia
- Decipher
- Depth Charge
- Easter Egg Haggle
- Eleusis Express
- Family Jeopardy
- Frisbee Golf
- Haggle
- Iron Chef Potluck
- Lost Sport of Olympia, The
- Mafia
- Murder Mystery Games
- Museum Scavenger Hunt
- Nomic
- Priest of the Parish
- Puzzle Scavenger Hunt
- Quotations
- Rewordable
- Scrabble Categories
- Super Babel
- 25 Letters
- Valentine's Story Slam
- Yukigassen

New Games

- Associations
- Cage Match
- Can I Buy You a Drink?
- Competitive Picnicking
- Counter Squirt
- Eleusis Express
- Ethicist Game, The
- Heartbreaker
- Inheritance Game
- iPod Dance Charades
- Lost Sport of Olympia, The
- Ministry of Silence
- Museum Scavenger Hunt
- Quizlinks!
- Rewordable
- Store
- Urban Bingo
- Weekend-Long Forbidden Words

Noncompetitive Games

- Acting Rhymes
- Adult Musical Chairs
- Alphabet Minute
- Band Name, Album Name, or Boat Name?
- Big Booty
- Butterfly or Bumblebee?
- Chain-Link Music
- Character Guessing
- Clap and Clapper
- Common Interests
- Compliments
- Consequences
- Cringe Party
- Epitaph
- Exquisite Corpse
- French Rhymes
- Geocaching
- I Never
- Make Your Own Pantomime
- Mr. Hit
- Name-Boggle Poetry
- One, Two, Three
- 1,000 Blank White Cards
- Pass the Orange
- Pictionary Down the Lane
- Psychiatrist
- Questions
- Questions R-and-G Style
- Read My Mind
- Resolutions
- Rhymes About
- Shag, Marry, Cliff
- Six Degrees of Kevin Bacon
- Six-Word Memoir
- Squeak, Piggy, Squeak
- Three Best
- Three Words
- Valentine's Story Slam
- Walrus
- What Are They Thinking?
- Would You Rather . . .
- Your Other Half

Online Games

- Arithmetic Croquet
- Blackjack
- Botticelli
- Breakfast Combo
- Butterfly or Bumblebee?
- Crambo, Version 2
- Encyclopedia
- 500 Rummy
- Gin Rummy
- How Why When Where
- Karaoke
- Mancala
- Multiple-Choice Trivia Game
- Nine Men's Morris
- Nocturnal Time Completely Lacking Noise
- Nomic
- Opposites
- Pinochle
- Poker Squares
- Poker, Texas Hold 'Em
- Reversals
- Reversi
- Shag, Marry, Cliff
- Six Degrees of Kevin Bacon
- Solitaire
- Walrus
- Word Links
- Would You Rather . . .

Silly Games

- Adult Musical Chairs
- Animal Attraction
- Balloon Football or Volleyball
- Baseball Bingo
- Big Booty
- Blind Man's Bluff Poker
- Bubble Wrap Kung Fu
- Can You Live With It?
- Charades
- Clap and Clapper
- Common Interests
- Contact
- Cringe Party
- Current-Events Trivia
- Dancing Cheek to Cheek
- Dozens, The
- El Dorado Omega Johnson
- Four on the Couch
- Game, The
- Get Down, Mr. President
- Hallway Bowling
- Head Splinter
- Human Battleships
- I've Always Thought BBQ Panda Cubs Would Be Delicious
- iPod Dance Charades
- Jail
- Just a Minute!
- Karaoke
- Knotty Problem, A
- Limbo Dance Contest
- Not OK
- Oh, Hell
- One, Two, Three
- 1,000 Blank White Cards
- Pass the Orange
- Pictionary Down the Lane
- Police Lineup
- Questions R-and-G Style
- Rat-Fink
- Sardines
- Secret Signals
- Song Scramble
- Squeak, Piggy, Squeak
- Sticky-Note Game, The
- Tabloid Trivia
- Unfortunately . . .
- United Nations
- What's Your Line?
- What?
- Who-Where-What
- Yankee Gift Swap, *Survivor*-Style, The
- Yoga Ball Jousting
- Your Other Half

Theatrical Games

- Acting Rhymes
- Adverbs
- Animal Attraction
- Art Charades
- Carnelli
- Charades and variations
- Compliments
- Counter Squirt
- Cringe Party
- iPod Dance Charades
- Just a Minute!
- Karaoke
- Mafia
- Make Your Own Pantomime
- Ministry of Silence
- Murder Mystery Games
- 1,000 Blank White Cards
- Police Lineup
- Psychiatrist
- Read My Mind
- Rhymes About
- Save Yourself
- Storyteller, The
- Tableaux
- Telephone Murder
- Trivia Fictionary
- United Nations
- Valentine's Story Slam
- What Are They Thinking?
- Who Am I?
- Your Other Half

Travel Games

- Alphabet Minute
- Alphabetical Quotations
- Ant and the Cricket
- Arithmetic Croquet
- Associations
- Band Name, Album Name, or Boat Name?
- Battleship
- Biography
- Botticelli
- Breakfast Combo
- Buzz
- Can You Live With It?
- Carnelli
- Celebrity
- Chain-Link Music
- Character Guessing
- Compliments
- Contact
- Crambo, Version 2
- Definitions
- Demolition Tic-Tac-Toe
- Dots and Boxes
- Dozens, The
- El Dorado Omega Johnson
- Epitaph
- Essences
- Ethicist Game
- Given Words
- Group Therapy
- Guess the Proverb
- Haiku Memoir
- Happy Days
- How Why When Where
- I've Always Thought BBQ Panda Cubs Would Be Delicious
- Labyrinth
- Liar's Poker
- Nocturnal Time Completely Lacking Noise
- One, Two, Three
- Opposites
- Psychiatrist
- Punch-Buggy
- Questions
- Questions R-and-G Style
- Reversals
- Rhymes About
- Situation Puzzles
- Six Degrees of Kevin Bacon
- Six-Word Memoir
- Sprouts
- Storyteller, The
- Syllepsis
- Three Best
- Three Lives
- Throwing Light
- Traveling Alphabet
- Trivia Bee
- Twenty Questions
- 25 Letters
- Unfortunately . . .
- Vowels
- What?
- Word Links
- Would You Rather . . .
- You Don't Say . . .

INDEX

A

Abbott, Robert, 138, 217
Ace-King-Queen, 336–37
Acting Rhymes, 159
Adult Musical Chairs, 16
Adverbs, 46
alcoholic beverage recipes
    Dark and Stormy, 156
    Icebreaker, The, 30
"Alice in Wonderland" party, 11
All Fours, 250, 251
Alphabet Minute, 155
Alphabetical Quotations, 163–64
Anagrams, 97
Analogies, 49–50
Ancient Japanese Art of
    Snowball Fighting, 319–20
Angel Biscuits recipe, 182
Animal Attraction, 32–33
Anomia, 268
Ant and the Cricket, The, 162–63
Apples to Apples board game,
    10, 90
Arithmetic Croquet, 213–14
Art Charades, 117–18
Assassin, 306, 317–18
Associations, 105
Axis and Allies, 293

B

Baby Bingo, 199
Baby Promises, 198
Baby Shower Games, 198–99
Baby Taboo, 198

Baby Words, 199
Back-to-Back Race, 321
Bad Sweaters party, 11
Badminton, 352–53
Balderdash, 100, 102
Balloon Football, 70–71
Balloon Volleyball, 70–71
Band Name, Album Name, or
    Boat Name, 92
Baseball Bingo, 211–12
Battleship, 282–84
   grids for, 377
   theme party, 11
Bezique, 259
Bidding games score sheet, 373
Big Booty, 31–32
Big Urban Game, 4
Biography, 62
biscuits recipe, 182
Black Lady, 239–41
Blackjack, 253–55
Blackout, 236–39
Blind Man's Bluff Poker, 210
Blindfolded Pictionary, 113–14
Blob Tag, 322
Bocce, 354–55
Book of Questions, The, 29, 167
Botticelli, 42–43
*Brain Games: the World's Best
    Games for Two,* 286
Brain Teasers, 212–13
Brainy Baseball, 72–73
Bratislava, 43
Breakfast Combo, 54–55
Bubble Wrap Kung Fu, 76
Bullshit, 210–11

Butterfly or Bumblebee?, 88
Buzz, 211

C

Cage Match, 86
Can I Buy You a Drink?, 34
Can You Live With It?, 91–92
Canasta, 245–48
Capture the Flag, 313–14
Capture the (Waterlogged) Flag,
    188–89
card games, 231–68
card games, common terms,
    233–34
Carnell, Jan, 131
Carnelli, 131–32
Carroll, Lewis, 213
Casino, 257–59
Categories, 139–41
Celebrity, 52–53
Chain-Link Music, 142
Character Guessing, 51–52
Charades, 37–40
   categories shorthand, 39
   variations, 40–41
Charles Ate a Goat Testicle in
    Algeria, 22–23
Chase the Ace, 235–36
Chicken Fights, 342
Childhood Games for Grown-ups
    party, 11
Chinese Handball, 336–37
Chop-a-Croc, 308
Christmas Off the Gold
    Standard, 197

Chutes and Ladders game board, 18, 197

Clap and Clapper, 23–24

Clark, Bob, 80

Classic Beach House Games, 305–6

Classic Outdoor Kid's Games, 321–22

Clumps, 53–54

Coast Guard and Smugglers, 335–36

Cold War party, 11

Come Out and Play festival, 2–4, 77

Common Ground, 145–46

Common Interests, 26–27

Competitive Picnicking, 185–87

Competitive Pumpkin Carving, 191–92

Compliments, 156

Consequences, 159–60

Conspiracy Theory party, 11

Contact, 108–9

Conway, John H., 272

Cookies, Martha Burgess's Ginger Butter, 51

Counter Squirt, 345–46

Coup d'Etat, 273–75

Cracker-Whistling Contests, 322

Crambo
    Version 1, 157–58
    Version 2, 158–59

Craps, 205–7
    vocabulary, 206

Cringe Party, 102–3

Croquet, 348–51
    terms, 350

Crosswords, 98–99

Cucumber Sandwiches recipe, 158

Current Events Charades, 40

Current-Events Trivia, 226–28

Cushion Dance, The, 167

D

Dancing Cheek to Cheek, 30

Dark and Stormy recipe, 156

de Bono, Edward, 278

Decipher, 275–77

Definitions, 107–8
    variations, 108

DeMers, Scott, 273

Demolition Tic-Tac-Toe, 271–72

Depth Charge, 279–82

Dictionary, 100–101
    variations, 101–2

Diplomacy, 293

Distract the Parents, 199

Divide and Conquer, 19–20

Do, Date, or Die, 87–88

Dodgeball, 321

Dory, Michael, 110, 187

Dots and Boxes, 278–9

Dozens, The, 87

Dudo, 204–5

E

Easter Egg Haggle, 180–81

Easter Egg Hunt, "Reverse," 182

Easter Keg Hunt, 183

Eat Poop You Cat, 116–17

Egg-in-the-Spoon Race, 321

El Dorado Omega Johnson, 309

Eleusis Express, 217–18

Encyclopedia, 61

English Majors party, 11

Epitaph, 107

Essences, 49–50

Ethicist Game, The, 94

Euchre, 255–56

Existential Rock Paper Scissors, 84–85

Expanda-Toe, 271

Exquisite Corpse, 125–26

F

Fall Pork Roast recipe, 70

Family Jeopardy, 196

Family Pictionary, 114

Fictionary, 101

Fingers, 58–59

500 Rummy, 243–45

Five Men's Morris, 286

Flashlight Tag, 322

Flyting, 87

Football, Balloon, 70–71

Footsteps, 282

Forbidden Words, 48

Forehead Stud, 210

Fortune-Cookie Charades, 41

Four on the Couch, 66–67

Four Square, 337

Four-Handed Pinochle, 261–63

Fox and Geese, 344

Fox and Hounds, 334–35

Freeze Tag, 322

French Rhymes, 161

French Toast, 54–55

Frisbee Golf, 323–24

G

Game, The, 310

Game Night, how to host, 7–11

Games magazine, 28

Games People Play, 114

Geocaching, 302–3

Geography, 136

Get Down, Mr. President, 310

Ghost, 103–4

Ghost in the Graveyard, 322

Gigantic Mechanic, 34

Gin Rummy, 241–43

Given Words, 164–65

Go Fish, 235

Go-Tag, 322

Golden, John, 217

GPS device, 4, 302–3, 313–14

Gradual Turn of Events, 197

Gramazio, Holly, 304

Grateful Guessing, 194

Gratitude Fictionary, 194

Great Minds Think Alike, 146–47

Greenvoss, Zach and Amanda, 275

Group Therapy, 92–93

Guacamole recipe, 226

Guess the Proverb, 62

Guggenheim, 139–41
    grid for, 372

Guggenheim Outdoors, 141

H

Haggle, 136–38

Haiku Memoir, 22

Halloween Ball, 192–93

Hallway Bowling, 65
Hangman, 272
Happy Days, 139
Hazard, 205–7
Head Splinter, 309–10
Heartbreaker, 173–74
Hearts, 239–41
Hide-and-Seek, "reverse," 67
Hoffman, David, 86
Holiday Trivia, 196
Hometown Quiz, 225
Horse (basketball game), 318
Horse (word game), 103–4
Horseshoes, 351–52
hosting a game night, 7–11
Hot Cockles, 168
How They Met, 159–60
How Why When Where, 55
Howard Stern Show, The, 17
Human Battleships, 184
Human Chess, 312

I

I Accuse, 44–45
I Doubt It, 210–11
I Never, 84
I've Always Thought BBQ Panda
    Cubs Would Be Delicious,
    310
Icebreaker, The (recipe), 30
icons explained, 6
Idiot's Delight, 71
Impromptu Games, 307–10
Indian Poker, 210
Inheritance Game, 195
Innes, Andrew, 268
invitation ideas, 9
iPod Dance Charades, 128
Iron Chef Potluck, 144–45
Italian Ice recipe, 340

J

Jail, 69–70
Jelly Doughnut Pudding recipe,
    143
Jeopardy, 5, 220, 229
    Family Jeopardy, 196
Jesse James, 314–16

Jimison, David, 329–30
Jinx, 309
Jotto, 106–7
Jump Rope Rhymes, 339
Just a Minute!, 126–27

K

Karaoke, 120–21
Kick the Can, 337–38
Kickball, 324–25
King, Stewart, 300
Kirsch, Melissa, 171
Klondike, 263–65
Knotty Problem, A, 18–19

L

L Game, The, 278
    board for, 376
Labyrinth, 286–87
    grids for, 386
Lap Game, The, 74–75
Lavigne, Sam, 195
Lawn Games, 348–55
Lemonade recipe, 315
Liar's Dice, 203–4
Liar's Poker, 207–8
Liebrary, 102
Life Saver on a Toothpick, 31
Limbo Dance Contest, 33
Literary Rebus, 118–19
Lobster Rolls recipe, 326
Lopez, Chloe, 300
Lost Sport of Olympia, The,
    347–48

M

Mad Libs, 159
Mafia, 132–35, 305–6
Make Your Own Pantomime,
    296–99
Malarkey, 100, 102
Mancala, 289–90
Manhunt, 316
Marco Polo, 338–39
Mardi Gras Costume Party and
    King Cake, 176–78
Mardi Gras King Cake recipe, 177

Martha Burgess's Ginger Butter
    Cookies, 51
Match Game, The, 61
Match the Match Ad, 57–58
McGonigal, Jane, 347–48
McQuillen, Nathan, 299–300
Mean Scrabble, 97
Medical or Law Dictionary, 101
Middle-School Dance party, 11
Midnight Madness, 312, 332
Miller, Charley, 64, 80, 86, 174
Ministry of Silence, 77–80
    cards for, 357–61
Monopoly game board, 18, 197
Monster Movie Charades, 40
Montague Blister's Strange
    Games, 76
Mora (or Morra), 58–59
Mother, May I?, 321
Mr. Hit, 28–29
Multiple-Choice Trivia Game, 222
Murder Mystery Games, 300–302
Murder Mystery Puzzles, 122–24,
    306
Museum Scavenger Hunt, 333

N

Name Boggle, 20–21
Name-Boggle Poetry, 195
Name Game, 23
New Rules for Classic Games, 139
New Year's Hangover, 197
9-5-2, 293–95
Nine Men's Morris, 285–86
    board for, 285
No-Equipment Baseball, 340–41
Nocturnal Time Completely
    Lacking Noise, 43–44
Noisemaker Charades, 41
Nomic, 148–52, 305
    rules for, 151–52
Not It, 308
Not OK, 308

O

Oh Pshaw, 236–39
Oh, Hell, 236–39
Old Maid, 235–36

Old-Fashioned Dance Party, 119
Old-Fashioned Lemonade recipe, 17
One, Two, Three, 90–91
One-Word Charades, 40
1,000 Blank White Cards, 299–300
Opposites, 89–90
Othello, 288

P

Party Games for Adults, 26
party recipes
   Angel Biscuits, 182
   Cucumber Sandwiches, 158
   Dark and Stormy, 156
   Fall Pork Roast, 70
   Guacamole, 226
   Icebreaker, The, 30
   Italian Ice, 340
   Jelly Doughnut Pudding, 143
   Lemonade, 315
   Lobster Rolls, 326
   Mardi Gras King Cake recipe, 177
   Martha Burgess's Ginger Butter Cookies, 51
   Old-Fashioned Lemonade, 17
   Rosemary–White Bean Dip, 106
   Scones, 103
   Tea and Pecan Shortbread, 85
   Toasted Pumpkin Seeds, 192
party theme ideas, 11
Pass the Orange, 30–31
Passover Trivia Quiz, 178–79
Password
   Version 1, 46–47
   Version 2, 47–48
Paterson, M. S., 272
Pathfinder, 286–87
Patience, 263–65
Pecan Shortbread recipe, 85
Physical Word Hunt, 76–77
Pictionary, 113–14
Pictionary Down the Lane, 116–17
Pin the Tail on the Donkey, 22
Pinochle, 259–61
   Four-Handed, 261–63

Pitch, 251–53
Poetry Fictionary, 102
Poison, 351
Poker Squares, 284–85
   grid for, 372
Poker, Texas Hold 'Em, 249–50
Police Lineup, 114–16
Pork Roast recipe, 70
Prediction Bingo, 73
Priest of the Parish, 189–91
Pritchard, David, 286
Profiles, 119–20
Protozoa, 43
"Proverbs" Dictionary, 101
Psychiatrist, 60, 306
Psychological Bingo, 25
Psychological Scavenger Hunt, 24–25
   grid for, 372
PubQuiz USA, 229
Pudding, Jelly Doughnut recipe, 143
Punch-Buggy, 308
Pussy Wants a Corner, 68–69
Puzzle Scavenger Hunt, 330–32

Q

Queen of Spades, 235–36
Questions, 29
Questions R-and-G Style, 91
Quizlinks!, 229–30
   answer sheet for, 371
Quotations, 156–57
Quotations Dictionary, 101–2

R

Race Charades, 40
Race Pictionary, 114
Rat-Fink, 208–9
Read My Mind, 132
recipes. *See* party recipes
Red Light, Green Light, 321
Red Rover, 321–22
Relay Race, 322
Resolutions, 171–72
Reversals, 147
"Reverse" Easter Egg Hunt, 182
Reversi, 288–89

Rewordable, 109–10
   letter cards for, 362–70
Rhymes About, 103
Ringoleavio, 325
Romeo, Mattia, 128, 346
Rosemary–White Bean Dip recipe, 106
Rosencrantz and Guildenstern Are Dead, 91
Rubenstein, Dan, 61

S

Sack Races, 322
Sackson, Sid, 136
Salvo, 282–84
Sardines, 67
Save Yourself, 143
Scarne, John, 231
Scavenger Hunts, 24, 326–28
   Easter Keg Hunt, 183
   indoor variation, 76
Schmittberger, Wayne, 139
Scones recipe, 103
Scrabble Categories, 104–5
Scramble, 97
Secret Signals, 215–16
Self-Portrait, 127
Set-Back, 251–53
Settlers of Catan, The, 293
Seven Up, 250–51
SFZero.org, 195
Shag, Marry, Cliff, 87–88
Sharks and Minnows, 341–42
She's So Fine . . ., 56–57
Shortz, Will, 4, 105
Shuttlecock, 352
Sight Unseen, 121
Simon Says, 321
Simon, Adam, 110, 187
Sink the Onesie, 199
Situation Puzzles, 122–24, 306
Six Degrees of Kevin Bacon, 228–29
Six-Word Memoir, 21–22
Slang Dictionary, 102
Slip 'n Slide Curling, 342–43
Sniderman, Stephen, 340
Socialbomb, 187
Solitaire, 263–65

Soltis, Daniel, 187
Song Scramble, 26
Southwell, Heather, 94
Spades, 265–67
Spoons, 208–9
Sprouts, 272–73
Squeak, Piggy, Squeak, 162
Stewart, Alisa, 229
Sticky-Note Game, The, 42
Stock, Gregory, 167
Stoopball, 337
Stoppard, Tom, 91
Store, 268
Storyteller, The, 165–66
Suber, Peter, 148
Super Babel, 138–39
Super Ghost, 104
Superstitions Dictionary, 101
Syllepsis, 97–98

T

Tableaux, 295–96
Tabloid Charades, 41
Tabloid Trivia, 225–26
Taboo board game, 10, 48
Tag, five variations, 322
Taste of America, 167–88
tea, how to make, 85
Telephone, 59, 116, 321
Telephone Murder, 59–60
Tetherball, 353–54
Texas Hold 'Em (poker), 249–50
That's the Way It Was, 197
theme party ideas, 11
This Is Your Life Trivia, 183–84
Three Best, 88–89
Three Lives, 103–4
Three Words, 75
Three-Legged Race, 321
Throwing Light, 160–61
Tic-Tac-Toe variations, 271–72
Tiered Charades, 41
Tiered Name Guessing, 41–42
Tinker.it, 187
Titanic party, 11

Toasted Pumpkin Seeds recipe, 192
Town Hunt, 332
Traveling Alphabet, 164
Trefry, Greg, 34, 128, 346
Triathlons and Relay Races, 343–44
Triomphe, 255–56
Trivia Bee, 224–25
Trivia Betting, 222–23
Trivia Fictionary, 223–24
Trivia games, 219–230
Trivia night, preparing for, 221
Trivial Pursuit cards, 222–23
TV Charades, 40
Twelve Men's Morris, 286
Twenty Questions, 20
21, 253–55
25 Letters, 98–99
    grid for, 372
Two Truths and a Lie, 17–18

U

Unfortunately . . ., 90
Ungame, The, 29
United Nations, 28
Up Jenkins, 67–68
Up the River, 236–39
Urban Bingo, 329–30
Urban Orienteering, 343

V

Valentine's Story Slam, 175–76
Varland, Scott, 187
Verbatim, 99–100
Vermicelli, 43
Victorian Parlor Games, 153–68
Volleyball, Balloon, 70–71
Vowels, 166–67

W

Wait Wait . . . Don't Tell Me, 226
Walcott, Karen, 43

Walrus, 84–85
Warner, Penny, 114, 146
Watson Adventures, 333
weekend games, 291–306
Weekend-Long Forbidden Words, 303–4
Weird Wordz, 100
Werewolf, 132–35
What Are They Thinking?, 86
What's the Scoop?, 124
    noncompetitive version, 124–25
What's Your Line?, 16–17
What?, 309
Wheelbarrow Race, 321
Whisper Pictionary, 113
Whitcher, David E., 279
Who Am I?, 20
Who-Where-What, 125
Wink Murder, 293
Wise and Otherwise, 101
Wiswell, Phil, 28
Wits and Wagers, 223
Word Factory, 99–100
Word Links, 48–49
Word Logic, 106–7
Word Squares, 98–99
Would You Rather . . ., 83–84

Y

Yankee Gift Swap, The
    Hallway Bowling variation, 65
    Survivor-Style, 172
Yo Mamma, 87
Yoga Ball Jousting, 75–76
You Don't Say . . ., 144
Your Other Half, 15
Yukigassen, 319–20

Z

Zabar, Eli, 143
zeugma, 97
Zobmondo!!, 83